48

9989

STUDIES IN COMMUNICATION

VOLUME 3

Culture and Communication:
Methodology, Behavior, Artifacts, and Institutions:
Selected Proceedings from the Fifth
International Conference on Culture
and Communication, Temple University, 1983

Edited by

SARI THOMAS

Temple University

A Volume in the Series
COMMUNICATION AND INFORMATION SCIENCE
Melvin J. Voigt, series editor

ABLEX Publishing Corporation
Norwood, New Jersey 07648

Library of Congress Cataloging-in-Publication Data

Culture and communication.

(Communication and information science)
Selected articles from the Fifth International Conference on Culture
and Communication, held in 1983 at Temple University.
Bibliography: p.
Includes index.
1. Communication—Social aspects—Congresses.
2. Intercultural communication—Congresses.
I. Thomas, Sari   II. International
Conference on Culture and Communication (5th : 1983 :
Temple University) III. Series.
HM258.C843   1986   302.2   86-10874
ISBN 0-89391-253-0

ABLEX Publishing Corporation
355 Chestnut Street
Norwood, New Jersey 07648

Contents

PART **IV**   **INSTITUTIONS**

Introduction

The original chapters included in this volume represent selections from over 300 papers presented at the 1983, Fifth International Conference on Culture and Communication (CCC). The CCC endeavors to provide a multi-disciplinary forum for the discussion of social theory and research with an emphasis on the role played by information (in its broadest sense) in cultural processes.

It has been the practice of the CCC to umbrella a variety of epistemological perspectives and, by doing so, to support non-mainstream work as well as more traditional themes and approaches. Although the 1983 program listed numerous topics with various methodological perspectives, this volume has been limited to four broad sections as described individually below.

The first section of this book, "Methodology and Philosophy of Social Science," covers a wide range of topics all of which address questions concerning the elicitation and organization of information in the context of scholarship. Farrel Corcoran's "Ideology and Consciousness: the Construction of Social Meaning" discusses the evolution of the construct of *ideology* and how this changing construct has been influential in the development of social theory. "The Technological Determination of Philosophy" by Paul Levinson suggests that classical philosophical thought is greatly a function of, if not determined by, the dominant technological systems of the period in which it was produced. Stella Ting-Toomey's "The 'Root Metaphors' Orientations" broadly addresses how universal metaphorical devices are relevant to epistemological activity.

Dealing specifically with theory of *mass* communication, Kevin Carragee, Mark Rosenblatt, and Gene Michaud trace the development of theory and research on how the mass media establish a program of relevant issues for society at large. Their article, "Agenda-Setting Research: A Critique and Theoretical Alternative," provides an analysis of the strengths and weaknesses of the important agenda-setting concept and suggests that a larger sociological context is required for a more complete and accurate understanding of the phenomenon.

The last two contributions in this section rely, in varying degrees, on the presentation of original research data to exemplify how largely qualitative, ethnographic methods may be used to secure more substantial information on communication behavior. Given that the history of communication research has been dominated by more superficial but perhaps expedient approaches in eliciting data on communicative activity, Stuart J. Sigman's "The Application of Ethnographic Methods to Communications Research" and Michelle A. Wolf's "Using Non-Traditional Methods to Assess Children's Understanding of Television" demonstrate the potential of this important methodological alternative.

This volume's second section, "Behavior," includes seven chapters addressing human interaction in various contexts. The first selection, Fumiteru Nitta's "'A Flower for You': Patterns of Interaction between Japanese Tourists and Hare Krishna Devotees in Honolulu," provides ethnographic data on a combination of two long standing areas of communication inquiry: intercultural interaction and persuasion. Through the use of an experiment, John A. Jones and James M. Vincent explore the effects of a particular communication event in "The Impact of Humor on Speaker Credibility in Funeral Eulogies."

In the context of interaction in formal business/industry, two theoretical analyses are offered. Robin E. Lester's "Organizational Culture, Uncertainty Reduction, and the Socialization of New Organizational Members" provides a thorough set of propositions regarding how appropriate social values are transmitted to organizational participants, while Nina Wishbow's "Applying the Concept of the Double Bind to Communication in Organizations" uses Bateson's classic model to elucidate interactional problems specific to organizational behavior.

With specific reference to mass communication's "effects" on behavior, Josephine R. Holz's "The Neo-Nazi March in Skokie: Communication and Consensus" details, through case study, how social understanding of an event can be related to the mass media's construction of that event. Similarly, Stanley J. Baran's experimental study, "Automobile 'Positioning' and the Construction of Social Reality," demonstrates how advertising may be more influential in creating social consensus than it is in actual marketing. Finally, a most current topic, "Video Games: Competing with Machines," is explored by Jarice Hanson through interviews with players. Hanson also ties this contemporary phenomenon into more traditional social theory on game and role playing.

"Artifacts," the third section, examines the resultant material commodities of communication processes. In the first chapter, David L. Graper examines the integration of lower-socioeconomic-status individuals into dominant U.S. worldview through "The Kung Fu Movie Genre: A Functionalist Perspective." Similarly, in "The Body and Femininity in Feminine Hygiene Advertising," Berkeley Kaite suggests that the evolution of "appropriate" roles for and self-concepts of American women is both reflected and taught in this specialized print "genre." Also, Ella G. Taylor and Andrea S. Walsh's " 'And Next Week—

Child Abuse!': Family Issues in Contemporary Made-for TV Movies" examines how "relevant" social issues are structured for mass consumption.

While the artifacts examined in the selections noted above might popularly be regarded as "apolitical" events, they are shown by the authors to contain implicit "politics" or ideological values. However, the next four chapters examine artifacts more explicitly related to "politics," persuasion, and "propaganda." In "The Moral Dilemma of Reporting Human Rights," Jarice Hanson and Christine Miller examine U.S. television's recent coverage of Central America with an eye toward the relationship between foreign policy and newsgathering operations. Veronica Schild also examines coverage of Central America, this time in the Canadian press. Her chapter, "The Coverage of El Salvador in the *Globe and Mail*," discusses the reconstruction of reality by the mainstream press. Graham Knight's "News of Talk, News of Riot" suggests how the recent coverage of events in Northern Ireland establishes an ideological stability. Lastly, "An Analysis of Anti-Handgun Propaganda" by Jerry M. Goldberg discusses the means by which a controversial cause (usually examined from the other side) is lobbied before government and the larger public.

The final section of this volume, "Institutions," regards certain formal cultural organizations in terms of their structural impact on society. In the first chapter, "The Role of Values in Supreme Court Opinions as Legal and Cultural Force," Candiss Baksa Vibbert analyzes a number of decisions and opinions by this ranking judicial institution to demonstrate their power as legitimators of social standards as well as purely legal precedents. In "From Ford to Carnegie: The Private Foundation and the Rise of Public Television," Ralph Engelman historically analyzes the role of two most major philanthropic institutions in the development of a particular endeavor to demonstrate the "merger" of public service and political control.

The three articles which follow all investigate mass-media institutions outside the U.S. Alexander F. Toogod in "Broadcasting as a Reflection of the Politicizing of German Culture" discusses how knowledge of Germany's special political character is essential to an understanding of its broadcasting regulation systems. In "Communications Multinationals in Subsaharan Africa: The Recording Industry in Kenya and Nigeria," Arnold S. Wolfe discusses a rarely treated African industry and explores the effects of foreign-based, multinational domination. Similarly, in Thomas L. McPhail's "Contemporary Canadian Communication Issues," the unique domination-related problems of Canada's role in the "Information Age" is investigated.

J.R. Rayfield's "The Language of Education and Revolutionary Policies in Formerly French West Africa" looks not at the mass media but at educational policies among emerging governments, and examines their import in establishing cultural balance and independence. Lastly, in "Local Telecommunications, Political Economy, and Enterprise Zones," Russell L. Stockard examines contemporary U.S. urban policy in the sphere of telecommunications and relates this to national economic development and regulation.

PART I

METHODOLOGY AND PHILOSOPHY OF SOCIAL SCIENCE

1

Ideology and Consciousness: The Construction of Social Meaning

FARREL J. CORCORAN

Northern Illinois University

Although coined almost two centuries ago, it is only recently that the word "ideology" is enjoying an undisputed popularity. It is not yet consistently defined and applied, however. Lately, there has been a major shift of interest in communication theory away from the behaviorist emphases of previous research approaches, towards the ideological problem of how messages are structured, how they function in the circulation and securing of dominant social definitions, and how communication can be analyzed as a process through which a particular culture is represented, maintained, or transformed. In American media theory, there has been a resounding absence of the notion of ideology. Specifically, the concept of cultural studies, of which ideology is a part, has been, as Carey (1979, p. 410) says, "generally misunderstood, ignored or misrepresented in the U.S." The purpose of this essay is to isolate and elucidate, against its historical background, the sense of ideology that predominates in modern Media Studies. The essay will also keep in sight the parallel notion of "consciousness" and explore recent attempts, particularly in European theory, to integrate the two, that is, to explain the subjective internalization of ideology in the formation of individual consciousness.

ORIGINS

Plato proposed the development of a critical process which would address common sense discourse, that system of misleading concepts evolved through custom, which today we would call ideological discourse, and deconstruct the seeming coherence between those concepts. His process of criticism involved what Laclau (1977, p. 7) calls "an operation of rupture," a rupture of the apparent obviousness of common sense discourse.

Although the term ideology did not emerge until the end of the eighteenth century, the seminal distinction between appearance and reality, which is basic to all theories of ideology today, is a constant theme in the development of European political philosophy. Machiavelli, for instance, articulating the dawning

3

critical consciousness of the emerging middle class, linked religion to power
and secular domination, and analyzed the social functions of religious thought
with a clarity that anticipated both Feuerbach and the early Marx:

> Our religion has glorified humble and contemplative men, rather than men of ac-
> tion. It has assigned as man's highest good humility, abnegation and contempt for
> mundane things . . . This pattern of life, therefore, appears to have made the
> world weak and to have handed it over as a prey to the wicked, who run it success-
> fully and securely since they are well aware that the generality of men, with para-
> dise for their goal, consider how best to bear, rather than how best to avenge,
> their injuries (quoted in Larrain 1979, p. 18).

The term "ideology" was created during the period of the French Revolution
by Antoine Destutt DeTracy, who used it to describe a new science, the science of ideas, Larrain, 1979, p. 27). It would have as its object the establishment of the origin of ideas. By overcoming religious and metaphysical prejudices, he hoped this would serve as a new basis for public education. Ideology,
along with grammar and logic, was to be a part of zoology and thus have a close
relation with the physical sciences (Miller, 1971, p. 27). The work of de Tracy
and his followers, who were called "the ideologists," was known in the new
American republic, at least by John Adams and Thomas Jefferson (Drucker,
1974, p. 13).

The term ideology was first given a negative connotation by Napoleon. Although he found himself on the same side as the "ideologues" during the Revolutionary period, he later became their target after he gained a position of absolute authority (Miller, 1971, p. 28). When they could not accept his despotic
excesses, Napoleon turned against them, using the description "ideologists"
with the derogatory meaning that they were unrealistic and doctrinaire intellectuals ignorant of the possibilities of politics (Larrain, 1979, p. 28).

In French political philosophy, the birth of this negative connotation is
linked to the fortunes of religion in general and to the Catholic Church in particular. In eighteenth century France, criticism of religion preceded criticism
of the State (Barth, 1976, p. 10). In the eyes of the ideologues, nothing endan-
gered social peace and the achievements of 1789 more than divisive religious
conflict and the siding of the State with religious authority for the purpose of
suppressing tolerance and freedom of conscience. Napoleon intended to found
the new political order of France on the traditional European basis of a religion
firmly rooted in the social order, which would sanction divinely ordained inequalities within a hierarchical social structure.

Among the pro-Bonapartist public, then, ideology came to connote something low and despicable, which, in the words of Walter Scott, Napoleon's biog-
rapher, prevailed "with none save hot-brained boys and crazed enthusiasts"
(Scott, 1887, p. 251). By 1812, contempt had blossomed into full-grown animos-
ity. In a speech to the *Conseil d'Etat* on his return from the disastrous Russian
campaign, Napoleon put the blame for his military catastrophe on the ideologues and the doctrines disseminated by them (Carlsnaes, 1981, p. 27).

To the present time, the concept of ideology has retained the connotation of an invective and accusation. Roucek (1944, p. 16) speaks of a "popular connotation of the term as visionary moonshine," and most modern dictionaries include the signification "theorizing of a visionary and impractical nature." Alongside the passive connotation is one of extremism and emotionalism: ideology is seen as "emotionally-charged beliefs about the substance of the 'good life' " (Mark, 1973, p. 3); a "force increasingly hostile to the advancement of civilization" (Feuer, 1975, Preface); "systems of beliefs that are implicitly totalitarian" (Halle, 1972, p. 6); "the product of a right- or left-wing stance, combined with a certain personality structure which predisposes a person to aggressive action, to dogmatic assertion and to Machiavellian practices" (Eysenck and Wilson, 1973, p. 310); or characterized by "bias, oversimplification, emotive language and adaptation to public prejudice" (Geertz, 1964, p. 47).

Although Napoleon was the first to give the term a derogatory association, Marxian usage incorporated a pejorative content into the concept of ideology itself (Carlsnaes, 1981, p. 28). This represents a return to a conception of ideology that is in line with Plato's notion of *Doxa* or common-sense discourse which, unlike philosophy and science, denotes sets of ideas not primarily conceived for cognitive purposes.

NINETEENTH CENTURY USAGE

During the nineteenth century there was a growing convergence between the term ideology and its negative content. This was taking place largely through the radical critique of religion by the so-called left-wing Hegelians, although without any formal connection with the term ideology. The transformation of Christianity into a dogmatic system was being described, for the first time, as responsible for alienation in society. Feuerbach went further by attempting to show that the attributes of the divinity, such as providence, goodness, love, and holiness, are really reifications of human attributes. As Feuerbach put it, "God is born in the misery of man" (Barth, 1976, p. 57). Religion was no longer seen either as a totally irrational belief or as an arbitrary invention of wicked priests trying to deceive the people. Feuerbach came close to the Marxian concept of ideology, which surpassed the critique of religion and asserted the negative and critical character of ideology.

Although Marx expressed unqualified appreciation of Feuerbach's work (Barth, 1976, p. 58), he criticized it for abstracting religion from the historical and social process. For Marx, the decisive explanation was that individuals are not inherently disposed to seek an illusionary satisfaction of desires in a god; social and economic conditions lead them to it. Marx was the first philosopher to make the connection between psychological distortions (previously analyzed at the level of superstitions, passions, and religious prejudices) and the historical development of an individual's social relations, with all their contradictions. When Marx finally arrived at his own general concept of ideology, it subsumed

not only religion but all forms of distorted consciousness, and it initiated a tradition of critically examining the negative, historical contradictions in a society in
relation to its dominant ideology. So, although non-Marxists use the term, often with a different meaning, most modern writers discussing cultural criticism
take into account the Marxian usage.

An ideology understands a culture within the framework of a set of assumptions which are characteristic of a specific social group but have probably spread
beyond it to other groups. It reflects a systematic orientation of thought, a point
of view derived from the conditions of existence and the forms of thought and
feeling of a particular group. Therefore, it is biased towards that group in a systematic and pervasive way, implicitly suggesting that a society which is not
structured in harmony with its characteristic forms of thought and conditions of
existence is not fully rational. As Marx puts it, an ideology "defends,"
"justifies," "legitimizes," "speaks for," or is an "apologia" for a particular group.
It is necessarily led to "conceal," "disguise," "mystify," or "misunderstand" its
subject-matter (Parekh, 1982, p. 30).

What of the social group to which an ideology is biased? Although Marx concentrated on class-based ideology, the dominant social group might be a nation,
a race, a linguistic group, a professional group, or even a subgroup within a
class. Thus, a history of Rome or India, which selectively interprets facts so as
to show the good leadership of the Patricians or the Brahmans and the chaos of
their opponents' leadership, defined either in terms of the objectively shared
conditions of existence (class-in-itself) or in terms of the awareness among people of common identity springing from their common experience (class-in-itself)
is of major importance to Marx (Marx and Engels, 1968, pp. 117f and 170–171).
His theoretical frame of reference was bounded by the three major classes of his
time—those who owned large amounts of land (earning income from ground
rents), those who owned capital (earning profit from interest), and those who
owned labor-power (earning income from wages). Other classes included the
petit bourgeoisie, whose role in the economic structure lay in the realm of the
circulation of commodities rather than their production; the professionals, who
provided the technical expertise for the social structure, trained qualified people, administered government, etc.; and the lumpenproletariat, the poor, the
unemployed, the homeless, the criminal, etc. Class-in-itself involves the objective existence of classes like these, based on a social structure produced by the
unequal social or economic conditions of existence. People's response to their
class situation gives rise to the secondary notion of class-for-itself, people becoming conscious of themselves as belonging to a specific group and struggling
against other classes in a process that produces collective self-consciousness.
Without this there is alienated consciousness, the sense of being a unidimen-
sional, highly fragmented, superfluous and instrumental being. This greatly-
weakened self-consciousness, Marx claimed, affects people's whole manner of
living.

THE MARXIAN CONCEPT OF CULTURE

The concept of culture implied here attacks the traditional theory of cultural autonomy. By emphasizing the ways in which culture reflects the labor process, Marx has changed the dominant concept of how human activity formed its world and how human consciousness was in turn formed by that world. Related, though distinctly different, attacks on cultural autonomy can be found more recently in Whorf's (1956) idea that language fashions culture and Innis's (1968) idea that technology shapes culture. Marx was their forerunner in bringing to an end the concept of culture as a separate and autonomous sphere of human activity.

Any approach to Marx's theory must begin with the proposition that a material base in society determines an ideological superstructure. In 1851, Marx wrote:

> Upon the several forms of property, upon the social conditions of existence, a whole superstructure is reared of various and peculiarly shaped feelings, illusions, habits of thought and conceptions of life. The whole class produces and shapes these out of its material foundation and out of the corresponding social conditions. The individual unit to whom they flow through tradition and education may fancy that they constitute the true reasons for and premises of his conduct (Marx and Engels, 1962, Vol. 1, p. 27).

Eight years later he wrote:

> The mode of production of material life determines the general character of the social, political and spiritual processes of life. It is not the consciousness of people that determines their being but, on the contrary, their social being that determines their consciousness (Marx, 1964, p. 51).

Since the death of Marx in 1883, the Marxist tradition has been divided over the extent to which the base "determines" the superstructure. "Vulgar" Marxism (Rader, 1979, p. xx) has interpreted the base-superstructure model in a narrowly deterministic way, since the idea of erecting something on a base implies that the base precedes and supports the superstructure which is later erected on it. Many critics reject this reductively economistic kind of analysis. Engels was the first to react against the oversimplification of the economic factor and the undialectical conception of cause and effect as rigidly opposite poles:

> According to the materialist conception of history, the *ultimately* determining factor in history is the production and reproduction of real life. Neither Marx nor I have ever asserted more than this. Hence, if somebody twists this into saying that the economic factor is the *only* determining one, he transforms that proposition into a meaningless, abstract, absurd phrase (Marx and Engels, 1975, p. 394).

The confusion has been confounded by the contention that there were "two Marxes," an "early" and a "mature" Marx, whose ideas are discontinuous

(Carlsnaes, 1981, p. 50), and by the fact that the fundamentalist version of the base-superstructure model, tending towards economic determinism, took root when less than half of what Marx had written was published and was favored by such political leaders as Lenin and Mao Tse Tung (Rader, 1979, pp. 4–5). More recent theorists, favoring the dialectical interactionism of Engels' model, point out, first, that Marx used a variety of expressions, such as "condition," "shape," "mould," and "form" to describe the base-superstructure relationship (Parekh, 1982, p. 26) and second, that the root sense of "determine" is "setting bounds" or "setting limits," rather than "to cause" (Williams, 1977, p. 34). Determinism, in recent writings, is seen as a complex and interrelated process of multiple, structured limits and pressures embodied in the whole social process itself.

Any approach to the Marxian theory of culture must also address the notion of "false consciousness." Without using the term, Marx and Engels had stressed the idea that people suffer from class-based illusions and mystifications. The term "false consciousness" appeared for the first time in a letter by Engels, ten years after the death of Marx:

> Ideology is a process accomplished by the so-called thinker consciously, it is true, but with false consciousness. The real motive forces impelling him remain unknown to him: otherwise it simply would not be an ideological process. Hence, he imagines false or seeming motive forces (Marx and Engels, 1962, p. 451)

An ideology, then, is essentially a body of thought giving a systematically biased and distorted account of its subject matter, but also with enough grains of truth to make it plausible. It has an empirical basis in the experience of a specific social group and it is normative for the rest of society, turning what is a fact for one group into an "ought" or "ideal" for all groups. Insofar as it presents an illusion or appearance of reality, it has obvious similarities with Marx's theory of fetishism; just as, at the level of the economic base, the products of work are given a life of their own by being fetishized, so social roles are reified in the ideological superstructure (law, politics, education, media, etc.). Not until the time of Lenin was the term ideology no longer taken as synonymous with false consciousness but given its own neutral meaning.

IDEOLOGY AS MYSTIFICATION

If the task of ideology is to bring about the logical transition from what is a fact for one group to what is a norm for others, it might reasonably be asked why ideology is so persistent, why so many individuals do not see through its distortions. Ideological explanations tend to misperceive and distort and mystify because they universalize a partial social point of view. The bourgeoisie, for instance, will argue that people are *by nature* possessive and that the bourgeois form of society, with its laws and institutions protecting private property, is *natural* to human kind. Here the limits of this point of view are taken as the limits of the world itself, as what is natural and self-evident. It would also, of course, suit the practical interests of the bourgeoisie if everyone behaved as bourgeois, thus eliminating any subversive challenge to the social structure. As Marx puts it, one need not take the narrow view that one class *explicitly* sets out to assert its own class interests: "it rather believes that the *particular* conditions of its liberation are the only *general* conditions within which modern society can be saved" (Marx and Engels, 1962, Vol. 1, p. 275).

In this sense, ideology legitimizes the class structure and becomes indispensable for its reproduction in a non-coercive way. The medieval serfs who accepted their inferior status as part of a God-given hierarchical order, or the slaves who believed in their owners' right to do with them as they pleased in Colonial America, or the bourgeoisie who accepted the principle of the Divine Right of Kings in pre-Revolutionary France, were all negative classes who internalized ideological beliefs that originated elsewhere and mystified their exploitation. In each case, the socio-cultural world was perceived as necessity and fate. In more recent times, the mystique of feminine fulfillment, according to Betty Friedan (1963, p. 68) was so powerful "that women grew up no longer knowing that they have the desires and capabilities the mystique forbids."

The most basic form of reasoning characteristic of ideological thought is the fallacy of reducing history to nature and presenting a prevailing practice or idea as "natural," "normal," "rational," "reasonable," or "necessary." This is why Marx was intensely suspicious of any reference to "nature" in philosophy, seeing this as a cloak for legitimizing a social practice (Parekh, 1982, p. 138). An ideology that has successfully universalized, naturalized, and dehistoricized the world-view of a particular social group then finds it easy to present the critic as naive, irresponsible, Utopian, or even as "an ideologist" (in the Napoleonic sense, of course), because one of the most striking aspects of ideology is that it is "critical towards its adversary but—uncritical towards itself" (Marx and Engels, 1975, Vol. 3, p. 181).

IDEOLOGY AFTER MARX

The evolution from a negative to a positive concept of ideology within Marxist theory was achieved by Lenin. If Engels was the first to react against the oversimplification and rigidification of cause and effect within the polarity economic base and ideological superstructure, Lenin leaned in the opposite direction, arguing that there is no need for analysis of superstructures themselves since they can be reduced to essential economic relations. As used by Lenin, the term ideology was no longer synonymous with false consciousness but assumed a neutral meaning. Bourgeois ideology, not ideology as such, was false. "To belittle the Socialist ideology in any way," he wrote, "to turn away from it in the slightest degree, means to strengthen bourgeois ideology" (Lenin, 1950, pp. 233–234).

The concept now included distorted, as much as true, forms of consciousness, which could be distinguished in practice only under the leadership of a centralized, vanguard party which would have a correct understanding of socialist theory. Lenin's thesis of the two ideologies, either of which excludes the other and which together exhaust the universe of ideology, contrasts sharply with the Marxian notion of ideology as contained solely within the bounds of bourgeois consciousness.

Marx's notion that definite forms of social consciousness correspond to the totality of relations of production, was pursued by Lukacs (1971) in his efforts to avoid the simple notion that a superstructural phenomenon such as literature directly reflects the base. Instead, he explored the refractions, transformations, or mediations which reveal the dialectical relations between "consciousness" and "society," thus giving impetus to the sociology of consciousness. Lukacs lent theoretical development to the notion of ideology as the reification of social relationships in the interest of one class. Ideology disguised these social relationships at the base of society by abstracting social processes and presenting them as natural laws of social development. Thus, all groups in society are "alienated," in the sense of looking on social relations as external forces to which they must resign themselves (Lukacs, 1971). Lukacs insisted on the importance of superstructures in the development of historical processes, but though he avoided Leninist economic reductionism, he has not avoided the accusation of class reductionism by contemporary Marxists (e.g., Laclau, 1977, p. 125).

Gramsci continued the trend away from a purely negative concept of ideology. Since superstructures are where people gain awareness of their positions in society, Marxism itself is a superstructure, just like every other class ideology (Gramsci, 1971, p. 366). The superiority of Marxism is based on its being the most conscious expression of social contradictions.

Gramsci's most important contribution to the theory of ideology is his analysis of the relationship between ideology and the state, based on the concept of hegemony, which today is recognized as one of the major turning points in cultural theory (e.g., Williams, 1977, p. 108; Hall et al, 1980, p. 35). The traditional definition of hegemony as political rule or domination of one state by another is expanded by Gramsci to both include and go beyond ideology. Ideology is a relatively formal and articulated system of meanings, values, and beliefs, the decisive form in which consciousness is at once expressed and controlled. A subordinate or negative class has nothing but this ideology as its consciousness since, as Marx pointed out, the production of all ideas is in the hands of those who control the primary means of production. The political power of a ruling class consists not simply in its monopoly of the repressive apparatuses of the state (tax collectors, the courts, the prison system, the army, police, etc.) but in its ideological hegemony over society as a whole. The ideological apparatuses of this hegemony are rooted not only in the state but what Gramsci termed "civil society," that is, in the "private" activities of citizens (in family, school, university, church, media, trade unions, political parties, etc.). Gramsci used the concept of hegemony to refer to the way in which "a certain way of life and thought is dominant, in which one concept of reality is diffused throughout society in all its institutional and private manifestations" (Cammett, 1967, p. 204).

The concept of hegemony views the relations of domination and subordination as what Williams (1977, p. 110) calls

> a saturation of the whole process of living . . . to such a depth that the pressures and limits of what can ultimately be seen as a specific economic, political and cultural system seem to most of us the pressures and limits of simple experience and common sense . . . . It thus constitutes a sense of reality for most people in the society, a sense of absolute because experienced reality beyond which it is very difficult for most members of the society to move, in most areas of their lives.

This hegemonic culture, embodying the lived dominance and subordination of different groups, has internal structures that are highly complex, through which it is defended, modified, or renewed. At any time, forms of oppositional culture exist which threaten its dominance and, in turn, are threatened with being neutralized or controlled or incorporated. Gramsci's concept of hegemony, then, moves cultural analysis beyond mere observation of superstructural "manipulation" by a dominant class. It recognizes that modern industrial societies have very complex links between political, economic, and cultural activities; between, for instance, the realities of electoral politics, "leisure" and "privacy," family, school, church, language or ethnic group, race, specific places of work and living, and the major communications systems. Gramsci would argue that the resultant learning within these practices is tied to a selected range of meanings and values which are the foundations of the hegemonic. Selective attitudes to self, to others, to a social order, and to the material world are consciously and unconsciously taught, resulting in effective self-identification with the hegemonic forms, either positively or with resigned recognition of the inevitable and the necessary. Instead of identifying with themselves, for instance, workers identify with symbols of authority and the lifestyles of the rich, famous, and powerful. Instead of identifying with their common educational goals, students identify with the institutional needs and training imperatives of employers.

Gramsci's thinking is peculiarly relevant to modern industrial societies in which the institutions of state and civil society have reached a stage of great complexity, in which the consent of the popular masses is required to secure the ascendancy of particular groups, in which earlier Marxist notions of economic or class determination of ideological superstructures are less persuasive. His influence has been particularly evident in the area of media studies, particularly in England (cf., Hall et al,. 1980), because of the role of communication systems in the process of hegemonic continuity. The suppression of ideological alternatives, once carried out exclusively through the legal system, is now seen to be achieved in part by the mass media in their ability to define the parameters of legitimate discussion and debate over alternative beliefs, values, and world views. Rarely is direct censorship needed; the more effective hegemonic process is the ability of media to define "what is legitimate, sane, reasonable, practical, good, true and beautiful" (Sallach, 1974, p. 166).

WHO KNOWS?

If the concept of ideology, whatever its variations, implies an obfuscation of actual social relations, from what sector can a critique be launched which will successfully remove the ideological veil which hides the features of a repressive society and thus dispel false consciousness? Orthodox Marxist theory has always maintained that Marx himself offered his critique of social reality from the proletarian point of view. Some recent writers have suggested that although he stressed the role of the negative class in every historical epoch as the best articulator of a critique (for instance, the bourgeoisie during the very early years of capitalism, before they became dominant, their mantle as negative class passed on in the nineteenth Century to the proletariat), and although Marx's own critique profoundly benefited from the proletarian point of view of his time, his critique was not essentially undertaken from that point of view (Parekh, 1982, p. 185). The point remains controversial.

Two writers who have developed the Marxist critique, while explicitly rejecting the mission of both the proletariat and the vanguard party in this task, are Mannheim and Marcuse. Mannheim argued that it is the mission of intellectuals to illuminate the nature of socially-bound interests which distort the thinking of all other social groups. Intellectuals alone are suited to this task because they form a classless group, "a social stratum which is to a large degree unattached to any social class" (Mannheim, 1936, p. 40). Marcuse had a similar mission for the intellectual. Advanced industrial culture is more ideological than its predecessors in the sense that the goods or services it produces "sell" the system of social relations as a whole. "The irresistible output of the entertainment and information industry carry with them prescribed attitudes and habits, certain intellectual and emotional reactions which bind the consumers more or less pleasantly to the producers, and through the latter, to the whole" (Marcuse, 1964, p. 12). For Marcuse, as for Mannheim, neither the proletariat nor the vanguard party are capable of the reformist task ascribed to them by Marx and Lenin respectively. Each is integrated into the existing system and suffers from false consciousness. The universities, along with oppressed minorities in the Third World, could be relied upon to provide an emancipated consciousness and carry on the task of political education (Marcuse, 1972, p. 28). This rejection of class and party as harbingers of enlightenment is echoed by Habermas (1970, p. 30), who suggests that the process of "petrification" of consciousness has progressed so far that it can be broken through today only "under the socio-psychologically exceptional conditions of university study."

IDEOLOGY AND PSYCHOANALYSIS

Traditional Marxist theory has been slow to explain how the conditioning of consciousness by social factors takes place, slow to develop a political psychology which would supplement the theory of ideology. Some attempts have been made, however, centered around the work of Freud, Reich, and Lacan.

Although the term ideology was not used by Freud, a psychological conception of ideology emerges from his conviction that most human acts in society respond to basic impulses and instincts and that the human mind tries to conceal this by giving a rational account of irrational behavior. The psychological mechanism of transposition or projection, for example, which, Freud (1958, p. 209) claimed, "is very commonly employed in normal life" as well as in paranoid states of mind, consists of an internal impulse which is concealed or distorted by its transposition in consciousness into the form of an external perception.

This mechanism matches, in an inverted way, the mechanism of ideology by which an external contradiction receives a distorted solution in the mind. Freud came close to a psychological theory of ideology near the end of his career in his analysis of the defense mechanism called "identification" and in his analysis of religion. A child, for instance, when overwhelmed by fear of an aggressor, may attempt to overcome the unbearable anguish by identifying with the personality of the aggressor. Freud saw this mechanism as one of the factors which could explain the attachment of oppressed people to the cultural ideas of their oppressors. In his analysis of religion, Freud followed Feuerbach in contending that human beings have always needed protection against the uncertainties of life and thus create gods with the traits of father figure.

Reich took the individual mechanisms of Freud a stage further by suggesting that they can have a collective impact in the form of an ideology. His analysis of German National Socialism, for example, suggests that extreme nationalism and racism could politically motivate a frustrated population whenever a rigid patriarchy and extreme repression of sexual impulses mold character structure in a particular way. Thus, he expanded traditional Marxist analysis by emphasizing that the determinations of the material structure of society alone are not sufficient to explain ideology. Reich made a systematic attempt to incorporate social influences into psychoanalytic theory and reveal the psychological processes which influence the social conditioning of consciousness. In his view, political psychology should try "to determine as completely as possible, the myriad intermediary links in the transforming of the material base into the ideological superstructure" (Reich 1976, p. xxviii).

Reich's conclusion was that the social structure is psychologically reproduced within the individual as a corresponding character structure and that this takes place primarily within the setting of the family, which provides the crucial mediation between ideology and the development of character. In addressing the question of why large numbers of people were mobilized by Fascism, Reich believed that the movement appealed to the authoritarian character structure of the middle-class family, which could share, via identification, with the greatness of the Fuhrer and the nation (Reich, 1970, pp. 75–79). Working-class families, not being as isolated from one another in working and living conditions, cultivated less rigid character structures, better able to resist the authority of exploiters, with the result that the largest core of followers of Fascism were rural, business, and white-collar middle classes (Reich, 1970, p. 13).

In Reich's view, then, ideology is embedded in character structure, the basic traits of which are formed in early childhood during the development of the superego. The patriarchal family is not only an economic unit but a transmitter of ideologies and an agent in the development of a submissive character structure. The ideological function of the family is experienced by its members as feelings of family responsibility. The wage-earner accepts unjust conditions of employment imposed by the employer and represses anger provoked by exploitation; women continue to serve as domestic servants in the family. These feelings of duty breed conservatism and the repression of social criticism by blocking the articulation of anger and frustration felt in the workplace, all in the interest of family responsibility. Ideologically reconciled to the existing social order, parents communicate their acceptance of social authority to their children.

Character structure is also determined within the family through its lifelong repression of sexuality and the association of unconscious feelings of guilt with sexual desires. The same psychological disposition is the basis of mass acceptance of class authority: by assimilating the external authority of sexual morals, the individual is predisposed to internalize and submit to authority in social life (Reich, 1970, pp. 30–1). In this way, the transmission of moralistic sexual attitudes within the family assumes political consequences, because the family "produces the authority-fearing, life-fearing vassal and thus constantly creates new possibilities whereby a handful of men in power can rule the masses" (Reich, 1975, p. 95).

Reich argued that his theory added a psychological dimension to Marx's theory of ideology by explaining how ideologies are reproduced within individuals through unconscious association with repressed impulses. The process is dialectical; the social conditions which force people to repress basic needs and emotions produce characterological submissiveness which readily accepts the relationships of authority that are taken for granted in dominant ideology (Cohen, 1982, p. 157). Thus Reich offers refinement to the traditional Marxist explanation of human nature as an embodiment of the history and structure of the social relationships within which it finds itself.

FRENCH STRUCTURALISM

While Reich's political psychology found its roots in Freud's theory of censoring mechanisms, many of the contemporary French analyses of the psychology of ideology find their roots in Freud's approach to language. His theoretical model of the unconscious suggests that it is the site of meaningful representations of experiences which can be consciously apprehended through language. Freud's method of analyzing the latent content of dreams (the whole range of thoughts which have been repressed) is characterized by unraveling the primary processes which govern the links between latent content and the manifest content which the dreamer can remember (Freud, 1958, p. 277).

Setting out to reinterpret Freud in the light of Saussurian linguistic theory, Lacan emphasized the mechanisms of condensation and displacement as the very mechanisms of language itself, through which the social construction of the individual subject takes place. Through condensation, one idea comes to represent a number of chains of meaning in the unconscious. Through displacement, an originally important idea is invested with psychic energy which is due to another drive-motivated ideal. Lacan linked condensation to metaphoric relations in language, whereby a conscious ideal is linked to a number of unconscious chains of meaning. And he linked displacement with metonymy, the linguistic ability to represent an idea by reference to only part of it. Much of this linguistic ability is initiated in a child's "mirror" phase of development, when the child, at about the age of six months, experiences itself as a fragmented mass of uncoordinated limbs and learns to identify with a mirror image of a complete, unified body. With its imaginary experience of wholeness and self-control, however, this recognition is actually based on mis-recognition, because children at this stage cannot distinguish between themselves and their object of imaginary identification (Lacan, 1977, p. 19).

This structure of mis-recognition has been taken up by Althusser, Laclau and others as one of the mechanisms at work in the process of ideology. The unformed infant becomes a subject through entering into language, a network of signifiers organized around certain culturally privileged signifiers which act as nodal points structuring the network in a definite way. The operation of ideology is explained in a similar way. Thus Althusser emphasized the relative autonomy of the ideological superstructure and created a space within Marxism for more serious analysis of how ideology signifies. In helping to bring to the fore the question of subjectivity and its importance for the working of ideology, Althusser introduced the concepts of misrecognition and interpellation.

Althusser (1965, pp. 231–235) defines ideology as

> a system (with its own logic and rigor) of representations (images, myths, ideas or concepts, depending on the case) endowed with a historical existence and role within a given society . . . In ideology people do indeed express, not the relation between them and their conditions of existence but the *way* they live the relationship between them and their real conditions of existence. In ideology, the real relation is inevitably invested in the imaginary relation, a relation that expresses a will (conservative, conformist, reformist or revolutionary), a hope or a nostalgia, rather than describing a reality . . . . Ideology (as a system of mass representations) is indispensable in any society if people are to be formed, transformed or equipped to respond to the demands of their conditions of existence.

Ideology, for Althusser, produces an account of the world which is the mystified form in which people experience their relation to the world. In a major break from Marx, Engels, and Lenin, Althusser contends that no matter what kind of society we live in, classless or class-divided, we cannot exist without a certain representation of our world and of our relations to it. Ideology is a structural feature of society. Althusser poses the question how are concrete individuals in society formed as subjects who "live" class oppression and accept them as "necessary" (Althusser, 1971, pp. 123–173). He answers by drawing on Lacan's concept of the "mirror" (Lacan, 1977). Just as an infant is confronted by the prefabricated "self" it will become in its "mirror" phase, so an ideological subject is formed as a subject by recognizing an image of the other as its own image. The function of ideology in adapting individuals to society's demands is achieved by constituting the individual as subject in the world—and not allowing the individual to be seen as the object or effect of the world. This takes place through the crucial act of individuals recognizing the illusion that the world and history were created for them, with the assurance that if they conform with what is required of them by society, all will be well. Thus, Althusser retains the materialistic notion of individuals being constituted as subjects by a pre-existing system of relations, but borrows the psychoanalytic notion of the "mirror" to explain how the roles of subject/object are reversed by ideology as individuals come to see themselves as subjects who live the relation with their real conditions as if they themselves were the "autonomous principle of determination" of that relation (Laclau, 1977, p. 100).

The notion of the subject is undoubtedly among the more obscure features of Althusser's philosophy (Callinicos, 1976, p. 65), as is his notion of "interpellation." Ideology transforms individuals into subjects by "that very precise operation which I have called interpellation or hailing and which can be imagined along the lines of the most commonplace everyday police (or other) hailing: 'Hey, you there' " (Althusser, 1971, p. 163). When individuals are interpellated as subjects, the ambiguity of the term "subject" emerges: "(1) a free subjectivity, a center of initiatives, author of and responsible for its actions; (2) a subjected being, who submits to a higher authority and is therefore stripped of all freedom except that of freely accepting submission" (Althusser, 1971, p. 169).

Laclau (1977, pp. 102–104), insisting on the plurality of ideologies available to a subject, suggests that different types of interpellations (political, aesthetic, religious, familial, etc.) may coexist even while being articulated within a unified ideological discourse and being a symbol of each other. In periods of stability, contradictions can be neutralized and absorbed by the dominant ideological discourse, as, for instance, between religious interpellations of an ascetic kind and an increasing enjoyment of worldly goods, without subjects "living" these as incompatible. In periods of crisis, however, when ideological contradictions in all their sharpness become translated into an "identity crisis," one sector may try to reconstitute a new ideological unity through a narrative version which denies all interpellations but one, and transforms this into a critique of the existing system and a reconstruction of the entire ideological domain.

The religious interpellation, for instance, may come to be a chief reorganizer of all familial, political, aesthetic, economic, and other aspects of culture. Examples of this can be seen in the rise of Wahhabism in eighteenth century Arabia, or of Khomeinism, or the Religious New Right in contemporary Iran and America.

IDEOLOGY AND SEMIOTICS

The linguistic theories of de Saussure have had an important influence in directing attention (mainly Lacan's) to Freud's approach to language and the unconscious. In a very different way, de Saussure has had an influence on recent semiotic attempts to understand how ideology has its effects. As Poulantzas (1971, p. 207) emphasizes, the social function of ideology

> is not to give agents a true knowledge of the social structure but simply to insert them, as it were, into their political activities supporting this structure. Precisely because it is determined by its structure, at the level of experience the social whole remains opaque to its agents.

How are our perceptions of social reality distorted? One tradition of ideological analysis would reply that the answer is to be found, not in surface forms but at the deep structural level where discourse is coded. This approach bypasses the traditional Marxian polarity of ideology and consciousness by emphasizing that ideology is profoundly "unconscious." Althusser alludes to this without going on to a specifically semiotic analysis:

> Ideology is indeed a system of representations but in the majority of cases these representations have nothing to do with 'consciousness'; they are usually images and occasionally concepts, but it is above all as *structures* that they impose on the vast majority of people, not via their 'consciousness' (Althusser, 1965, p.65).

Drawing on the Chomskian notion of generative grammatical rules, that is, a set of rules which, though finite, are capable of generating an infinite set of propositions (Chomsky, 1965), Veron views ideology *not* as a body of propositions of a certain kind but instead as a body of semiotic rules capable of generating a certain set of images and concepts and defining the constrictions to which their production is subject: "Ideology is a system of coding reality and not a determined set of coded messages within this system . . . . This way, ideology becomes autonomous in relation to the consciousness or intention of its agents" (Veron, 1971, p. 68).

Analysis of the latent organization of messages should arrive at rules of selection and combination of the signs which constitute a message. By disentangling these rules, we would arrive at the core of the message, that is, not only its denotative content or its connative (latent) style of expression but also what was not said but could be said. This latter category is referred to in semiotic theory as paradigmatic analysis (Fiske and Hartley, 1978, pp. 50–51). It is foreshadowed in Marx's interest in exploring an individual's underlying *forms* of thought, the general limits within which thought remains "confined," "bounded," "restricted," "shut up," or "imprisoned" (Parekh, 1982, p. 126). It is implicit, though left unexplored, in modern American theories of "agenda-setting" in the media (Sallach, 1974, p. 169; Saldich, 1981, p. 26). It is evident also in attempts to emphasize the family as an important ideological apparatus which imposes closure on meaning, thus delimiting children's mental horizons and fixing them within a particular ideology (Larrain, 1979, p. 167).

TO BE A CRITIC

The analysis of ideology is currently one of the fastest growing areas within media studies. To be a critic of ideology, however, presents a major epistemological problem. If ideology is so all-persuasive, how can one be liberated from it? If ideology appears to be in opposition to science, as a pre-scientific mode of cognition, how can one be sure to be engaging in scientific as opposed to ideological theoretical practice? If ideology is a form of thought resulting from the universalization of a partial and narrow social point of view, it would seem that critics can rise above their limiting assumptions if they are acutely aware of and concerned to transcend them. Marx believed, rather optimistically, that one could become a "free agent of thought" and, with enough self-consciousness and self-criticism, look at society from *any* stand-point (Parekh, 1982, p. 27). The following theses would be important: Critics should investigate, with a rigorous critical attitude, the inner structure of society rather than its phenomenal forms, be aware of how their own position in society mediates their relations with what is being studied, and avoid ahistorical concepts or methods of investigation or ways of understanding the prevailing social order (Parekh, 1982, p. 143).

Yet a doubt remains as to where critics of ideology can be found: within a negative class (Marx and Engels), or within a vanguard party committed to raising the consciousness of that class (Lenin), or within the ranks of intellectuals who are (supposedly) free of class ties (Mannheim and Marcuse). Yet the characterization of intellectuals as somehow above ideology is itself an ideological position, as is the general academic belief that methodologies and agenda for study are uninfluenced by social bias. The social theorist brings to the study of society a specific social point of view, a body of attitudes, assumptions, and interests which shape the selection, organization, and interpretation of the subject matter. The ideological view of the academic denies the social mediation of knowledge, thus overlooking a powerful source of bias, and views universities as transcendental institutions in no way shaped by society. As Althusser (1971, pp. 163–164) contends,

> what takes place in ideology seems therefore to take place outside it. That is why those who are in ideology believe themselves outside ideology: one of the aspects of ideology is the practical denegation of the ideological character of ideology by

ideology: ideology never says "I am ideological." It is necessary to be outside ideology, that is, in scientific knowledge, to be able to say: I am in ideology (a quite exceptional case) or (the general case) I was in ideology.

The precise relationship between "science" and "ideology" is a crucial aspect of the epistemological question which underlies much of recent media study: How do I know that my critique is not itself ideological?

REFERENCES

Althusser, L. (1965). *For Marx*. London: New Left Books.

Althusser, L. (1971). *Lenin, Philosophy and Other Essays*. London: New Left Books.

Barth, H. (1976). *Truth and Ideology*. Berkeley, CA: University of California Press.

Callinicos, A. (1976). *Althusser's Marxism*. London: Pluto Press.

Cammett, J. M. (1967). *Antonio Gramsci and the Origins of Italian Communism*. Stanford, CA: Stanford University Press.

Carey, J. W. (1979). "Mass Communication Research and Cultural Studies." *In* J. Curran, M. Gurevitch, and J. Woollicott (Eds), *Mass Communication and Society*. Beverly Hills, CA: Sage.

Carlsnaes, W. (1981). *The Concept of Ideology and Political Analysis*. London: Greenwood.

Chomsky, N. (1965). *Aspects of a Theory of Syntax*. Cambridge, MA: MIT Press.

Cohen, I. H. (1982). *Ideology and Consciousness*. New York: New York University Press.

Drucker, H. M. (1974). *The Political Uses of Ideology*. London: MacMillan.

Eysenck, H. J., and Wilson, G. D. (1973). *The Experimental Study of Freudian Theories*. London, Methuen.

Feuer, L. S. (1975). *Ideology and the Ideologists*. Oxford, England: Blackwell.

Fiske, J., and Hartley, J. (1978). *Reading Television*. London: Methuen.

Freud, S. (1958). *The Standard Edition of the Complete Psychological Works of Sigmund Freud*. London: Hogarth.

Friedan, B. (1963). *The Feminine Mystique*. New York: Norton.

Geertz, C. (1964). "Ideology as Cultural System." *In* D. E. Apter (Ed.), *Ideology and Discontent*. New York: Free Press.

Gramsci, A. (1971). *Selections from the Prison Notebooks*. Lawrence and Wishart.

Habermas, J. (1970). *Towards a Rational Society*. Boston, MA: Beacon.

Hall, S. et. al. (1980). *Culture, Media, Language*. London: Hutchinson.

Halle, L. J. (1972). *The Ideological Imagination*. Chicago, IL: Quadrangle Books.

Innis, H. A. (1968). *The Bias of Communication*. Toronto, Ontario: University of Toronto Press.

Lacan, J. (1977). *Ecrits: A Selection*. New York: Norton.

Laclau, E. (1977). *Politics and Ideology in Marxist Theory*. London: New Left Books.

Larrain, J. (1979). *The Concept of Ideology*. London: Hutchinson.

Lenin, V. I. (1950). "What is to be done." *In Selected Works*. Moscow: Progress Publishers.

Lukacs, G. (1971). *History and Class Consciousness*. Cambridge, MA: MIT Press.

Mannheim, K. (1936). *Ideology and Utopia: An Introduction to the Sociology of Knowledge*. New York: Harcourt, Brace.

Marcuse, H. (1964). *One Dimensional Man: Studies in the Ideology of Advanced Industrial Society*. Boston, MA: Beacon Press.

Marcuse, H. (1972). *Counter Revolution and Revolt*. Boston, MA: Beacon Press.

Mark, M. (1973). *Modern Ideologies*. New York: St. Martin's Press.

Marx, K. (1964). *Selected Writings in Sociology and Social Philosophy*. New York: McGraw Hill.

Marx, K., and Engels, F. (1962). *Selected Works*, Vol. 1. Moscow: Progress Publishers.

Marx, K., and Engels, F. (1968). *Selected Works*, Vol. 1. London: Lawrence and Wishart.

Marx, K., and Engels, F. (1975). *Selected Correspondence*. Moscow: Progress Publishers.

Miller, K. B. (1971). *Ideology and Moral Philosophy*. New York: Humanities Press.

Parekh, B. C. (1982). *Marx's Theory of Ideology*. Baltimore, MD: Johns Hopkins University Press.

Poulantzas, N. A. (1971). *Political Power and Social Classes*. London: New Left Books.

Rader, M. M. (1979). *Marx's Interpretation of History*. New York: Oxford University Press.

Reich, W. (1970). *Mass Psychology of Fascism*. New York: Farrar, Strauss & Giroux.

Reich, W. (1975). *Sexual Revolution: towards a Self-Regulating Character Structure*. New York: Simon and Schuster.

Reich, W. (1976). *Character Analysis*. New York: Simon and Schuster.

Roucek, J. S. (1944). "A History of the Concept of Ideology." *Journal of the History of Ideas*. 5, 479–488.

Sallach, D. L. (1974). "Class Domination and Ideological Hegemony." *In* G. Tuchman (Ed.), *The TV Establishment*. Englewood Cliffs, NJ: Prentice Hall.

Saldich, A. R. (1981). "Electronic Democracy: How TV Governs." *In* C. Lowe (Ed.), *Television and American Culture*. New York: H. W. Wilson.

Scott, W. (1887). *The Life of Napoleon the Great*. Philadelphia, PA: Lippincott.

Veron, E. (1971). "Ideology and Social Sciences: A Communicational Approach." *Semiotica 3*, 68.

Whorf, B. L. (1956). *Language, Thought and Reality*. Cambridge, MA: MIT Press.

Williams, R. (1977). *Marxism and Literature*. Oxford, England: Oxford University Press.

2

The Technological Determination of Philosophy

PAUL LEVINSON

Fairleigh Dickinson University

This paper advocates neither a strict technological nor a media determinism. Indeed, this paper subscribes to no determinism at all, in the sense that determinism has come to mean a single-cause explanation of history in which all manner of human events are seen as satellites of one, underlying, controlling activity, such as economics in the case of Marx or expression of sexual energy in the case of Freud. This paper rejects these determinisms because Marx and Freud were both right—as are other determinisms such as those focused on food (Tannahill, 1973), disease (e.g., McNeill, 1976), geography (Toynbee, 1934–1954), and communications technology (Innis, 1951; McLuhan, 1962)—that is, this paper admits the obvious case that human events are the product of a complex and interacting plurality or ecology of factors, in which economics, sexuality, and the others figure most amply but not exclusively. In fact, the number of elements and their real and possible interactions and permutations that determine the course of human events are so close to being infinite that history is, in principle, quite indeterminate, and the future quite unpredictable. This has the nice result of leaving the world open for the exercise of human free will and rationality.

Still, this awesome plurality of determinants should not blind us to the individual factors that make up this plurality, and what we can learn by studying these factors in isolation. Ecologists often remark that taking an organism out of its environment and dissecting it teaches us very little about what the organism is "really" like. True, in that dissected organisms are not living organisms, and the most profound feature of organisms is that they are alive. But not true, in that dissection may disclose something interesting, say, about the organism's cellular composition, which may increase our understanding of the organism in life. Bearing in mind the limitations and possible value of such analyses which separate the subject from its myriad-cause environment, this paper removes philosophy from its living matrix of connected ideas, logic, politics, personalities, etc., and looks at the growth of philosophy from the standpoint of one human activity. We ask, in what ways has the history of philosophy been a product of dominant media of communication?

PATTERNS OF MEDIA CHANGE

In considering the relationship of media and philosophy throughout history, we use, with one exception, the account of media developed by Harold Innis (e.g., 1951) and Marshall McLuhan (e.g., 1962), which portrays the history of communications as a fluctuation between oral, acoustic, ambiguous, impermanent modes of communication, on the one hand, and written, visual, clear, permanent vehicles, on the other. Situating this fluctuation in actual (Western) history, Innis and McLuhan find oral environments dominant until the Age of Pericles, written modes in the ascendant from Greece until the decline of Rome, orality resurgent in the Dark Ages, written culture rethroned through the development of print in the Renaissance, to be challenged and overthrown anew by electronic media in the twentieth century (this last chapter is mostly McLuhan's contribution).

This ping-pong model of media history, however, is in need of a crucial refinement. For rather than an endless series of pendulum swings to oral and written polarities, the development of media seems better described as a series of swings growing less and less extreme—i.e., each shift to oral carrying more and more written characteristics, and vice versa, in a dialectic-like pattern—culminating in a cessation of swinging, or a balanced environment of oral and written media (see Levinson, 1979). In history, surely the orality of the Dark Ages had more net literacy than the primal orality of preliterate times; currently, electronic computers promote visual literacy in their modes of data display, print-outs, etc. This dialectic adjustment of Innis and McLuhan, however, has relevance to a media determination of philosophy only in the twentieth century. For although prior swings to oral or written modes may have brought along more of their opposite number than Innis and McLuhan allowed, the Dark Ages were still sufficiently oral, and early modern times still sufficiently written, that we may reasonably conclude that these environments were dominated by either oral or written characteristics. The environment of our own day and age, however, is dominated not only by orality revived by electronic media, but by a mixture of oral and written, which, as the example of the computer attests, is indeed the full consequence of the electronic revolution. And in accordance with the Innisonian/McLuhanesque premise that media environments determine other aspects of human existence (in this case, philosophy), we should expect that the mixed media environment of the twentieth century may have important consequences for current philosophy.

PHILOSOPHY: PRE-LITERATE TO PRE-ELECTRONIC

Pre-literate conceptions of the world, as Innis and McLuhan have emphasized, are mythic rather than realistic. In the absence of any ready recording system, the human need for permanency and security is satisfied by myths, which run like sinews through the past, present, and future. The few logical constructions of the world which do exist similarly answer a need for order and containment in cultures which have none in a physical sense, and these pre-literate worldviews tend to be all-at-once attempts to explain the diversity of existence in terms of single, underlying substances or principles. Thus we find, among the pre-Socratics, Thales' reduction of all existence to water, Anaximenes' philosophy of air, and Anaximander's surprisingly modern implication of incoherent matter. A bit later and more sophisticated is the Pythagorean identification of essential truth as numerical relations or "number," various Eleatic renditions of metaphysical "Oneness," and Heraclitus' conflation of being and not-being, the one and the many, into a single "becoming." These mystical, time and space binding monisms are just what we would expect of philosophies responding to acoustic, ambiguous, impermanent communication environments.

The revolutionizing impact of the alphabet on Greek philosophy is foreseen by Socrates in his searing attack on writing as destructive of established intellectual modes in the *Phaedrus*—a critique which, fortunately or unfortunately, was unheeded by Socrates' pupil Plato who troubled to write it down. Plato, like St. Augustine and Hegel after him, is a pivotal figure in a media history of philosophy, propounding a system at once mythic and mystic in its far-reaching, underlying essences, yet decidedly unmonistic (indeed, tripartite) in its rigidly held divisions.

The harvest of the written word in ancient philosophy awaits Aristotle, who, building upon the atomism of Socrates' contemporary, Democritus, is the epitome of the cool, detached assayer, patiently putting the many parts of the world into their proper places. In Aristotle, we have the dissector, the classifier, the sorter—the tireless investigator with all the time in the world who gets to the bottom of things, the true nature of things, by analysis. Such an analytic approach to external reality mirrors the alphabet's dissection of spoken fluency into discrete letters; at the same time, the speed and convenience of alphabetic writing provides a ready means for keeping track of the numerous data of analyses, conferring an intellectual confidence necessary for science and lacking in insecure oral societies.

As suggested above, St. Augustine signals the beginning of the slide back into orality, with the resurgence of mystic faith and decline of mundane analysis that acoustic ascendancy entails. At the other end of the Age of Faith, the other saint, Thomas Aquinas, immerses himself in the writings of Aristotle and signals a rediscovery of rational vision and division.

But the Renaissance of detached and detaching reason is the prerogative of the printing press which, in putting iron authority behind the power of the alphabet, gave the written word bite as at no time before in its history. Two early progeny of the explosion of permanent words from the press are Descartes and Bacon: the first an architect of supreme separatism and mechanism in his mind/body dualism, the second out-classifying and out-gathering even Aristotle in the view that we can attain truth through a process of endless amalgamation of experience called induction. Locke, Berkeley, and Hume in their own ways elaborate the atomistic, associationist approach of Bacon—though Berkeley gives it an idealist twist (holding that sensations, not material objects, are the ultimate pieces of reality), and Hume troubles to point out that the association-ist, inductivist technique of gathering numerous experiences cannot, on logical grounds, ever lead to anything like a general truth. With induction thus in ruins, it is left to Kant to rescue and nearly perfect rational empiricism in an intricate, delicately interacting system that slices existence into internal cogni-tive structures and external experiences, things-in-themselves and the appear-ances of things, realms of intellect, practice, and feeling and the like. Written at the height of the Age of Writing and of Reason, Kant's philosophy in many ways remains unsurpassed in its unflinching attempt to wrest a coherent, logically explainable world-picture from the immense multiplicity and complexity of ex-istence.

Successor to the master of written rationality is Hegel, who, as implied above, inherited and applied Kant's focus on reason and categorization, but also sticks a tentative toe into the on-coming Electronic Age with his un-Kantian mystic talk of the pre-ordained unfolding towards the Absolute. The first elec-tronic medium, the telegraph, was of course still a decade or two away, yet electricity was very much in the air in Hegel's day, and indeed Hegel (1970, pp. 220 ff.) even wrote a few lengthy passages on the subject. The telegram itself, as McLuhan (1964, p. 222) aptly points out, ushered in the age of fear and anxiety, and thus Kierkegaard's discovery of angst as the underlying thread of existence. Nietzche's aphorisms, both in subject and style, continue the anti-vivisectionist outlook of electronically-inspired philosophy, but the widely read empiricism and inductivism of J.S. Mill (not to mention the success of nine-teenth century empirical/analytic science itself) reminds us that print and its impact did not disappear with advent of electronic existence. The stage was set for the pluralism of both media and philosophy in the twentieth century.

MIXED CURRENTS OF MEDIA AND THOUGHT

The introduction of telegraphy and photography in the first half of the nine-teenth century were the first salvos of the Electronic Age. But a series of impor-tant advances in the process of printing during this time—and the invention of the linotype a bit later in the nineteenth century—meant that, even at the out-set, the electronic era would not be an unqualified triumph of resurgent oral forms, but rather a mixed environment with written as well as oral presence. Thus in addition to visual Mill versus acoustic Nietzsche, we find in the nine-teenth century a powerful realism and objectivity characteristic of print sensi-bilities operating right alongside the rushes of romanticism and idealism en-couraged by instantaneous (emotion-paced) speed and all-at-once imagery.

The twentieth century, of course, has been dominated more by electronic than by print media, and thus by philosophies that may be considered electronically induced or inspired. The two salient examples are Existentialism, which in its more somber moments discerns the underlying, unifying essence of all existence to be nothing, and Wittgenstein, whose linguistic philosophy attempts to reduce all reality and knowledge to permutations of word usage. Wittgenstein is especially interesting, because his linguistic philosophy of the 1930s and 1940s (which, perhaps not so incidentally, was never written but spoken in classroom lectures) reverses the atomistic and analytic philosophy of his one written work, the *Tractatus* of 1922. Thus in Wittgenstein we have the personification of electronic conversion.

The less flamboyant print philosophies of the twentieth century have been represented primarily by logical positivism, which with its epistemic denial of anything not given in sensory (read usually visual) experience, and indeed its total equation of the sensible (as in perceivable or visible) with the sensible (as in reasonable), has been a print philosophy par excellence, and a darling of science. Popper's evolutionary epistemology offers a more balanced and systematic rational empiricism, which stands in much the same relation to logical positivism as Kant's philosophy did to British empiricism two centuries earlier.

TECHNOLOGICAL SHAPING OF IDEAS

The above of course is but the broadest of speculation, and in want of extensive historical examination (such as the type provided by Eisenstein (1979) in specification of hypotheses about the printing press first raised by Innis and McLuhan) if it is to be taken seriously as even a partial explanation of the development of philosophy. And yet the notion that technologies of communication, whose very function is to transmit ideas, should have had some effect on the formal growth of ideas, that is, philosophy, seems to me not at all trivial or unlikely. Surely a circle-shaped channel of communication would be more conducive to dissemination of circular than square ideas.

As I have argued at length elsewhere (Levinson, 1982), all technologies are material embodiments of human ideas (e.g., an automobile embodies human theories about metallurgy, combustion, travel, etc.), and communication technologies have a dual ideational character in that they are embodiments of ideas about how to transmit other ideas (books embody a strategy or idea about how to communicate—to publish, say, rather than video-tape—the ideas about romance, philosophy, or occasionally communication presented in their pages). Thus, media and ideas are intimately related, and we should not be surprised to find at least some of this relationship obtaining between media and philosophy.

REFERENCES

Eisenstein, E. L. (1979). *The Printing Press as an Agent of Change*. New York: Cambridge University Press.

Hegel, G. W. F. (1970). *Philosophy of Nature*, translated by A. V. Miller. Oxford, England: Clarendon Press. First published in 1817.

Innis, H. A. (1951). *The Bias of Communication*. Toronto, Ontario: University of Toronto Press.

Levinson, P. (1979). "Human Replay: A Theory of the Evolution of Media." Ph. D. dissertation, New York University.

Levinson, P. (1982). "What Technology Can Teach Philosophy." *In* P. Levinson (Ed.), *In Pursuit of Truth: Essays on the Philosophy of Karl Popper*, pp. 157–175. Atlantic Highlands, NJ: Humanities Press.

McLuhan, M. (1962). *The Gutenberg Galaxy*. New York: Mentor.

McLuhan, M. (1964). *Understanding Media*. New York: Mentor.

McNeill, W. (1976). *Plagues and Peoples*. Garden City, NY: Anchor Press.

Tannahill, R. (1973). *Food in History*. New York: Stein and Day.

Toynbee, A. J. (1934–1954). *A Study of History*. London: Oxford University Press.

Wittgenstein, L. (1922). *Tractatus Logico-Philosophicus*, transl. by C. K. Ogden. London: Routledge & Kegan Paul.

3

The "Root Metaphors" Orientations: Implications for Intercultural Communication Researchers

STELLA TING-TOOMEY

Rutgers University

Human actions are grounded in the symbolic constructs which give rise to social meanings. This process of reality construction is framed within the larger context of a cultural system. Culture, as a system of symbols and meanings, mandates how activities and events around an individual should be interpreted and understood. Pepper (1942) argues that humans' "sense making" processes can be basically classified into four distinct world hypotheses or world orientations: *mechanism, formism, organicism, and contextualism*. These coherent sets of assumptions are grounded in the root metaphors (that is, machine, form, organ, and context) of everyday, "common sense" observations.

Metaphor, in this context, is defined as a "creative form which produces its effect through a crossing of images . . . the processes of comparison, substitution, and interaction between the images" (Morgan, 1980, p. 610). These images, myths, rituals, and postulates are the basic properties of a unique cultural system. It is culture which provides the basis for a meaningful system of human actions; and cultural norms are oriented toward movements and patterns for actions. Images and symbolic forms such as verbal and nonverbal codes constitute the cultural galaxies of a meaningful human interaction system.

The objective of this essay is to develop systematically the relationships between Pepper's (1942) root metaphors and theory-building and research in intercultural communication. Specifically, the paper is developed in three sections: (1) Pepper's four sets of root metaphors—machine, form, organ, and context—are introduced; (2) the relationships of metaphorical functions—metaorganization function, perceptual influence function, and behavioral expressive function—to culture are explored; and (3) the implications of the root metaphors of "machine" and "organ" to intercultural communication research are discussed. Fundamental to the theme of this essay is the notion that human "sense making" process structures one's categorization process, perceptual process, and expressive process of the universe surrounding oneself. Metaphorical images of machine, form, organ, and context, will influence how one conceptualizes the twin constructs of communication and culture in the context of intercultural communication research.

WORLD HYPOTHESES

According to Pepper (1942), humans' "sense making" references are ultimately derived from four distinct "root metaphors"—the origins of everyday common sense observations.

Mechanism or mechanistic thinking has been labeled as "experimental thinking" (Bartlett, 1958). Its root metaphor is that of the machine. A mechanistic thinker views the world around him/her as possessing discrete and separate ontological existence. S/he is interested in positing the question of "why" in everyday thinking, and believes in the supremacy of causal reasoning and speculation of people's motives for actions. *Formism* or formistic thinking has been labeled as "everyday thinking" (Bartlett, 1958). Its underlying root metaphor is "similarity." A formistic thinker conceptualizes the world around him/her based on the principles of similarity and typification. Events are placed and cataloged closely together because of their definitions, commonalities, and "ideal forms of types" (Pepper, 1942, pp. 179–180). A formistic individual attempts to define or approximate the ideal way of doing things through comparative and categorization processes. S/he is interested in positing the question of "where" things belong together and how they typify one another.

Organicism, or organistic thinking, has been previously labeled as "systems thinking" (Angyal, 1965) and "patterned thinking" (Dienes and Jeeves, 1965). The root metaphor for organicism is the "organic process." The organistic thinker possesses "the thinking of the artist." S/he perceives the world around him/her as interconnected events of a larger process. The world unfolds to the organicist as a series of patterned constellations. The system thinker believes that there is an inherent totality in all expressed forms. S/he is primarily interested in the question of "how" patterns or puzzles are fitted together in a fixed picture. Finally, *contextualism* or contextual thinker has been labeled as "relational thinking" (Lee et al., 1963). Its root metaphor is the "ongoing act" or "dynamic dramatic active event" in its context (Pepper, 1942, p. 232). For the contextualistic thinker, it is the context that gives rise to any symbolic meanings. Meanings are embedded in a fluid context that is subject to reconstruction and co-creation. For the contextualists, context is a constantly changing phenomenon; it is not a constant variable. S/he conceptualizes the world or reality around him/her based on a wide variety of perspectives. They will not follow one absolute truth. S/he is mainly interested in the question of "how" the fluid, interactive symbolic process of human interaction works against a constantly changing backdrop.

Thus, each of the world hypotheses constitutes a rather unique and distinct perspective of structuring and interpreting experiences beyond and within an individual. When translating these four basic root metaphors to intercultural communication setting, two major questions await to be addressed: First, what functions do metaphors serve in the context of culture? Second, what are the implications of the four root metaphors to intercultural communication research?

METAPHORICAL ORIENTATIONS AND CULTURE

In order to answer the first question, one has first to define culture. Culture, in this essay, is simply defined as "a system of symbols and meanings" (Schneider, 1976). Culture is concerned with "a body of definitions, premises, statements, postulates, presumptions, propositions, and perceptions about the nature of the universe and man's place" (Schneider, 1976, p. 203). The core set of assumptions and values point to a "relatively unified set of shared symbolic ideas associated with one or more patterns of social ordering" within a system (Olsen, 1978, p. 161). Cultural values, norms, and ideals are expressed through shared symbolic activities and actions. Symbolic activities in turn, are stemmed from the "subjective culture" of an individual *in situ* within the larger social-cultural contexts.

The concept "subjective culture" derives its origin from Triandis (1972). According to him, "subjective culture" is defined as a cultural group's characteristic way of perceiving the human-made part of its environment. How an individual experiences his/her social environment, categorizes his/her experiences, perceives and expresses his/her group's norms, values, rules, and roles, are all aspects of subjective culture.

Metaphor, which is a linguistic transference device, is intricately linked to the subjective cultural system. The use of metaphors such as machine, form, organ, and context, and the emphasis one places on respective root metaphors, will have a strong influence on how one perceives reality and social order. Different epistemological orientations, in turn, will impact on how one views communication and culture in the context of intercultural communication research. If one views culture from the root metaphor of "machine," one is assuming that culture has an objective, ontological existence. If one views culture from the root metaphor of "organ," one would focus on the mutually interdependent parts that constitute the whole. This section presents the specific functions that metaphors serve in culture. The next section of this essay provides a general analysis of Pepper's root metaphors (in particular, the "machine" metaphor, and the "organ" metaphor) to intercultural communication research.

As a language tool, metaphor basically serves the following three basic functions: metaorganizational function (Maruyama, 1965), perceptual influence function, and behavioral expressive function (Bednar and Hineline, 1982). The metaorganizational function of metaphors refers to the individual's categorization process of social experiences based on a set of implicit criteria within one's head. These implicit criteria are generated and developed through the value premises (such as desirable modes, means, and ends) and normative patterns of culture. As Schneider (1976, p. 203) notes, "where norms tell the actor how to play the scene, culture tells the actor how the scene is set and what it all means. Where norms tell the actor how to behave in the presence of ghosts, gods, and human beings, culture tells the actors what ghosts, gods, and human beings are and what they are all about." The normative rules and patterns of a culture interact with the subjective culture of an individual and influence the categorization principles of how one structures the events around him/her.

The perceptual influence function of metaphors refers to the individual's selective filtering process between self and social reality. In employing particular sets of metaphors (for example, "machine," "operation," "action-reaction," "design," "measurement," and "control"), these figurative forms can either provide focus and sharpness to a particular image or "picture" of reality out there, or they can "reframe" reality in such a way that they may release our conventional modes of thinking concerning certain concepts or ideas (for example, viewing culture as "form" as versus viewing culture as "context"; or viewing organization as "culture" as versus viewing culture as "organization"). These dual sub-functions of "perceptual directing" and "perceptual reframing" (Bednar and Hineline, 1982, p. 11) orient our attentions toward new focus of study. In the context of intercultural communication research, the use of vivid metaphorical images in the research setting, may produce and generate new insights to problems that have never been noticed before by the ethnographer or the anthropologist.

Finally, according to Bednar and Hineline (1982, p. 6), the behavioral expressive function of metaphors refers to the different means of metaphorical usage such as elaboration, conciseness, translation, and invention. Elaboration refers to the "intensity, emotive force, richness of detail, and verbal power of metaphorical images." Conciseness, according to these authors, refers to the compact yet complete nature of the metaphorical act. Translation refers to the association of familiar concepts with the radical and the new. Invention refers to the use of an entire new metaphor to express what has never been expressed before.

Metaphor, in short, is a reality creation and a reality-capturing symbolic tool. Transferring the various functions of metaphors to the study of culture, the following sets of questions can be deduced. On the relationship between metaorganization function of metaphor and culture, one can ask: What kinds of dominant metaphors do the cultural members in the system use to structure and organize their social experience? Do particular modes of metaphors hold particular "logics" in different cultural systems? Do cultural members in different cultures classify information or symbolic events based on different metaphorical models (for example, linear model, decision-making tree model, hierarchical model, circular or spiral model)?

On the relationship between perceptual influence function of metaphor and culture, one can posit the following questions: Can ethnographers or participant observers be imprisoned by their own cultural metaphors to the extent of not perceiving the key metaphors that are present in an alien culture? How can a researcher go about identifying and explaining the uses and implications of dominant metaphors in different cultures? Are such variables as status, social class, or mass media more influential than others in initiating and spreading metaphorical trends in diverse cultural settings? How do metaphors become transferred from one speech community to another?

Finally, on the relationship between expressive function of metaphor and culture, the following questions can be asked: How do individuals from different cultures achieve metaphorical alignment and consensus in a system? How can an ethnographer use cultural metaphors effectively to integrate oneself to the research community? Can we make a distinction between "metaphorical competence" and "metaphorical performance" in a speech community? If yes, what are the implications of such distinctions? The next section addresses some of the critical issues stemming from the use of machine-form root metaphors and organ-context root metaphors in intercultural communication research.

ROOT METAPHORS: RESEARCH FUNCTIONS

According to Kuhn (1970, p. 175), the term "paradigm" refers to the "entire constellation of beliefs, values, techniques, and so on, shared by the members of a given community." The configurations of how one conceptualizes social reality and formulates a favored world view are, oftentime, based on the ground assumptions and values of a cultural system. Pepper's four metaphorical orientations—mechanism, formism, organicism, and contextualism—represent four preferred views of the universe. These four world perceptual orientations also correspond to the findings or observations of the Western versus the Eastern perspectives. For example, Hall (1976) divides different communication systems on a continuum of low-context and high-context cultures. Low context culture refers to a group of cultures which value individual orientation, rational logic, and overt communication patterns, and maintain heterogeneous normative structure (for example, Germany, Scandinavia, and United States). High context culture, on the other hand, refers to a group of cultures which value group orientation, spiral logic, and covert communication patterns, and maintain a homogeneous normative structure (for example, China, Japan, Korea, and Vietnam). The low context cultures operate primarily from the "machine-form" root metaphors. The high context cultures work predominantly from the "organ-context" root metaphors. Countless other intercultural studies (Barnlund, 1974; Benedict, 1946; Condon, 1977; Hofstede, 1980; Hsu, 1981; Nakane, 1970; Okabe, 1981; Stewart, 1971; Triandis, 1972) have supported this observation and divided the Western versus the Eastern world views as either "classification universe" and "relational universe" (Maruyama, 1965), "horizontal society" and "vertical society" (Nakane, 1970), or "masculine culture" and "feminine culture" (Hofstede, 1980). All these cultural

taxonomies have been derived in part through the direct and indirect use of the "machine-like" root metaphor in the Western world view; while the Eastern world view operates from predominantly the "organistic-like" metaphorical mode.

Based on the "machine" root metaphor, the following assumptions can be deduced: (1) individuals respond to their outer reality in a law-like, "mechanistic" manner (mechanism); (2) reality assumes an objective, ontological existence separate from the individual cultural members; and (3) individuals process external information through classification, typification, comparison, and contrast procedures (formistic thinking). Based on the "organ" root metaphor, we can posit the following three assumptions: (1) individuals sustain and create symbolic reality within a rule-like, patterned structure (organicism); (2) reality assumes a subjective and an intersubjective existence and is manifested through the interactive process of symbolic discourse; and (3) individuals process streams of information or behavior *in situ* with the flow of the social and cultural contexts (contextual thinking).

In extending these basic assumptions of the "machine" metaphor and the "organ" metaphor to intercultural communication inquiry, the machinery image in essence represents the "outsider inquiry" mode, while the organismic image represents the "insider inquiry" mode (Evered and Louis, 1981). Three critical issues are addressed, based on these two distinctive modes of social science inquiry: (1) the aim of intercultural communication research; (2) the investigator's role in the inquiry process; and (3) the knowledge structures that are acquired through these two metaphorical modes of research.

From the machinery imagery of research, the aim of intercultural communication research is viewed as a purposeful, rational activity. The machine model is based on mechanical concepts such as "operational definition," "control," "design," "prediction," "cause-effect," and "measurement." The machine performs its duties through law-like routines, mechanistic movements, and cause-effect outcomes. "Outsider inquiry" pursues a means-ends relationship in the study of communication and culture; and the concepts of communication and culture are assumed to maintain objective, observable characteristics that are identifiable and explainable. In contrast, from the organismic imagery of research, the aim of intercultural communication inquiry is viewed from a goal-emergent model perspective. The images of organismic-systems, such as words like "immersion," "experiential," "sensitized concepts," "idiographic," "contextual," "thickness," and "density of description," reflect an insider mode of inquiry. An "organism" is a "living entity in constant flux and change, interacting with its environment to satisfy its needs" (Morgan, 1980). Culture, when viewed from the organismic metaphorical mode, regulates changes and stability through the movements of mutually interdependent elements within the system. Intercultural researchers, in this context, are primarily interested in observing and understanding the interrelationships of activities that maintain stability and regulate change in the social environment.

The investigator's role in the outsider mode of inquiry is that of a detached observer. This role is derived from the assumption that the phenomenon under study is objectively detached from the observer. The investigator's role in the insider mode of inquiry is that of a participant observer. This role is stemmed from the assumption that the act under study is symbolically represented. Researchers have to be physically present to capture the true meanings and implications of a particular symbolic act in relationship to its larger social and cultural settings.

Finally, knowledge structures that are produced under the mechanistic mode are usually law-like principles aiming for wide generalizability and application. Knowledge structures that are acquired under the organismic imagery attempt to present interpretive truths based on particular symbolic events and situations. The logic of such knowledge structures can be applied to particular situations within the complex fabric of local culture.

This essay has addressed two primary issues of metaphor to culture: The first issue concerns the basic functions of metaphor to culture, and the second issue concerns the paradigmatic functions of root metaphors to intercultural communication research. Root metaphors embody different aspects of viewing social reality and favored world views. By exploring different meanings and implications of root metaphors to culture, this essay contributes to a sense of appreciation and awareness of how metaphorical images direct our thinking process, and ultimately "frame" our picture of the universe.

REFERENCES

Angyal, A. (1965). *Neurosis and Treatment: A Holistic Theory*. New York: J. Wiley.

Barnlund, D. C. (1974). "The Public Self and the Private Self in Japan and the United States." *In* J. C. Condon and M. Saito (Eds.), *Intercultural Encounters with Japan*. Tokyo: Simul Press.

Bartlett, F. C. (1958). *Thinking: An Experimental and Social Study*. New York: Basic Books.

Bednar, D., and Hineline, J. (1982). "The Management of Meaning through Metaphors." Paper presented at the annual convention of the Academy of Management Assoication, New York.

Benedict, R. F. (1946). *The Chrysanthemum and the Sword: Patterns of Japanese Culture*. Cleveland, OH: World.

Condon, J. C. (1977). *Interpersonal Communication*. New York: Macmillan.

Dienes, Z. P., and Jeeves, M. (1965). *Thinking in Structures*. London: Hutchinson.

Evered, R., and Louis, M. A. (1981). "Alternative Perspectives in the Organizational Sciences: Inquiry from the Inside and Inquiry from the Outside." *Academy of Management Review 6*, 385–395.

Hall, E. T. (1976). *Beyond Culture*. New York: Anchor.

Hofstede, G. H. (1980). *Culture's Consequences: International Differences in Work-related Values*. Beverly Hills, CA: Sage.

Hsu, F. L. K. (1981). *Americans and Chinese: Passages to Differences*, 3rd ed. Honolulu, HI: University Press of Hawaii.

Kuhn, T. S. (1970). *The Structure of Scientific Revolutions*. Chicago, IL: University of Chicago Press.

Lee, L., Kagan, J., and Rabson, A. (1963). "Influence of a Preference for Analytic Categorization upon Concept Acquisition." *Child Development 34*, 433–442.

Maruyama, M. (1965). "Metaorganization of Information." *Cybernetica 4*, 55–60.

Morgan, G. (1980). "Paradigms, Metaphors, and Puzzle Solving in Organization Theory." *Administrative Science Quarterly 25*, 605–622.

Nakane, C. (1970). *Japanese Society*. Berkeley, CA: University of California Press.

Okabe, R. (1981). "Culture Assumptions of Communication Theory from Eastern and Western Perspectives: The Cases of Japan and the United States." Paper presented at the annual convention of the Speech Communication Association. Anaheim, CA. (November).

Olsen, M. E. (1978). *The Process of Social Organization,* 2d ed. New York: Holt, Rinehart & Winston.

Pepper, S. C. (1942). *World Hypotheses: A Study in Evidence*. Berkeley, CA.: University of California Press.

Schneider, D. (1976). "Notes Toward a Theory of Culture." In K. H. Basso and H. A. Selby (Eds.), *Meanings in Anthropology*. Albuquerque, NM: University of New Mexico Press.

Stewart, E. C. (1971). *American Cultural Patterns: A Cross-Cultural Perspective*. Pittsburgh, PA.: University of Pittsburgh Press.

Triandis, H. C. (1972). *The Analysis of Subjective Culture*. New York: John Wiley & Sons.

4

Agenda-Setting Research: A Critique and Theoretical Alternative

KEVIN CARRAGEE
Denison University

MARK ROSENBLATT
ABC Radio News, New York

GENE MICHAUD
University of Pennsylvania

AN HISTORICAL REVIEW OF THE AGENDA-SETTING PERSPECTIVE

The agenda-setting perspective derives its theoretical framework principally from Walter Lippmann's seminal work, *Public Opinion*. Lippmann (1922) argued that mass communication helps to shape the "pictures in our heads." These pictures produced by the media create a pseudo-environment and contribute to the formation of public opinion on the issues confronting society. Given the emphasis on attitude change and the direct effects model in early communication research, Lippmann's provocative interpretation of the media's important role in structuring the cognitive images of sociopolitical reality was largely ignored in the late 1940s and 1950s.

The reemergence of the concerns articulated by Lippmann is traceable to a number of researchers both inside and outside the communication field. Lang and Lang (1968) stress the cumulative impact of mass mediated information in shaping the political images of the public in the period between elections. They argued:

> the mass media structure issues and personalities. They do this gradually and over a period of time, and thus this impact seems less spectacular than the shift or crystallization of a particular vote decision. We cannot help but believe that, indirectly, by creating a political climate, a sense of urgency, an image of parties and candidates, etc., they do influence votes (*Lang and Lang, 1968, p.19*).

Nimmo (1970) advanced a consonant position by stating that the media helps set the public agenda by defining and legitimizing those issues which are open for public debate. Edelman (1964, p.5) argued that "for most men, most of the time, politics is a series of pictures in the mind placed there by television news, newspapers, magazines, and discussions. The pictures create a moving panorama taking place in a world the mass public never quite touches." White (1972) characterized the power of the press as "primordial" in setting a public agenda. Political scientists Cobb and Elder (1971) emphasized the importance of the agenda-building process in defining those issues and alternatives which become legitimate concerns of public policy debate. They also argued that the press plays a significant role in shaping the public agenda. The proposed agenda-setting of the press is perhaps most succinctly articulated by Cohen (1963, p.13): "It [the press] may not be successful in telling people what to think, but it is stunningly successful in telling its readers what to think about." This growing concern with the agenda-setting role of the press was reflected in empirical communication research beginning in the early 1970s.

McCombs and Shaw (1972) provided the first testing of the agenda-setting function of the press. Their research hypothesis reflected this concern: "While the mass media may have little influence on the direction or intensity of attitudes, it is hypothesized that the mass media set the agenda for each political campaign, influencing the salience of attitudes toward the political issues" (McCombs and Shaw, 1972, p.177). Their study was designed to compare the actual content of the media with what voters in Chapel Hill, North Carolina said were the important issues in the 1968 presidential campaign. A content analysis of the media provided the data for media coverage, while a survey of voters supplied the information on public perceptions of issues. This methodological approach has dominated agenda-setting research to the present. By correlating the media's emphasis with voters' judgments, McCombs and Shaw found that the media appeared to have a highly significant impact on what voters considered major issues.

The striking correlations found in the Chapel Hill study were to generate over fifty empirical investigations of agenda-setting in the next eight years. The weight of this research suggests a more complex relationship between the media agenda and the public agenda than was initially advanced by McCombs and Shaw. In part, the interest in the agenda-setting hypothesis reflected a shift from questions of opinion formation to the media's role in the development of cognitions about issues. Moreover, the appeal of the agenda-setting function indicated a growing disaffection with the limited effects model (see Klapper, 1960) which had previously dominated mass communication research. The dissatisfaction with this model contributed to a sense of urgency in the development of agenda-setting research.

The initial wave of empirical studies into the agenda-setting role of the press revealed some of the components of this process. Funkhouser (1973) found a strong positive correlation between specific issues presented in news magazines and voter's perceptions of their most important concerns. Mullins (1973) analyzed young voter's perceptions of important issues and their relationship to media content. He found high positive correlations between media content emphasizing certain issues and the student rankings of the importance of these issues. In this way, the initial research following the McCombs and Shaw study supported the agenda-setting hypothesis. Despite these early findings, a number of methodological problems involving this hypothesis began to surface. Concerning McCombs and Shaw's methods, for example, their chosen sample maximized media effects because it consisted only of undecided voters (Becker et al., 1975, p.42). Early research on agenda-setting, including the McCombs and Shaw study, employed a static design which was unable to establish causal direction. The question of whether or not the media sets or reflects the public agenda could not be determined through methods employed by early researchers in this area. In addition, Funkhouser admits to using "soft methodology:" reliance on Gallup public opinion polling for public perception of issue salience and a review of *The Reader's Guide to Periodical Literature* to determine media emphasis on issues. Given these methodological concerns, the initial agenda-setting research was seen as inconclusive.

Later studies, which lacked an integrative framework, attempted to explore the agenda-setting process. Tipton et al. (1975) investigated media agenda-setting on the state and local levels. Their principal contribution was the introduction of cross-lagged correlations. This technique attempts to establish causal direction by evaluating the agenda-setting function over time. The assumption being tested is that the cause (agenda-setting) measured at one time will have a stronger effect on public opinion at a second time; correspondingly, public opinion measured at one time should have a noticeably weaker effect on the agenda presented by the press at the second time. This statistical method comes closest to establishing whether or not the media sets the public's agenda or if, in fact, the inverse is true. Although the use of cross-lagged correlations is an advance over past static designs, it is important to keep in mind that, as Westley (1976) points out, correlational data does not conclusively demonstrate a causal relationship. Tipton et al. (1975) found that on a state or local level the media do *not* present as consistent a view of election campaigns as they do on a national level. Overall, the study indicated that there was no consistent evidence that the media serve a causal agenda-setting function on the state and local levels. It should be noted, however, that this study failed to include a content analysis of news presented on the major local television station. This shortcoming casts doubt on the significance and generality of the findings.

McLeod et al. (1974) noted that previous agenda-setting research had ignored an important range of influences. They posit that agenda-setting operates only under certain conditions and that past research had failed to take into account the impact of individual differences on the process of agenda-setting. McLeod et al. demonstrate the existence of three distinct agenda: individual issue salience, perceived issue salience of others, and community issue salience. Weaver (1977) articulates a critical individual difference which influences the media's ability to set an agenda. He identifies this concept as an individual's need for orientation. In simple terms, this concept refers to an individual's need to seek information in the media in order to better understand his/her environment. A number of studies using this construct, including Weaver et al. (1975) and Cohen (1975), found that a high-need orientation led to an enhanced agenda-setting effect. While these researchers were identifying individual characteristics which influence agenda-setting, other studies were developing additional concepts which helped change the emphasis of agenda-setting research.

McClure and Patterson (1976) investigated the possibility that the use of different media might influence the agenda-setting process. They contrasted high and low media exposure as well as the differences in content between television and newspaper coverage of a campaign. They found no support for the agenda-setting hypothesis among heavy television users. However, McClure and Patterson indicated that issues most emphasized in newspapers were identified as important among heavy newspaper readers. This study demonstrated that the agenda-setting function is not only related to the degree of media exposure, but also to the media to which one is exposed. McClure and Patterson speculated that the lack of a noticeable television agenda-setting effect was a product of the television news format which functions principally as a headline service lacking in-depth coverage.

The trend towards greater specificity and the limitations of the agenda-setting hypothesis was continued by Benton and Frazier (1976). They advanced a three-level conceptualization of agenda-setting. Level one is where most of the research has centered. It has concerned itself with a broad set of issues. Level two involves sub-issues which include specific problems, while level three focuses on specific information about these sub-issues. Benton and Frazier found that newspapers set agenda for their readers across all three levels. However, they noted that television did not serve an agenda-setting function on levels two and three. This line of research further indicates limitations which serve to restrict the generality of the agenda-setting hypothesis.

These limitations were underscored in a number of subsequent research efforts, the most important of which was conducted by the originators of the agenda-setting hypothesis—McCombs and Shaw. McCombs (1977) attempted to address a major weakness in the Chapel Hill study, the problem of causal direction, through the use of cross-lagged correlational analysis. The results were ambiguous. The study found that newspapers did perform an agenda-setting function for their readers; in contrast, the data from television news supported the opposite notion, that the public's agenda was influencing the media's agenda. Moreover, Westley (1978) argues that closer scrutiny of the cross-lagged correlational data indicates there is little support for the contention that newspapers perform an agenda-setting function. Westley contends that the amount of change in the public agenda between the first and second measurements was insufficient to support any hypothesis concerning the agenda-setting function of the press. Other empirical studies have demonstrated equally inconclusive results. Williams and Larsen (1977), in a study of agenda-setting in an off-year election, found that a significant agenda-setting effect was limited to newspaper coverage of local issues. The results, however, are questionable because the Williams and Larsen study did not employ a longitudinal design. In another study focusing on the agenda-setting process in primary elections, Williams and Semlak (1976) found no support for the agenda-setting hypothesis. Atkin and Heald (1976), in a study evaluating the effects of political advertisements, discovered moderate positive correlations between the amount of television ad exposure and voter's recognition of candidates and issues. Patterson (1980), in a massive content analysis and panel survey of 1,236 voters during the 1976 presidential election, indicated that there was a significant correlation between the agenda set by the media and the voter's perception of important aspects of the campaign. Clearly, to this date, the major empirical finding concerning the agenda-setting hypothesis are both conflicting and inconclusive.

The problems inherent in agenda-setting research have not gone undetected by those involved in these studies. McCombs (1981), in an overview examining these methodological and theoretical problems, writes:

> The burgeoning number of sub-concepts used to operationalize the public agenda, media agenda, and their relationships define dozens of subhypotheses, each detailing the idea of an agenda-setting role of mass communication in a different way. It is this great variety of detail, which one could pessimistically say approaches near chaos, that underscores the appropriateness of a literature review at this stage in the history of agenda-setting research (McCombs, 1981, p. 210)

As part of this review, McCombs characterizes present agenda-setting research as exploratory and fragmentary. This 1981 study explores the many methodological inconsistencies that have developed in past agenda-setting research.

Despite the acknowledged importance of the temporal variable in agenda-setting research, there has been little consistency in the formulation and application of the time-frame concept in these studies. Eyal et al. (1981) call for a more precise definition of the temporal variable and for a consistent application of this concept to future research. They also argue that agenda-setting research must abandon static designs in favor of longitudinal studies utilizing either cross-lagged correlational techniques or path analysis. DeGeorge (1979) points to another inconsistency within past agenda-setting research: the type of questioning employed within the design. Certain studies have adopted forced-choice question construction, while others have employed open-ended questioning. DeGeorge suggests that the selection of different questioning techniques may lead to differences in conclusions.

Still another limitation of agenda-setting research is the variety of contingent conditions attached to the original hypothesis. Winter (1979) articulates a series of contingent conditions, including the level of media exposure, the role of interpersonal communication and the need for orientation, which influence the agenda-setting process. Most studies indicate that a high level of media exposure and a high need for orientation facilitate agenda-setting. The role and influence of interpersonal communication on agenda-setting are unresolved. Mullins (1973), Shaw (1974) and Atwood et al. (1976) claimed that interpersonal communication served to increase the agenda-setting effect. On the other hand, McCombs and Shaw (1972), Weaver et al. (1975) and Miller et al. (1976) found that interpersonal communication weakens the power of the mass media to set the public agenda.

Winter (1979) points to a further methodological problem in agenda-setting research. Past studies have often failed to identify the specific source of media information and the extent of user exposure to that medium. Instead, these studies have tended to use aggregate data which Winter characterizes as inadequate. Aggregate data may obscure the true nature of the agenda-setting effect, according to Winter. He suggests that, at the very least, future research should take into account the amount of interpersonal communication, measures for the need for orientation, and the amount and kind of exposure to media. Clearly, such methodological criticism indicates a need for a reorganization of agenda-setting research.

McCombs and Shaw (1980) attempted to address the criticism leveled at agenda-setting research and propose directions for additional studies. Summarizing earlier research, they acknowledged the following contingent conditions which influence the agenda-setting process: the need for orientatio.., media use and level of exposure, the role of interpersonal communication, and the existence of intrapersonal, interpersonal and community agendas. In addition, they cite research by Eyal (1980) which suggests that the degree of obtrusiveness, that is the degree to which respondents have personal contact with an issue, impacts on agenda-setting. Eyal found no agenda-setting function relating to obtrusive issues, while determining a considerable agenda-setting effect for unobtrusive issues. Eyal's study continues the trend in agenda-setting research for uncovering additional contingent conditions.

McCombs and Shaw call for a broader theoretical approach to agenda-setting. This approach would attempt to explicate those variables which accelerate or inhibit agenda-setting. In their view, this perspective would bring together the effects tradition and the uses and gratifications approach in mass communication. They offer a transactional model which focuses on both differences within the media and individual differences. In such an approach, "the perceived salience of an issue is the outcome of the individual's scanning behavior" (McCombs and Shaw, 1980, p.20). McCombs and Shaw concede that other contingent conditions may surface in the use of this transactional model. The purpose of this approach is to verify what McCombs and Shaw call "a social anchoring theory of agenda-setting:"

> Agenda-setting can be conceptualized as one step of society's ongoing process of achieving a level of social consensus which allows peaceful functioning and reason-

able adaptation to change. Healthy societies exist somewhere between issue anarchy and total issue conformity (McCombs and Shaw, 1980, p.28).

They posit that "In a sociological sense, one might argue that agenda-setting is a
macro-case of balance theory" (McCombs and Shaw, 1980, p.31). It is important to note that this approach changes the traditional focus of agenda-setting
research away from how the press sets the public agenda to a concern with how
an individual *balances* personal, interpersonal, and media issues into a spectrum of cognitive images. This constitutes a summation of eight years of
agenda-setting research.[1]

The integrative framework advanced by McCombs and Shaw (1980) fails to
consider a number of problems which severely limit the explanatory power of
their theoretical approach. Despite the attempt to integrate past research into a
uses and gratifications strategy which would lead to a social anchoring theory,
this perspective neither responds to past problems nor suggests a fruitful way to
conduct future research. Recent agenda-setting research has uncovered a list of
contingent conditions which influence the agenda-setting process and
McCombs and Shaw point out that the use of their transactional model is likely
to identify even more of these conditions. As additional contingent conditions
emerge and are accounted for in the agenda-setting paradigm, this perspective
becomes increasingly situational and thus severely restricts the nature of generality in this research. Moreover, the attempt to link agenda-setting with a uses
and gratifications model is highly problematic. Although an exhaustive critique
of the uses and gratifications approach is beyond the scope of this paper, we
should point out that Swanson (1977) and Elliott (1974) note the severe theoretical and conceptual weaknesses of this research strategy. In our view, the
wedding of one problematic methodology with still another can only serve to
weaken the resulting theory. Finally, the view of agenda-setting as a macro-
case of balance theory is fraught with obvious problems. Like consistency
theory, this approach to agenda-setting will only uncover exceptions to the very
phenomenon that agenda-setting research once attempted to explain.

A REVISED PERSPECTIVE ON AGENDA-SETTING RESEARCH

What follows is an exploratory attempt to integrate the useful aspects of agenda-
setting research into a productive framework. The present methodological
problems which characterize this perspective are directly traceable to its narrow scope. The adoption of an institutional perspective, examining how media
messages are produced and presented, reveals the media's power to shape pub-

---

[1]Clearly, interest in the agenda-setting hypothesis has continued. See, for example, Stone and
McCombs (1981) and Semlak and Williams (1982). The McCombs and Shaw (1980) study, however,
provides the most comprehensive effort at a reorganization of agenda-setting research and proposes
new directions for future research. Subsequent research has worked within this framework.

lic perceptions of reality. The consonant and cumulative nature of media messages suggest that powerful media institutions perform an essentially hegemonic function. This entire process results in a severely restricted presentation of ideas, values, and beliefs.

It is important to keep in mind that, despite important shortcomings, the agenda-setting approach has contributed to a more advanced understanding of the media's role in society. On a theoretical level, it has helped to change the emphasis of mass communication research away from the study of short-term attitudinal effects to a more longitudinal analysis of social impact. This is no small contribution. However, agenda-setting research has failed to grasp the implications of this change in emphasis.

The absence of clear theoretical formulations has led to the adoption of methodological approaches which are inherently unable to evaluate the basic assumption of the agenda-setting perspective—that the media structure public perceptions of reality. For example, McCombs and Shaw along with other researchers characterize agenda-setting as the ability of the media to make specific issues salient among the public. This definition of agenda-setting is considerably narrower than the one offered by political scientists. Cobb and Elder (1971) emphasize that the agenda-setting process produces a range of issues open for public debate. They define agenda as "a general set of controversies that will be viewed as falling within the range of legitimate concerns meriting the attention of the polity" (Cobb and Elder, 1971, p.905). McCombs and Shaw's approach reduces the focus of agenda-setting to the specific issues presented in the media rather than to an examination of the range of possible concerns transmitted by the media to the public. In our view, the principal agenda-setting power of the media lies in their ability to set the parameters for public debate by legitimizing and emphasizing a certain range of issues to the exclusion of others. By focusing attention on a limited range of concerns, the media effectively structure the public agenda. Mass communication researchers have concentrated on a reductionistic view of the agenda-setting process; their emphasis on short-term issue salience obscures the larger, more important consideration. The fundamental assumption of agenda-setting research is that the media shape the public's cognitive images of social and political reality. These images are not simply the product of the media's attention to specific issues, but are rather a result of the range of alternatives offered by the media.

The present microscopic view of agenda-setting has led to a series of seemingly endless methodological problems. These problems involve the controversy over causal direction and the large number of contingent conditions which may influence the agenda-setting process. These debates have shifted the focus of agenda-setting research away from the important ability of the media to set the boundaries of public discussion. Further attempts to clarify the problems of causal direction and the impact of individual differences *within* the present narrow definition of agenda-setting will not serve to explicate the real power of the media to influence public perceptions of society. While the debate rages around narrowly defined methodological issues, the substantive theoretical questions in agenda-setting research go unanswered. This is but one indication of the elevation of methodological issues over theoretical clarity in the field of mass communication.

Nowhere is this process more evident than in an examination of media content. Content analysis has repeatedly shown that the emphasis of television news is not on issues; it focuses instead on the non-substantive aspects of important events. Yet, agenda-setting research has continued to examine the issues presented in television news. Moreover, the non-substantive emphasis has led many researchers to conclude that television news has no agenda-setting effect. This finding is a direct result of the narrow confines in which agenda-setting research has been conducted. If one looks beyond this faulty conceptualization, it becomes apparent that television's emphasis on non-substantive matters may constitute an important influence on public perceptions of socio-political reality. Given an expanded framework, we would suggest that the real agenda-setting function of television news is that it trivializes potential issues of public concern and, therefore, presents a severely truncated range of alternatives.

A significant shortcoming of agenda-setting research has been its failure to examine the institutional framework within which the media form their agenda. The principal controversy surrounding agenda-setting research has been characterized by "either/or" statements of causality: either the media set an agenda *for* the public, or the media reflect an agenda set *by* the public. This ignores the very real possibility that the media agenda is a product of the institutional framework within which it is created. Agenda-setting research has consistently accepted the media agenda as a given without considering the process by which the agenda is constructed. Additionally, the debate over causal direction overlooks the inherent power of media institutions to establish a limited number of concerns and to portray these concerns as the only range of options available for public discourse.

Increasingly, some theorists have appealed for a more contextual approach to the study of mass communication (see, for example, Williams, 1974, 1981; Golding and Murdock, 1978). This approach attempts to place the study of mass communication within a larger social framework. Within this framework, an analysis of the processes by which media messages are constructed within institutional settings becomes important. A number of researchers including Tuchman (1974) and Gitlin (1979, 1980) have argued that the media's decisive role is the perpetuation of hegemony; that is, the structure of the media and their content serve to legitimate the status quo and limit the range of ideas open for public discourse. Tuchman (1974, p.31), for example, states that:

> the organizational structure of newswork set the frame in which news personnel cover or create news stories, helps to establish a professional ideology that insists upon the political neutrality of TV newswork, and ultimately encourages hegemony.

It is this hegemonic process that should be the focus of agenda-setting research, not the microscopic study of the transmission of specific issues and their short-term effects on individuals.

It was Gramsci (1971) who initially articulated the concept of hegemony; this concept is based upon the belief that those who dominate major institutions in society will use their influence, power, and privilege to maintain the existing social order. Among these major institutions are the communications media. Sallach (1974), in an analysis of Gramsci's work, states that the hegemonic process involves the propagation of certain ideas, values, and beliefs which support and reinforce the position of a powerful elite. Moreover, this process "involves not only the inculcation of its values and the censorship of heterodox views, but also and especially the ability to define the parameters of legitimate discussion and debate over alternative beliefs, values and world views" (Sallach, 1974, pp.165-166). Hegemony does not simply depend on censorship or coercion but rather rests on the power to shape the nature of public discussion through the imposition of specific boundaries. Thus, debate does take place, but it is limited by the ideological constraints imposed by those who control institutions which perpetuate hegemony. Gitlin (1979) argues in a similar fashion that powerful media institutions sanction not only the types of issues raised, but also the alternatives to the issues as well. Both the issues and their alternatives must fall within predetermined and narrow parameters. Issues which fall outside these parameters are rarely if ever voiced through powerful media institutions. In this view, the news media have become the "core systems for the production and distribution of ideology" (Gitlin, 1980, p.12). These considerations should play an important part in the evaluation of the media's role in American society.

The organizational influences on newswork and their effect on news content—so prominently explored in the work of Tuchman (1974, 1978) and Gitlin (1980)—have largely been ignored by agenda-setting researchers. A significant body of research does, however, exist in this area and the compelling need is to integrate this research into the agenda-setting perspective. Future research concerning the agenda-setting influence of the media should carefully analyze the processes by which news is produced. At present, our effort is to suggest that past studies examining the nature of newswork offer significant insights for the future development of the agenda-setting perspective. Moreover, in our view, an analysis of the production of news helps to reveal the hegemonic processes evident in newswork.

A large number of studies have examined the organizational influences on newswork. Breed's classic study (1955) documented the existence of an implicit socialization process in the news room and its effect on the presentation of news. Gans (1979), Tuchman (1978), Altheide (1974) and Epstein (1973) have provided organizational analyses of newswork. These researchers share the belief that news is socially constructed by journalists within organizational and bureaucratic settings; in turn, these settings influence the definition of news and the nature of newswork. Epstein (1973, p.25) for example, points out that both the selection and editing processes do not simply reflect news events but are rather the product of organizational policy:

> To describe news as mirroring events thus necessarily involves seriously neglecting the importance of the chain of decisions made both before and after the fact by executives and newsmen or, in a word, the organizational process.

Furthermore, Epstein argues that news producers play a crucial role in determining both the content and form of network news. Producers are the key link between management and reporters; they see their main task as enforcing the standards of the network organization (see also Batscha, 1975). Finally, Elliott (1973, p.257), in a case study of the production of a television documentary, succinctly points to the existence of organizational constraints and their effects:

> What is said is the unplanned product of following accepted production routines within established organizational systems. As a result, it must be expected that what is said will in the main be fundamentally supportive of the socio-economic structure of the society in which those organizations are set.

Traditional journalistic values, procedures and techniques—which are a product of the organizational structure of media institutions—significantly determine the sources of news. Altheide (1974), Wicker (1975), Batscha (1975), Tuchman (1978) and Gans (1979) have noted the common tendency among journalists to seek and depend on official sources of information. These sources are often governmental and are tied to the existing power structure. Moreover, the increasing bureaucratic centralization of the news media has only helped to strengthen the symbiotic relationship between journalists and corporate and governmental bureaucracies (see Fishman, 1980).

Gans (1979, p.128) ties the journalistic dependency on governmental sources for information to the emphasis on efficiency in news organizations; that is, the governmental instruments of the news conference and the press release serve to expedite the tasks of journalists. For Tuchman (1978), the anchoring of the news net and the reliance on "beat" reporters—the very organizational techniques which routinize newswork—increase journalistic reliance on official sources of information. Altheide (1974, p.16) argues that "the main news sources for local [television] stations are the dominant institutions and officials." Finally, Fishman (1980) contends that centralized news organizations have a bureaucratic affinity with other large institutions.

Others have noted that the concept of objectivity in American journalism has also contributed to a reliance on official sources of information. Batscha (1975, p.60) explicates this relationship:

> The professional criteria of obectivity and neutral reporting discipline the correspondents to look to the political center. This is reinforced by their concept of television's national and heterogeneous audience, by the complimentary attitudes of their colleagues, employers and competitors; and by their perceptions of audi-

ence expectations. Centrism reinforces the status quo or at the most accepts modifications of that status quo. In seeking to occupy the middle ground, the correspondents have again a propensity to balance opposing viewpoints, intimating that the truth is found somewhere in-between. Too often bias is perceived to occur automatically when the correspondent veers away from the center; as a result, the center itself becomes a journalistic bias.

Wicker (1975, p.39) makes the same point by noting that objective journalism almost always favors establishment positions. In sum, the close relationship between journalists and their news sources, which are primarily governmental and official, legitimizes and strengthens the status quo by providing information that largely reflects the perspectives of those holding institutional power. Other viewpoints are systematically excluded or minimized by the institutionalized and routinized nature of newswork.

Under these conditions, groups lacking institutional power find it difficult to place issues on the news agenda. Groups outside of the existing power structure have limited access to the news media, while those holding institutional power have frequent and easy access. Tuchman (1977, p.52), for example, argues that the:

> Organizational and professional practices entail the stratification of news as a social resource. Those with the most economic and political power have the most access to the news processes and the most power over reporters. Those with the least economic and political power in the society are subject to the power of reporters.

Molotch and Lester (1974) and Altheide and Johnson (1980) point out that groups whose political and social ideas do not conform to the normative values prescribed by existing powerful institutions must resort to dramatic means (e.g., demonstrations) in order to gain a public forum. Such tactics, however, may obscure the issues that these groups seek to raise. For example, Halloran et al. (1970), in a case study of a British anti-war demonstration, note that the press focused attention on the form of the demonstration rather than the substantive issues raised by it. In effect, media coverage served to divorce the demonstration from its antecedent political and ideological framework. Similarly, Gitlin's (1980) investigation of news reporting concerning the New Left and Morris's (1973, 1974) analysis of news treatment of the feminist movement suggest that the media's coverage of social movements perpetuates hegemonic ideology.

Given the viewpoints presented above, the need to integrate institutional analysis of the media within the agenda-setting perspective is clear. One product of this type of analysis is to help clarify the debate over causality which has plagued agenda-setting research. In our view, the news media agenda is largely a result of the organizational decision-making process. Moreover, this institutional process serves to legitimate and perpetuate the existing social order. Clearly, comprehensive research is needed to investigate both the processes by which media messages are produced and the long-term effect of this content on public perceptions of socio-political reality.

It is apparent that present agenda-setting research has failed to provide a comprehensive understanding of the role of the news media in shaping the "pictures in our heads." This failure is tied directly to its narrow focus on media content and short-term cognitive effects. What is needed is a comprehensive approach which takes into account the organizational structure of the institutions which produce media messages and their function with social, political, and economic systems. This type of analysis reveals the real power of the media to shape messages which are consonant with the views of those who dominate the existing power structure. As such, the managers of the major media organizations play a pivotal role in the legitimization and maintenance of the dominant institutions within society.

The consonant and cumulative nature of media messages leads to the establishment of parameters. These parameters severely truncate the range of ideas and issues which can be raised in public debate. The news media not only transmit certain norms, values and beliefs, but additionally define and amplify legitimate alternatives. These alternatives, however, must fall within established parameters. Consequently, a whole range of opposing viewpoints are systematically ignored or distorted. Thus, the range of issues which fall within the parameters are presented as the entire spectrum of possible choices. In this way, the illusion of a "free marketplace of ideas" is maintained. By controlling the selection of issues admissible to public discourse, the news media structure social, political, and economic communication. This structuring is largely hegemonic in nature and has been largely overlooked in mass communication research.

REFERENCES

Altheide, D. L. (1974). *Creating Reality*, Beverly Hills, CA: Sage.

Altheide, D. L., and Johnson, J. M. (1980). *Bureaucratic Propaganda*. Boston, MA: Allyn and Bacon.

Atkin, C. K., and Heald, G. (1976). "Effects of Political Advertising." *Public Opinion Quarterly 40*, 216-228.

Atwood, L. E., Sohn, A., and Sohn, H. (1976). "Community Discussion and Newspaper Content." Paper Presented to the Association for Education in Journalism, University of Maryland.

Batscha, R. M. (1975). *Foreign Affairs News and the Broadcast Journalist*. New York: Praeger.

Becker, L. B., McCombs, M. E., McLeod, J. M. (1975). "The Development of Political Cognitions." In S. H. Chaffee (Ed.) *Political Communication: Issues and Strategies for Research*. Beverly Hills, CA: Sage, 20-63.

Benton, M., and Frazier, P. J. (1976). "The Agenda-Setting Function of the Mass Media at Three Levels of Informational Holding." *Communication Research 3*, 261-275.

Breed, W. (1955). "Social Control in the Newsroom: A Functional Analysis." *Social Forces 33*, 326-335.

Cobb, R. W., and Elder, C. D. (1971). "The Politics of Agenda-Building: An Alternative for Modern Democratic Theory." *Journal of Politics 33*, 892-915.

Cohen, B. C. (1963). *The Press and Foreign Policy*. Princeton, NJ: Princeton University Press.

Cohen, D. (1975). "A Report on a Non-Election Agenda-Setting Study." Paper Presented to the Association for Education in Journalism, Ottawa, Canada.

DeGeorge, W. F. (1979). "Conceptualization and Measurement of Audience Agenda." Setting the

Agenda for Agenda-Setting Research: An Assessment of the Priority Ideas and Problems." Paper prepared for the American Association for Public Opinion Research, Buck Hills Fall, PA.

Edelman, M. (1964). *The Symbolic Uses of Politics*. Urbana, IL: University of Illinois Press.

Elliott, P. (1973). "Mass Communication—A Contradiction in Terms?"*In* D. McQuail. (Ed.), *Sociology of Mass Communications*, New York: Penguin, 237-258.

Elliott, P. (1974). "Uses and Gratifications Research: A Critique and a Sociological Alternative."*In* J. G. Blumler and E. Katz (Eds.), *The Uses of Mass Communications: Current Perspectives on Gratifications Research*. Beverly Hills, CA: Sage, 249-268.

Epstein, E. J. (1973). *News From Nowhere*. New York: Random House.

Eyal, C. (1980). "Time Frame in Agenda-Setting Research: A Study of the Conceptual and Methodological Factors Affecting the Time Frame of the Agenda-Setting Process." Ph.D. dissertation, Syracuse University.

Eyal, C., Winter, J. P. and DeGeorge, W. F. (1981) "The Concept of Time Frame in Agenda-Setting." In G. Cleveland Wilhort and H. de Bock (Eds.) *Mass Communication Review Yearbook 2*, Beverly Hills, CA: Sage, 212-218.

Fishman, M. (1980). *Manufacturing the News*. Austin, University of Texas Press.

Funkhouser, G. R. (1973). "The Issues of the Sixties: An Exploratory Study in the Dynamics of Public Opinion." *Public Opinion Quarterly 37*, 62-75.

Gans, H. J. (1979). *Deciding What's News*. New York: Vintage Press.

Gitlin, T. (1979). "Prime Time Ideology: The Hegemonic Process in Television Entertainment." *Social Problems 26*, 351-267.

Gitlin, T. (1980). *The Whole World is Watching: Mass Media in the Making and Unmaking of the New Left*. Berkeley, CA: University of California Press.

Golding, P., and Murdock, G. (1978). "Theories of Communication and Theories of Society" *Communication Research 5*, 339-355.

Gramsci, A. (1971). *Prison Notebooks*. New York: International Publishers.

Halloran, J., Elliott, P., and Murdock, G. (1970).*Demonstrations and Communication: A Case Study*. Harmondsworth, England: Penguin.

Klapper, J. (1960). *The Effects of Mass Communication*. New York: Free Press.

Lang, K., and Lang, G. E. (1968). *Politics and Television*. Chicago, IL: Quadrangle Books.

Lippmann, W. (1922). *Public Opinion*. New York: MacMillan.

McClure, R. D., and Patterson, T. E. (1976). "Print vs. Network News." *Journal of Communication 26* (No.2), 23-28.

McCombs, M. E. (1977). "Newspapers Versus Television: Mass Communication Effects Across Time." *In* D. L. Shaw and M. E. McCombs (Eds.), *The Emergence of American Political Issues: The Agenda-Setting Function of the Press*. St. Paul, MN: West, 89-105.

McCombs, M. E. (1981) "Setting The Agenda For Agenda-Setting Research: An Assessment of the Priority Ideas and Problems." In G. Cleveland Wilhoit and H. de Bock (Eds.), *Mass Communication Review Yearbook 2*, Beverly Hills, CA: Sage, 209-211.

McCombs, M. E. and Shaw, D. L. (1972). "The Agenda-Setting Function of Mass Media." *Public Opinion Quarterly 36*, 176-187.

McCombs, M. E., and Shaw, D. L. (1980). "An Up-To-Date Report on the Agenda-Setting Function." Paper presented to the International Communication Association, Acapulco, Mexico.

McLeod, J. M., Becker, L. B., and Byrnes, J. E. (1974). "Another Look at the Agenda-Setting Function of the Press." *Communication Research 1*, 131-166.

Miller, A., Erbing, L., and Goldbert, E. (1976). "Front Page News and Real World Cues: Another Look at Agenda-Setting by the Media." Paper presented to the American Political Science Association.

Molotch, H., and Lester, M. (1974). "Accidents, Scandals, and Routines: Resources for Insurgent Methodology." *In* G. Tuchman (Ed.), *The TV Establishment*. Englewood Cliffs, New Jersey: Prentice-Hall, 53-65.

Morris, M. B. (1973) "Newspapers and the New Feminists: Black-Out as Social Control?" *Journalism Quarterly 50*, 37-42.

Morris, M. B. (1974). "The Public Definition of a Social Movement: Women's Liberation" *Sociology and Social Research*. 57, 526-543.

Mullins, L. E. (1973). "Agenda-Setting on the Campus: The Mass Media and Learning of Issue Importance in the 1972 Election." Paper presented to the Association for Education in Journalism, Fort Collins, CO.

Nimmo, D. (1970). *The Political Persuaders*. Englewood Cliffs, New Jersey: Prentice-Hall.

Patterson, T. E. (1980). *The Mass Media Election: How Americans Choose Their Presidents*. New York: Praeger.

Sallach, D. (1974). "Class Domination and Ideological Hegemony." *In* G. Tuchman (Ed.), *The TV Establishment*. Englewood Cliffs, New Jersey: Prentice-Hall, 161-173.

Semlak, W. D., and Williams, W., Jr. (1982). "A Further Consideration of Political Gratifications, Avoidances and Agenda-Setting." Paper presented to the Eastern Communication Association, Hartford, CT.

Shaw, E. F. (1974). "Some Interpersonal Dimensions of the Media's Agenda-Setting Function." Paper presented at the Conference on the Agenda-Setting Function of the Press, Syracuse University.

Stone, G. C., and McCombs, M. E. (1981). "Tracing the Time Lag in Agenda-Setting." *Journalism Quarterly*, Spring 1981, 51-56.

Swanson, D. L. (1977). "The Uses and Misuses of Uses and Gratifications." *Human Communication Research 3*, 214-221.

Tipton, L. P., Haney, R. D., and Basehart, J. R., (1975). "Media Agenda-Setting in City and State Campaigns." *Journalism Quarterly 52*, 15-22.

Tuchman, G. (1974). "Introduction." *In* G. Tuchman (Ed.), *The TV Establishment*, New York: Prentice Hall, 1-39.

Tuchman, G. (1977). "The Exception Proves the Rule: The Study of Routine News Practices." *In* P. Hirsch, P. Miller and F. G. Kline (Eds.), *Strategies For Communication Research*, Beverly Hill, CA: Sage, 43-62.

Tuchman, G. (1978). *Making News: A Study in the Construction of Reality*. New York: The Free Press.

Weaver, D. H. (1977). "Political Issues and Voter Need for Orientation." *In* D. L. Shaw and M. E. McCombs (Eds.), The Emergence of American Political Issues: The Agenda-Setting Function of the Press, St. Paul, MN: West, 107-119.

Weaver, D. H., McCombs, M., and Spellman, C. (1975). "Watergate and the Media: A Case Study in Agenda-Setting." *American Politics Quarterly 3*, 458-472.

Westley, B. H. (1976). "What Makes It Change." *Journal of Communication 26*. (No.2), 43-47.

Westley, B. H. (1978). "Review of the Emergence of American Political Issues: The Agenda-Setting Function of the Press. *Journalism Quarterly 55*, 172-173.

White, T. H. (1972). *The Making of the President*. New York: Bantam.

Wicker, T. (1975). *On Press*. New York: Viking.

Williams, R. (1974). *Television: Technology and Cultural Form*. New York: Schocken.

Williams, R. (1981). *The Sociology of Culture*. New York: Schocken.

Williams, W., Jr., and Larsen, D. C. (1977). "Agenda-Setting in an Off-Election Year." *Journalism Quarterly, 54*, 744-749.

Williams, W., Jr., and Semlak, W. D. (1976). "Campaign "76: The Agenda-Setting Effects of Television Network News and a Local Daily Newspaper on Interpersonal and Intrapersonal Agendas During The New Hampshire Primary." Paper presented to the Speech Communication Association, San Francisco.

Winter, J. P. (1979). "Contingent Conditions and The Agenda-Setting Function." Setting the Agenda for Agenda-Setting Research: An Assessment of the Priority Ideas and Problems. Paper prepared for the American Association for Public Opinion Research, Buck Hill Falls, PA.

5

The Application of Ethnographic Methods to Communications Research: A Case Study with Discussion

STUART J. SIGMAN
State University of New York at Buffalo

The intent of this paper is to provide some initial perspective for answering the question: "Why employ ethnographic methods in (mass) communication research?" I begin by contrasting two sets of observations made on separate occasions in two nursing homes. The subsequent discussion of some analytically relevant considerations of these two cases serves as an illustration of some general features of ethnographic research, and provides groundwork for answering the question.

The excerpts from my field notes are as follows:

(A)
I am walking through the corridor and stop at the two-bed room near the nurse's station. Mrs. O'Hara is watching her television; Sarah Allan, her roommate, is screaming as usual, and is restrained in her bed. Mrs. O'Hara calls me over to her chair, which I go to. We watch the TV for a few minutes; a news flash comes on to give the "latest news" on Pope John Paul's condition. I hadn't heard anything about this earlier in the day; it seemed that the Pope was shot during one of his usual audiences . . .

I walk up to the fourth floor. Several of the nurses are standing in the kitchen area (behind the nurse's station) listening to a radio. Nurse Dana asks me if I have heard and I tell her that I just found out . . . The fourth floor is its usual quiet self. The lounge is empty except for two residents; one is intently staring at the television, and the other is looking out a window on the opposite wall.

. . . (On the first floor) I observe several of the women from the activities room enter the chapel. I do not follow them in. Most of the first floor corridor is empty. Many of the patients have drawn the curtains around their beds (in their rooms) and are watching their televisions.

(B)
I am sitting with several women from "A" section, who are watching TV, when news that President Reagan has been shot is broadcast . . .

After lunch, the "E" women return to the living room. Mrs. Bergman turns on the television (I later find out it is Mrs. Axelrod's). Miss Peace says: "It's a shame to hear these things practically every day." Bergman replies: "Yes, dear, it is."

On "B" I observe several residents enter Mrs. Bellack's room (hers is the deluxe two-bed room). Some sit on the edge of her bed—while others rearrange the chairs near the two desks in order to see Bellack's TV.

The first series of observations was made in a geriatric facility owned and administered by the Catholic Church in Philadelphia, a nursing home which I will refer to here as Sisters of Faith Home (SFH). The latter observations were made at People's Home (PH), a private-profit nursing home also located in Philadelphia. The data, which consist of taped interviews, observational field notes, and excerpts from medical records, were collected during a nine-month period from 1980 to 1981.

There are a number of similarities and differences in the patients' media exposure and use which are exemplified by the above citations. On first reflection, the observational notes seem to be about television viewing in two nursing homes under fairly comparable circumstances, i.e., "special" or nonscheduled broadcasts concerning assassination attempts on the lives of public officials. However, there are also some differences apparent in terms of the number of people observed watching television as well as in the general viewing context. In order to begin to analyze the possible significance of these contrasting data, I will describe briefly what appear to me to be some salient aspects of the television viewing events at SFH and PH covered by the citations. After this, I will need to consider how these particular events can be related to other instances of television viewing which I observed at each institution, to examples of patient exposure to other mass media, and to details about social life in general in each nursing home.

During the broadcast of the assassination attempt on President Reagan, PH residents and staff created small viewing groups in the bedrooms, in the lounges (which are allocated one to each ward), in the corridors, and even in the main living room and dining room. Several residents were asked by the activities personnel if they would allow their television sets to be removed temporarily from their bedrooms and set up in one of the common areas. Most of the residents agreed once they were given assurances that the sets would be securely locked and later returned. For several days after the assassination attempt (and for several days after the initial broadcasts of the return of the Iranian hostages) residents visited their neighbors' rooms for brief periods so as to catch a glimpse of the unfolding drama, or sat with each other and with staff members before one of the television sets provided by the nursing home in the lounges.

The structure of the above scenes seems to contrast markedly with what I observed at SFH. My field notes reveal the following: A few patients could be found in each of the floor lounges which contained a television set; most of the residents, however, remained in the bedrooms and watched their own sets. From time to time, I noticed a staff member popping her head into a patient's room or into one of the lounges in order to catch a brief glimpse of the special broadcasts. For the most part, however, I observed staff members listening to portable radios at the various nurse's stations.

I will not become inordinately "microscopic" in my descriptions and, in fact, I do not have much more in the way of detailed behavioral observations. If this had been my initial research goal though, detailed micro-descriptions could certainly have been generated concerning who turned each television on, how it was decided which channel to watch, where people aligned themselves spatially, and so on. As I will suggest below, I did not begin my investigations at People's Home and Sisters of Faith Home at this level of analysis because there was no basis for knowing at the outset the possible contribution that such data could make to the nursing home ethnographies at large. For present purposes, at least superficially, there appear to be a number of differences in how patients at SFH and PH watched television under the conditions mentioned. To consider the possible significance of these differences, there are a number of more general differences between social life at SFH and PH that need to be presented.

First, there is the physical or locational context for everyday television viewing at SFH and PH.

(In "A" lounge, People's Home)
Mrs. Polo's nurse is sitting next to Mrs. Kriegel. She points out to Kriegel that she's wearing two different shoes. She tells her to uncross her legs and shows her the two different shoes. The two aides on the opposite end of the room start laughing and Mrs. Kriegel laughs too. She then says it doesn't matter, she's not going anywhere. The nurse asks her what would happen if she went out with two different shoes, and she begins to laugh. A picture of the Pope appears on the television, and one of the aides asks: "Why would anyone want to hurt the Pope?" Another aide says: "He really is a Pope of Peace. It's crazy." Mrs. Polo's nurse says that celebrities are going to have to wear a protective bubble with a helmet; she makes a gesture of the entire body with her hands. Lillian Goldstein stands up and says: "That would be just terrible." One of the aides says: "You think so?" Mrs. Goldstein responds yes.

(Sisters of Faith Home)
I take a general tour throughout the facility while lunch is being served. I am struck by the number of patients who are eating in their rooms (instead of the main dining room or one of the floor lounges). There are many television sets on; sometimes more than one in each room.

(People's Home)
I see Suzy Weiss leave her room (on "E" section) and take her usual after-lunch walk through the "E" and "A" corridors. After about ten minutes, she stops in Mrs. Katz's room (on "E"), and walks to an empty chair near the window. Mrs. Katz is leaning over her tray, finishing her meal, sitting at the edge of her bed.

Both women say hello (I stay back, near the entrance to the room); they complain about the food, etc., etc. After a few seconds, they fall silent and watch the TV which has been on since before Weiss entered the room.

(Interview with Miss Taylor, nurse, SFH)
"The end lounges (on each of the floors) are really, I wouldn't call them a total waste; but they're hardly never used. You sometimes get one patient at a time in there. There's a TV, so they go in to watch if they don't have their own."

(Mid-morning, PH)
I take a general tour through the wards. I do not stop to talk to any of the patients. I want to get a sense of the various activities during the morning (about 10:30 a.m.). I notice that the nurses have already taken most of the ambulatory patients and placed them in the lounges. The residents on "A" are all seated around the television, in two concentric semi-circles. The "C/D" lounge is less organized; patients are placed in all directions; the television is on and seems (to me) to drown out the noises from some of the screaming residents. Several of the "B" women who usually sit out by the dining room are in Mrs. Brenner's room, watching a game show on her television.

The above citations provide the initial indication that SFH residents viewed television in their own rooms (privately or solitarily), and PH residents did this in one of the ward lounges or in the living room or with a group. This description is not intended to suggest that I never saw SFH residents viewing television in one of the ward lounges with their peers present, or PH residents watching television alone in their bedrooms. However, both in terms of numbers of patients and in terms of preferences expressed by the residents (and, incidentally, the staff) of each facility, there appeared to be a tendency toward solitary viewing at Sisters of Faith Home and group viewing at People's Home.

These initial impressions can be considered in a bit more depth. Most of the residents who sat in the lounges at SFH during the day were placed there by the staff; they had been defined by the staff either as seniles or as "halfway" patients who were not alert enough to attend the arts and crafts program which was conducted off the residential floors. The remainder of the non-active residents were allowed to remain in their rooms all day. Most of the bedrooms at SFH contained four beds, and it was not uncommon to see several residents in the same room at one time and all watching television. Interestingly, however, the residents tended to view their *own* television sets even when the same program was being played on those of their roommates:

(After lunch, second floor, SFH)
Margaret enters her room (followed by me) and turns on her television set (near the window). She puts her pocketbook on her bed, and then excuses herself, saying she has to go to the bathroom. She tells me to sit down, which I do (on her bed). One roommate is sleeping in bed. The other two are in the chairs near their beds (only Stacy Howard has a physical restraint on). I say hello to both women, who say that it's good to see me again. I tell them the same. I ask them what they

are watching and both say (I think) "The Price Is Right." They are watching their own TV sets. Margaret returns from the bathroom, and turns the dial on her set to "The Price Is Right." There is no sound coming out of her set, and I ask her if it's broken. Before Margaret can answer, Stacy says: "It saves electricity." Margaret says: "It's cheaper, Stu." I ask Margaret if this is really so, and she says, yes.

As reported by other resident informants, multiple television viewing was not intended to increase one's sightlines, but rather was an implicit claim for (1) privacy, or a withdrawal from the company of others, and (2) a demarcation and utilization of one of the few personal possessions at the nursing home:

(Interview with Mrs. McDonald, second floor resident, SFH)
"We can each have our televisions going and it doesn't matter. The TV is mine. I don't worry about everyone else here; they can watch theirs if they like."

(Interview with Mr. O'Hara, fourth floor resident, SFH)
I ask Mr. O'Hara if he ever watches television in a group, with some of his floor-mates, for example, and he responds: "Well, if there's someone doesn't have a TV, I wouldn't be mean about it."

PH residents did also view television privately in their rooms. This usually occurred during the day while those patients who took their meals in their rooms were eating, or at night while the residents were lying in bed ready to fall asleep. It is important to note, however, that it was just as common for residents to invite each other into their rooms to watch television together, especially (it seemed to me) in the early evening after dinner. Although there were few four-bed rooms and many more doubles at PH, roommates usually shared the viewing of a single television set, and often alternated days for whose set would be turned on:

(Interview with Mrs. Klein, "E" resident, People's Home)
"If we're watching the same program we watch the same TV. It's silly otherwise. One night we use mine, and the next time Trudy will say: "It's my turn." We like living together. We get along—which is better'n what you can say for most room-mates. We sometimes invite Mrs. Bath from across the street, y'know, the uh corridor; we sit around together and talk or just watch the TV."

In addition to this, there were several locations at PH in which commingling between patients and staff members was apparently sanctioned and encouraged by the latter. The television seemed to provide a focus for conversational interaction between the two populations:

(In "A" lounge)
Suspenseful organ music is heard on the television as one of the nurses walks into the lounge to distribut medicine.
   Nurse: What was that suspense I just heard?
   Aide: Where?
   Nurse. Weren't you watching? Were you watching?
   Private nurse: I was showing her these pictures. (Points to an envelope that says Kodak on it.)

Aide: Oh, what's his name wants to know who had who took the checks from in his drawers and only Murdock had the key.

Nurse: Sean? Sean?

Aide: Yeah, Sean.

Private nurse: God, this has been going on for thirty years.

Gloria: It's the same story for thirty years.

Private nurse: It is, isn't it!

(In "A" lounge)

The television is tuned in to a news program. It is just after noon, and several residents still have their food trays.

Private nurse: Oh, she had a baby.

Aide: Who?

Private nurse: Patty Hearst.

Mrs. Polo: No big deal.

Nurse: No big deal?! She just had a baby.

Polo: Oh, a baby, Congratulations.

Nurse: Not me, Miz Polo, Patty Hearst.

If we hold the specific observational differences between SFH and PH in abeyance for a moment, an initial analytic point may be made at this juncture. Lull's (1980) analysis of the different social uses of television may be used here to suggest lines of differences in SFH and PH patient use of the media. Lull delineates a type of "structural" use of television by suggesting that the medium may be employed by individuals as an environmental resource:

> It is a companion for accomplishing household chores and routines. It contributes to the overall social environment by rendering a constant and predictable assortment of sounds and pictures which instantly creates an apparently busy atmosphere (Lull, 1980, p.202).

At the "relational" level, however, television may be used to facilitate and sustain interpersonal contexts:

> Television viewing is a convenient family behavior which is accomplished *together*. The medium is used to provide opportunites for family members or friends to communally experience entertainment or informational programming (Lull, 1980, p.203).

Employing Lull's terminology, the television may be said to serve a companionship use at SFH, and a group or interaction focus use at PH. Certainly, the informant quotes I have collected at each facility[1] can be seen to bear this out.

But we may question beyond the differences regarding the patients' apparent uses of and gratifications derived from the media. Why do such differences as exemplified by the initial set of contrasting observations exist for the two

---

[1] In the present report, I am using the informant quotes to illustrate a point, and I am not specifically analyzing their "factualness."

nursing homes? To what other behavior in each nursing home are these television uses in the respective facilities related?

It was noted above that much television viewing at People's Home took place with residents interacting with staff members or with peers. I also observed residents engaging in other types of media-related behavior in group contexts:

> (In living room, 3:15 p.m.)
> Mrs. Bergman is sitting on the wooden chair in area 4. She is reading the paper out loud. It looks as if she is doing this primarily for Mrs. Axelrod. She occasionally puts the paper down to make a comment about a particular article and receives acknowledgment from Mrs. Axelrod, as well as from Mrs. Fink and Mrs. Pearl sitting on the sofa in area 4.

Although both SFH and PH staff members showed movies to their residents, only residents of the latter facility attended in large numbers (as high as 65% of the total resident population for some films, as compared to 35% at SFH). The PH staff members considered one of their principal goals to be that of providing opportunities for peer social contact for as many residents as was possible. PH residents were encouraged, and, in turn, insisted that they sit with their friends, usually ward-mates, at the various film screenings.

A great deal of conversation at PH was spent by the residents talking about the media, and about events depicted by the media. The media provided frameworks for conversation while all were jointly watching over an extended period, or while residents were greeting each other, sitting with each other, etc. It is important to note here that, from the staff's perspective, the purpose of the group media viewing was not necessarily to provide residents with information but to provide them with a context for peer (and staff) socializing.[2]

In contrast, most of the conversations among the active patients of SFH concentrated on the work in the arts and crafts program. Those residents who were not regulars of the activities program tended to emphasize for me the "friendships" they had with staff members over those with other residents, and they reported minimal interaction with the latter. Both actives and non-actives suggested that the arts program was where peer contact with nonsenile patients was possible, and that, as a result, there was very little visiting between bedrooms.

Those individuals who did not attend the activities programs at SFH remained on the floors except for morning chapel services, physical or speech

---

[2] It should be noted that most of these conversations about events depicted in the media were carried on when residents were not in the staff members' presence (with the exception of talk about soap operas). Sigman (1979) suggests that there existed rules for conversational behavior at People's Home, one of which proscribed outside-home topics. Staff members suggested that, for the most part, residents were not interested in current events or things outside the nursing home. They generally discouraged talk about personal lives, historical events, current news, and so on, although they encouraged residents to socialize with each other (with or without the television.)

therapy, or an occasional visit to speak with the social workers. These residents remained in their rooms all day, watching television "alone" or (quite literally) just staring into space; occasionally I observed them walking or wheeling themselves on an endless back-and-forth tour of the corridors, or sitting in one of the floor lounges. Only the activities participants were permitted by the nurses to travel the elevators on their own, and so the other residents were confined to their respective floors.

Although there was a news and discussion hour a few times each week, few of the SFH patients were solicited by the nurses or aides to attend. Also, the news hour was taken up, not with discussion, but with a staff member's reading aloud from the local newspaper.

In order to more fully contextualize some of the above comments, it is necessary to place the differences discussed in a still larger analytic framework. For example, the above contrast can be related to the general patterning of patient careers (life courses) at each facility. SFH staff members suggested that the behavioral expectations that were placed on residents in the facility were responses to "individual" or "personality" characteristics of the patients, and were *not* based on the ward to which the patient had been assigned or the immediate peer group. Staff members insisted that it was impossible to provide any generalizing statements about their charges, for each of the residents was considered to be his/her own "individual."

This contrasts with the situation at People's Home. There, staff members held differing expectations for the residents relative to the section to which a bed assignment was made. There was an assumption among the staff members at PH that a ward assignment was not a mere residential slotting (a place to sleep) but was also, and perhaps more importantly, an implicit message about the patient's degree of "competence." This was conceived by the staff members to include the patient's interest and ability to interact in appropriate ways with others, and the probable acceptance of the individual into one of the ward-specific social groups. It is interesting to note that I never had difficulty at People's Home in inducing staff members to make generalizations about various patients. The staff members did not hesitate to speak with me in terms of *categories of patients*.

(Interview with Mrs. Richter, administrator at PH)

SJS: Can we go through each of the sections, you tell me about the type of patients there?

Richter: "C/D" is very disoriented, confused, noisy and most are incontinent. They are management problems. They touch other persons' things. They go into other patients' rooms. "A" is kinda the halfway house. There are some there not as confused as others. Some have been there a long long time, and many have deteriorated over time. The people are confused, but not real management problems. "B," "new B," "E" and "A/E" are basically the same. New "E," "A/E," the newest, is the plushest. Traditionally a new wing brings a plusher feeling . . . you get demanding prima donnas.

Another set of differences which can be described here concerns each institution's structuring of residential wards and the beliefs about the role of nursing homes held by each administration.

As noted, People's Home was operated as a private and profit-making facility. In apparent consequence of the profit orientation, the directors of this facility aimed at making the home maximally appealing to its various customers. The owner and the administrator of PH told me that private nursing homes were able to maintain some competitive edge over other geriatric facilities by providing a physically appealing building which attracted a variety of types of clients. They also agreed that private nursing facilities drew applicants from a pool of individuals who sought particular services and special facilities for relatives who were to be institutionalized. At PH, the satisfaction of these presumed customer demands was seen by the administration to require the implementation and employment of a ward system which provided the different physical locations of the facility with differing definitions. *Thus, each section of People's Home was designated as appropriate for a different category of patient.*

The segregation of patients was one of the institution's ostensible selling points. This segregation enabled each patient to commingle with selected peers and to receive treatment from health professionals who specialized in the care of selected types of patients. Interestingly, when the residents and their families were interviewed by the social workers (or by me) concerning the decision to apply to PH, they referred to the nursing home as *primarily a place for meeting and socializing with other people*, i.e., as a residential community.

Sisters of Faith Home can be seen to have been organized on a different basis. When SFH staff members were asked to talk about distinctive features of the nursing home, they referred first and foremost to the numerous health programs which were made available to patients, and which extended beyond those required by state and federal regulations for skilled care licensure. Although the residents' social and emotional needs were considered vital, the institution as a whole was seen as a health-care facility, not a residential or social one.

Unlike PH, SFH was not based on a ward system. SFH consisted of six residential floors, but none of the six was specifically allocated for a certain type of patient. The absence of differential ward criteria was justified on the grounds that this decreased the lag time between the application to and entry into the facility; patients did not need to be matched to particular wards, and could be randomly assigned beds. In addition, staff members claimed that patients should be treated as individuals, and that a ward system served only to label and group people.

The various contrasts I have presented can now be integrated. Solitary television viewing at SFH may be used to fulfill a privacy and companionship purpose for residents. It is important to note, however, that it apparently does so because of (or, congruent with) a patterning of social behavior at the *institu-*

tional level which regulates and justifies an individualized approach to residents' careers, and which places emphasis in the facility on the staff's servicing of patients over the patients' peer contacts. That is to say, private television viewing functions within a system of interaction which discourages or minimizes patient-patient socializing in general. Television viewing at People's Home, on the other hand, appears to be used by residents as a direct means for companionship and interaction. Thus, it serves a group creation (and/or maintenance) function; residents are provided with peer group contact as well as non-task interactions with staff via the presence of a television set in the main lounges. Moreover, it is congruent with an institutional emphasis on group-defined social life. Those who do not view television in the lounges are encouraged to seek out friendships through room visits, through conversation in the living room or dining area, through group TV watching in the bedrooms, and so on.[3]

In brief, differences in individuals' uses of the media can be systematically related to the structure and function of each institution's residential positions, to general expectations for patient careers, and to general expectations for staff-patient relationships.

It should be reiterated that I did not enter either SFH or PH with the idea of using them as field sites in which to conduct observations on media-related behavior in institutional settings. Rather, my concern for doing ethnographies of nursing homes has been with analyzing recruitment procedures, i.e., the interactions concerning patient selection and room assignments, and the communicational implications of particular recruitment outcomes (cf., Sigman, 1982). Nevertheless, I have made observations of individuals' and groups' newspaper reading, television viewing, film attendance, and the like. I did not start out expecting these kinds of data to be important. In terms of the general patterning of social relationships at each facility, however, they did emerge as significant. Although it is probably true that some of the lacunae in the above analysis might have been eliminated had I begun fieldwork with the aim of systematically studying the patients' media exposure, the fact that I did not and yet was able to generate some initial perspective owes a debt to what is at the core of ethnography: its non-a priori and flexible nature. Ethnography is an emic method, not in the sense that it is exclusively or primarily concerned with social actors' statements and perceptions (cf., Agar, 1980), but rather in the sense that it represents a systematic attempt to derive analytic units directly

---

[3] This process in fact has two interrelated institutional consequences: It serves to provide residents with a group of peers (a clique, buddies, friends—all such terms have been used by staff and patients) for sustained sociable contact, which is one of the ostensible reasons for entering People's Home in the first place. In addition, such group formation implies bound aries, more specifically, it defines those certain others with whom residents (depending on ward affiliations) do not have to sustain contact. In point of fact, residents were discouraged from prolonged interaction with out-group members, particularly those individuals not from their own wards.

from the observational field instead of through the imposition of pre-existing coding or ranking systems (Pike, 1967).

The ethnographic investigator enters the field with acknowledged biases, expectations, and hunches regarding behavior which may be important for understanding the particular research question. However, the end result of an ethnographic investigation is likely to look different from what was originally expected or proposed. An ethnographic study requires the researcher to be adaptable while collecting data so as to *generate units of behavior integral to the social scene actually isolated for study*. These units are not necessarily the ones which the researcher focuses on initially when first entering the field. Although I had no hypotheses (or research questions) regarding the mass media and interpersonal behavior when I began my work at SFH/PH, a cerain willingness to explore such data as a result of my day-to-day contacts with the residents and personnel has provided a welcome end product. Certainly, the mass-media behavior has shed a distinctive light on the issue of patient careers more generally, and, not unimportantly, the general ethnographic study of institutional recruitment procedures and social relationships has contextualized and provided for the significance of the media behavior discussed.

As defined above, ethnographic flexibility, i.e., the non-a priori character of ethnography, can be seen in terms of (1) the investigator's freedom to amend questions and hypotheses once actual field work has begun, and (2) the *continuous* requirement to make selections of observational contexts, informants, and behavioral levels for analysis. At the same time, such flexibility implies considerable methodological responsibility on the part of the researcher. To take one example, the ethnographic report should contain an explicit statement regarding the various choices which comprise a particular study. After being "in the field" for a period of time, and after having performed several ethnographically based investigations, the researcher needs to consider his/her "biased" (consistent and patterned) research selections. Does the investigator tend to avoid male informants, for example, or engage in interviews with male social actors which seem less productive than other interviews? Is there a consistent avoidance of certain spatial locations, or a preference for observing only certain types of individuals and only in certain social settings? In many instances, it is important for the experienced researcher to be aware of such obtrusive selections so that they can be modified (or their influence "controlled" for) in future work. Perhaps more importantly, however, the acknowledgment of such selections is important for the investigator's readers and critics to understand the full context of the data generation. While the ethnographic researcher should not be held to a rigid research protocol prior to the start of the study, s/he nevertheless must be held accountable for the various selections made once the study is under way. These selections give shape to and become part of the final written document.

Implicit in the above discussion is the general notion that ethnography is grounded in contextual description. As communication researchers, we cannot always assume in advance the boundaries of interaction. The boundaries of a media event—its integrity as a unit of behavior for investigation—should not be limited by the space-time dimensions of activity commencing with the turning on of a television set (or the picking up of a newspaper) at one point, and at some later juncture the turning of it off. Deciding to engage in mediated communication, negotiating with others for a claim to the media technology (TV sets, newspapers), etc., are not peripheral to mass media behavior; they are constituent partials or units. In addition, the act of watching a television set is part of a larger social event; as a behavior unit unto itself (i.e., as a heuristic category isolated by the researcher) it also exists as one constituent unit of some larger unit of communication behavior. In an ethnographic study, the researcher must consider not only the rules which sustain a particular interaction event (e.g., rules for television viewing) but the rules for the presence or absence of this event (e.g., when people are or are not allowed to view television), and the relationship of this event to other events separated in space and time. In the present context, group viewing during the presidential assassination attempt can be related to group oral reading of newspapers, which in turn can be related to patients' patterns of room visiting and their explanations for entering this particular nursing home.[4] This is in part what Geertz (1973) means by "thick description." Ethnographic investigations attempt to be holistic; observations sample behavioral rules across interaction situations, sustained social relationships across discrete moments of interaction, and so on. *These selected events form part of a larger message system; the observational present (i.e., the immediate physical setting of an interation) is a constituent of the encompassing episode.*

Many of the naturalistic studies concerned with television have focused on the family context. Given the anticipated audiences of most programs, this is a reasonable and appropriate research site (see Lull, 1980). It is not, however, the only natural (non-experimental) context for media behavior to be observed. Moreover, it is not the only natural context in which the mass media are integrated into persons' social relationships with others. Ethnographic investigations need to tap the various social situations, institutional contexts, and geographic locations which can be identified by viewer-users themselves as occasioning (or forbidding) the use of the mass media, and as salient to the issue of media behavior.

---

[4] The family and its television viewing are only part of the patterning of information flow throughout an entire neighborhood or community. The interpersonal relationships sustained by the mass media occur on the playing field, in the school lunchroom, by the office water cooler, and so on. However, it cannot be assumed that participation in the messages exchanged in one of these situations is quantitatively or qualitatively equivalent to those found in another context. A social system, and by implication, its message transmission system (i.e., communication) are characterized by a division of labor (see Durkheim, 1933, 1938; Aberle et al., 1950; Kemper, 1972). See also Golding and Murdock (1978, p. 349), who criticize and characterize mass communication theories which involve a "mistaken location of the mass media at the center of social life."

A behavior unit derives meaning from the constellation of social relationships, actors' intentions and goals, societally imposed definitions of the situation, physical contexts, and so on, of which it is part. In the present discussion, for example, the two institutions can be seen as contexts which give shape to and thus provide for the significance of the varying behaviors observed. In this respect, the importance of the contrast method, which articulates the context embeddedness of social forms, must be noted:

> The student is told that he must consider any feature of social life in its context, in its relation to the other features of the particular social system in which it is found. But he is often not taught to look at it in the wider context of human societies in general . . . Without systematic comparative studies anthropology will become only historiography and ethnography. Sociological theory must be based on, and continually tested by, systematic comparison (Radcliffe-Brown, 1958, p.110).

Harkening back to de Saussure, Agar (1980, p.21) similarly writes:

> We cannot define the universe of possibilities without examining the range of patterns that exists. This principle is itself an illustration of the yet more general idea of definition by contrast. One defines something by systematically contrasting it with what might have occurred, but did not.

The accusation that is often lodged against ethnographic methods as being solely a descriptive technique thus fails to consider the possibility of testing research hypotheses through careful selection of *multiple research field sites*, and through *comparative observations and interviewing*. Moreover, such contrast analyses allow one to rule out alternative solutions and interpretations of data, and to phrase generalizations which are applicable to a variety of situations and contexts. The contrast method can also be used to test observer reactivity by accounting for the different roles assumed and the different interaction formats followed by the "same" individual in contrasting contexts.[5]

Finally, ethnography should not simply be equated with naturalistic observation, since the inclusion of informants' verbalizable meanings for their actions, of "thick" contextualized descriptions, and of contrast analyses as above are hallmarks primarily of ethnographic practice (see Fetterman, 1982). In this light, the distinctive status of ethnographic interview data should be briefly noted.

As evidenced in the above comparative analysis, informant reports are a necessary adjunct to the researcher's descriptions of observed behavior. Fetterman (1982, p.18) points out, in his paper on the diffusion of ethnographic methods to

---

[5] The current research concern with the uses of new technologies, as in the case of social interaction in video arcades, is an interesting and important one. I would suggest, however, that comparative data with other recreational contexts, such as pool halls, would place the use of new technologies in a new perspective, and would in fact provide a means for ascertaining their novel contributions (if any) to social interactional and relation forms.

the field of education, that one of the factors which distinguishes ethnography from other "naturalistic" studies is the concern for phenomenology: "Phenomenology requires that investigators be guided by the insider's viewpoint, the emic perspective." Although it is inaccurate to imply that emicity is always equivalent to verbalizability, it is true that a primary concern in anthropological work is to give comparable status to the researcher's observations and to the meanings, explanations, and significances of this behavior for informants. Radcliffe-Brown, (1964, pp.234-235) writes:

> In explaining any given custom it is necessary to take into account the explanation given by the natives themselves. Although these explanations are not of the same kind as the scientific explanations that are the objects of our search yet they are of great importance as data. . . . The reason given as explaining an action is so intimately connected with the action itself that we cannot regard any hypothesis as to the meaning of a custom as being satisfactory unless it explains not only the custom but also the reasons that the natives give for following it.

As several writers have suggested, however, informants cannot always provide evidence for system patterning. This is because of their lack of awareness of the phenomena of interest to the investigator, or an inability to generate a general rule. Radcliffe-Brown (1965) therefore writes that interview data are subject to scrutiny and cannot be taken as "face valid" evidence for particular behavioral patterns. Birdwhistell (1971, chapt. 3, p.27) also writes that an informant's answer to the questions posed by the investigator "provide further data for analysis, not an acceptable conclusion to . . . analytic research." For these reasons, the identities of ethnographic informants must be known and understood by the investigator. Furthermore, in order to use the reports of an informant, the researcher must be aware of the particular individual's relationship to the social system, his/her attitudes towards the resultant status and towards the verbal reports that are provided, and his/her consistency or inconsistency of response over time. Ethnogaphic interview data must also be analyzed with reference to the researcher's emerging knowledge of the contexts which elicit particular statements from cultural participants, and, whenever possible, should be cross-referenced with observational material. Birdwhistell (1977, p.107) summarizes the ethnographer's approach to informants thus:

> An informant, if used as an access to cultural values, needed to be understood in terms of the relationship the person had to the society he or she represented. Terms such as "sample" or "respondent" as used in certain types of opinion polling or as a source of auxiliary data in an experimental situation are not substitutable for knowledge about the investigator's source of data. Informants are not rats; all too often they learn in a single session.

In brief, I have attempted to outline some components of an approach which must be taken in order to create an ethnographic study of the mass media, and what constitutes ethnography.

REFERENCES

Aberle, D. F., Cohen, A. K., Davis, A. K., Levy, M. J., Jr., and Sutton, F. X. (1950). "The Functional Prerequisites of a Society." *Ethics 60*, 100-111.

Agar, M. H. (1980). *The Professional Stranger*. New York: Academic Press.

Birdwhistell, R. L. (1971). "Body Motion." *In* N. McQuown (Ed.), *The Natural History of an Interview*. University of Chicago Library, Microfilm Collection of Manuscripts on Cultural Anthropology.

Birdwhistell, R. L. (1977). "Some Discussion of Ethnography, Theory and Method." *In* J. Brockman (Ed.), *About Bateson*, pp.101-141. New York: Dutton.

Durkheim, E. (1933). *The Division of Labor in Society*. New York: Free Press.

Durkheim, E. (1938). *The Rules of the Sociological Method*. Chicago, IL: University of Chicago Press.

Fetterman, D. M. (1982). "Ethnography in Educational Research: The Dynamics of Diffusion." *Educational Researcher, 11*, 17-22, 29.

Geertz, C. (1973). *The Interpretation of Cultures*. New York: Basic Books.

Golding, P., and Murdock, G. (1978). "Theories of Communication and Theories of Society." *Communication Research, 5*, 339-356.

Kemper, T. D. (1972). "The Division of Labor: A Post-Durkheimian Analytical View." *American Sociological Review, 37*, 739-753.

Lull, J. (1980). "The Social Uses of Television," *Human Communication Research 6*, 197-209.

Pike, K. L. (1967). *Language in Relation to a Unified Theory of the Structure of Human Behavior*. The Hague: Mouton.

Radcliffe-Brown, A. R. (1958). *Method in Social Anthropology*. Chicago, IL: University of Chicago Press. 1958.

Radcliffe-Brown, A. R. (1964). *The Andaman Islanders*. New York: Free Press.

Radcliffe-Brown, A. R. (1965). *Structure and Function in Primitive Society*. New York: Free Press.

Sigman, S. J. (1979). " 'Who Pushed the Button to Drop the A-Bomb?': Contexts and Conversations in a Nursing Home." Paper presented to the International Communication Association, Philadelphia.

Sigman, S. J. (1982). "Communication and Social Recruitment in Two Nursing Homes." Paper presented to the Society for Applied Anthropology, Lexington, Kentucky.

6

Using Non-Traditional Methods to Assess Children's Understanding of Television

MICHELLE A. WOLF
San Francisco State University

Mass communication scholars who examine how children interact with mediated content have begun to recognize the importance of developmental notions and their potential utility in terms of media theory, and researchers argue that the vast array of logical abilities which develop may affect children's understanding of, learning from, and eventual use of mediated content (Wartella et al., 1979). In much of the latest research on television and children negotiation of mediated content is conceptualized as a complex activity which presents children with a sense-making task vis à vis the mediated sounds and symbols (Roberts and Bachen, 1981). Anderson and Smith (In press) refer to this task as a problem of "cognitive continuity," arguing that children's approaches to solving this problem are both active and unexpectedly sophisticated.

One problem with the vast majority of these recent research endeavors is that, despite the recognition of the active nature of the "viewing" *process*, researchers generally employ traditional methods and fail to use models which are truly process-oriented. As such, those who use these methods cannot collect the data necessary to permit an examination of children relating to mediated content which actually focuses on the event in its own terms. Such a study would necessarily look at this activity as a *process* involving constructive cognition which flows from a frame of reference that is quite different from cognitive activities undertaken by adults.

Those who do not seek to establish a child-oriented frame of reference confront the problem of "adultocentrism," of assessing children's performance against an adult yardstick, which demands for its solution simplification techniques for dealing with children's responses that appear on the surface to be inadequate (Blank et al., 1978, p.64). Traditional research models adopted from the physical sciences and applied to the study of human development in an adult-oriented manner embody "the science of the strange behavior of a child in a strange situation with a strange adult" (Bronfenbrenner, 1977, pp. 277-278). In order to distinguish between linguistic and cognitive competence, one must examine children as they are actually negotiating tasks in a range of situations which demand or at least allow for a wide variety of response alternatives (Campbell and Wales, 1975).

This paper addresses the need for alternative ways to conceptualize how children relate to cognitive tasks such as negotiating mediated content. Nontraditional methods of assessment that were developed during a ten-month naturalistic study of how individual members of a group of children interacted with one another and with televised content are presented. The utility of these methods is discussed in terms of how they contribute to the researcher's ability to deal adequately with the limitations of language-based, non-process-oriented measures of children's cognitive skills.

CONCEPTUAL FRAMEWORK

Methodological Issues and the Study of Children

A number of social scientists have addressed various issues concerning research methods that are suitable for assessing children's cognitive skills. In their critical analysis of traditional methods, Goffman and Parkhurst (1980) highlight three problem areas. First, they say that researchers who argue that children's cognitions become increasingly more complex may actually be measuring the development of vocabulary and abstraction rather than cognition in general. Second, researcher's questions may pose problems in that children who do not understand them are likely to behave in an expected or predictable manner. A third problem area stems from the assertion that adults who examine children's cognitive skills are likely to infer that what children say about an experience is equivalent to what they actually thought during that experience.

Donaldson (1978, p.69) believes that the way children interpret classical tests is influenced by at least three factors, including knowledge of language, assessment of what adults expect or intend, and how children would represent the (physical) situation to themselves if an adult were not present. The conclusion offered, that young children's interpretive processes differ from those of older children, is anchored in a variety of language-based observations. For example, young children are more limited in their language abilities and less confident in their own verbal skills. In addition, they are often unable to distinguish when or when not to give primacy to language. Furthermore, they may not pay scrupulous attention to language in its own right.

From critical points such as these, one can see some patterns in the issues that have been raised. Three general problem areas address the important factors which researchers must take into account when attempting to assess children's cognitive skills. These areas involve the way that adults interpret children's behavior and responses to task demands, children's understanding of what is expected of them, and the way in which questions are posed to children. Each of these is considered in the following sections.

Interpretation of Children's Behavior and Responses

Among the many elements which are not dependent upon language are the perception and manipulation of objects (categorization, estimation of distances, and the like), conceptual identification of objects, evolution of new intellectual skills (assimilation and accommodation of available responses to novel situations), development of perceptual categories and generalization skills, and discovery of rules (Oléron, 1977, pp. 67-76). In short, cognitive operations emerge independent of language (Siegel, 1977, p. 402). It is not surprising, then, that when children are asked to talk about their thought processes or behavior, a particular response may be assessed by an adult to be either adequate or inadequate in a relatively insensitive fashion.

Despite "inadequate" responses to adult questions, some researchers lead one to believe that children are quite sophisticated in their thinking. For example, Blank et al. (1978, p. 63) found that four- or five-year-old children are able to think clearly and to be "extraordinarily articulate" if their verbal skills are not confounded by other demands and are evaluated apart from other abilities. This verbal sophistication is much more likely to be evident in situations where children and researchers are familiar with one another and when children's preferred and most appropriate response modes are fully understood by the adult (Wolf, 1982, p. 20). But even before children begin to express their ideas and thoughts verbally, they do seem to comprehend more than is superficially evident. That is, comprehension emerges earlier than does production (Nelson, 1979, p. 310; Oviatt, 1980, p. 104). Children learn to *mean* before they learn to *speak,* and they later learn to *speak* because they have first learned to *mean* (Halliday, 1975, p. 9).

It seems, then, that traditional studies of cognitive development often measure verbal skills, in many cases without acknowledging the dangers of accepting children's apparent lack of understanding at face value (Reid and Frazier, 1979, p. 9; Lovell and Ogilvie, 1960, p. 117). Recognition of this dilemma has led to efforts to expand response options so that children can better communicate their perceptions of tasks. For example, one study of the acquisition of relational terms underscored the need for new measures and criteria used to determine the appropriateness of utterances which are constrained by traditional linguistic measures of the grammaticality (i.e., acceptability) of sentences (Donaldson and Wales, 1970, p. 265).

Other researchers make the point that elements of context may cause some measurement problems. Rose and Blank (1974, p. 499) argue that contextual cues which seem insignificant to adults may strongly influence children's performance, noting that "any behavior gains its meaning from the setting and circumstances in which it is embedded." This is further supported by an earlier study in which Smith (1970) observes that children's responses to complex tasks reveal not only linguistic and situational decoding skills, but also holophrastic understanding.

One approach to dealing with some of these problems centers on the use of nonverbal measures of understanding. In his analysis of covert versus overt measures of understanding, Denzin (1971) argues that covert methods require children to demonstrate skills through symbolic encounters and conversations, while overt measures look at children's conversations with others, declarations of behavioral intention, gestures, movements, and actual, real-life perform-ance. The use of overt measures may be even less revealing for specific sub-groups, such as those in low income groups, who appear to have twice as much trouble verbally encoding their thoughts as they do acting them out (Feagans and Farran, 1981, p. 725).

The need for nonverbal measures is stressed by others as well (Cole et al., 1971, p. 78; Furth, 1975, p. 218), especially when nonverbal messages are the focus of study (Byers and Byers, 1972, pp. 7-9). This becomes quite important in the face of mediated visual content. The essential points are that nonverbal tasks enable one to control the variables which are irrelevant to the operations, being tested (Siegel, 1977, p. 403) and that simplification techniques for nonadequate responses must be explored (Blank et al., 1978, p. 87).

Children's Understanding of What is Expected

In a reference to Piaget, Robinson (1981, pp. 167-168) argues the following:

> In none of this work has there been any attempt to analyze whether or not the child understands what he is doing, Piaget's egocentric child does not *understand* that for communication to be successful, the message must meet the listener's in-formation requirements; evidence that the child frequently does meet these re-quirements does not decrease the potential validity of this aspect of the concept of egocentrism.

This supports the notion that the way children interpret tasks may be affected by a number of variables, such as when information handling capacities are overloaded (Shatz, 1977, pp. 294-295), or when researchers' actions toward task materials suggest that they are thinking about a different attribute than what they linguistically expressed to children under study (McGarrigle and Donaldson, 1974, pp. 347-348).

Factors such as these underscore Donaldson's (1978, p. 60) assertion that adults tend to speak in an egocentric manner, in that they assume that they are understood by children. When this problem is controlled, there is strong evi-dence that more traditional assessments of children's cognitive abilities are in-correct (Donaldson, 1978, pp. 17-18). According to Gelman (1979, p. 901), preschoolers operate from a different logic which cannot be detected in tradi-tional tasks designed from an adult perspective. In fact, some research indicates that children often judge statements that are quite different from those that adults believe to be the point of focus (Donaldson, 1978, p. 63).

Some studies attribute child-adult differences to the relative salience of ob-jects of attention (Levin et al., 1980, p. 661), or to the assumption that children understand problems of perspective in verbal communication (Robinson, 1981, p. 182). Others point to various situational effects such as the existence of ele-ments that are not directly perceivable to children (Siegel et al., 1978, p. 22).

In the area of task understanding, one variable that must be considered is the quality of instructions. Donaldson (1978, p. 96-109) suggests that instructors, in a school situation, for example, can help by teaching language as a system that contains options, or rules. To this end, one should carefully display the *structure* of the task, help children to recognize it themselves, and recognize the constructive role of error by replacing inadequate rules.

Similarly, the conclusion that young children employ a simple response strategy that utilizes what they know best led Shatz (1978, pp. 298-299) to call for more direct feedback and identification of "stop action markers," or signals indicating that a certain action is inappropriate. These suggestions are a function of the assertion that young children bring "preferred representational heuristics" to the task of understanding and responding to words spoken to them.

Posing Questions to Children

Also methodologically important is how researchers present questions to children. It appears, for example, that although children will generally model their own speech after the way adults relate to them (i.e., simple, single answers to simplistic questions), they are capable of much more (Blank, 1975, pp. 254-257). Rosen and Rosen (1973, p. 55) argue that "given a challenge that they cannot meet from their existing vocabulary, they make efforts to use language creatively and inventively." The authors add that concerns with the non-adultness of language often prevent the adult from listening to and accepting what children express (Rosen and Rosen, 1973, p. 65).

To deal with children's developing language, Cazden (1972, pp. 25-27) suggests that adults should value thoughtful and unique verbal responses because children are aided by what they are encouraged to say rather than simply by what they hear. Practice, then, seems to be important. The nature of questions posed is another key factor, since question-asking "provides direct confrontation to the child's point of view, thus leading the child to restructure his thoughts" (Siegel and Saunders, 1979, p. 169). Open, direct questions can be simple, complex, or embedded, and a question-asking model should consider the linguistic structure of the question, the psychological function of the question-asking process, the cognitive processes activated by the question, the strategies used by adults, and the way in which responses are evaluated (Seigel and Saunders, 1979, pp. 172-184).

The techniques used in the question-asking process are important variables to consider. Almy and Genishi (1979) suggest that one examine the effects that pacing, reflection, countersuggestion, and following-through have on children's reponses to adult questions.

The questions posed in the present study are based on a question-asking model which was developed as a means of stimulating critical thinking about television (Wolf et al., 1982). The model is divided into five stages, with the earlier ones tapping lower-level skills. Each stage is subdivided into three levels of questions which encourage generalization/observation, explanation, and prediction/evaluation level responses. The questions at these three stages are labeled "who/what," "why," and "suppose," and are ordered in terms of the sophistication of the required or desired response, thereby establishing an overall progression of sophistication between and within each of the five stages.

When posing questions to children, the response demands should permit nonverbal as well as verbal response options. This is especially true for media researchers, since they often deal with a medium that provides children with visual images to be perceived, processed, and often retained as personally constructed images. And, since predominant concerns with regard to children and television center on what is learned from nonverbal as well as verbal content, language may not adequately represent cognitions. Children should be encouraged to *show* as well as to *tell*, and the researcher must use all available means, such as role playing or drawing, to encourage well developed responses from children.

Considering all the above, this paper now turns to the question of:

What research strategies *are* best suited for an examination of how children make sense of mediated content?

METHOD OF DATA COLLECTION

Overview of Research Methods

The research methods employed in this study are qualitative in nature, with various types of observational and interviewing procedures serving as the major techniques used for data collection. Seven trained assistants worked with the primary researcher, who spent a total of ten successive months (December 1981 to September 1982) with a total of 109 4 twelve-year-old children. The children were met at a day care/summer camp facility and groups studied ranged in size from 40 to 85 on any given day. The researchers worked with sub-groups of this population, and often had daily contact with groups of 5 to 10 children, as well as with single individuals. There were 65 males, including 3 four-, 11 five-, 15 six-, 11 seven-, 7 eight-, 9 nine-, 2 ten-, 5 eleven-, and 2 twelve-year-old boys. Of the 44 females, there were 2 four-, 10 five-, 7 six-, 6 seven-, 5 eight-, 4 nine-, 5 ten-, and 5 eleven-year-old girls. The majority of children were from white, Protestant, middle- or upper-middle class families. About 20% were from black or Mexican-American lower-class backgrounds. At least one researcher was in the field for an average of eight to ten hours per week.

The researchers engaged themselves in a wide range of activities with the children. During the first two months, they rarely watched television, despite the fact that, at any given time, some children did so with regularity. This period of time was focused on getting to know the children and observing their interactions with one another, as well as attending to any indications of the way in which mediated content appeared to be integrated into individual and group activities. A camera and video playback equipment were used during the last five months of the study. All spatially confined interactions were audio taped, and various outdoor activities were videotaped on a weekly basis from May through September. Both audio and video tapes were transcribed for data analysis.

Description of the Major Phases of the Field Research

The study was divided into two major phases, with a well defined transition between them. Phase One was essentially a "non-viewing" phase. During this time, researchers visited the facility and simply joined the children in whatever activities were ongoing. For the first three weeks of the study, researchers were primarily observers, walking around the various areas of the grounds and watching the children engage in a wide variety of outdoor play activities. Journals of field notes were kept, and regular meetings were held to discuss and compare observations.

As time passed, we were invited to play with the children, and within five weeks we were *expected* to play. Beginning at this point and continuing for approximately the next two months of study (January and February, 1982), the researchers functioned primarily as participant observers, having been integrated into daily activities, but still not accepted as "members" of the group.

In early March we began the process of becoming more fully integrated into the group in that we made efforts to participate in conversations and activities that had previously been confined to children only. Our penetration extended beyond simple participation in play activities as we made directed efforts to actually "become" daycare participants. At this point, it was not unusual for us to bring snacks and to share the children's "juice time." Our goal was to remove the barriers which separated us from the children as fully as we could and to look for signs of more complete acceptance. During this period, we began to make visits to the TV room and to watch afternoon shows with the children.

By the beginning of April, we seemed to be accepted as participants, almost as peers. We discussed the need to look for a comfortable entry point to bring in video equipment so that we could begin the second phase of the study, which was to focus more directly on viewing specific televised shows. One day, a young boy reacted to a show we were watching by commenting that even he could make one that was better. Another child offered to see if his parents would allow him to bring in their video playback equipment, noting that they had a camera we might be able to use. He returned two days later with bad news, and I said that I might be able to secure some equipment for our use.

Equipment was brought in, and several children, recalling the boy's proclamation, challenged him to the task of making a better television show. This began the onset of an unexpected transition phase of research, that of making our own TV shows. As a group and as individuals, we thought of stories for possible shows. All stories were audio recorded and told a second time in terms of what the shows would "look like" if they were on television. Four stories were selected for production. Each production lasted, at the most, two days. The children were in charge of the productions from beginning to end, and those who had trouble operating the camera gave explicit instructions as to what they wanted the shots to "look like."

After this phase, the school year was coming to a close, and the final phase of the research began in late May when the school term ended and the summer camp program began. Most of the school year children returned for the summer, and were joined by a number of new children. We spent the summer watching shows which were recorded according to the children's requests.

During Phase Two, which involved more concentrated and directed interaction with mediated content, several methodological concerns were kept in mind. These have been previously detailed (Wolf, 1982; Brown and Deloache, 1978) and are summarized as follows. First, we were careful to note and deal with the children's understanding of the viewing and question-asking situation. The goal was to be sure the children were comfortable with the question-asking environment, understood the questions posed, and felt free to ask questions themselves. Regular efforts were made to provide the children with a wide range of response alternatives that varied across visual and verbal dimensions. The viewing or talking environment was open to children's nonverbal demonstrations of responses to questions, to acting out their responses to questions whenever possible, and to drawing or role playing when they were unable to express themselves in other ways.

Second, we varied our assessment framework during the course of the study. The open, free-flowing character of the study acknowledged the fact that, even within a single age level or developmental range, children differ in their abilities and behavior and that such differences might only be evident if the methods are flexible and the activities and interactions are tailored with respect to the individual child. For example, a variety of methods were used when asking children to remember visual, nonverbal elements of mediated content. In some cases, we addressed particular shows or advertisements as they were being viewed, as well as content seen the previous day, several days before, a week before, and so on. Memory was tapped via a number of strategies, including, for example, assessing the children's ability to reconstruct visual elements through their own verbal descriptions, creating pictures, adding to or correcting our nonverbal depictions, and comparing mediated content to real life. When focusing on children's perceptions of body-motion behavior, we were likely to present the children with a variety of activities which permitted them to demonstrate their sense-making skills at several different points in time. Exercises included, for example, discussing expressions while viewing, viewing a particular expression again for clarification or further evaluation, listening to audio without video (and asking, for example, if anyone could show how a particular character might or should look), looking at video portions of the content without audio, and creating pictures of nonverbal expressions.

A third methodological concern involved efforts to study the same process in a range of situations. Since we were limited to a single setting, we were somewhat confined in this area. However, we did seek to go beyond considering simply the direct act of negotiating mediated content. We also attended to instances in which mediated content appeared to be used in play and other social activities. In addition, older children kept journals of their television usage and discussed their logs with the researchers.

RESEARCH FINDINGS AND DISCUSSION

The presentation and discussion of results is divided into two sections. The first issues focus on the general research strategies and methods which were developed in response to the basic concern of what it means to "view television" from a child's frame of reference. The second section involves more specific considerations of measures of understanding alternative means of assessing children's cognitive processes, and posing questions to children.

Approaching a Child's Frame of Reference

The first five months of observation provided basic information in a number of areas which contributed to our general understanding of what it means for children to "view television." The insights that emerged were a function of increasingly more intense involvement in the day-to-day lives of the children, through participation in and sharing of such routines as enjoying snacks together at 4:00 P.M. and revealing private "secrets" to which only a few were privy. Such interactions were pursued not so much by consciously developing strategies or making decisions to do this or that, but by genuinely *experiencing* a situation which was guided by its own set of rules, *children's* rules. In order to do this, one must suspend previously learned "adult rules," many of which are so well ingrained as to be "natural," automatic, and often difficult to perceive. This process is much like the one children are required to progress through on the way to becoming fully operational and socialized adults. To learn our rules, they must be actively and intensely involved in, or exposed to, our routines. For us to learn their rules, to be able to really share meaning with them, we must take a few steps back and do the same.

The areas of discovery which proved to be most important when beginning to address our methodological concerns of cognitive assessment are these: (1) individual personalities and cognitive skills; (2) familial and home environmental factors; and (3) consumer and general social orientations.

The earliest observations revealed a great deal about the children's overall personal and interpersonal communication styles. Their daily behavior served as indices of personal characteristics such as fears, weaknesses, strengths, and desires, and provided clear examples of how the different children went about meeting basic needs (for example, ways of attracting praise and avoiding rejection for their behavior).

In a more academic vein, the children revealed their cognitive skills in other ways. For example, the results of more traditional (school-oriented) opinions and assessments of the children's thought processes were observed in the form of evaluations, grades based on "objective" tests, and school assignments en route to such destinies as parents, wastebaskets, and bedroom drawers. Our own opinions of the children's thinking abilities were based on how cognitions were presented in a variety of experiences, such as instances in which reading, writing, or drawing grew out of individual or group pursuits. Careful observation and notations of the resources children used when relating to peers and caretakers who escorted them to and from the facility revealed a great deal about communicative abilities.

These observational notes were used to illuminate many of the findings concerning the ways in which the children perceived mediated content. For example, most of the overly shy or socially reticent children fared well on more personalized cognitive tasks. When "exposed" in public, these children often required special attention and efforts geared toward dispelling their fears of openly expressing their opinions and feelings.

Growing awareness of the children's social rules, communication styles, and cognitive skills was complemented by efforts to gain some understanding of their home environments. We took careful notes and followed up on references to parents, siblings, family matters, and household rules, and made regular contact with caretakers who came to pick the children up each day. Most of the parents walked about the grounds to find their children, and were open to questions which indicated our interest in truly knowing their children.

Information about family life clarified some seemingly puzzling perceptions of mediated content. For example, one day when talking about *The Fall Guy*, I asked no one in particular how old the show's main character probably was. One six-year-old boy replied, "They don't tell that . . . I guess he's 14." A second boy, five years old, offered his speculation, saying, "I'd guess he's 32." Interestingly, the first boy came from a large minority family with no father at home. It is likely that any one of his several older brothers, who were often mentioned in almost reverential terms, was the only close "father figure" he had. The oldest of these brothers was, according to an earlier report, 14. The second boy, on the other hand, had no brothers, and his father was 32.

Two additional outcomes of the regular interactions with the children facilitated the development of the research methods later used to understand how the children processed television. The first involved establishing an atmosphere of *trust* in which the children were most likely to freely express themselves. For example, several girls made up and told stories that focused on their own relationships with their mothers. All of these stories were told in the first person and involved situations in which the main character, a young girl, engaged in "bad" behavior. In each case, the mother confronted the girl, was sympathetic to her plight, suggested an alternative way of dealing with the problem, and absolved her from any crimes. Each story ended with a scene in which the girl and mother, reunited in the home, engaged themselves in some sort of parent-child intimacy. Because the children trusted us, they communicated aspects of their persons and environments which helped us to deal with them not only at their level, but also as individuals characterized by a unique mix of feelings, opinions, and ways of looking at the world. Thus, we could integrate our own goals with their needs.

The second of the two additional outcomes of the early observational period involved the numerous opportunities to gain insights in the area of consumer orientations and materialistic predispositions as they were revealed in personal possessions, play, and various interpersonal behavior and comments about, or miscellaneous reactions toward, clothing and general physical appearances. These observations were further complemented by data collected from games which were introduced, such as "going to the store" and "what to give my friend for his/her birthday." This information was consulted in conjunction with perceptions of advertisements and the overt appearance of televised characters.

In short, one cannot take on a child-oriented frame of reference until one knows the child well. The need for a backdrop, a perspective against which one can evaluate or more clearly understand children's perceptions of me diated content, cannot be emphasized strongly enough.

Measures of Understanding

Discussion of the results based on the data from the directed viewing experiences which ran the course of the summer is necessarily general, in light of the sheer amount of data that were collected. The areas of consideration include verbal and nonverbal measures of understanding and the use of a naturalistic research setting.

Several patterns emerged in terms of how the children processed verbal versus visual content and expressed themselves in visual and verbal modes. To begin, it was evident that their limited vocabularies meant they could not directly negotiate a number of words and phrases. In most cases, however, the children understood the content as a whole and got the gist of the unfamiliar verbal expression from the context in which it was used. For example, not one child could define the word "leper" when it was used in an episode of *Happy Days*, but the group admitted that a leper colony was indeed an unfortunate place to be. In addition, misunderstanding verbal labels, as in the case of a child who insisted that the main character in *The Fall Guy* was a "stuckman," did not affect the behavior or role of the referent of the misunderstood term; he was still "a guy who can jump from buildings and stuff without hurting himself." In situations like these, the words are essentially unimportant; they are conventions developed so that people can talk about things.

A second trend was that the children understood and used a number of words that were markedly different from conventional adult usage and understanding. For example, one child's insistence that dogs *do* talk may have been interpreted as a lack of media-reality understanding, whereas for this child, a bark was synonymous with "dog talk." A more pervasive difference in children's versus adult's word usage centered on the appropriate terms for designating particular types of media fare. For almost half the children, the terms "program," "movie," "show," and for many, even "commercial" were interchangeable. While talk and activities during actual viewing experiences revealed that the children made the distinctions at a more conceptual level, one can see how it would be easy to conclude that the children would not distinguish between, for example, a television program and a commercial. And if this assumption were pursued by asking the children just what the differences were, it is likely that the same conclusion would be offered. This is because many of those same children had trouble expressing the differences between commercials and programs when asked about them in terms of simple, straightforward, verbal questions.

Throughout the study, whenever language appeared to be insufficient as a means of expression for the children, various measures of understanding were explored. When watching a Charlie Chaplin movie, for example, the children were encouraged to create their own messages in a nonverbal way. This show additionally proved useful for guessing or talking about how various actions were negotiated. Providing words from their own vocabularies, the children further demonstrated their own verbal decisions and usage patterns. In other instances, we darkened the video and imagined the sights we were likely to be missing.

Frequently, we used drawing materials as a means of expression, as in a case when one six-year-old girl simply could not manage to find the words she needed to explain the differences between cartoon and real people. The pictures she drew quite clearly revealed many important distinctions between the two, and in fact, after making several sketches, she was able to discuss the content in a manner that previously seemed beyond her range.

Nonverbal measures such as picture-drawing were often complemented by physically-oriented activities which, when they involved talk, were structured so that the children were the ones to select the words. We imagined that we were in shopping malls, window shopping, and deciding which stores to patronize; and we pretended that E.T., who had never seen television as we know it, wanted to learn how he could be sure that he was watching a comedy and not another type of program. On some days, we decided to be little kids trying to make sense of adult conversations that we were overhearing, imagining what they might be saying and how we would attach meaning to those words. We also created our own television shows, and often, when viewing network shows, we tried to guess what we would see immediately after commercial breaks. We even made efforts to duplicate specific shots in mediated content, explaining where the lights, camera, and visual events would be, and we made our own commercials in a big cardboard television, selecting our products from a grab bag and making purchases with paper money.

Demonstrations of their relatively sophisticated skills in negotiating television provided further support for the contention that children know more than some research results indicate; they simply require more appropriate media for expressing this knowledge. Time and again, their intuitions concerning the construction of mediated content were surprisingly accurate. For example, one four-year-old girl explained a dream-based idea for a program which involved a number of monster-type characters. When asked how we would make the creatures and things (special effects), she replied: "Oh, you know, Michelle, we'll just draw some of those pictures . . . like on TV . . . not real people, just pictures of them and the other things . . ." My consistent lack of understanding led her to the work area where she picked up a pad and drew a few hurried pictures in the corner and explained: "See? If you make lots of little pictures, and move the pages real fast, flip 'em, that's how we could get a cartoon." Apparently, she had a concept of animation, but when I later introduced the word, it was quite foreign.

Clearly, the research procedures used, at some point, required posing language-based questions to the children. However, great care was taken to respect those personal expressions which were grounded in some sort of child-oriented logic. When children's responses did not seem to make "sense" and additional queries did not help to pave the way to more clear expression, the situation was often one in which there was some specific lack of understanding in one of two areas: knowledge of some formal, technical aspect of a production, or absence of some real world experience which would clarify a social convention. For example, when Janet of *Three's Company* walked around the house as if crippled and the audio track responded with uproarious laughter, several children who did not know she had painted her toenails did not understand what was so funny until the situation was explained.

When questions were asked and answered and there were no apparent gaps in understanding, but the answers were nevertheless puzzling, we repeatedly realized that there were serious, valid, logical alternative responses to nearly any question that seemed to have a more specialized, "correct" answer. To discover how the children arrived at such responses, we played the devil's advocate, hoping to reveal the systems of logic that were operating. For example, we had some trouble understanding why so many children laughed when a realistic character was hurt. A series of questions over several days finally provided at least one explanation; we found that the children often laughed at actions they could not conceive of experiencing themselves without suffering more serious bodily harm than was evident from the program. Our general impression was that they laughed either because they were uncomfortable with the event or because they recognized its absurdity. Whether they felt sorry for the character, felt awkward in relation to the situation, or thought the whole thing was silly or unrealistic, they knew the differences between situations that could and could not happen in real life.

The insights gained from this research would not have been possible without the use of a naturalistic environment. Observations of the children as they were in the *process* of negotiating production and narrative conventions in a *real* viewing situation served as ongoing indices of their appreciation (e.g., favored content, sense of humor), understanding of narrative and production conventions and use of other nonverbal television conventions (e.g., the use of establishing shots to designate locale), knowledge of the levels of reality at which the conventions operated, understanding of specific plot levels and genres, perceptions of audio techniques, critical evaluations, and memory processes with respect to mediated content.

REFERENCES

Almy, M., and Genishi, C. (1979). *Ways of Studying Children*, 2d ed. New York: Teacher's College Press.

Anderson, D. R., and Smith, R. (In press). "Young Children's TV Viewing: The Problem of Cognitive Continuity." *In* F. J. Morrison, C. Lord, and D. F. Keating (Eds.), *Advances in Applied Developmental Psychology*. New York: Academic Press, in press.

Blank, M. (1975). "Eliciting Verbalizations from Young Children in Experimental Tasks: A Methodological Note." *Child Development 46*, 254-257.

Blank, M., Rose, S. A., and Berlin, L. J. (1978). *The Language of Learning: The Preschool Years*. New York: Grune & Stratton.

Bronfenbrenner, U. (1977). "The Ecology of Human Development in Retrospect and Prospect." *In* H. M. McGuire (Ed.), *Ecological Factors in Human Development*, 275-286. Amsterdam: North-Holland.

Brown, A. L. and DeLoache, J. S. "Skills, Plans and Self Regulation." In R. S. Siegler (Ed.), *Children's Thinking; What Develops?* 3-35. Hillsdale, NJ: Erlbaum.

Byers, P., and Byers, H. (1972). Nonverbal Communication. *In* C. B. Cazden, V. P. John, and D. Hymes (Eds.), *Functions of Language in the Classroom*, 3-31. New York: Teacher's College Press.

Campbell, R., and Wales, R. (1975). "The Study of Language Acquisition." *In* R. Sinclair (Ed.), *Children and Language: Readings in Early Language and Socialization*, 3-22. London: Oxford University Press.

Cazden, C. B. (1972). "The Issue of Structure." *In* C. B. Cazden (Ed.), *Language in Early Childhood Education*, 23-34. Washington, D.C.: National Association for the Education of Young Children.

Cole, M., Gay, J., Glick, J. A., and Sharp, D. W. (1971). *The Cultural Context of Learning and Thinking: An Exploration in Experimental Anthropology*. New York: Basic Books.

Denzin, N. K. (1971). "The Logic of Naturalistic Inquiry." *Social Forces 50*, 166-182.

Donaldson, M. C. (1978). *Children's Minds*. London: Croom Helm.

Donaldson, M., and Wales, R. (1970). "On the Acquisition of Some Relational Terms." *In* J. R. Hayes (Ed.), *Cognition and the Development of Language*, 235-268. New York: John Wiley and Sons.

Feagans, L., and Farran, D. C. (1981). "How Demonstrated-Comprehension Can Get Muddled in Production." *Developmental Psychology 17*, 718-727.

Furth, H. G. (1975). "Thinking Without Language." *In* S. Rogers (Ed.), *Children and Language: Readings in Early Language and Socialization*, 209-222. London: Oxford University Press.

Gelman, R. (1979) "Preschool Thought." *American Psychologist, 34*, 900-905.

Goffman, J. M., and Parkhurst, J. T. (1980). "A Developmental Theory of Friendship and Acquaintanceship Processes." *In* W. A. Collins (Ed.), *Development of Cognition, Affect, and Social Relations*, 197-254. Hillsdale, NJ: Erlbaum.

Halliday, M. A. K. (1975). *Learning How to Mean: Explorations in the Development of Language*. London: Edward Arnold.

Levin, I., Gilat, I., and Zelniker, T. (1980). "The Role of Cue Salience in the Development of Time Concepts: Duration Comparisons in Young Children." *Developmental Psychology 51*, 661-671.

Lovell, K., and Ogilvie, E. (1960). "A Study of the Conservation of Substance in the Junior School Child." *British Journal of Educational Psychology 30*, 109-118.

McGarrigle, J., and Donaldson, M. (1974). "Conservation Accidents." *Cognition 3*, 341-350.

Nelson, K. (1979). "The Role of Language in Infant Development." *In* M. H. Bornstein and W. Kessen (Eds.), *Psychological Development From Infancy: Image to Intention*, 307-338. Hillsdale, NJ: Erlbaum.

Oléron, P. (1977). *Language and Mental Development*. Hillsdale, NJ: Erlbaum.

Oviatt, S. L. (1980). "The Emerging Ability to Comprehend Language: An Experimental Approach." *Child Development 51*, 97-106.

Reid, L. N., and Frazier, C. F. (1979). "Children's Interactional Experience With Television Advertising as an Index of Sophistication: A Symbolic Interactionist Study." Paper presented to the Advertising Division of the Association for Education in Journalism, Houston.

Roberts, D. F., and Bachen, C. M. (1981). "Mass Communication Effects." *Annual Review of Psychology 32*, 307-356.

Robinson, E. J. (1981). "The Child's Understanding of Inadequate Messages and Communication Failure: A Problem of Ignorance or Egocentrism?" *In* W. P. Dickson, (Ed.), *Children's Oral Communication Skills*, pp. 167-188. New York: Academic Press.

Rose, S. A., and Blank, M. (1974). "The Potency of Context in Children's Cognition: An Illustration Through Conservation." *Child Development 45*, 499-502.

Rosen, C., and Rosen, H. (1973). *The Language of Primary School Children*. (School Council Project on Language Development in the Primary School.) London: Cox & Wyman.

Shatz, M. (1977). "The Relationship Between Cognitive Processes and the Development of Communication Skills." *Nebraska Symposium on Motivation, 26*, 1-42.

Shatz, M. (1978). "On the Development of Communicative Understandings: An Early Strategy for Interpreting and Responding to Messages." *Cognitive Psychology 10*, 271-301.

Siegel, L. S. (1977). "The Relationship of Language and Thought in the Preoperational Child: A Reconsideration of Non-Verbal Alternatives to Piagetian Tasks." *In* J. F. Magary, M. K. Poulsen, P. J. Levinson, and P. A. Taylor, (Eds.), *Piagetian Theory and Its Implications for the Helping Professions Emphasis: The Handicapped Child*. 402-414. Los Angeles, CA: University of Southern California Press.

Siegel, A. W., Kirasic, K. C., and Kail, R. V. (1978). "Stalking the Elusive Cognitive Map: The Development of Children's Representations of Geographic Space." *In* I. Altman and J. F. Wholwill (Eds.), *Human Behavior and Environment: Advances in Theory and Research* Vol. 3: *Children and the Environment*, 223-258. New York: Plenum Press.

Siegel, I. E., and Saunders, R. (1979). "An Inquiry Into Inquiry: Question Asking as an Instructional Model." *In* L. G. Kate (Ed.), *Current Topics in Early Childhood Education*, Vol. 2, 169-194. Norwood, NJ: Ablex.

Smith, C. (1970). "An Experimental Approach to Children's Linguistic Competence." *In* J. R. Hayes (Ed.), *Cognition and the Development of Language*, 109-135. New York: John Wiley and Sons.

Wartella, E., Alexander, A., and Lemish, D. (1979). "The Mass Media Environment of Children." *American Behavioral Scientist 23*, 33-52.

Wolf, M. A. (1982). "The Role of Mental Imagery in the Child's Processing of Mediated Content: Some Qualitative Research Strategies and Suggestions for Study." Paper Presented to the Mass Communication Division of the International Communication Association, Boston.

Wolf, M. A., Abelman, R., and Hexamer, A. (1982), "Children's Understanding of Television: Some Methodological Considerations and a Question-Asking Model for Receivership Skills." *Communication Yearbook 5*, 405-431.

PART II

BEHAVIOR

7

"A Flower For You": Patterns of Interaction between Japanese Tourists and Hare Krishna Devotees in Honolulu

FUMITERU NITTA

University of Hawaii

INTRODUCTION

The activities of Hare Krishna members in Honolulu met strong opposition in the late 1970s, but members continue to distribute flowers and religious literature, and to solicit donations from tourists in Waikiki and at Honolulu International Airport. Opposition consisted mainly of objection to the "aggressive" and "intimidating" tactics devotees use when dealing with Japanese tourists. This approach has apparently been very effective in soliciting large contributions from them. A Honolulu newspaper reported an incident about which a Japanese tourist complained to police:

> A 22-year-old Hare Krishna devotee was arrested yesterday 40 minutes after a Japanese tourist told police a man in Waikiki reached into her purse, took money and then demanded $20 from her husband.
> The woman said she and her husband were walking along Kalakaua near Kaiulani Avenue when they were accosted at 2:10 p.m. by a man who wanted a donation in return for a flower. She took a dollar from her purse but the man refused it, saying words similar to "No, that's not the American style. Give me $20". He reached into her purse and took more than $20, she told police. The man then demanded $20 from her husband, she said, but a passerby intervened (Honolulu Advertiser, December 13, 1977).

Only a few Japanese visitors, however, report or complain to police after donating large sums of money. Attempts initiated by the Hawaii Visitors Bureau and the Waikiki Improvement Association to put solicitation to an end resulted in legislation enacted in 1979 which "Makes it misdemeanor to impede or obstruct any person in a public place for the purpose of begging or soliciting alms" (Honolulu Advertiser, February 10, 1979). Additional legislation made it illegal to reach into, take, hold, or touch the belongings of any other persons. However, distributing religious literature and flowers, and soliciting charitable donations are all acts that are constitutionally protected by the First Amendment.

As a result of the legislation, Hare Krishna devotees modified their tactics. Their approach to Japanese tourists is no longer so "aggressive", but they are still said to obtain large donations.

JAPANESE TOURISTS IN HAWAII

For Japanese tourists Hawaii is now reportedly the most popular destination within the United States and the fourth worldwide, following Taiwan, South Korea, and Hong Kong (Honolulu Advertiser, May 13, 1980). In 1982 approximately 750,000 Japanese tourists visited Hawaii. This number constituted 74% of total eastbound tourists and 17% of the total tourists visiting Hawaii that year.

Most Japanese tourists stay about five days in Hawaii and American visitors about ten days. Yet the total expenditure of the Japanese well exceeds that of the average Americans (*New Encyclopedia of Traveling to Hawaii*, 1975). The relative short stays of the Japanese visitors are due to their difficulty in taking longer vacations from work.

Japanese tourists do much shopping everywhere they travel. Many of the purchases are souvenirs for relatives and friends in reciprocity for kind treatment or as returns for *sembetsu* (sending off) gifts received before leaving Japan. The favorable yen-dollar exchange rate is another reason for the popularity of shopping and of travel abroad itself.

As visitors who spend large amounts of money, the Japanese have established a reputation in the local tourist trade as being desirable clients. Although there is some seasonal variation in the number of Japanese visitors, throughout the year they are a major component of the Hawaii tourist industry.

HARE KRISHNA

The Hare Krishna movement, known officially as International Society for Krishna Consciousness (ISKCON), was founded by an Indian guru named A. C. Bhaktivedanta Swami Prabhupada, who came to New York from India in 1965 "—to spread the message of Krishna to the West and revitalize the ancient Vedic culture in India and throughout the world" (Brooks, 1979, p. vii). Since then nearly 5,000 have become members, and there are now 108 ISKCON centers or temples worldwide. It is estimated that the growth rate of new devotees is about 500 per year, and is increasing (Brooks, 1979, p. vii).

Brooks (1979) and Daner (1974) both characterize the Hare Krishna movement as a counter-culture and revitalization movement. Before being converted to Hare Kirshna, many of the American cult members were familiar with other non-traditional religions such as Self-Realization Fellowship, Zen, and Divine Light Mission. It seems that the Hare Krishna movement attracts those who are not satisfied with the traditional religions and values of the American mainstream. Once converted, devotees follow an ascetic religious life based on the four "principles" prohibiting meat-eating, intoxication, gambling, and sex (except for married devotees to whom sexual relations are allowed once a month for procreation).

Devotees believe that violating any of the four principles results in loss of one's spiritual qualities. It appears, then, that the Hare Krishna devotees have a distinct sub- or counter-culture with ideals and ways of life fundamentally different in several respects from that of American society.

The Honolulu ISKCON temple, founded in 1975, is the religious center for approximately 200 devotees. Of these, about 50 celibates live in the temple compound; other married members live outside the temple.

SANKIRTAN

Hare Krishna devotees ideally live an ascetic religious life isolated from what they call the "material world," but it is impossible for them to maintain absolute isolation from the surrounding community. There is, in fact, a Hare Krishna activity called *sankirtan* which prescribes that devotees venture into the "material world." *Sankirtan* is one of the most important religious practices of the cult. Regarded as highly religious training, it is also a " 'supreme welfare activity' performed for the benefit of the society at large" (Brooks, 1979, p. 56). Also regarded as a service to Krishna, *sankirtan* comprises the activities by which Hare Krishna is known to most Americans: public chanting, preaching, distributing religious literature, and seeking monetary donations.

Although *sankirtan* is obviously important to the goals of the cult, members of the cult who were interviewd state that it requires strong will power and determination on their part and often results in great "spiritual strain." Devotees encounter various difficulties while participating in *sankirtan*. For example, Sauri (his cult name), my key informant, who is a male Caucasian in his 20s, has experienced some physical attacks and has been injured several times. He now carries a small camera with him in order to take pictures of assaulters for later display to police.

Physical attacks and confrontations, however, do not often occur. More common are negative responses, or more frequently, no response at all on the part of the people who are solicited. The result of my casual statistical observations shows that only about 18% of all tourists of whatever cultural or ethnic background responded with a led donation. Others flatly rejected the offered flowers or totally ignored the offerers.

According to informants in the travel industry, Japanese visitors are usually warned upon their arrival here against possible "harassment" by members of a religious group in Waikiki. Bus escorts of some Japanese travel firms may point to the Hare Krishna devotees participating in *sankirtan* in Waikiki as the bus passes them. Sauri and other cult members are well aware of this cautioning process.

SANKIRTAN IN WAIKIKI

Sankirtan in Waikiki usually takes place in front of Liberty House, a department store where there is a long stretch of sidewalk, approximately 180 feet, without much cross traffic. The flow of pedestrian traffic, therefore, is rather smooth and constant in both directions. By court injunctions and city ordinance, *sankirtan* in Waikiki is limited to the public sidewalk area. This means that it is allowed only on the outer half of the sidewalk in front of the store. The other half of the sidewalk, closer to the building, is the private and commercial property of Liberty House, although the general public is allowed to walk there.

The number of devotees who may participate in *sankirtan* in Waikiki is limited to a "maximum of six devotees at any time with the exception of Friday and Saturday nights between the hours of 6:00 P.M. and 9:00 P.M." Usually four or five devotees operate in front of Liberty House during the day.

After numerous observations, it became clear that the *sankirtan* in Waikiki is dexterously planned. The devotee, for example, does not approach a walking tourist by giving religious literature and then asking for a donation. Instead, he presents a flower (usually a rose or a plumeria blossom). This approach is used for both Caucasian and Japanese tourists.

Offering a flower to a stranger in Waikiki is not an act that strikes tourists as being unusual. Those who are unfamiliar with Hare Krishna may well interpret the proffered flower as a Hawaiian way of welcoming visitors. Moreover, the flower appears to have the special attribute of helping establish a tie between the devotee and the tourist, because unlike printed advertising brochures, flowers are not ordinarily distributed on the street. The reaction of the recipients of flowers governs further action. If a tourist rejects the flower, the episode ends.

If the tourist accepts the flower and subsequently stops walking, the devotee asks a number of stereotyped questions and then explains what he or she is doing there. Only after these steps are taken does the devotee begin to seek a donation. The whole interaction of *sankirtan* between the Hare Krishna devotee and the tourist may take several minutes, depending on the response from the tourist.

My observations of *sankirtan* interactions showed that the responses of Japanese tourists differed from those of Caucasians and that, presumably as a result of the differing responses, the tactics the devotees used with the Japanese also differed from those used with others. For the purpose of comparison, a typical interaction pattern between devotees and Caucasian visitors is described and then contrasted with encounters between the devotee and the Japanese tourist.

Interaction Between the Devotee and Caucasian Tourists

Before offering a flower to a walking couple, usually to the woman, the devotee approaches them and asks, "Have you got a flower yet?" If the couple responds, smiling and slowing down, the devotee approaches more closely and asks the woman if she is married. The devotee then pins the flower in the woman's hair according to what he explains is a Hawaiian custom, on the left side if she is married and on the right if she is single. If the male tourist has not stopped walking, the devotee puts out his hand to shake with him. Sometimes the devotee pins another flower on the man's shirt.

Pinning flowers on the tourists and subsequent handshaking are accompanied or followed by the question, "Where are you from?" A short conversation may evolve from the answer; the devotee may comment, for example, that he has been there. Depending upon the existence of some common knowledge of or shared experiences regarding the couple's home town, the conversation may continue for a few minutes.

Self-introduction follows. The devotee often says he is a student participating in a contest or marathon to collect money for food or educational programs for the poor in India. As the devotee introduces himself, he often points to an ID card attached to the strap of the shoulder bag he carries. The card bears an identifying photograph and includes in large type the letters ISKCON.

By the time the devotee reaches this point in his approach, he takes a colorfully-decorated candle out of his shoulder bag and presents it to the tourists. According to Sauri, it costs 60 cents for them to make each candle. As he presents it, the devotee says it is not for sale but is available in exchange for a donation, usually asking for $5. The devotee also suggests that the tourists may choose a candle of another color if desired.

If the tourists like the candle but do not want to give the sum of $5, negotiation takes place, the devotee allowing them to bargain as low as $3. When tourists are willing to pay between $3 and $5 but prefer a candle of another color, they are taken to a spot on the sidewalk where boxes of candles and other paraphernalia are kept, where they make a selection.

If the couple is not interested in the candle for $3 or more, the devotee retrieves it. The tourists may then give some small coins to the devotee. Most Caucasian tourists give one dollar, if anything. After receiving the money, the devotee presents them with an ISKCON magazine entitled "Back to Godhead." Some Caucasian tourists decline to receive the magazine and leave the area, even though they have given a donation.

Interaction with Japanese Tourists

For two reasons, the description that follows is limited to interaction between Sauri and Japanese tourists. First, Sauri is the most skillful devotee in soliciting Japanese tourists, despite the fact that he is a Caucasian. He conducts his entire approach to Japanese tourists in the Japanese language. Second, Sauri has been responsible for many of the controversial incidents involving Japanese tourists.

Whether involving Japanese or Caucasian tourists, interaction sequences can be divided into seven segments to which I have assigned the titles: Location of targets, Presentation of flower, Familiarization, Explanation, Solicitation of donation, Intensification/Negotiation of solicitation, and Completion. Most segments have further subroutines. Although both interaction sequences follow a similar general pattern, most subroutines used with Japanese differ from those used with Caucasians. Although my description gives the impression that each segment is distinctive and that one follows another, in an actual *sankirtan* interaction two connected subroutines or segments may take place simultaneously. Thus, for example, presentation of flowers and hand-shaking may be done at the same time by the devotee. The following description of each of the seven segments is given in consecutive order.

Location of targets: Targets are spotted at least ten to fifteen feet away. This allows the devotee to make sure that he has a flower with a hairpin attached to it so that he may pin the flower in the hair of a female or on the clothing of a male. The devotee then approaches the targets or walks along with them as he prepares to present the flower.

Presentation of flower: To Japanese tourists, Sauri says, "*Purezento age masu*" (the equivalent of the English "A flower for you"). Like Caucasian tourists, few Japanese accept the flower. One difference seen at this segment, however, is that even though the flower is rejected by the Japanese tourists, Sauri does not give up and turn to other targets. Instead, he persists and follows the targets to "present" the already rejected flower, attaching it to the Japanese woman's hair as both he and the couple walk along. This mode of presenting the flower has never been observed with a Caucasian woman. After Sauri has attached the flower, some Japanese women slacken their pace if they notice it; some simply keep walking without change in pace.

If the Japanese woman keeps walking with the flower in her hair, Sauri says to her, "*Age mashita yo*" ("I have given you the flower") and/or "*Kaeshite kudasai*" ("Please return it to me"). When the woman notices that she has received the flower against her will, she often stops and tries to return it. Very few walk away with the flower. As two Japanese friends, middle-aged women who recently visited here, told me when they were warned against *sankirtan*, "For Japanese, it is difficult to walk away with the flower."

Sauri then approaches the tourists more closely and the latter in turn attempt to return the flower. However, Sauri will not receive it, despite his request to return it. Noticing his intention not to receive the flower, the Japanese woman may then try to put it in his shoulder bag. In order to cope with this action from the tourist, Sauri swings his shoulder bag to evade the attempt. At the same time he extends a pamphlet written in Japanese, which the male tourist may accept. Sometimes the pamphlet is given immediately after Sauri presents the flower.

This interaction of the tourist's attempting to return the flower and Sauri's tactics of declining to receive it has never been observed between Caucasian tourists and Sauri or any other Hare Krishna devotee. Other subroutines similarly differ.

Familiarization: When the Japanese tourists accept the flower or become "stuck" with it, Sauri extends his hand to shake hands with the male. This act, it seems, is planned to stop the target, who is still slowly walking. He then asks, *"Doko kara desu ka"* ("Where are you from?"). Instead of waiting for an answer, however, Sauri often adds immediately, "Tokyo, Osaka, Nagoya . . .?" This question-answer approach is then followed by a series of other questions and comments:

"Hanemūn desu ka" (Are you on a honeymoon?")
"Okusan kirei desu ne!" ("Your wife is beautiful")
"Okusan joyū desu ka?" ("Is your wife an actress?")
"Okusan moderu desu ka?" ("Is your wife a model?")

To these flattering questions and comments most Japanese women smile and may respond in a manner a little more relaxed than before. Sauri then adds, *"Watashi Keio"* ("I am a graduate of Keio University). Japanese tourists may respond to the statement by uttering *"Ho!"* or *"Hee!"* showing that they are impressed. Keio is a prestigious private university in Tokyo. To the last statement Sauri further adds, *"Wata shi ima sensei"* ("I am now a teacher"). In Japan, teaching is often referred to a "sacred profession," and the teacher is one of the most highly respected professionals. It is interesting to note in this connection that to Caucasian tourists Sauri and other devotees introduce themselves as students.

Explanation: Sauri then goes on to explain what he wants from the Japanese tourists. By this time he has in his hand another copy of the Japanese edition of the small pamphlet, the first copy of which he had already given to the Japanese. The pamphlet in Sauri's hand is open so that some pictures of food programs for poor people in India are visible. As he points out these pictures, Sauri briefly describes the programs. Visible at the same time, in front of photos in the pamphlet, is a bundle of American bills placed on the open pages. On the outside is a $20 bill, which may give the impression that the whole bundle consists of bills of the same denomination.

Solicitation of donation: When soliciting Caucasian tourists, Sauri presents a candle at this point, but he does not do so with Japanese tourists. Instead, he says, *"Sukoshi kifu onegai shimasu"* ("We request a small donation"). Then, as he points to the bundle with the $20 bill, he adds, *"Daitai niju doru gurai"* ("About $20 is an appropriate amount"). If the Japanese tourists reach for their wallets or purses, Sauri sometimes adds the statement: *"Nihonjin wa tottemo shinsetsu desu ne"* ("Japanese people are very kind indeed"). However, although a few Japanese tourists comply with Sauri's solicitation at this point and make a donation, many apparently hesitate to give $20. If the target now begins looking for a certain kind of bill, Sauri often assists by pointing at one, probably a $20. During my observations it was often difficult to identify the denomination of bill given by tourists. The amount, however, could be inferred from

Sauri's reaction, because he seldom accepts from Japanese tourists small amounts such as the one dollar which he readily accepts from Caucasians.

Intensification/negotiation of solicitation: For this segment of the interaction sequences, two labels are assigned because interaction between the devotees and Caucasian and Japanese tourists differs sharply. Negotiation is applicable to interaction with Caucasian tourists, as described earlier, and intensification refers to interaction with Japanese.

At this point of solicitation, should the Japanese tourists start to leave, Sauri resorts to tactics which he uses only with them. He first says, *"Chotto matte"* ("Wait a minute"). As he himself stated in one of my interviews with him, he then raises his voice. His smile, maintained up to that moment, disappears and now he assumes a sullen expression. If the reaction of the Japanese is not favorable or, as often happens, is not overt, he glares at them, moving even closer.

At this moment, in the face of rather unexpected behavior by a strange Caucasian male who speaks Japanese quite well, most Japanese tourists seem not to know what to do. They often pause or seem frozen on the spot. Some simply stand there without doing anything except to look around and at Sauri. Some look in the direction they were walking several minutes earlier. The glaring and staring may last for a few minutes if the Japanese do not respond favorably.

Completion: It is not wholly clear how large a donation Sauri regards as acceptable from a Japanese. In one interview with him and a female devotee from Japan, they estimated the average donation at one dollar from Caucasians and at ten from Japanese. However, several Japanese tourists whom I interviewed immediately after they made donations told me they had each given $20.

Sometimes Sauri stands silently staring at one partner, generally the male, conveying the idea that he is waiting for an acceptable donation. The female, who has been watching the whole interaction from several steps away, walks up to Sauri and makes a donation. Apparently she has concluded that the only course of action is to accede.

Very few Japanese tourists who have gone this far with Sauri in his routine leave without donating. When Sauri receives an acceptable amount he again smiles and looks friendly, and presents the targets with a candle, thanks them and they part company.

DISCUSSION AND INTERPRETATION

Japanese behavioral pattern

Takie S. Lebra describes the Japanese as "extremely sensitive to and concerned about social interaction and relationships", a circumstance to which she gives the name "social preoccupation" (Lebra, 1976, p. 2). Lebra contrasts this social preoccupation of the Japanese with what she calls "unilateral determinism," in which there is a prime mover, a cause, origin, or purpose. In unilateral determinism, social influence flows unilaterlly from center to periphery. The socially preoccupied Japanese is more aware than are Westerners of influence flowing both ways between himself and his object. Lebra (1976, p. 7) calls this orientation "interactional relativism." In other words, the outcome of a social interaction involving a Japanese is strongly contingent upon the nature of the interaction and of the parties involved in it.

In analyzing Japanese society, Nakane (1970, p. 26) states that vertical principles of rank and hierarchy dominate all relationships and are the actuating principle in creating cohesion among group members.

Lebra (1976, p. 77) argues that solidarity among the Japanese is easier to create among unequals on a hierarchical basis than it is among equals. She attributes this circumstance to a strong motivation to elevate one's status, which, although putting peers into fierce competition, induces superior and inferior to play complementary roles.

In a symmetrical relationship in which exactly equal actors interact, Ego may have too much uncertainty about how Alter acts, and Ego may thus be unable to take action. "Ego's humility might be taken advantage of and reacted to in arrogance, whereas Ego's status display might arouse enmity. A vertical relationship does away with this uncertainty and riskiness since the actions of a superior and inferior Alter are more predictable." Lebra (1976, p. 77) contends that this last point accounts for the greater Japanese propensity toward "complementarity" rather than toward "symmetry" in social interaction.

The strong tendency of the Japanese toward group orientation and their group affiliation needs have long been recognized. From this perspective, it is understandable that the Japanese put more stress on the group than on the individual. As a result, "The Japanese individual ordinarily does not consider it frustrating to bow to group will. He has been carefully trained to acquiesce" (Kerlinger quoted by Saint-Jacques 1971, p. 88).

Relevant here are not group orientation or group affiliation needs of the Japanese as such. Rather, it is the result of training and socialization for them. Consequently, the Japanese have a tendency to give in to another's will quite easily. This tendency is clearly reflected in one of the frequently used colloquial expressions, "shikata ga nai" (it cannot be helped).

It is evident that the dealing with Caucasian tourists sankirtan solicitation takes places within the American framework. For the devotee to suggest $20 as a donation from an American is an outrageous request. Similarly, it may well be that many of the Japanese approached by Sauri sense that the suggested donation is high.

However, it is also probable that Japanese tourists, unfamiliar with circumstances in a foreign country, are not sure what the appropriate donation might be. This ambiguity seems to be reinforced by Sauri's intensifying tactics, used only during his solicitation of Japanese.

It is useful to note again that protests about Hare Krishna activities and attempts to stop their "aggressive and unruly solicitation" have been made by local rather than Japanese people. One reason appears to be that Japanese do not wish to take the time and trouble to protest or report to the police. Also, the so-called non-confrontational tendency of Japanese people (Lebra, 1984) seems to be evident.

In a letter to State Senator Nishimura, Hiromu Nojima of the Hawaii Visitors Bureau gives the following reasons why Japanese tourists "still fall prey to these aggressive solicitations": 1) they are unable to express refusal because of a handicap in communication, and 2) being in a foreign land, they feel that they must not displease the local people.

These statements are Nojima's own interpretations, and not the Japanese tourists' views. It is apparent that his first statement is not altogether accurate, because at least the solicitation of Sauri is conducted entirely in the Japanese language so that no linguistic communication handicap exists. Rather, the Japanese are simply unable to refuse. Moreover, it is difficult to imagine that Japanese tourists hold the view described in Nojima's second statement. It is more probable that they behave according to the cause and effect sequence created by Sauri and other Hare Krishna devotees in encounter with Japanese.

The following is a more plausible interpretation of Japanese responses seen during *sankirtan*. First, Japanese tourists appear to become socially paralyzed when they are approached and solicited by Sauri. Lebra describes what she calls "social paralysis" as a Japanese behavioral pattern taking place when a Japanese encounters and interacts with a stranger whose cultural identity and social status are unknown and/or rather ambiguous. A culturally ambiguous individual, she argues, may "paralyze" the usual and normal behavioral patterns of the Japanese, leaving them with no readily available course of action (Lebra 1980, personal communication).

From the Japanese point of view, Sauri is indeed culturally ambiguous. He speaks fluent Japanese but is Caucasian. Sauri also presents himself as a graduate of a prestigious university in Tokyo and says he is a teacher. Despite this prestigious personal background, he solicits large donations of money, behavior incongruent with his declared status, and does so along the busy main thoroughfare of Waikiki. A lack of norms in this intercultural situation seems also to promote "social paralysis" on the part of Japanese visitors.

Second, another set of influencing factors related to the foregoing may usefully be discussed following the concept of "complementary interaction" pattern (Sluzki and Beavin, 1977; Watzlawick et al., 1967). Interactional complementarity along with symmetry were first introduced by Gregory Bateson (1958) in relation to what he termed schismogenesis.

Both symmetrical and complementary schismogenesis are sequences of social interaction in which A's behavior and action are stimuli for B's, which in turn become stimuli for more intense behavior and action on the part of A, and so forth. These two patterns of interaction have subsequently come to be referred to as simply symmetrical and complementary interaction without reference to schismogenesis.

The two concepts can be described as relationahips based on either equality or difference. In the first case, the behavior of each party tends to be similar, while in the second case one party's behavior complements that of the other. Thus, symmetrical interaction is characterized by equality and minimization of difference, while complementary interaction is based on the maximization of difference (Watzlawick et al., 1967, pp. 68-69).

There are two different positions in complementary interaction, one occupying the superior, primary, or "one-up" position, and the other the correspondingly inferior, secondary, or "one-down" position. The two positions are of an interlocking nature in which dissimilar but fitted behaviors evoke each other (Watzlawick et al., 1969, p. 69).

The two concepts have been used by some interactionally oriented psychiatrists in the context of "control theory." It is the belief that all persons, implicitly or explicitly, are constantly attempting to define the nature of their relationships. One such communicative behavior that is viewed as an attempt to define the nature of relationships is associated with complementary interaction. In such interaction, the party who occupies the "one-up" position is in control or in charge, while the other who occupies the "one-down" position is accepting or being taken care of (Sluzki and Beavin, 1977, p. 72).

What will be most likely to happen in culture contact where two different groups of people interact with one another? Bateson (1972, p. 68) predicts that symmetrical differentiation takes place in "cases in which the individuals in the two groups A and B have the same aspirations and the same behavioral patterns, but are differentiated in the orientation of these patterns." He further predicts that complementary differentiation takes place in "cases in which behavior and aspirations of the members of the two groups are fundamentally different."

From the above discussion, it can be safely assumed that behavioral patterns and aspirations of Hare Krishna devotees and Japanese tourists are fundamentally different. Throughout interaction with the Japanese, Sauri uses persistent, aggressive, demanding, and compelling tactics. The behavior of the Japanese is generally: 1) minimal verbal response in a low and weak tone of voice; 2) usually no questions asked by them; 3) no decisive refusal; and 4) finally, compliance with Sauri's requests and demands.

Sauri plays an active role and the Japanese are usually passive. He does what the Japanese call *makushi tateru* (to talk or argue volubly and furiously), not allowing them a chance to speak. This behavior on the part of Sauri makes the Japanese remain listeners. Even when he asks questions such as "Where are you from?", he often gives no opportunity for the Japanese to respond. This complementary pattern of interaction becomes escalated and intensified.

We may note again that Sauri first gives flowers and then pamphlets, which the Japanese tourists receive, and thus he establishes a giver-receiver relationship. When attempts are made by the Japanese tourists to give the flower back,

Sauri rejects it, thus remaining a giver. During the Familiarization segment, Sauri takes the position of a talker, asking questions and making flattering comments. At this time he becomes "one-up" by introducing himself as a graduate of a famous Japanese university and as a teacher. In this routine, Sauri is the talker and flatterer; the Japanese are listeners and receivers of flattery.

During the Intensification segment when Sarui raises his voice, sulks, the glares at Japanese tourists, interaction is now intensified, bringing his targets to immobile silence and, finally, compliance with his request for money.

Thus, Saru remains the solicitor and the Japanese remain "solicitees" throughout. Clearly, Sauri reacts to the reactions of the Japanese, whom he described as being "so polite that they don't know how to say no" and takes advantage of their responses.

Japanese behavioral patterns, which devotees in turn react to and take advantage, of, result in Japanese tourists consistently giving substantially larger donations than do Caucasian tourists. Such behavioral patterns on the part of Japanese tourists include "social paralysis," non-confrontational management, and a tendency to react and interact in a complementary manner with one another in interprersonal relations.

It is also clear that solicitation behavior of Hare Krishna devotees is motivated by and based on values and teachings of the cult which differ significantly, not only from those of the Japanese, but also from those of the Americans. In this regard, the controversy seems, in part, to stem from differences in behavioral patterns and cultural values beetween Japanese tourists and Hare Krishna devotees.

REFERENCES

Bateson, G. (1958). *Naven*, 2d ed. Palo Alto, CA: Stanford University Press.

Bateson, G. (1972). *Steps to an Ecology of Mind*. New York: Ballantine.

Brooks, C. (1979). "The Path to Krishna." Unpublished MA thesis. University of Hawaii.

Daner, F. J. (1974). *The American Children of Krsna*. New York: Holt, Rinehart & Winston.

Lebra, T. S. (1976). *Japanese Patterns of Behavior*. Honolulu, HI: University Press of Hawaii.

Lebra, T. S. (1980). Personal Communication.

Lebra, T. S. (1984). "Non-Confrontational Strategies for Management of Interpersonal Conflicts in Japan." *In* E. Kraus, T. Rohlen, and P. Steinhoff (Eds.), *Conflicts in Japan*. Honolulu, HI: University Press of Hawaii.

Nakane, C. (1970). *Japanese Society*. Middlesex, England: Penguin.

New Encyclopedia for Traveling to Hawaii (Hawai Ryoko no Tameno Shinhyakka) (1975). Tokyo: Economic Salon.

Saint-Jacques, B. (1971). *Structural Analysis of Modern Japanese*. Vancouver, B.C.: Evergeen Press.

Sluzki, C. E., and Beavin, J. (1977). "Symmetry and Complementarity." *In* P. Watzlawick and J. H. Weakland (Eds.), *The Interactional View*. New York: Norton.

Watzlawick, P., Beavin, J. H., and Jackson, D. D. (1967). *Pragmatics of Human Communication*. New York: Norton.

8

The Impact of Humor on Speaker Credibility in Funeral Eulogies

JOHN ALFRED JONES
University of Illinois at Chicago

JAMES M. VINCENT
Moody Bible Institute

Can a speaker win laughter from an audience attending a funeral? If so, what impact will the use of humor have on the eulogizer's credibility? This study investigates the usefulness of including humorous material to benefit speaker credibility within one speech event, the funeral eulogy. The standard eulogy is devoid of humor (Stevens, 1961), and authorities recommend that the speaker exercise caution and restraint in the use of humor during a serious speech event (Monroe, 1939; Gray and Braden, 1965; Bryant and Wallace, 1976).

Brownlow and Davis (1974) classify three major purposes for the eulogy: (1) to express appropriate personal and audience grief; (2) to deepen appreciation and respect for the deceased; and (3) to give the audience strength for the present and hope for the future. As one of its functions, humor provides relief from concentrated mental effort and tension (McBurney and Wrage, 1965). Grimes (1955) theorizes that mirth results from the resolution of tension after a surprise insight. Therefore, if humor's effectiveness is based on creating and then allaying tension, humor may be particularly helpful in the funeral setting. Humor should, in fact, reduce stress as the mourners manage to dispel their grief.

Within the funeral setting, the mourners during the eulogy have feelings of respect, love, and loss toward the deceased person (Brownlow and Davis, 1974). The principle of cognitive balance can be applied to the funeral eulogy. To the extent the source, either a minister or friend, reflects the same attitudes as the mourners during the message of praise for the deceased, the listeners should increase their positive regard for the source, thus assigning higher speaker credibility.

The present study tests three main hypotheses concerning the influence of humor on speaker credibility in a funeral eulogy:

1. The source of a humorous-appropriate funeral eulogy will rate higher in credibility than the source of a no-humor eulogy.

2. The source of a humorous-appropriate funeral eulogy will rate higher in credibility than the source of a humorous-inappropriate eulogy.
3. The source of a no-humor funeral eulogy will rate higher in credibility than the source of a humorous-inappropriate eulogy.

PROCEDURE

Two hundred twenty-two undergraduates enrolled in beginning communication and sociology courses at the University of Illinois in Chicago participated in this study. Each class was assigned to one of three experimental conditions: exposure to a funeral eulogy with serious content, exposure to a funeral eulogy with humorous-appropriate content, or exposure to a funeral eulogy with humorous-inappropriate content.

Ego Involvement

Ego involvement by the subjects similar to that experienced by attending an actual funeral presented an important concern of this study. The funeral of President Kennedy was selected. To personalize the death of the president, the subjects first watched a short documentary of Kennedy's active life as president: giving speeches, shaking hands of young and old, showing his role as loving father and husband, and encountering national crises. Footage of young people and minorities crying in anguish after learning of Kennedy's death demonstrated the appeal of the president and helped invoke greater ego involvement. This sentimental documentary was culled from a longer twenty-minute documentary to emphasize the charisma of the man. New narration and music were added to the film which ran six minutes and was entitled *A Sound of Drums*.

In addition, the subjects watched a preliminary eulogy. This eulogy was the actual speech delivered by Senator Mike Mansfield (Eulogies by Leaders, 1963). This short two minute forty-five second maudlin eulogy evoked memories of the humanity of the President and was included to increase ego involvement. Within the design, this eulogy was used to test whether the populations of the three experimental groups were similarly representative samples within the total population employed. Credibility ratings assigned to the speaker of the preliminary eulogy were expected to be similar across the three groups.

Conditions

All three groups participated in this sequence: (1) viewing the documentary, (2) viewing the preliminary eulogy, (3) completion of Part I of the testing instrument consisting of credibility scales, (4) viewing the selected test eulogy–serious content, humorous-appropriate content, or humorous-inappropriate content, and (5) completion of Part II of the testing instrument for credibility of the main eulogy source, scales to measure perceived content, and a scale to measure appropriateness of the humor.

The Test Eulogies

In creating the test eulogies, the serious content presentation was based on the eulogy delivered originally by Richard Cardinal Cushing of Boston during a mass for the slain president (The Transcript of Cushing's Eulogy, 1963). In the present study, the source in all three conditions was allegedly a United States senator who knew the president as a colleague. Cushing's eulogy was edited to remove all references to Scripture and religion. New text was inserted only for ease of transitions.

In the humorous-appropriate eulogy, anecdotes told by and about the president and witticisms by the president were added to the serious version. Seven humorous items were included (Adler, 1964; Adler, 1965; "The Transcript of Cushing's Eulogy," 1963).

In the humorous-inappropriate eulogy, seven items were added to the serious version. Most were inappropriate because of their unsympathetic stance toward the President. Like the humorous-appropriate eulogy, the serious portion of the text was edited to maintain close equality in time for the three versions of the eulogy. Both humorous conditions included serious sentences not in the original serious version to provide transitions to and from the humorous items. The three versions of the eulogy had identical salutations, and three of the four first paragraphs were identical.

The same professional actor/announcer delivered the three test eulogies which were videotaped. He was instructed to glance away from the camera sometimes, upward at other times, as if he were looking at an audience on a main floor and in a balcony. He stood behind a wooden lectern with the Great Seal of the United States over his right shoulder on a wooden panel backdrop. A U.S. flag appeared off to his left in angle shots.

The preliminary eulogy was delivered by a communications professor employing the same setting. This presentation was, also, videotaped. Both men wore glasses and were appropriately older men.

Pilot Study

In a pilot study, ego involvement elicited by the documentary and preliminary serious eulogy was tested. Thirty-three undergraduate students randomly were assigned to two groups. The subjects recorded their responses on two semantic differential scales: happy-sad, and joy-grief. Ratings clearly indicate that feelings of sadness and grief appropriate to a funeral setting developed in the two testings and no significant difference in those feelings appeared between the two groups. Subjects in both groups also rated the content of the preliminary eulogy and the test eulogy on a serious-humorous continuum. Both the humorous-appropriate and the humorous-inappropriate eulogies were rated significantly more humorous than the serious preliminary eulogy ($p<.005$). Subjects also were asked to rate the two humorous test eulogies on a humorous-appropriate: humorous-inappropriate scale. The humorous-appropriate eulogy was preceived as appropriate and the serious-inappropriate as inappropriate ($p<.005$).

Next, a panel of three communication experts was asked to evaluate the humorous versions of the test eulogies. Each humorous item in each test eulogy was evaluated. Ratings were recorded by asking the evaluators to assess the speaker's attitude toward the deceased on two scales: sympathetic-unsympathetic, and friendly-unfriendly. Results showed high humorous-appropriate ratings for the items in the humorous-appropriate eulogy; however, five of the items in the humorous-inappropriate eulogy received positive ratings. Two positive items were retained for realism to an actual speaking situation based on the assumption that no eulogizer would intentionally choose humor that was inappropriate. Four new inappropriate items replaced other items. Using the panel a second time, the humorous-inappropriate items received a negative score of -56 compared with $+1$ for the original. This negative version was now selected as the inappropriate-humor eulogy.

Testing Instrument

The testing instrument, titled "Speaker Evaluation Form", contained two parts. Part I of the booklet included fifteen semantic differential scales to measure the credibility of the source of the preliminary eulogy across five dimensions (McCroskey et al., 1974; Burgoon, 1976). Part II included the same credibility scales to evaluate the source of the test eulogy. The scales were randomly reversed so the two sets of scales would not appear identical. In addition, three items were used to measure the perceived content of the test eulogy, and a final scale was included for measurement of the perceived appropriateness of the humor.

Administration

Subjects were only told that the study would determine how a funeral eulogy can affect the listener's feelings toward a speaker. After being introduced by the course instructor, the administrator presented identical oral instructions to all three sample groups. The documentary and preliminary eulogy followed the oral instructions. Subjects completed Part I of the booklet, and, next, viewed the second eulogy, which was one of the three test treatments. After this viewing, subjects completed Part II of the test booklet.

RESULTS

A t-test was performed on the independent variable of appropriateness of humor to determine whether subjects in treatments two and three (the two humorous treatments) differed significantly in their perceptions. A one-way analysis of variance using the F-ratio measured the significance of differences among the three sample groups on ego involvement, perception of humorous content, and ratings of overall credibility of the preliminary-eulogy source. In addition, results for ratings of overall credibility and the five credibility dimensions for the source in the three treatment eulogies were subjected to separate analyses of variance. For all statistical tests the probability of sample error was required to be less than .05 for significance.

The Scheffe procedure evaluated which pair(s) of sample groups differed significantly. Assuming the three groups were from the same population, the harmonic means method of the Scheffe procedure was used (Williams, 1979).

Involvement and Perception of Humor

To determine whether the first half of the presentation, consisting of a film documentary and short eulogy, had created the desired salience for subjects in all three conditions, two scales measured the effective responses of the experimental subjects that were considered relevant in a funeral setting: happy-sad and grief-joy. A Pearson Correlation test for the two items produced a correlation coefficient of 0.5994. Based on this moderate correlation, the two were combined for an analysis of variance among the three subject samples. Z-scores for the two items were added to produce the independent variable "ego involvement." Results indicated the differences among the three groups were not significant ($F = 2.97$, $p < .054$), and that subjects were emotionally involved, experiencing feelings of sadness and grief when their eulogy treatment began.

Subjects in groups two and three heard humorous items in their eulogies. A one-way analysis of variance measured whether subjects in conditions two and three perceived the content as humorous. A significant effect occurred, with $p < .005$, indicating the perceptions of subjects in groups two and three were significantly different from those in group one, the control group. A t-test measured the extent to which subjects in conditions two and three regarded the humorous material as appropriate to the eulogy. With the "appropriate" label closest to the first space (1) on the semantic differential, group two had a mean of 2.43; group three, 4.19. The difference was significant at the .005 level, with $t = 6.67$.

Overall Credibility

To evaluate the statistical significance of results for the three main hypotheses, a mean credibility score for each of the three subject samples was calculated by summing the 15 mean scores of the individual credibility scales. An analysis of variance was performed on this mean score to determine whether any of the groups differed significantly in its overall credibility ratings from another. Data showed a significant effect had occurred among the three conditions, with $p < .01$ (Table 1). Subjects in the humorous-appropriate condition rated their source significantly higher in credibility than subjects in the no-humor group rated their source. Credibility ratings by subjects in the humorous-appropriate group also were significantly higher than those by subjects in the humorous-inappropriate group.

The results supported the first two research hypotheses. There is evidence that the source who includes humorous-appropriate content in a eulogy will be rated higher in credibility than will a source who has no humorous content or

Table 1.   Analysis of Variance Summary for Overall Credibility Ratings

Analysis of Variance

Source	Degrees of Freedom	Sum of Squares	Mean Squares	F Ratio*
Between Groups.........	2	5,116.91	2558.46	14.57
Within Groups	219	38,454.33	175.59	
Total...................	221	43,571.24		

Treatment Means for Overall Credibility

No-Humor Content	Humor. Appropriate Content	Humor. Inappropriate Content
72.90$_a$	84.67$_b$	76.75$_a$

*$p < .005$.
Means with different subscripts are sigificantly different at the .01 level.

one who includes humorous-inappropriate material. Results fail to support the third research hypothesis. In fact the inverse was found: the source who included humorous-inappropriate material received higher ratings than the source who excluded humor, although the difference was not statistically significant.

Individual Credibility Dimensions

Table 2 displays the credibility ratings of significant difference among the three testing conditions. The table also depicts the significant difference among groups for the five dimensions of credibility.

In each dimension, means for the three items were summed. Thus the maximum character mean score for the three seven-interval scales would be 21; the lowest would be 3. This range exists for all five dimensions, since each dimension is a cluster of three items. (Treatment means are shown for the five dimensions in Tables 3 through 7).

Table 2.   Findings of Superior Credibility Ratings Overall and Among the Five Dimensions

	Credibl.[a]	Char.[a]	Competn.[b]	Socib.[a]	Compos.[a]	Extrov.[b]
Condition						
Serious			↑ HumorIn			
Humorous App.	↑ HumorIn ↑ Serious	↑ HumorIn ↑ Serious	↑ HumorIn	↑ HumorIn Serious	↑ Seri.	↑ Seri.
Humorous In.				↑ Serious		↑ Seri.

↑ Significantly higher rating than
[a]The groups differ significantly at the .01 level.
[b]The groups differ significantly at the .05 level.

Table 3.   Analysis of Variance for the Character Dimension of Source Credibility

Source	Degrees of Freedom	Sum of Squares	Mean Squares	F Ratio*
Between Groups.........	2	317.72	158.86	13.73
Within Groups	219	2,534.63	11.57	
Total...................	221	2,852.36		

Treatment Means for Character Dimension		
No-Humor Content	Humor. Appropriate Content	Humor. Inappropriate Content
15.49$_a$	17.49$_b$	14.94$_a$

*$p<.005$.
Means with different subscripts are sigificantly different at the .01 level.

Analysis of variance showed that the three groups differed significantly in their ratings of the character items ($p<.005$). The Scheffe procedure indicated the humorous-inappropriate group had statistically higher character mean scores than the humorous-inappropriate and no-humor groups. The no-humor and humorous-inappropriate groups did not differ significantly; however, observed difference was in the predicted direction (Table 3).

Subjects also differed significantly in their ratings of competence items, with $p<.005$ (Table 4). Ratings for the sources in the humorous-appropriate and no-humor conditions were significantly higher than those in the humorous-inappropriate condition. Although ratings for the humorous-appropriate source were higher than those for the no-humor source, as predicted, the difference was not significant.

For the sociability dimension, subjects exposed to the humorous-appropriate and humorous-inappropriate conditions marked their sources

Table 4.   Analysis of Variance for the Competence Dimension of Source Credibility

Source	Degrees of Freedom	Sum of Squares	Mean Squares	F Ratio*
Between Groups.........	2	324.59	162.29	11.90
Within Groups	219	2,986.58	13.64	
Total...................	221	3,311.17		

Treatment Means for Competence Dimension		
No-Humor Content	Humor. Appropriate Content	Humor. Inappropriate Content
16.79$_a$	17.75$_a$	15.06$_b$

*$p<.005$.
Means with different subscripts are significantly different at the .05 level.

Table 5.   Analysis of Variance for the Sociability Dimension of Source Credibility

Source	Degrees of Freedom	Sum of Squares	Mean Squares	F Ratio*
Between Groups.........	2	735.51	367.75	29.63
Within Groups	219	2,718.44	12.41	
Total..................	221	3,453.95		

Treatment Means for Sociability Dimension

No-Humor Content	Humor. Appropriate Content	Humor. Inappropriate Content
11.67$_a$	16.67$_b$	14.62$_c$

*$p<.005$.
Means with different subscripts are significantly different at the .01 level.

significantly higher ($p<.01$) than subjects who evaluated their source in the no-humor condition. In addition, the source who included humorous-appropriate material in his eulogy was rated significantly higher in sociability than the source who included inappropriate humor. Interestingly the no-humor source was rated significantly lower in sociability than the humorous-inappropriate source (Table 5).

Within the composure dimension, only the source of the humorous-appropriate eulogy received a significantly higher rating than the no-humor source ($p<.01$). Evidence was lacking, however, that sources using either appropriate humor or no humor will be rated higher in composure than the source using inappropriate humor in a eulogy (Table 6).

Examining the extroversion dimension, ratings in the humorous-appropriate condition were significantly higher than those in the no-humor condition, and ratings in the humorous-inappropriate condition were significantly higher than

Table 6.   Analysis of Variance for the Composure Dimension of Source Credibility

Source	Degrees of Freedom	Sum of Squares	Mean Squares	F Ratio*
Between Groups.........	2	142.21	71.11	6.16
Within Groups	219	2,528.86	11.55	
Total..................	221	2,671.07		

Treatment Means for Composure Dimension

No-Humor Content	Humor. Appropriate Content	Humor. Inappropriate Content
15.08$_a$	17.21$_b$	16.13$_{ab}$

*$p<.005$.
Means with different subscripts are significantly different at the .01 level.

Table 7.   Analysis of Variance for the Extroversion Dimension of Source Credibility

Source	Degrees of Freedom	Sum of Squares	Mean Squares	F Ratio*
Between Groups.........	2	91.33	45.66	4.64
Within Groups	219	2154.13	9.84	
Total...................	221	2245.46		

Treatment Means for Extroversion Dimension

No-Humor Content	Humor. Appropriate Content	Humor. Inappropriate Content
13.77$_a$	15.48$_b$	15.42$_b$

*$p<.05$.
Means with different subscripts are significantly different at the .05 level.

ratings in the no-humor condition ($p<.05$). Data failed to show that ratings of sources who use either appropriate humor or no humor were significantly higher than ratings of a source who uses inappropriate humor (Table 7).

DISCUSSION

Evidence from this study supports the hypothesis that the source who interjects humor that is relevant and positive to the deceased during a funeral eulogy is accorded greater credibility than the source who refrains from humor. This finding was supported further when four of the five credibility dimensions were compared across the three testing conditions.

In the early stages of this research, it was theorized that the use of appropriate humor by a eulogizer may cause the listener to regard this source as being warmer and more compassionate than the source who decided to forego humor in the eulogy. The humor appears to form a bridge by which the source, through an indirect appeal to the listener's thoughts and feelings, can make more intimate contact with the listener than a source who declines to include humor. Ratings were significantly higher for both humor conditions in the sociability and extroversion dimensions than for the serious condition, which supports the idea that lack of humor may hinder a serious-eulogy source.

Results also support the hypothesis that the inclusion of appropriate humor in a eulogy produces higher overall credibility for the source than does inappropriate humor. This relationship was supported in three of the five credibility dimensions. However, no significant differences appeared between the two sources within the dimensions of composure and extroversion. Perhaps inappropriate humor in a eulogy will not adversely influence evaluations of a humorous-inappropriate source in these two dimensions.

Further, no significant differences were found in the overall credibility ratings when a eulogy of serious content was compared with a eulogy of humorous-inappropriate content, nor in four of the five credibility dimensions. Only in the competence dimension did the source who delivered the serious-content eulogy receive ratings significantly higher than the source who included humorous-inappropriate content. In its strongest sense, this finding suggests that a speaker may experiment with occasional humor in a eulogy and not fear that the audience will assess speaker credibility poorly, even if the humor is accidently inappropriate.

At least two possible explanations emerge to explain the failure of the audience in this study to provide a truly critical evaluation of the humorous-appropriate eulogy. First, in one's grief the listener at a funeral can be expected to cling to words of hope and recollections of love. So the inappropriate content may have been misperceived. Second, the subjects may have forgiven the source's indiscretions as unintentional. Since the source remained respectful and praised the deceased whenever he did not deliver a humorous anecdote, witticism, or pun, and the source resumed his serious mood after each humorous-appropriate item, the audience may have concluded that the speaker meant well, did not intend to be inappropriate in his remarks, and, the audience may have chosen to overlook the indiscretions.

REFERENCES

Adler, B. (1964).*The Kennedy Wit*. New York: Citadel Press.

Adler, B. (1965). *More Kennedy Wit*. New York: Citadel Press.

Brownlow, P., and Davis, B. (1974). "A Certainty of Honor: The Eulogies of Adlai Stevenson." *Central States Speech Journal*. 25, 217-224.

Bryant. D. and Wallace, K. (1976). *Oral Communication: A Short Course in Speaking*. 2nd ed. Englewood Cliffs, NJ: Prentice-Hall.

Burgoon, J. (1976). "The Ideal Source: A Reexamination of Source Credibility." *Central States Speech Journal*. 27, 200-206.

"Eulogies by Leaders," (1963). *New York Times* sec. 1, p. 4.

Gray, G., and Braden, W. (1965). *Public Speaking: Principles and Practice*, 2d ed. New York: Harper and Row.

Grimes, W. (1955). "The Mirth Experience in Public Address." *Speech Monographs*, 22, 243-255.

McBurney, J., and Wrage, E. (1965). *Guide to Good Speech*. Englewood Cliffs, NJ: Prentice-Hall.

McCroskey, J., Holdridge, W., and Toomb, J. (1974). "An Instrument for Measuring the Source Credibility of Basic Speech Instructors." *Speech Teacher*. 23, 26-33.

Monroe, A. (1939). *Principles and Types of Speech*. New York: Scott Foresman.

Stevens, W. (1961). "On Using Humor in Public Speech." *Today's Speech*. 9, 10.

"The Transcript of Cushing's Eulogy." (1963). *New York Times*. sec. 1, p. 4.

Williams, F. (1979). *Reasoning With Statistics*, ed. New York: Holt, Rinehart and Winston.

9

Organizational Culture, Uncertainty Reduction, and the Socialization of New Organizational Members

ROBIN E. LESTER
Northwestern University

Much of the "traditional, managerially-oriented" literature on organizations (as described by Pacanowsky and O'Donnell-Trujillo, 1982; Putnam, 1982) has tended to give only a passing nod to the processes by which new organizational members are socialized, and has, instead, generally assumed that all the components of organizational life are in place, and the mechanisms for interaction are well-established, uninterrupted, and continuous. One of the virtues of the recent enthusiasm for a cultural approach to the study of organizations may well be a renewed interest in the ontogenetic processes by which particular cultures develop within organizations, and the processes by which cultural values, norms, and beliefs are transmitted to new organizational participants. What follows is exploitative, in that aspects of organizational life which have become the focus of attention for cultural approaches to the study of organizations are modified for adoption as theoretical constructs capable of varying along dimensions, and thus, capable of being embedded in a covering law causal model.

The socialization of new participants in organizations can be expressed, from a managerial perspective, as fundamentally an issue of "how to melt these guys down into right-thinking people." To phrase this traditional view in more euphemistic traditional language, one of the central features of the socialization process is the achievement of some degree of congruence between individual and organizational values, or identification by the individual with the organization and its aims (Katz and Kahn, 1978). At a more concrete level, managerial concerns lie in the transmission of behavioral norms deemed appropriate for the expression of organizational goals and values (Van Maanen and Schein, 1979).

While such a managerially oriented description may at first appear callous or even manipulative, this conceptualization of the socialization processes may not necessarily be so discrepant from the fundamental aims and needs of the individual who first enters the world of a particular organization. Viewed from the perspective of the new member, it is possible to draw an analogy between the individual's first interactions with the organization as an entity and the initial interaction phase of a dyadic interpersonal relationship. This analogy may be particularly apt for the new organizational participant, who is not yet familiar enough with the specific component parts of an organization to generate more than a global, undifferentiated perception of the organization as an external entity, much in the same way individuals generate relatively undifferentiated perceptions about other individuals as strangers. Indeed, just as interpersonal initial interaction sequences often produce only vague recall of general impressions, recollections of newly encountered organizations are likely to consist almost entirely of such general demographic features as organizational size, physical location and setting, industry, and ownership.

If one views socialization processes in organizations from this initial interaction perspective, it is reasonable to assume that those considerations which guide interpersonal interactions also hold in the organizational situation. That is, such processes as the reduction of uncertainty about the other (Berger and Calabrese, 1975), in this case, the organization, are fundamental to the acquaintance process of the new participant. The ability to generate confident inferences, in terms of *post hoc* explanations and *a priori* predictions, becomes central to the individual interacting with an organization for the first time. However, as opposed to the more general notion of uncertainty advanced by Berger and Calabrese (1975), and later modified to embrace notions of behavioral versus cognitive uncertainty (Berger, 1979), it can be argued that the new organizational participant's uncertainty is highly specific with respect to two domains.

Of fundamental concern to the new organizational participant is the notion of predicting one's own probable success or failure in a particular organizational role. That is, the individual attempts to reduce evaluative uncertainty about the likelihood of succeeding or failing in organizational life. One of the most critical elements in reducing this type of evaluative uncertainty may well be the ability to reduce uncertainty about what specific behaviors will be rewarded or punished in the organization.

Hence, one can propose a bifurcated notion of uncertainty centering around, first, the notion of predicting one's own success or failure in an organization; and second, what specific action from among the behavioral choices in any given situation is likely to be deemed the most appropriate by superiors in the organization, the most likely to be rewarded, and hence, to lead to organizational success.

While specific outcomes of increased or decreased levels of behavioral and evaluative uncertainty are intriguing to consider, such plausible dependent variables as job affect, turnover, stress, and productivity will, for the time being, be left to the realm of speculation. This paper, as a first attempt at formulating a model of socialization centering around notions of uncertainty reduction will, instead, focus on eight exogenous factors hypothesized to affect uncertainty levels. Further, the paper will treat those organizational attributes closely related to the cultural aspects of organizational life more extensively than individual variables, which might predict differences in uncertainty reduction between individuals within the same organizational setting.

Beginning first with the notion of reducing evaluative uncertainty, it should be noted that uncertainty can be reduced in either one of two directions; one may become increasingly certain that one will experience either success or failure in an organization. Since this immediately presents problems in formulating a linear causal model, a choice has been made to discuss this construct in terms of the certainty or confidence one feels that one is likely to *succeed*, or be positively rewarded within an organizational context. Given this conceptualization, evaluative confidence can be diminished by either high levels of uncertainty or by increasing confidence in negative outcomes.

The major factor hypothesized to affect evaluative confidence is behavioral certainty, or the degree to which one feels one can predict what one behavior from among the alternatives for any given situation will be the most highly valued by organizational superiors. While this notion of behavioral certainty includes traditional aspects of task certainty, including knowledge about specific actions requisite for successful task completion, it is also intended to subsume less formal aspects of organizational life, e.g., dress, jargon, and social style, not generally included in traditional conceptualizations of task certainty.

Expressed axiomatically, it can be said:

Axiom 1: As behavioral certainty increases, evaluative confidence will increase; decreases in behavioral certainty will produce decreases in evaluative confidence.

One organizational factor which directly affects levels of evaluative confidence is the degree to which an individual perceives variance or a broad range of potential gains or losses as a function of participation in an organization. Expressed as an inverse relationship, it is proposed:

Axiom 2: PBAs the perceived variance of potential gains and losses for participation in an organization increases, an individual's level of evaluative confidence will decrease. Decreases in the perceived range of available potential gains and losses will increase evaluative confidence.

While perceived gain-loss variance operates primarily at the organizational level, we can observe some intra-organizational differences. For example, in the case of two new employees at an advertising agency, it may well be that greater potential salary increases, promotional levels, and job risks exist for the individual who joins a creative staff, as opposed to one who begins work with a research department. Given these intra-organizational differences, we would expect the latter individual with lower perceived variance in available gains and losses, to be more confident with respect to evaluation than the former, who ought to experience more evaluation anxiety as a function of "having more at stake."

This same relationship should hold when comparing participants across organizations, so that given two individuals who join two different advertising agencies, we would expect the one who joins the firm with the greater possibilities for advancement to experience *less* evaluative certainty or confidence. It should be noted that the perception of variance of potential gains and losses for participation in any particular organization may be closely tied to older, more mundane, organizational variables such as size or hierarchical structure. Further, perceptions of variance in potential gains and losses are not necessarily tied directly to the actual range of positive and negative rewards available to an individual. Such factors as an organization's rhetorical stress on the potential for achievement or on negative sanctions, such as pay cuts or layoffs, may be more influential than objective data on the actual probability of success or failure.

An organizational attribute which is likely to affect both evaluative and behavioral uncertainty in participants is the availability of performance feedback indicators. Such feedback mechanisms may take either a highly formal form, as in the case of standardized training review procedures, or an informal flavor, as a spontaneous compliment from a superior. In either case, such performance feedback indicators tend to inform the individual which previous behavior is valued and which is not, and often suggest a general level of evaluative standing within the organization. Hence,

Axiom 3: Increases in performance feedback indicators will produce increases in both behavioral certainty and evaluative confidence; decreases in the availability of performance feedback will reduce both behavioral certainty and evaluative confidence.

Given this model's formulation of evaluative confidence, it could be argued that negative feedback actually ought to increase evaluative uncertainty. However, two factors are important to consider. First, even negative feedback will reduce behavioral uncertainty, and thus, should ultimately increase evaluative confidence. Second, it should be considered that organizational superiors rarely provide negative feedback until the point of dismissal. Hence, if we were simply to divide organizational feedback into positive and negative performance evaluations, the former would very likely outweigh the latter.

Both the availability of feedback indicators and behavioral certainty are often increased by organizational initiation rituals. Again, such rituals can vary greatly with respect to the degree of formality, as in the case of structured training programs lasting for a specified period of time. Initiation rituals can, however, operate in much more subtle ways, as in requiring new recruits to learn specific terms and labels. Mastery of such organizational jargon carries with it an implicit education about what features are salient in organizational life and what values underlie the attention given to these specific details. In the case of either formal or informal initiation rituals, it can be said:

Axiom 4: Increases in participation in organizational initiation rituals will produce increases in both behavioral certainty and performance feedback available to an individual.

A third organizational factor which is likely to impact behavioral certainty is the clarity of an organization's sense of self-identity and superordinate goals. This sense of identity can be likened to Deal and Kennedy's (1982) notion of a strong culture. That is, to the extent that there is one overarching principle which guides everyday organizational behavior, there will be a reduction in the individual's uncertainty about which behavioral choice to select in any given situation. Thus, guiding maxims which illustrate a fundamental organizational value, such as "IBM means service" or G.E.'s "Progress is our most important product," not only focus attention on consenually agreed upon aims of the organization, but serve to indicate probable preferred responses to everyday occurrences. Hence:

> *Axiom 5:* Increases in organizational identity and goal clarity will increase behavioral certainty; decreases in the clarity of organizational identity and goals will cause decreases in behavioral certainty.

The clarity of organizational identity and goals will depend both on the degree to which there is a consensus about the fundamental nature, character, and purpose of the organization, as well as the degree to which this sense of identity and purpose is communicated to rank and file participants.

Organizational stories and sagas are yet another cultural mechanism for conveying to new organizational participants what behavioral acts are rewarded or punished (Martin, 1980). In a sense, such stories provide specific scripts (Abelson, 1976) which allow individuals to infer hypothetical level propositions about the likelihood of certain outcomes, given particular actions.

It should be noted that from an information theory perspective (Shannon and Weaver, 1949), positive stories (stories in which some particular behavior was rewarded) provide more uncertainty reduction than negative stories, since when the positive desirability of one behavior is illustrated, it reduces a greater number of behavioral alternatives in an uncertain situation. Thus, a story which tells how a new employee wore grubby jeans to the office and was promptly fired eliminates only one response from among the set of clothing possibilities. However, if we learn that another employee consistently wore three piece suits from Saks and was promoted, a "best choice" is suggested, and more alternatives are eliminated. However, except for founding hero stories, it would appear that negative stories, like rule enforcement modes of motivation, predominate in American business organizations. Nonetheless, in either the case of positive or negative stories, at least one choice from among the set of behavioral options is eliminated, and hence:

> *Axiom 6:* Increases in the number and frequency of telling of organizational stories will increase behavioral certainty; decreases in organizational story telling will decrease behavioral certainty.

An intervening variable which may be expected to determine at least partially an individual's evaluative confidence is the perceptions of one's own influence. Perceived influence, in the context of this model, is intended to subsume the degree to which one believes one has power, both formal and informal, to control decision outcomes and the behavior of others. Thus:

> *Axiom 7:* Increases in one's own perceived influence will increase evaluative confidence; decreases in perceived influence will decrease evaluative confidence.

One exogenous factor which can vary significantly across both organizations, as a function of their specific cultures, and across individuals located within a single organizational culture is amount of communication. Between organizations there can be significant differences in the amount of ongoing communication activities. Amount of organizational communication can be seen to vary as a function of such traditional variables as task interdependence, organizational size, and the physical setting in which an organization operates. Additionally, within any given organization, individual differences arise in the degree to which any one person engages in communication activities, based on differences in such job dimensions as task coordination demands and physical centrality (Monge, Edwards, and Kirste, 1978; Lester, 1981).

Regardless of organizational or individual determinants of communication, the amount of communication will have a direct effect on both behavioral certainty and perceived levels of influence. The former relationship is intuitively appealing, assuming that communication activities generally carry some information content likely to reduce behavioral uncertainty; that is, the more communication an individual has with other organizational participants, the more likely it is that information will be gleaned abut what are more or less desirable behavioral responses to uncertain situations.

Amount of communication might also be expected to affect one's own as well as others' perceptions of an individual's degree of influence. The early small group network studies conducted by Leavitt (1951), as well as later experimental studies of small group leadership (Bavelas et al., 1965), have clearly illustrated a relationship between the amount of communication engaged in by an individual and perceptions by others of that individual's degree of influence. Such perceptions of influence on the part of others probably set up self-fulfilling prophecies, such that an individual comes to have a greater sense of his own influence as a function of more communication activity. Additionally, recent organizational network studies have begun to suggest a direct relationship between total communication and self-perceptions of influence. Hence:

> *Axiom 8:* Increases in the total amount of communication activities engaged in by an individual will produce increases both in that individual's behavioral certainty and level of perceived influence in the organization.

It should be noted that informal communication might have a stronger effect in both of these relationships, since, as is suggested by attribution theory arguments (Jones and Davis, 1965), stronger inferences will be drawn if formal requirements cannot be cited as situational causes for any particular communicative activity. In other words, information gained during informal interactions is more likely to produce confident inferences about appropriate behavioral norms within an organization than information transmitted via such channels as formal meetings, presentations, or written memoranda. Similarly, informal communication, not dictated by specific job requirements, would seem more likely to produce greater changes with respect to one's own perceived level of influence, since, again, individuals would be unable to attach external attributions, such as job requirements, to the attention of co-participants.

Having thus considered the effects produced by organizational factors, those effects determined more by individual attributes and experiences can be considered. First, it can be argued that one's relative status (Pacanowsky and Heald, 1976), or the formal status of one's position relative to the total vertical hierarchical string in which one is located, will directly affect one's perceived level of influence, such that:

> *Axiom 9:* Increases in relative status will produce increases in one's own perceived level of influence; decreases in relative status will decrease perceived influence.

Two additional factors dependent on an individual's experience and attributes are likely to determine the degree to which one perceives the availability of alternatives for organizational participation. First, the degree to which one has had prior relevant experience in similar organizations will affect the degree to which alternative participative opportunities are recognized, such that:

> *Axiom 10:* Increases in relevant prior experience will produce increases in the perceived availability of alternatives for organizational participation.

Similarly, the degree to which one possesses extra-organizational links to other, similar organizations will increase one's awareness of other organizational alternatives available for participation:

> *Axiom 11:* Increases in extra-organizational links to other, similar organizations will produce increases in perceived available alternatives for organizational participation.

From a social exchange theory perspective, it can be argued that increased awareness of available alternatives, for organizational participation will directly affect an individual's subjective sense of participative dependence, such that:

> *Axiom 12:* Increases in the perception of available alternatives for organizational participation will decrease an individual's subjective sense of participative dependence; decreases in the perception of available alternatives will increase in the perception one's participative dependence.

This proposition basically acknowledges the possibility of organizational participants scanning for participative alternatives in much the same manner that interpersonal theorists argue an individual might "shop around" for a romantic, dyadic partner from among the pool of available potential partners (Blau, 1964; Roloff, 1981). Certainly such market factors as the supply of and demand for persons with particular organizational skills might also be expected to influence the perceptions of available participative alternatives. Regardless of the sources of perceived alternatives and their consequential reduction of subjective sense of participative dependence, it can be said that:

> *Axiom 13:* Increases in participative dependence will produce decreases in evaluative confidence; decreases in participative dependence will increase evaluative confidence.

These thirteen axiomatic propositions taken together specify a causal model which predicts and explains levels of evaluative confidence for new organizational participants (Figure 1). As a next step in the theory construction process, it seems reasonable to consider the period of time during which this kind of model might operate. Certainly length of time spent within a particular organizatonal context could be expected to alter such independent variables as participation in initiation rituals, relative status, and extra-organizational links. However, there seems little reason to abandon as unimportant the notions of behavioral and evaluative uncertainty after some fixed temporal period of participation. Indeed, organizational life may continue to proceed through various cycles and phases of increasing and decreasing levels of uncertainty, so that something analogous to a "personal phase" model of organizational participation along these same lines might be advanced.

This model, as it stands, represents a rought first approximation of a theory of socialization; as such, it attempts to incorporate both organizational and indi-

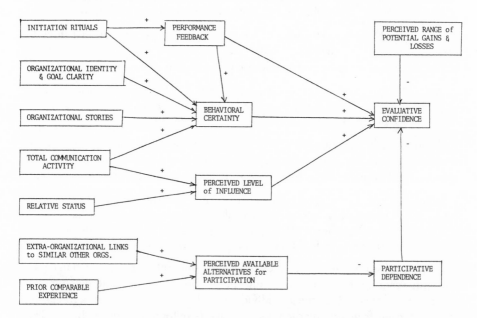

Figure 1. Uncertainty Reduction and Organizational Socialization: A Preliminary Formulation.

vidual factors as determinants of the behavioral and evaluative uncertainty experienced by new organizational participants. Having begun from a model borrowed from interpersonal communication theory, it is intriguing to consider that this may represent an occasion when organizational theory can repay the loan with interest. That is, dichotomizing uncertainty into evaluative and behavioral components and introducing concepts of participative dependence and perceived variance in potential outcomes may not only enhance our understanding of organizational life, but may inform the study of uncertainty reduction in interpersonal relationships as well.

REFERENCES

Abelson, R.P. (1976) "Script Processing in Attitude Formation and Decision Making." In J.S. Carroll and J. W. Payne (Eds.), *Cognition and Social Behavior*. Hillsdale, NJ: Erlbaum.

Bavelas, A., Hastorf, A., Gross, A., and Kite, W. R. (1965) "Experiments on the Alteration of Group Structure." *Journal of Experimental Social Psychology 1*, 55-70.

Berger, C.R. (1979). "Beyong Initial Interaction: Uncertainty, Understanding, and the Development of Interpersonal Relationships." In H. Giles and R. N. St. Clair (Eds.), *Language and Social Psychology*. Baltimore, MD: University Park.

Berger, C.R., and Calabrese, R.J. (1975). "Some Explorations in Initial Interaction and Beyond: Toward a Developmental Theory of Interpersonal Communication." *Human Communication Research 1*, 99-112.

Blau, P. (1964).*Exchange and Power in Social Life*. New York, NY: John Wiley.

Deal, R.E., and Kennedy, A.A. (1982) *Corporate Cultures*. Reading, MA: Addison-Wesley.

Jones E.E., and Davis, K.E. (1965). "From Acts to Dispositions: The Attribution Process in Person Perception." In L. Berkowitz (Ed.), *Advances in Experimental Social Psychology* (Vol. 2). New York: Academic Press.

Katz, D., and Kahn, R.L. (1978). *The Social Psychology of Organizatons*. New York: John Wiley & Sons.

Leavitt, H. (1951). "Some Effects of Certain Communication Patterns on Group Performance." *Journal of Abnormal and Social Psychology 46*, 38-50.

Lester, R.E. (1981). "Embedding Network Analysis Constructs in a Theoretical Framework: A Preliminary Formulation of a Model of Intraorganizatonal Communication Behavior." Paper presented at the Western Speech Communication Association, San Jose, CA.

Martin, J. (1980). "Stories and Scripts in Organizational Settings." Stanford University Graduate School of Business Research Paper Series, Research Report No. 543 (Revised).

Monge, P.R., Edwards, V., and Kirste, K. (1978). "The Determinants of Communication Structure in Large Organizations." In B.D. Ruben (Ed.), *Communication Yearbook 2*. New Brunswick, NJ: Transaction Books.

Pacanowsky, M.E., and Heald, G.R. (1976). "Environmental Change, Perceived Uncertainty, and Communication Volume in Organizations." Paper presented at the International Communication Association; Portland, OR.

Pacanowsky, M.E., and O'Donnell-Trujillo, N. (1982). "Communication and Organizational Cultures." *Western Journal of Speech Communication 46*, 115-130.

Putnam, L.L. (1982). "Paradigms for Organizational Communication Research: An Overview and Synthesis." *Western Journal of Speech Communication 46*, 192-206.

Roloff, M.E. (1981). *Interpersonal Communication: The Social Exchange Approach*. Beverly Hills, CA: Sage.

Shannon, C. E., and Weaver, W. (1949). *The Mathematical Theory of Communication*. Urbana, IL: University of Illinois Press.

Van Maanen, J., and Schein, E.H. (1979). "Toward a Theory of Organizational Socialization." In B.M. Staw (Ed.), *Research in Organizational Behavior*, Vol. 1; Greenwich, CN.: JAI Press.

10

Applying the Concept of the Double Bind to Communication in Organizations

NINA WISHBOW
Carnegie-Mellon University

This paper addresses issues in research utilizing the concept of double bind to deal with conflict and stress in organizations. The double bind concept originated with Bateson et al. theory of the origin of schizophrenia. To Bateson *et al.* (1972, p. 202) citing Russell's theory of Logical Types, schizophrenia develops as a result of a child's inability to interpret and respond appropriately to paradoxical messages sent by the mother. The crux of the double bind as they describe it is that the mother chronically sends paradoxical messages to the child, messages that are internally inconsistent, specifying one type of meaning at the verbal level, and another at the emotional level. For example, they relate the story of a schizophrenic whose mother's requests for affection were accompanied by physical rigidity, backing away, and other nonverbal messages signifying retreat (Bateson et al., 1972, p. 213). The child could neither respond to the mother's message nor ignore it. Schizophrenia develops when the child, who is chronically subject to such confusion, retreats into a world where symbols and symbolic logic are construed in a highly idiosyncratic manner. The schizophrenic develops difficulty in assessing his or her own messages, thought and perceptions, as well as those of others (Bateson et al., 1972, p. 208).

From this early explanation of the origin of schizophrenia, the double bind was expanded to incorporate situations in which all members of the family are seen as victims and victimizers in a cyclical, chronic conflict. The concept changed from a description of pathology, i.e., schizophrenia, to a description of more "generic" family conflict. In the revised version of the concept, there may be a "victimizer" who precipitates a conflict, but after the onset of the situation, "victim" and "victimizer" trade roles. The constituents of the family double bind are enumerated by Watzlawick et al. (1967) as:

1. A situation involving people who are in close contact with one another and depend on each other to varying degrees and for various reasons.
2. Within that situation, parties send paradoxical messages to one another.
3. Finally, the nature of the paradox serves a function, and thus, no one can talk about the paradox because to do so would mean having to resolve the conflict that the paradoxical messages conceal.

For example, an alcoholic husband may continually be told to stop drinking by his wife, but continually refuse to do so. The couple's behavior is a cycle: The husband drinks, they fight about his drinking, he reforms temporarily but soon continues drinking. The alcoholism disguises the fact, perhaps, that the couple cannot deal with one another as individuals. The wife's admonitions to her husband to stop drinking are ambivalent (one could say paradoxical) messages because they disguise the fact that she could not relate to him if he stopped drinking. And the husband's attempted reform, likewise, is paradoxical because his drinking is the only way he can get his wife to respond to him.

Note that since Bateson, *et al.*'s (1972), p. 208) original description of the double bind as a paradox, the paradox has remained a crucial ingredient in subsequent formulations. However, in an organization, the complexity of the roles an individual must play is increased, and the paradox is not an adequate concept for describing complex sets of choices. Further, in an organization, individuals can experience binds from messages which are clear, rational, and definitely not ambivalent. Often in an organization, an individual is not troubled as much by the "real meaning" of others' messages as by the uncomfortable suspicion that no matter what he or she decides to do, the action taken will lead to disastrous consequences. The organizational double bind (ODB), thus, is better conceptualized as a dilemma. A dilemma in ordinary speech is a puzzle with numerous constituents, whereas a paradox is merely a dual-level message. In particular, the double bind may be expressed as a complex constructive dilemma, a situation in which an individual is confronted with a number of possible response choices, all of which appear to lead to undesirable consequences. The key to solving an ODB, then, is to "go through the horns of a dilemma" that can have lots of horns.

Although this formulation contrast with the original concept of double bind, there are still similarities and continuity between the family double bind and the ODB. Solutions for the ODB, even when it is construed as a dilemma, seem the same as solutions for a paradox. To resolve a dilemma, one has to add choices to the set of alternatives , i.e., "go through the horns of the dilemma." When one adds choices to the limited set of response alternatives, one achieves what Rabkin (1976, p. 296) calls a "saltus," a creative "leap" in one's thinking which produces alternative behavior that in turn produces a relatively satisfactory outcome. Solving a dilemma might also be called, in Watzlawick's (1978) terms, "reframing" a problem, or "investing a given situation with a new meaning that is just as appropriate or even more convincing than the one originally attributed to it." Reframing, for the purposes of this paper, might be understood as redefining a dilemma into a "tamer" problem with one or more pathways to a solution.

Reformulating an ODB from a paradox into a complex constructive dilemma captures the logic of communication problems in public institutions. In an organization, one can encounter numerous (unsatisfactory) possibilities for responding to a message, and similarly, one can add terms to a complex constructive dilemma, so that one can actually construct triple binds, quadruple binds, and so on. Applying the double bind concept to organizations becomes a matter of: (1) enumerating the possible choices organizational members have for responding to a given situation and (2) finding the reasons why these choices consistently result in negative reactions on the part of other people. Generally, negative reactions result because an individual has violated others' expectations. According to Katz and Kahn (1978) the expectations people have for their own and others' behavior in organizations center around roles they and others are supposed to enact, rules that are stated either explicitly in the organization or are implicitly understood, and values which people either possess as individuals or share with the institution.

When "doing one's job" conflicts with other people's rules, roles or values, no doubt the consequences will be disastrous. Downs (1967, p. 100) notes that bureaucracies tend to promote "conserverism" and constrain innovation. He also mentions several other "laws" of bureaucratic activity, including the tendency for all bureaus to become more "conserveristic" over time (Downs, 1967, pp. 165–166), and for their innovators to behave more like conservers as the length of time the innovator spends within one position in the organization increases. An ODB may occur when a nonconserver finds himself or herself surrounded by a group of conservers. An innovator in such a setting immediately confronts a dilemma. Obviously enough, his or her values conflict with the values of others and in order to express innovative ideas, he or she will have to find strategies for presenting them which transcend the conflict of values, e.g., strategies that express commonality with co-workers. In discussing a plan with others in the organization, he or she may decide upon such presentational tactics as:

1. Tell Jones that his superior heard of the idea and said "damn the cost."
2. Let word get around to Smith that my idea is really bringing an old, revered managerial concept back into vogue.

As a result of resolving a double bind, the individual in the example can actually improve the organization. This notion is in keeping with Bacharach and Lawler's (1980) assertion that conflict and its resolution are creative. It may be the case that people resolve double binds by rethinking the roles they enact, the values they possess, or the rules they live by, and that such rethinking leads to a qualitatively different set of perceptions and reactions towards others individuals and other problems.

From the above example, it may seem that double binds arise and are resolved routinely. However, a double bind may be impossible to resolve. Unresolved ODB's may produce stress and culminate in irreversible damage. For example, Stewart (1979) describes the opening of the Bay Area Rapid Transit System in San Francisco, in 1972. The transit system was designed to connect two districts in the San Francisco Bay area through an underwater tunnel. Completion of the plans ran months and millions of dollars over the proposed schedule and budget. Facing pressure from the public, the Board of Directors wanted a rapid completion of the system. When three engineers complained that the switching system was not yet completed and that it would fail in its present condition, they were accused of self-aggrandizement by those at the top of the organization (Stewart, 1979, p. 112). Their attempts to communicate upward were considered to be efforts at "climbing" by the Board of Directors. The engineers reported their complaints to an outside agency—they were forced to "flee the field," and they were subsequently fired (Stewart, 1979, p. 122–127).

Stated as a dilemma, the nature of the engineers' bind was that: (a) they needed to report the system failure to maintain their identities as professionals, and (b) that to be treated like "good" employees they were supposed to keep their complaints to themselves. The only way they could find to get out of the situation was to escape it. However, there may have been alternative solutions. Had they found a way to (c) draw attention to the problem in a way that the organization would sanction, they might have prompted the Board to take constructive action. Attempting to resolve the problem presented by the engineers may have created a "bind" of sorts for the Board of Directors, but it would have prevented the subsequent whistle-blowing incident.

The purpose of this paper is not to propose easy answers to the ODB, but to introduce a framework for future research. This framework consists of viewing an ODB as a complex constructive dilemma caused by conflicting organizational rules, roles, and values. The following section of the paper reviews studies on the ODB utilizing this framework, and suggests directions for future research based upon the critique.

Abeles (1976) reports repeated failure of researchers to arrive at any conclusive evidence that the causes for double bind interaction can be isolated in a laboratory. Dell (1980) asserts that the failures of such studies to identify causes for double binds is due primarily to the inapplicability of research approaches which examine logical-positivist relations between causes and effects. The problem becomes somewhat clearer when one considers that there are no particular variables that make "necessary and sufficient" conditions for a double bind.

Only one laboratory research study on the ODB will be used to illustrate the problem. Polite (1972) hypothesized that the more control an individual has within an organization, the more controlled by the organization that individual will feel. Subjects were placed in one of two conditions: (1) either they had control, and they were allowed to select their supervisor in a simulated organization, or (2) they were not given control, and were assigned to a supervisor. Confederate supervisors told the subjects to write papers after consultation with style texts. It was predicted that subjects who selected their supervisors would feel greater pressure to perform, and that these individuals would consult the style guides. However, the study failed to support the research hypotheses. Polite argued that either the task was too simple, or the measurement (the papers) was not strong enough. However, giving the subjects "control" is merely a laboratory operationalization of a double bind. For example it would seem that giving subjects control should not affect their behavior if they see no reason to associate this control with their role in the organization. Thus, Polite's study does not ask questions relating to the establishment and maintenance of organizational roles, rules, or values. Instead, he assumes that people who have control automatically feel more loyal to those who give them control. In trying to operationalize an ODB "objectively," he evidently eliminated every possibility for one to occur.

In order to study double binds in laboratory research, one must simulate conditions in which organizational members are aware of each others' expectations, and insure that these expectations conflict. Although it may appear grossly "unscientific" (or at least grossly unfair) to take people with conflicting ideas and expectations and deliberately place them in organizationally defined relationships, it seems that this would at least operationalize an ODB. Laboratory researchers exploring the organizational double bind, then, might create such obviously dilemma-ridden situations as: Mixed-sex organizations that are run by females; assembly-lines in which "employees" are forbidden to specialize or form a hierarchy of jobs on the line, and white-collar bureaus in which an "incompetent" confederate has been planted, and who is defended to the other employees by a confederate "director." The double bind concept is designed for examining the clarity of role definitions (or the lack of it), the freedom for others to have different values, and problems that can arise when organizational rules become too rigid.

It would seem that descriptive research has been more fruitful in detecting and attributing causal factors to ODBs. It may be useful to consider utilizing descriptive research studies on the ODB as models for future laboratory studies since descriptive research has focused on "real-world" issues which empirical research tends to deflect. However, as in laboratory research, descriptive studies can become too focused on analyzing specific behavior and less concerned with factors in organizational life that may actually make a difference. For example, while it is an interesting critical analysis of a film, the content-analysis of Frederick Weisman's film, *High School* by Benson (1980) misrepresents the concept of double bind, and one could argue, the purpose of conducting research on the double bind. The film *High School* depicts the repression of high school students and their families by school administration and teachers. In one scene in the movie a parent is seen asking an administrator why his daughter failed a course when she had received all high grades on her papers. The administrator replies by telling him that he "understands" his daughter's problem, leaving the parent speechless because the claim is so obviously false (Benson, 1980, pp. 245–246). Benson calls the film a statement on a social problem, and evidently finds it socially "relevant." However, Benson's critique has only focused on the behavioral manifestations of a double bind situation, and he does not seem to notice that Weisman tends to blame all communication problems on the administration. The director's camera glosses over the fact that these people, too, are hemmed in by necessary constraints. Rather than ask what features of high school *modus operandi* create dilemmas for interactants, Benson asks what features of interactants' behavior, objectively, "look like" a double bind. The result of Benson's focus on behavior rather than rules, roles, and other constraints is that supposedly "objective" (behavioral) data is used to prove a very "subjective" point—the point that the administration is victimizing everyone.

The descriptive studies which appear more successful at describing ODB situations start from the level of organizational rules and values before attempting to identify the meaning of particular behavior in the double bind situation. Marcus (1972), examines problems which were present in establishing boundaries in supervisor-subordinate relationships in the American army during the 1960s. At that time, many enlisted men and officers were similarly educated. At that time, many enlisted men and officers were similarly educated. The high numbers of educated enlisted men caused problems because the supervisors wished to treat them as equals, rather than subordinates. The confusion caused by these mixed values and confused role relationships, according to Marcus (1972, p. 272), helped maintain the army-established differences between the enlisted men and the officers, albeit in a way which was mystifying and distressing for all parties involved. Marcus suggests that transcriptions of conversations may help to identify the confusing types of messages that are symptomatic of double bind communication, but does not try to draw any necessary connection between the behavior of individuals in the double bind situation and who is to "blame" for the bind.

A second example of research that seems oriented in the "right" direction is by Hall (1974), who suggests that news agencies are in a bind between fulfilling their sense of social responsibility and maintaining their professional commitment to impartiality. Hall notices that political and economic elites are more public, vocal, and supportive of the status quo. As well, they are more able to give and control the kind of information broadcasters need. Hall's study, like Marcus's, identifies a problem—in this case, one of mixed values that leads to a dilemma on the part of the broadcasting agency—but he does not try to attribute the double bind to overly-particular causes.

In general, it seems that descriptive research is the best way for research on the ODB to proceed. Descriptive research eliminates the problems of operationalization and control present in the laboratory, and avoids the problem of experimental ethics in field research. Yet, field research may also be useful because it is guaranteed to deal with the rules, roles, and values that govern real organizations, real people, and real problems.

Given that the double bind concept helps clinicians diagnose and treat problems in families, it becomes tempting to try to step in and "fix" similar problems in organizations. However, the double bind was developed in the context of analyzing interaction in the small group, the family, and for all but the already-trained within a given organization, consultation using the double bind may not be worthwhile. Two examples, given below, illustrate this point.

In a field study, Hirschhorn and Gilmore (1980) entered an organization which seemed on the verge of collapse. The researchers used a family therapy model to guide their help of the organization. They diagnosed the organization as having grown and changed too rapidly, and concluded that many of the employees were experiencing role ambiguity and "boundary problems," i.e., that the organization had not reorganized its departments to adapt to other kinds of changes it had recently experienced. Hirschhorn and Gilmore helped members of the organization renegotiate their roles and reestablish order. However, successful as their attempt was, it should not be considered a viable paradigm for applying the concept of the double bind to organizations. This type of application calls for training in both organizational consulting and double-bind therapy, and one can only guess which doses of which the researchers used. In fact, Hirschhorn and Gilmore (1980, pp. 35–36) found that their consultation efforts were debilitated by the strictness of the family/organization analogy. Organizations, they argue, are more complex than families, and stepping into an organization to fix interactional problems simply becomes too confusing. Finally, even though Hirschhorn and Gilmore are trained consultants, they had problems establishing their credibility with all relevant coalitions and ran the risk of becoming part of some of these coalitions (Hirschhorn and Gilmore, 1980, p. 35).

Ferris (1975) also attempted to change the structure of an organization using double-bind prevention principles. He reorganized several high-school English classes, giving students more freedom to direct their own studies and establish their own criteria for success. Students were more satisfied with Ferris' class, and teachers of high-school students might be interested in his results. However, any individual from a different profession who used Ferris' format may not have had as much success in guiding this type of research. As well, Ferris was the only teacher in his study who used his double bind-prevention principles, and the degree of his success may not be replicable.

It seems that only those with training in the setting in which the change effort takes place should attempt applied work with the ODB. However, there may be small-scale types of change efforts which could be conducted by trainers in a classroom format. Such efforts might include:

1.   Training people in "metacommunication." Watzlawick et al. (1967) talk about "metacommunication" as the way people can most effectively get out of binds. Simply put, "metacommunication" is talking about the nature of the bind—a difficult art, since one of the features of a bind is that there are implicit rules against talking about them.

2.   Training managers to plan explicit statements of role expectations for new employees. Certain types of organizations seem more prone to role ambiguity than others. For example, workers in a research and development

unit are rarely given deadlines or specifications for output, and are continually creating their own jobs. Helping these individuals cope with the dozens of constraints they face may help them think of creative approaches to their jobs. In all likelihood, such help may be best provided by those with authority in the organization.

3. Finally, Wagner (1978) suggests that a major cause of double binds in organizations is that most employees never have an opportunity to express their irrational, emotional side. Wagner suggests that organizations should provide time during the week for employees to convene for the simple purpose of relaxing and letting go.

REFERENCES

Abeles, G. (1976). "Researching the Unresearchable: Experimentation on the Double Bind." In C. E. Sluzki and D. C. Ransom (Eds.), *Double Bind: The Foundation of the Communicational Approach to the Family*, 113–150. New York: Grune and Stratton.

Bacharach, S. B., and Lawler, E. (1980). *Power and Politics in Organizations*. San Francisco, CA: Jossey-Bass.

Bateson, G., Jackson, D. D., Haley, J., and Weakland, J. (1972). "Toward a Theory of Schizophrenia" (1956). In G. Bateson *(Ed.)*, *Steps to an Ecology of Mind*. New York: Ballantine.

Benson, T. (1980). "The Rhetorical Structure of Frederick Weisman's 'High School.'" *Communication Monographs 47*, 233–261.

Dell, P. (1980). "Researching the Family Theories of Schizophrenia: An Exercise in Epistemological Confusion" *Family Process 19*, 321–335.

Downs, A. (1967). *Inside Bureaucracy*. Boston, MA: Little, Brown and Co.

Ferris, W. P. (1975). "The Incidence and Prevention of Double-Binding Communication Patterns in the Secondary School." Unpublished dissertation, Rensselaer Polytechnic Institute.

Hall, S. (1974). "Media Power: The Double Bind." *Journal of Communication 24* (No. 4), 19–26.

Hirschhorn, L., and Gilmore, T. (1980). "The Application of Family Therapy Concepts to Influencing Organizational Behavior." *Administrative Science Quarterly 25*, 18–37.

Katz, D., and Kahn, R. L. (1978). *The Social Psychology of Organizations*, 2d ed. New York: John Wiley and Sons.

Marcus, G. E. (1972). "The Double Bind and the Military Organization—a Special Case." *ETC 29*, 269–273.

Polite, C. (1972). "Control: The Double-Bind in Organizational Power." Unpublished dissertation, Michigan State University.

Rabkin, R. (1976). "Critique of the Clinical Use of the Double Bind Hypothesis." In C. E. Sluzki and D. C. Ransom (Eds.), *Double Bind: The Foundation of the Communicational Approach to the Family*. New York: Grune and Stratton.

Stewart, L. (1979). "The Ethnography of a Whistle-Blowing Incident: Implications for Organizational Communication." Unpublished dissertation, Purdue University.

Wagner, J. A., III. (1978). "The Organizational Double Bind: Toward an Understanding of Rationality and its Complement." *Academy of Management Review 3*, 786–795.

Watzlawick, P. (1978). *The Language of Change*. New York: Basic Books.

Watzlawick, P., Beavin, J. H., Jackson, D. D. (1967). *Pragmatics of Human Communication*. New York: Norton.

11

The Neo-Nazi March in Skokie: Communication and Consensus

JOSEPHINE R. HOLZ

National Broadcasting Company, New York[1]

Recent research has begun to indicate that the most significant effects of the mass media may have to do not with their immediate impact on audience attitudes and behavior but with their long-term effects on audience cognitions—assumptions, perceptions, and beliefs—and that these cognitive effects might be associated not so much with propaganda or other purposely persuasive messages but with mass-communicated news or even entertainment (Becker et al., 1975; Clarke and Kline, 1974; Gerbner and Gross, 1976; Holz and Wright, 1979; Wright, 1975). A key example of recent work using this approach to the study of mass communication effects can be found in the growing body of research on the "agenda-setting" function of the news media (e.g., Benton and Frazier, 1976; Bowers, 1973; Funkhouser, 1973; McCombs and Shaw, 1972; McLeod et al., 1974; Palmgreen and Clarke, 1977; Tipton et al., 1975). A number of related studies, primarily by British sociologists and communication theorists, have examined the manner in which mass media depictions can more generally shape audience conceptions and beliefs (Halloran et al., 1970; Hartmann and Husband, 1974).

What these works all have in common is a focus on the role of mass communication in the social construction of reality (Berger and Luckmann, 1967). All knowledge about "reality" can be said to be socially constructed, in that it is shaped by the culture in which it is based. The social construction of reality is a process in which communication plays an essential role, since social reality is a consensual reality, based on shared assumptions and perspectives, and since it is through communication that shared perspectives are produced and maintained (Mead, 1934). According to Festinger (1954), the establishment of consensus about the nature of reality is one of the primary motivations for engaging in interpersonal communication. With the development of increasingly sophisticated and ubiquitous forms of mass communication, the mass media have also come to play a significant part in the social construction of reality, particularly in regard to those aspects of reality with which people have little or no direct contact themselves.

In a society as pluralistic and geographically dispersed as the United States, the development and maintenance of a minimal degree of consensus or shared

---

[1] This article was written before the author joined NBC.

social reality is more than a little problematic, since the various groups and collectivities that make up our society cannot and do not all directly communicate with one another. In this context, it has often been suggested that the mass media have come to play a significant role in the creation of a consensual social reality by providing a common set of symbols, images, and definitions to which different groups can all orient themselves. There has been comparatively little empirical research, however, directly aimed at examining this assumption.

In order to examine the role of mass communication in the development of a common social reality among different social groups, a case study of a specific event which had received a considerable amount of mass media attention—a march by a group of neo-Nazis, planned for the town of Skokie, Illinois, in the summer of 1978—was carried out. The major purpose of the study was to determine whether and in what respects people with different social characteristics and with different degrees of interest and different opinions about the event, might nevertheless have developed common conceptions about it, and what roles mass and interpersonal communication may have played in this development. The study examined the beliefs, conceptions, and opinions about the event expressed by a sample of persons geographically distant from the event and thus largely dependent on mass communication for their information about it, and compared their views with the images, descriptions, and definitions of the event presented by the mass media sources relied upon by most members of the sample studied.[2]

THE NEO-NAZI MARCH

As Lang and Lang (1968) have noted, the processes by which a collective definition of reality arises are best observed in situations that are not as yet clearly defined, where a degree of novelty, choice, conflict, or crisis creates a problem. The planned Skokie march seemed an appropriate research topic, since it had become a national controversy by the time this study was undertaken, in June, 1978, two or three weeks before the event was scheduled to take place. A number of factors had made the Skokie march an issue of considerable interest and concern to the national news media and to many people beyond those immediately involved. For one thing, the population of Skokie was said to include a high percentage of Jews and, more specifically, survivors and relatives of victims of World War II Nazi concentration camps. The town of Skokie fought the planned march in the courts, including the Supreme Court; and the American Civil Liberties Union, an organization dedicated to upholding human and civil rights and one with a substantial Jewish membership, defended the neo-Nazis in court. At issue was the constitutional status of the march—whether it was a legitimate expression of free speech and thus protected by the first Amendment, or a form of provocation and incitement to

---

[2] The reader is referred to Holz (1981) for the larger study from which this report is taken.

Skokie's residents. As the case made its way through the courts, the militant Jewish Defense League announced their intention to forcibly stop the march from taking place, even if it were legally condoned.

As it turned out, although the Supreme Court eventually refused to overturn lower court decisions supporting the neo-Nazis' right to demonstrate in Skokie, the neo-Nazis decided to hold a rally in Chicago's Marquette Park instead, where they had also succeeded in overturning Chicago ordinances that would have impeded such a gathering. The neo-Nazis held their rally in Chicago on July 9, 1978.

METHODOLOGY

The research methodology consisted of two major components. First, in order to determine the beliefs, conceptions, and opinions about the Skokie march held by people distant from the event, a random sample of 192 residents in the suburban Philadelphia area were interviewed by telephone between June 18 and June 29, 1978, two to three weeks before the Chicago rally took place. Through a combination of closed and open-ended questions, respondents were asked about their awareness, interest, beliefs, and opinions about the upcoming march and neo-Nazis in general; their usual patterns of news media use; and their demographic characteristics.

The second major component of the study consisted of a content analysis of all reports about the events leading up to and including the planned march and any other neo-Nazi activities in those news media most often cited as primary sources of information about the Skokie march and neo-Nazism by the respondents interviewed: the *New York Times*, the *Philadelphia Bulletin*, the *Philadelphia Inquirer*, the three evening national television news programs (as summarized in Vanderbilt University's *TV News Index and Abstracts*), and *Time* and *Newsweek* magazines. All relevant content appearing from January, 1977, (the first year in which references to the Skokie march were found in these news media) through July 10, 1978 (the day after the neo-Nazi demonstration was finally held) was collected and analyzed.

In addition, several specific television programs mentioned as sources of information by the respondents were also studied: a segment of CBS-TV's "Sixty Minutes" program, originally broadcast February 20, 1977, which featured a report about the neo-Nazi movement in the U.S.; an installment of the former public television program "Black Perspective on the News," broadcast in the Philadelphia area on September 30, 1977, on which Frank Collin, the leader of the neo-Nazi group planning the Skokie march, and David Duke, a Ku Klux Klan leader, were interviewed; and an episode of the fictional "Lou Grant" television series which was apparently based on the Skokie march incident.

FINDINGS

Mass Media Depictions of the Skokie March and the Neo-Nazis

While there were some differences among the different news sources in the coverage they provided of the Skokie march and related matters, these were primarily differences in the relative amounts of coverage given to the subject as a whole (see Table 1). For example, of the three newspapers examined, the *New York Times* published a substantially greater number of articles about the Skokie march and other neo-Nazi issues and events (89 articles) than either the *Philadelphia Inquirer* (55) or the *Bulletin* (34). This finding is, of course, consistent with the *Times'* role as a newspaper of national scope and the two Philadelphia dailies' roles as primarily local news media.

Despite the differences in the amounts of news coverage given to the Skokie march and related subjects in the different media sources, however, considerable similarity was found in their treatment of the event, in terms of the relative emphases given to its various aspects (see Table 1). For example, the topic most frequently mentioned in all three newspapers and referred to second-most often in the television news stories was the characterization of Skokie as a "predominantly Jewish" town and/or the home of many ("thousands") survivors of World War II Nazi concentration camps.

Frequent references to the legal actions and decisions related to the march, the ACLU, and the neo-Nazi group's leader, Frank Collin, were also found in most of the sources examined. References to the possibility or occurrence of violence at the march were made in less than one-fourth of all the articles on Skokie in each newspaper and in an even smaller fraction of all the television news reports about the incident. All reports which mentioned a specific group as the likely instigators of any violence cited either the Jewish Defense League or the Skokie residents, and none indicated that the neo-Nazis themselves would be the instigators.

As for the specific terms used to refer to the event itself, the vast majority of the media reports in all sources examined labelled the event planned for Skokie as a "march," though the terms "rally" and "demonstration" were occasionally used. The group planning to hold the "march" was usually referred to as the "National Socialist Party of America" or "the American Nazi Party," and, though the specific number of members in the group was rarely mentioned, its size, when noted, was described as "small," "tiny," or "a handful." Of those few reports that did give specific figures for the group's membership, none put their number at over 100.

Few newspaper articles or television news reports attempted to place the neo-Nazis and the Skokie march within a broader context. Reports referring to the existence of groups espousing Nazism in other parts of the country or the world were few in number, and no more than a couple gave any indication as to

Table 1. Percentage of News Reports about Skokie "March" and Other Neo-Nazi Activities Referring to Specific Major Themes

Themes	Newspapers			National TV News*		
	NY Times (N=89)	Inquirer (N=55)	Bulletin (N=34)	ABC (N=11)	NBC (N=7)	CBS (N=9)
A. Characteristics of Skokie: many Jews and Holocaust survivors	65%	55%	59%	55%	71%	44%
B. Characteristics of neo-Nazis						
1. Involved in Skokie/Chicago						
a. Leader Frank Collin	48	50	38	18	29	22
b. Size of group/march	24	18	26	0	14	0
c. Presence or absence of community support	2	0	15	9	0	0
2. Throughout USA						
a. General references	3	8	9	9	0	0
b. Ties or similarity to KKK	9	8	18	9	0	0
3. Throughout world/general	1	3	3	0	0	0
C. Issues and decisions related to litigation						
1. Court decisions	47	50	56	73	84	56
2. ACLU's involvement	37	28	35	18	29	11
3. Reasons *for* allowing "march"	22	28	29	9	0	11
4. Reasons *against* allowing "march"	10	20	24	0	0	0
D. Characteristics of event						
1. Possible or actual violence	20	23	21	18	14	11
2. Planned or actual counter-demonstrations	13	10	24	9	29	11
3. Chicago as alternative site	17	15	9	45	29	22
E. Public expressions of support for Skokie and Jews	7	3	0	0	0	11
F. Other neo-Nazi activities and events						
1. Confrontations, conflicts, arrests	15	13	6	0	14	0
2. St. Louis march	4	5	0	0	0	0
3. "Black Perspective on the News"	4	5	9	0	0	0
4. "Murders by avowed neo-Nazis	0	3	9	0	0	0

Note: News reports were multiply coded, so figures do not total 100%.
*Note small *N*'s. Percentages for comparison purposes only.

the size of these other groups. Those few that did estimated that there might be up to 2,000 such persons in the U.S. or referred to their numbers as "small" and "tiny."

There were few reports in the news sources studied that offered any explanations as to why neo-Nazi groups might exist in this country, what their sources of funding might be, what motivates people to join such groups, or what characteristics might be shared by such persons. Those few reports which did touch on such questions generally presented a picture of the neo-Nazis as psychologically disturbed individuals or social misfits. For example, the "Sixty Minutes" television program segment about neo-Nazis in the U.S. featured an exclusive interview with a former neo-Nazi leader who was said to have spent most of his life in reform schools and prisons, often in a straitjacket and padded cell. In the "Lou Grant" show episode about a neo-Nazi group involved in a Skokie-like incident, the Collin-like neo-Nazi leader ended up by committing suicide.

Public Beliefs and Opinions about the March and Neo-Nazis

Of the 192 persons in the Philadelphia area interviewed shortly before the scheduled Skokie march, 88% reported some awareness of the incident. Unsurprisingly, Jewish respondents and more highly-educated respondents, who expressed more interest in the incident than other subgroups in the sample, were significantly more likely than others to report having heard about the march (Tables 2 and 3). Nevertheless, 79% of Catholics and 65% of respondents with no more than a high-school education, the two subgroups who expressed the least interest in the incident, had also heard about it.

There was no significant relationship between respondents' usual frequency of news media use and their frequency of awareness about the "march," though nearly all the respondents (97%) said they got most of their information about the event from the news media. Choice of newspaper, however, did make a significant difference in the probability of respondents' having heard about the incident, with all regular *New York Times* readers reporting an awareness of the march, while readers of the local papers were less likely to have heard about it

Table 2.   Awareness of Skokie March, by Respondent Religion and Education Level (Question: "Have you heard about a march that a Nazi group is planning to hold in Skokie, Illinois, some time soon?")

Answer	Religion*			No. Years of Education†		
	Jewish ($N=61$)	Catholic ($N=52$)	Protestant ($N=66$)	12 or less ($N=43$)	13-16 ($N=95$)	over 16 ($N=46$)
Yes	95%	79%	89%	65%	92%	98%
No	5	21	11	35	8	2

*$p<.05$
$eta=.21$
†$p<.01$
$gamma=-.45$

Table 3.   Interest in Skokie March, by Religion and Education Level (Question: "How interested have you been in keeping up with the news about the Skokie march? Would you say you've been: very interested, somewhat interested, or not at all interested?")

	Religion*			No. Years of Education		
Answer	Jewish (N = 56)	Catholic (N = 31)	Prostes- tant (N = 43)	12 or less (N = 28)	13-16 (N = 85)	over 16 (N = 45)
Very interested	54%	23%	12%	25%	31%	28%
Somewhat interested	44	35	58	36	48	58
Not at all interested	2	42	30	39	21	14

*$p<.0001$

(Pearson $r = .21$, $p<.01$). Controlling for religion and education level reduced but did not eliminate this association.

Of those who had some awareness of the event, over 60% replied that Skokie had been selected as the site for the march because of its predominantly Jewish or large Holocaust survivor population. Jewish respondents and those who had completed college were more likely to give this answer, but a majority of Catholics and Protestants and nearly half those respondents with no college training also offered this response (Table 4). Knowing the special characteristics of Skokie's population was not associated with higher frequencies of news media use, and *Times* readers were not significantly more likely than local newspaper readers to know about Skokie's characteristics.

Of those who had heard about the march, 52% thought it should not be allowed to take place, while only 33% thought it should be allowed. Respondents differed in their opinions according to religion, education level, and age, as had been expected, with Jewish, lesser-educated, and older respondents tending to hold negative opinions. However, age level was the only variable of the three to show a statistically significant relationship with respondents' opinions, and religious affiliation showed the weakest association of the three (Table 5).

Table 4.   Respondents' Information about Skokie, by Religion and Education Level (Question: "Why do you think the Nazis selected Skokie as the place for the march?")

	Religion*			No. Years of Education†			
Answer	Jewish (N = 58)	Catholic (N = 41)	Prostes- tant (N = 49)	12 or less (N = 28)	13-15 (N = 39)	16 (N = 48)	over 16 (N = 45)
Large Jewish or Hol- ocaust survivor population	81%	51%	51%	46%	56%	60%	80%
Other/don't know	19	49	49	54	44	40	20

*$p<.01$
†$p<.05$
gamma = $-.36$

Table 5. Correlation between Opinions on Skokie March and Religion, Education, and Age (Pearson Product-Moment Coefficients)

Respondent Characteristics	r	p
Religious Affiliation (Jewish/non-Jewish)	.14	n.s.
Education Level (college/no college)	−.17	p = .05
Age (50 or over/under 50)	.38	p < .001

While respondents' religion, education level, and age were to varying degrees associated with their awareness, interest, and opinions about the Skokie march, there were a number of other beliefs and conceptions about the march and the neo-Nazis that did not differ significantly or systematically according to these respondent characteristics. For example, most respondents (55%) thought there would be from 100 to over 1,000 neo-Nazis participating in the planned march. Of those willing to make a prediction, nearly three-fourths believed there would be fighting at the "march," and 9 out of 10 of these thought that persons other than the neo-Nazis themselves would be the ones to start it.

About half of those respondents who gave estimates of the number of neo-Nazis in the U.S. as a whole, guessed that there were over 2,000, or "very many," neo-Nazis in the country. However, almost two-thirds of the sample did not think the neo-Nazis posed a serious threat to the nation. When asked "what kind of people" were likely to be members of Nazi-type groups, 45% of the respondents chose to describe them in psychological terms, ranging from "lonely" and "insecure" to "disturbed," "crazy," and "psychotics." Only 15% described them in demographic or socioeconomic terms, and only 12% characterized them in terms of their political ideology.

On all these items, religion, education level, and age made little systematic difference in respondents' answers. For the most part, these beliefs were also unassociated significantly or linearly with respondents' frequencies or patterns of news media use or cited information sources.

DISCUSSION

All in all, there were systematic differences, as expected, among respondents in different religious, educational, and age categories, in their degree of interest in the neo-Nazi march planned for Skokie, in the frequency with which they reported having heard about the march and about Skokie's special characteristics, and in their opinions about whether or not the march should be allowed. However, it is noteworthy that respondents who differed in these respects did not differ significantly in many of their conceptions and beliefs about the march and neo-Nazism, which were largely consistent with the messages, either explicit or implicit, that the mass media conveyed about these subjects.

Furthermore, though Jewish and more highly-educated respondents were more likely to have heard about the march, it is significant that a majority of the respondents in all other religious and educational categories had also heard about it. This means that a considerable number of those respondents who claimed to have had little or no interest in the event had nevertheless become aware of it. Similarly, though religion and education level were associated with the frequency with which respondents described Skokie as a predominantly Jewish or Holocaust survivor community, a majority of the non-Jewish respondents and nearly half the least-educated members of the sample characterized the town in the same terms. It may be recalled that this aspect of the incident was the most frequent theme or "angle" in the news reports about the march.

The fact that the various news media sources available to the respondents all presented a very similar picture of the march is not insignificant in this regard. Thus, while readers of the *New York Times*, which carried more reports about the march than the local newspapers did, were more likely to have heard about the incident, they were not much more likely to "know" that Skokie's population was "predominantly Jewish." Since all three newspapers gave top priority to this item of information, those readers of the different papers who had heard about the event at all were equally likely to have heard about this aspect of it.

In some cases, it would seem that the implicit messages conveyed by the news media may have affected audience members' beliefs and conceptions more strongly than more explicit messages did. For example, most respondents' estimates of the likely size of the upcoming march were much higher than the figures given by the news media, none of which exceeded 100. However, such specific figures were infrequently presented, and though some of the descriptive terms applied to the size of the group indicated that they were few in number, the use of such terms as "march" and "rally" to describe the event and references to the neo-Nazis as the "National Socialist Party of America" all connoted large numbers of paticipants. Furthermore, the sheer amount of news coverage given to the incident may itself have led people to conclude that significant numbers of people must be involved.

About three-fourths of those questioned believed there would be fighting at the march, and most believed that the neo-Nazis themselves would not initiate it. Again, while explicit references to violence were found in a relatively small proportion of the news reports, references to planned counterdemonstrations and to arguments that the march was a form of provocation and incitement served as additional indications that violence was likely. Even the very use of such terms as "march" and "rally" may automatically connote violence and disruption to news audiences, since it was largely in terms of the expectation or occurrence of violence that such forms of civil protest had been found newsworthy in the past (Gans, 1979).

Most respondents described the neo-Nazis in negative psychological terms, a characterization consistent with those few mass media reports which attempted to provide more general information about such people and their motivations. The media's depiction of the neo-Nazis as a collection of psychologically maladjusted individuals rather than a coherent political or social group may also have led to or reinforced most respondents' beliefs that such persons presented no serious threat to the country, despite many respondents' large estimates of their total number.

CONCLUSIONS

All in all, it would seem that people with different background characteristics and different opinions and degrees of interest regarding the Skokie march had nevertheless come to share a number of beliefs and assumptions about it, conceptualizing it in rather similar terms. In these respects, the members of the different social groups into which respondents were categorized shared a collective definition of the situation and thus, to some extent, a common social reality, despite their differences of opinion. And their common view of reality can be traced to the picture of the event constructed for them by their primary sources of information about the incident—the mass media.

In order for the mass media to construct a common public reality for diverse social groups, the different media sources drawn upon by different groups must present essentially the same picture of reality. And numerous studies of mass media content have indeed concluded that the major media organizations do seem to provide essentially similar fare to their respective audiences (e.g., Gans, 1979; Gerbner and Gross, 1976; Glasgow University Media Group, 1976; Schlesinger, 1978; Sigal, 1973). The results of our analysis of the mass media's depiction of the Skokie march lend further support to this conclusion. The mass media thus limit the possible social realities individual audience members can select for themselves by presenting a limited and relatively homogeneous selection of public realities to begin with.

This is not to suggest that everyone exposed to this common public reality (see Tuchman, 1978) will come away with exactly the same picture of the world. Processes of selective exposure, perception, and interpretation do operate to filter messages received from the mass media through audience members' existing values, attitudes, and beliefs (Hyman and Sheatsley, 1947). Nevertheless, in the case of those aspects of reality with which people have only mass-mediated contact, selective perception and interpretation by audience members necessarily occurs within the already defined and delimited context of the public reality constructed by the mass media. While the media do not have the power to determine the exact content of the social realities that different individuals construct, by controlling what information is made available and how it is presented and defined, they limit the range of interpretations that audiences can make (Ball-Rokeach and DeFleur, 1976). If different group-specific definitions of reality evolve in response to the same mass-communicated "facts," they will constitute different versions of the same basic reality. To the extent that these group-specific beliefs are more alike than different, the members of different social groups or aggregates can still be said to share a common social reality.

REFERENCES

Ball-Rokeach, S., and DeFleur, M.L. (1976). "A Dependency Model of Mass-Media Effects." *Communication Research 3*, 3–21.

Becker, L. B., McCombs, M. E., and McLeod, J. M. (1975). "The Development of Political Cognitions." *In* S. H. Chaffee (Ed.), *Political Communication: Issues and Strategies for Research*, 21–63. Beverly Hills, CA: Sage.

Benton, M., and Frazier, P. J. (1976). "The Agenda Setting Function of the Mass Media at Three Levels of 'Information Holding'." *Communication Research 3*, 261–274.

Berger, P., and Luckmann, T. (1967). *The Social Construction of Reality: A Treatise in the Sociology of Knowledge*. Garden City, NY: Anchor.

Bowers, T. A. (1973). "Newspaper Political Advertising and the Agenda-Setting Function." *Journalism Quarterly 50*, 552–556.

Clarke, P., and Kline, F. G. (1974). "Media Effects Reconsidered: Some New Strategies for Communication Research." *Communication Research 1*, 224–240.

Festinger, L. (1954). "A Theory of Social Comparison Processes." *Human Relations 7*, 117–140.

Funkhouser, G. R. (1973). "The Issues of the Sixties: An Exploratory Study in the Dynamics of Public Opinion." *Public Opinion Quarterly 37*, 62–75.

Gans, H. (1979). *Deciding What's News: A Study of CBS Evening News, NBC Nightly News, Newsweek, and Time*. New York: Pantheon.

Gerbner, G., and Gross, L. (1976). "Living with Television: The Violence Profile." *Journal of Communication 26*, (No. 2), 172–199.

Glasgow University Media Group. (1976). *Bad News*. London: Routledge and Kegan Paul.

Halloran, J. D., Elliott, P., and Murdock, G. (1970). *Demonstrations and Communication: A Case Study*. Harmondsworth, England: Penguin.

Hartmann, P., and Husband, C. (1974). *Racism and the Mass Media: A Study of the Role of the Mass Media in the Formation of White Beliefs and Attitudes in Britain*. Totowa, NJ: Rowman and Littlefield.

Holz, J. R. (1981). "Communication about the Skokie 'March': A Case Study in the Social Construction of Reality." Unpublished dissertation, Annenberg School of Communications, University of Pennsylvania, 1981.

Holz, J. R., and Wright, C. R. (1979). "Sociology of Mass Communications." In A. Inkeles, J. Coleman, and R. H. Turner (Eds.), *Annual Review of Sociology 5*, Palo Alto: Annual Reviews, 1979, 193–217.

Hyman, H., and Sheatsley, P. (1947). "Some Reasons Why Information Campaigns Fail." *Public Opinion Quarterly 11*, 412–423.

Lang, K., and Lang, G. E. (1968). *Politics and Television*. Chicago, IL: Quadrangle.

McCombs, M. E., and Shaw, D. L. (1972). "The Agenda-Setting Function of Mass Media." *Public Opinion Quarterly 36*, 176-187.

McLeod, J. M., Becker, L. B., and Byrnes, J. E. (1974). "Another Look at the Agenda-Setting Function of the Press." *Communication Research*, 131–165.

Mead, G. H. (1934). *Mind, Self, and Society*. Chicago, IL: University of Chicago Press.

Palmgreen, P., and Clarke, P. (1977). "Agenda-Setting with Local and National Issues." *Communication Research 4*, 435–452.

Schlesinger, P. (1978). *Putting "Reality" Together: BBC News*, Beverly Hills, CA: Sage.

Sigal, L. V. (1973). *Reporters and Officials*. Lexington, MA: D.C. Heath.

Tipton, L., Haney, R. D., and Basehart, J. R. (1975). "Media Agenda-Setting in City and State Election Campaigns." *Journalism Quarterly 52*, 15–22.

Tuchman, G. (1978). *Making News: A Study in the Construction of Reality*. New York: Free Press.

Wright, C. R. (1975). *Mass Communication: A Sociological Perspective*, 2nd ed. New York: Random House.

12

Automobile 'Positioning' and the Construction of Social Reality

STANLEY J. BARAN
San Jose State University

A developing trend in mass communication research is the analysis of how people's perceptions of their environments relate to corresponding media portrayals (see, for example, Gerbner et al., 1980). In such cases, the media's impact is assessed not so much from the perspective of direct effects on behavior and attitudes, but rather from the perspective of how they influence their consumers' conception of their social reality. Usually, research of this nature is addressed to violence, crime, and race (see Gerbner et al., 1977; Tan and Tan, 1979) respectively.

Other research, however, has centered on the construction of social reality with respect to more intimate phenomena such as personal attractiveness and sex appeal (Tan, 1979; Kenrick and Gutierres, 1978), personal problems (Buerkel-Rothfus and Mayes, 1981), and careers (Beuf, 1974). What these and similar works tend to demonstrate is that individuals' understanding of the world and the appropriateness of their behavior in it are at least in part dependent on the pictures of that world represented in the media. This study is similarly geared to an analysis of this general relationship and, in particular, to the case of automobiles.

The automobile has long been considered a "supericon of popular culture" (Neuman, 1973). Cultural and critical scholars who examine the placement of the car in our society often interpret it as traditionally representing something "heavily masculine" (Neuman, 1973), satisfying our want for "privacy, power, and plushness" (Brake, 1974). Jeansonne (1974), Gammage and Jones (1974), and Kettler (1973/74) speak persuasively to the auto's meaning as something more than a vehicle of transportation. In a rare *empirical* investigation, Felson (1978) examined the assumption that people make "invidious distinctions" among automobile types, evaluating their owners on some prestige hierarchy. He discovered that such distinctions do exist. There was not, however, a simple relationship of car value or size to owner status. This led Felson to speculate, "We would conjecture that advertisers, each motivated to exaggerate its own product's quality, collectively confuse the public's ability to distinguish among consumer goods. Moreover, the prosperity of modern society allows enough budgetary leeway so that the average consumer can develop personal stylistic tastes and idiosyncracies." In other words, as expense has become less of a factor in car selection, other "qualities" of various vehicles are highlighted by their promotors.

Automobile advertising is one of the most common forms of advertising in the mass media. The automobile manufacturers and their dealers spend in excess of 175 million dollars a year to purchase television ad time alone (*Broadcasting*, March 24, 1980, p. 59). Much of the advertisers' persuasive effort is given to "positioning" the specific make of car, i.e., providing a given vehicle with its own supposedly *individual* character. While, from one perspective, this "positioning" may be seen as just a marketing strategy, it simultaneously has sociological import in terms of how people view the culturally-important car and car-owners in the real world.

For example, Doob and Gross (1968) and Chase and Mills (1973) have demonstrated that driver frustration with and aggression toward other drivers are often functions of the others' automobile brand. The present study similarly examines, in a somewhat different context, whether and how individuals attribute specific social behavior to others, based solely on the make of automobile that these other individuals drive.

PROCEDURE

The measurement instrument was administered to an introductory broadcasting class at the University of Texas in the guise of a "study in fiction writing" for an English professor teaching *English 341, The Short Story*, an actual course at the university. The students were told that their identities would not be attributed to their specific responses and were instructed to write their names on the back of the instrument. For their participation, subjects were to be awarded extra credit on an exam.

Two versions of the instrument were administered to 86 students. Both were identical in format and content, but in one version, the automobile in question was a Chevrolet Camaro and, in the other, it was a Honda Accord, two autos of roughly similar interior size. The two versions were randomly distributed to the students and both instructed subjects to do the following:

> Please complete the following episode as you think it might occur. Please be as realistic as possible, as this is an assignment in character motivation and actualization. Use the space provided at the conclusion of the introductory paragraphs.

The following is the episode which subjects were instructed to complete:

> The date had been a moderate success. The movie was entertaining, the meal satisfying, and the conversation flowed effortlessly. In all, a good first date. In fact, each had remarked to themselves that, as far as initial encounters go, each had had worse. But now it was that awkward time. They sat uncomfortably, fidgeting, making pained small talk. His (Camaro or Honda Accord), parked behind her

apartment, never seemed so small. The next move was his. What to say, what to do? It may have been only their first date, but he was not willing to let it end. But there would be other dates with her. He was frozen in self debate. After a few agonizing moments of indecision, he . . .

Once completed, the responses were read by a naive coder who was instructed to evaluate the behavior of the male automobile owner in the completed story and to classify his actions in one of three ways: *LESS*—he chose to end the date with a simple "Good night, may I see you again," a handshake, or some other conventional method of leave-taking; *KISS*—he chose to end the date with a kiss and then to take his leave; and, *MORE*—he opted for physical contact over and above a simple kiss. His success in his chosen behavior was not to be judged, only his actions. For example, a male who kissed his date goodnight and placed his hand on her chest only to be rebuffed was classified as *MORE*, even though he received "only" a kiss. A male who attempted to leave with a simple "May I see you again" but who was embraced and kissed by his date was classified as a *LESS*.

A second coder rated every fifth response and the two sets of evaluations were consistent in more than 92% of the cases.

After the coding was completed, the responses were identified as either Camaro responses or Accord responses and chi-squares and z scores were computed. ($P = <.05$ for all reported differences.)

RESULTS

Of the 86 respondents, 45 completed the Camaro version of the short story and 41 the Accord. There were 49 males and 37 female respondents. Table 1 presents the breakdown of responses by auto type and end of date behavior. As can be seen, the respondents projected no difference between Camaro and Accord owners in terms of the option *KISS*, but Accord owners were much more likely to end the date with a simple "good night" or a handshake, and whereas Camaro owners were seen as significantly more physical at the end of the date

Table 1. Respondents Predictions of Date Ending Behavior as a Function of Automobile Brand Ownership[a]

Predicted Behavior	Automobile Ownership	
	Camaro	Accord
Less	9	16
Kiss	18	18
More	18	7

[a]$x^2 = 6.63$, $2df$, $p < .05$
$C = .28$, $p < .05$

($x^2 = 6.63$, $2df$, $p < .05$). A contingency coefficient was computed to assess the extent of the relationship between respondents' predictions of the car owners' behaviors and the type of auto attributed to those characters. These two variables proved to be significantly related ($C = .28$, $p < .05$).

In addition, a z-score was computed to test for the difference between the proportion of Camaro owners in the *MORE* category and the proportion of Accord owners who so behaved. Forty percent (18 of 45) of the respondents saw the Camaro owner as attempting to secure more than a kiss, while 17% (7 of 41) saw the Accord owner acting this way. This proved to be a statistically significant difference ($z = 2.92$, $p < .001$).

Chi-square analyses of male ($x^2 = 5.93$, $2df$) and female ($x^2 = .81$, $2df$) respondents' observations showed no significant differences between their projections of Accord and Camaro owners' behavior. However, when the data were examined in terms of the proportion of males and females who saw the Camaro owner maneuvering for more than a kiss, some interesting results surfaced. No significant differences appeared for the females—12% of the Camaro respondents predicted an overzealous male date and 10% predicted an overzealous Accord owner. Fifty-seven percent (16 of 28) of the male respondents, however, saw the Camaro owner as maneuvering for more than a good night kiss while only 24% (5 of 21) saw the Accord owner so behaving ($z = 2.32$, $p < .001$).

DISCUSSION

While all respondents "met" exactly the same young man, those who met him in his Camaro judged his behavior differently from those who met him in his Accord. Although this study was not administered immediately after experimental subjection of respondents to automobile advertisements, it seems quite reasonable to assume that the respondents' evaluations in this study were media-based nonetheless. (In fact, it might be argued that artificial, experimental media exposure of such a study creates its own validity problems.) While a Camaro may not be innately a more aggressive auto than an Accord, it has been positioned as such by its promoters. General Motors' 1982 promotional materials for the Camaro, for example, claimed: "This is Camaro. An aggressive new road car designed to capture your imagination. It's sleek and lean." Honda Accord, on the other hand, is touted as "further proof that a sportive car's lively performance doesn't have to detract from its efficiency and commonsense advantages." These themes are echoed in both autos' respective television and print ads.

In his critique of the Gerbner *et al.* violence cultivation analysis (1977), Newcomb (1978) faults the earlier work for, among other things, suggesting that there may be in television "subtle patterns against whose influence we may all be somewhat defenseless." He contends that Gerbner and his colleagues err in their belief that the audience interprets television's "environment of symbols" as they, the researchers, do.

A similar argument may be raised against the analysis presented here. Even though the promoters of the two vehicles in question attempted to position them in specific ways, the researcher cannot assume that his or her respondents read the advertisers' symbols in those specific ways. To help insure that the promoters' symbols were indeed the respondents', a content analysis of the short stories written by the respondents might be conducted to ascertain if the Camaro respondents used more "aggressive" words, phrases, and illusions in their stories and if the Accord respondents used more "sensible, reliable, and practical" ones in theirs. In a less systematic analysis of the responses, it appeared that there was, in fact, no uniform pattern of word usage. Thus, we know only that Camaro owners were projected as behaving differently from Accord owners. Respondents made their reports of the character's behavior presumably without conscious reflection of the brand of car (the only difference in the way the male was represented), presumably without consciously calling to mind the advertising campaigns associated with Camaros or Accords, and presumably without consciously attributing either high or low aggression to the cars' owners. But when asked to define a situation—how a boy will end a date— they defined it in ways that very specifically and very logically refer back to the advertisers' positioning of their respective vehicles.

REFERENCES

Beuf, A. (1974). "Doctor, Lawyer, Household Drudge." *Journal of Communication 24* (No. 2), 142–145.

Brake, R. (1974). "Space, Motion, and Comfort in the Contemporary Automobile." *Journal of Popular Culture 8*, 155–161.

Buerkel-Rothfuss, N. L., and Mayes, S. (1981). "Soap Opera Viewing: The Cultivation Effect." *Journal of Communication 31* (No. 3), 108–115.

Chase, L. J., and Mills, N. H. (1973). "Status of Frustrator as a Facilitator of Aggression: A Brief Note." *Journal of Psychology 84*, 225–226.

Doob, A. N., and Gross, A. E. (1968). "Status of Frustrator as an Inhibitor of Horn-Honking Responses." *Journal of Social Psychology 76*, 213–218.

Felson, M. (1978). "Invidious Distinctions Among Cars, Clothes, and Suburbs." *Public Opinion Quarterly 42*, 49–58.

Gammage, G., and Jones, S. L. (1974). "Orgasm in Chrome: The Rise and Fall of the Automobile Tailfin." *Journal of Popular Culture 8*, 132–147.

Gerbner, G., Gross, L., Eleey, M. F., Jackson-Beeck, M., Jeffries-Fox, S., and Signorelli, N. (1977). "TV Violence Profile No. 8: The Highlights." *Journal of Communication 27* (No. 2), 171–180.

Gerbner, G., Gross, L., Morgan, M., and Signorelli, N. (1980). "The 'Mainstreaming' of America: Violence Profile No. 11." *Journal of Communication 30* (No. 3), 10–29.

Jeansonne, G. (1974). "The Automobile and American Morality." *Journal of Popular Culture 8*, 132–147.

Kenrick, D. T., and Gutierres, S. (1978). "Influence of Mass Media on Judgments of Physical Attractiveness: The People's Case Against Farrah Fawcett." Paper presented at the American Psychological Association, Toronto.

Kettler, R. R. (1973/74). "The Recalled Icon." *Indiana Social Studies Quarterly 26*, 45–51.

Neuman, D. J. (1973). "The American Courtship of House and Car." *Journal of Popular Culture 7*, 155–161.

Newcomb, H. (1978). "Assessing the Violence Profile Studies of Gerbner and Gross: A Humanistic Critique and Suggestion." *Communication Research 5*, 264–282.

Tan, A. S. (1979). "TV Beauty Ads and Role Expectations of Adolescent Female Viewers." *Journalism Quarterly 56*, 283–289.

Tan, A. S., and Tan, G. (1979). "Television Use and Self-Esteem of Blacks." *Journal of Communication 29* (No. 1), 129–135.

13

Video Games: Competing with Machines*

JARICE HANSON
University of Massachusetts, Amherst

It has been estimated that tens of thousands of electronic games now operate across the United States, and that these machines take in more than eight-billion dollars worth of quarters a year ("Using Electronic Games to Challenge Kids," 1981). The popular press has reported both positive and negative effects of video game playing, particularly concerning the effects these games have on children. However, most of the reports have been based upon fear and speculation rather than scientific study.

What seems to confound many parents and writers is the application of technology for game playing purposes. Game playing has traditionally included elements of socialization, competition, role playing, and fantasy—all items which could be considered in discussions of video games, but it appears that when technology replaces other persons in the game structure, the rewards of "gaming" become more questionable. This paper attempts to place video game playing within the traditional approaches to game playing, while realistically monitoring the amount of play and the perceived role of the video game in society.

WHAT DO WE KNOW ABOUT VIDEO GAME PLAYING BEHAVIOR?

Video games have become the center of much controversy in cities and towns across the United States. Many communities have drawn up ordinances and have passed legislation restricting the use of video games by young people. In Marlborough, Massachusetts, youths under the age of 18 are prohibited from using arcades at night and during school hours, and, in Illinois, children under the age of 15 are prohibited from playing public video games ("Town Zaps Video Games," 1981). In Coral Gables, Florida, a permit was given for the establishment of a video parlor, but the permit specified that a policeman must stand guard at all times. In Midland Park, New Jersey, where pinball machines have been banned since 1950, there are currently three court cases concerning video games pending ("Town Zaps Video Games," 1982), and in Mesquite,

* I wish to thank Dr. Walter Zakahi, Assistant Professor in the Department of Communication, Rutgers University, for his assistance in developing this paper.

Texas, the city council went so far as to bring up their case to the Supreme Court ("Video Games—Who's In Charge?" 1982).

While much of the controversy reminds one of the fears parents expressed about their children spending time in pool halls several decades ago, a more contemporary fear is that video game playing may "teach gambling and breed aggressive behavior" ("Battle for America's Youth," 1982). Even the Surgeon General, C. Everett Koop, has stated: "American youths are becoming addicted to video games . . . the games may be hazardous to their health" ("Battle for America's Youth," 1982).

Other common fears have been articulated by psychiatrists and other doctors who have seen symptoms in children such as "tensions, sleeplessness and dreams having to do with killing, eliminating, or destroying" ("TV Games Zapping Kids' Minds?," 1982). A less eloquent statement was provided by television talk show host Phil Donohue, who stated on one of his shows that "video games are contributing to the dumbing of American textbooks," and hence, "to the dumbing of American schoolchildren."

But are these fears well-founded? Joseph A. Dunne, President of the National Council on Compulsive Gambling, has stated that as yet, there are no statistics on how many children are overly involved in video game playing, nor do we know the ages of the children playing. Still, in general, gamblers start between the ages of 11 and 13 ("Electronic Games: Who Wins or Loses?," 1981), a fact difficult to ignore when watching children of these ages playing games, and casually observing their level of involvement.

Another common complaint is that parents feel their children are "wasting too much time" by playing video games. One psychologist however responded; "with or without video games, wasting time is a part, a good part, of what childhood is all about" ("Wasting Time," 1982).

While research is as yet not extensive, many professionals in the area of child development see positive aspects of video game playing. Video games, they conclude, teach hand/eye coordination, introduce children to computers which are necessary tools for the future, and allow children who are not athletically inclined to become "masters" of a skill.

Dr. Lee Salk, a Manhattan psychologist, thinks that video games have an indirect intellectual value since; "the child must sort out shapes, forms, colors and movements." Others believe that video game playing may give an outlet to work out aggression in a socially approved manner. Joyce Hakansson, project manager for computer software at the Children's Television Workshop applauds the games as ways to get children working with new technology ("Using Electronic Games to Challenge Kids," 1981).

Dr. Mitchell Rosenthal, President of Phoenix House, a rehabilitation center in Manhattan thinks that the word "addiction" is overused. "These games don't change the level of consciousness as drugs do, but they can be narcotizing, and they can be the focus of ritualized or obsessive behavior."

The little research conducted thus far with adult video game players generally involves the level of stress associated with playing the games. It has been determined that a person seated in a chair, will elevate pulse rate to as much as 60 beats per minute, with blood pressure increasing to as much as 220 mm within one minute of play.

However, the advocates for video game playing for youths *or* adults come from physical and occupational therapists, who see the skill/pleasure components as critical to development. As one doctor has stated: "Video games are fun, an important factor in occupational therapy where pencil-pushing tasks produce tedium and frustration" ("Video Games May Aid Brain-Injured," 1982). Paraplegics have had great success practicing wheelchair navigation with a joystick similar for games which simulate driving.

Renee O'Kaye and Anthony Hollander, two New York occupational therapists tested the effectiveness of multi-sensory stimulation upon children who were considered to be "learning disabled." After six weeks of structured sessions, they tested childrens' motor accuracy, eye-hand coordination and kinesthic awareness. All scores had greatly improved over the six week sessions ("Electronic Games Help the Handicapped," 1982).

The Epilepsy Center at Johns Hopkins uses specially wired Atari sets to determine effects of anticonvulsant drugs on learning and ability. Dr. Eileen Vining, associate director of the center says; "the advantage of the games is that children are eager to make their best efforts in eye-hand coordination tests."

Dr. Edward Friedman, a Manhattan optometrist says; "Under professional supervision, playing video games can help to make fine visual judgements in a hyperactive child who is easily distracted and who has a reduced attention span" ("Games Exercise Mental Ability," 1982).

Similarly, video games have been found to be worthy adjuncts to specialized training, and the U.S. Army has effectively used video games for instructional purposes. Because the Atari video game system has the same controls, telescopic sights, firing and tracking procedures, as well as the same target identification problems as the new M2 troop transporter, the Army has opted to use the video games to train personnel, citing lower costs of video game equipment as more practical than instituting the M2 simulator ("Video Games Train Army," 1982). The Army has also used two software systems familiar to video game players, such as the game "Battlezone" which is a training device "which doesn't appear to be one," and "Combat," which has also been used by the Naval Aerospace Medical Research Lab for performance testing.

The idea that the military would be interested in using gaming devices for training is certainly not new. Military war games have been useful training experiences for centuries, and several popular games have used similar strategies. Chess, for example, is similar to a war-strategy game, and has been played since the eighteenth century. More recently (and escalating in the 1960s) popular games became even more widely played. The average player in the

1960s tended to be male, highly educated, and interested in the military, history, or was a collector of military figurines (Levy, 1978, p. 43). Popular games in the 1980s seemed to take war strategies and place them in outer space.

VIDEO GAME PLAYING AND TRADITIONAL GAME PLAYING THEORIES

Two of the earliest areas of research on play involve both Schiller and Spencer's theories of play as surplus energy, and play as a time to recharge energy. Hall proposed that play was used by the child to recapitulate phylogenetic behavior and thus acquire the skills of his ancestors for his own mastery of the environment. Many theorists of the nineteenth century were influenced by the Darwinian point of view, such as Groos (1901), who stated that those animals who survive are best able to cope with prevailing conditions and that, if animals play, play is therefore useful for the practice of skills, i.e., developing competence.

However, it was Huizinga (1955) who identified the "play element" within culture, and who recognized that play is incorporated into all aspects of life. Huizinga determined that we could not just speak of Man in terms of reason (*Homo Sapiens*), and work (*Homo Faber*), but also in play (*Homo Ludens*).

Other researchers took the approach of ascertaining what types of people engage in leisure activities, such as games (Clarke, 1956), while still others have examined the influence of variables such as status, prestige, and occupation on leisure activities (Reissman, 1954; Havinghurst and Feigenbaum, 1959; Gerstl, 1961; and Bishop and Iheda, 1970). The findings of these studies point conclusively to the fact that members of certain groups, be they classes or occupations, participate in different activities.

Meyersohn (1969) specified three approaches to the study of leisure; (1) activities, (2) expenditure of time and money, and (3) meaning. Neulinger and Breit (1969) have stated: "We are interested in how people want to spend their time and money, and how much satisfaction they get from spending it the way they do." It is particularly interesting to note that the work of these writers reflects a concern for the economy which is often an understated variable. Today, with recessionary influences changing lifestyle patterns for so many people, particularly in the amount of available money for leisure, the expenditure of money for game playing may be viewed as a more important indicator of involvement than might normally be considered in determining trends.

A variation on the proposals suggested thus far comes from the work of Stephenson (1967), who postulated the "Play Theory of Mass Communication." Stephenson's main thesis is that "mass communication allows people to become absorbed in subjective play" (Stephenson, 1967, p. 67). Based in large part on the work of Huizinga, Stephenson determined that *communication-pleasure* is at the root of the enjoyment of any form of mass communication. Stating that "play has little gain for the player except in self-enhancement," Stephenson (1967, p. 68) effectively tied together concepts of psychological dependence upon mass media and on the social control provided by mass media. His theory states that mass communication has two functions: (1) to foster mutual socialization and (2) it "rocks the boat,"—to be in the forefront of change in status quo conditions. "The achievement of mass communication lies in the way it short-circuits older beliefs, substituting new values for them" (Stephenson, 1967, p. 70).

While video games are not in themselves forms of *mass* communication, they do share certain characteristics with forms of mass communication. First, they are a mediated form of entertainment, and secondly, they use traditional forms of technology heretofore used for the consumption of mass communication messages. As interactive systems are developed, video games will continue to share more similarities than differences with other forms of mediated entertainment.

A STUDY OF VIDEO GAME PLAYERS

We conducted a study to compare respondents' attitudinal and lifestyle patterns with the amount of time they played video games, the number of games they played, and the types of games played, to see if personal use of time and attitude toward leisure was different when playing video games. It was assumed that age, sex, and computer literacy might influence responses, therefore these items became important variables in understanding the data.

More specifically, the following questions were posed:

- What factors influence acceptance or rejection of video game playing for the individual?
- How much money do video game players spend on video games, and is money an indicator of addictive behavior?
- According to Stephenson's "Play Theory" what "communication-pleasure" is experienced while playing video games? Is it more appropriate to discuss video game playing as it compliments game theory or media theory?
- Does technological apprehension (fear of technology) influence acceptance of video games for traditionally interpersonal uses?
- Why do people say they play games? Can we believe them?

Methods

The questionnaire used in this study was patterned after Lieberman's Playfullness Scale (1977), and was adapted to measure (1) frequency of play, (2) amount of time participating in game playing, (3) preference for types of games, (4) meaning, and (5) attitude toward leisure (Meyersohn, 1969).

Two hundred individuals were questioned by a team of 20 interviewers who were instructed to go to bars, malls, arcades, restaurants, or any other place where video games were present, to observe whether the subjects were playing alone or with someone, the game being played, and the level of apparent involvement with the game. Interviewers were instructed to approach subjects who would fit the following categories, and report equal numbers of respondents in each category: (1) male under 21, (2) female under 21, (3) male over 21, (4) female over 21. After individuals were finished playing a video game, they were approached and asked a series of questions. Respondents ranged in age from 7 to 62.

Data were analyzed to determine frequencies of responses, correlations of specific items, and cross-tabulations of age, sex, and attitudinal and lifestyle data.

Results

Of the 200 subjects, 110 were male, 90 were female. It was sometimes difficult for interviewers to find women playing video games in malls or arcades who were over 21, so the sample of these women were found in restaurants, bars, and train terminals. All other age groups were questioned in the above-named areas as well as in arcades, student centers, and fast-food restaurants.

Male respondents appeared to play video games significantly more often than did female respondents, with younger males playing more often than any other age or sex group. While female respondents *usually* played only one or two games, the patterns of usage in the number of games played was not significant, though the amount of money spent weekly did indicate that males pay more for games per week (on the average, males pay $3.75/wk. while females pay only $2.50/week) (see Table 1).

Table 1. Frequency of Play: Number of Games Per Week (All Percentages Indicate Percent of the Sample of 200 Respondents)

	0-1	1	2	3	4	5	6	7	8	9	10
Male	19	4	22	9	7	28	2	9	1	0	0
%	9.5	2.0	11.0	4.5	3.5	14.0	1.0	4.5	0.5	0	0
Female	35	4	28	7	4	3	1	2	0	0	1
%	17.5	2.0	14.0	3.5	2.0	1.5	0.5	1.0	0	0	0.5

Number of Different Games

	0-1	1	2	3	4	5	6	7	10	12
Male	1	11	26	18	32	7	4	1	2	3
%	0.5	5.5	13.0	9.0	16.0	3.5	2.0	0.5	1.0	1.5
Female	1	23	22	19	16	2	3	1	1	0
%	0.5	11.5	11.0	9.5	8.0	1.0	1.5	0.5	0.5	0.0

Amount of Money Spent Per Week: To Nearest Dollar

	<$1	1	2	3	4	5	8	10	12
Male	13	15	14	18	14	28	2	4	0
%	6.5	7.5	7.0	9.0	7.0	14.0	1.0	2.0	0
Female	4	38	21	11	2	7	1	3	1
%	2.0	19.0	10.5	5.5	1.0	3.5	0.5	1.5	0.5

When contrasting the number of games played per week with a preference for indoor or outdoor activity, it becomes apparent that video game players tend to prefer participating in activity indoors, and tend to play a greater variety of games. While no significant correlation was found to indicate that these individuals who prefer to stay indoors tended to own their own games, there was also no correlation with the amount of money spent on video game playing. Therefore, it could be interpreted to mean that indoor activity does not necessarily indicate the level of interest in video games, or the willingness of the respondent to purchase a home system (see Table 2).

While women in general preferred to play against someone else rather than against the machine, they also demonstrated a higher level of computer knowledge than did male respondents (see Table 3).

Both males and females who reported receiving some *relaxation* from video game playing, tended to have less active lifestyles than other respondents, while individuals who reported that playing video games was *challenging* tended to lead more active lifestyles. Interestingly, there were no major differences between male and female respondents regarding "relaxing" or "challenging" responses to video game playing, but individuals (male and female) who did not have any computer literacy overwhelmingly listed video games as more "challenging" (see Table 4).

Perhaps the most surprising finding of the sex bias between perceiving video games as "relaxing" or "challenging" was revealed when participants listed their favorite video games. Men tended to name more games of skill and defen-

Table 2.   Level of Activity/Preference for Indoor—Outdoor

Number of Games Played Per Week	Prefers Indoor	Prefers Outdoor
0-1	12	4
	6.0%	2.0%
1	41	10
	20.5	5.0
2	26	10
	13.0	5.0
3	18	12
	9.0	6.0
4	10	6
	5.0	3.0
5	18	17
	9.0	8.5
8	1	2
	0.5	1.0
10	6	1
	3.0	0.5
Column Total	132	63
	66.0%	31.5%

% of sample of 200

Table 3.

Prefer to Play Alone or With Someone	Alone	With Someone
Males	69	38
%	34.5	19.0
Females	31	56
%	15.5	28.0

Computer Literacy	Knows How to Operate Computer	Does Not Know How to To Operate Computer
Males	40	63
%	10.0	31.5
Females	42	43
%	21.0	21.5

% of sample of 200

Table 4.   Perceived Use By Sex

How Relaxing Is

Playing Video Games?	Very	Moderately	Somewhat	Rarely	Never
Male	4	18	42	22	21
%	2.0	9.0	21.0	11.0	10.5
Female	6	17	22	20	22
%	3.0	8.5	11.0	10.0	11.0

How Challenging Is Playing Video Games?

Male	62	16	9	18	3
%	31.0	8.0	4.5	9.0	1.5
Female	31	23	15	11	7
%	15.5	11.5	7.5	5.5	3.5

% of sample of 200

sive positions ("Pong," "Asteroids," "Galaxian") while women preferred games with more animation ("Ms. Pac Man," "Donkey Kong Jr."). The overwhelming favorite however (for both sexes) was "Pac Man," though few male respondents (1.5%) listed "Ms. Pac Man" in their top three choices.

Open-ended responses to the question "Why do you play video games?" generated interesting answers which seemed highly biased by age. While popular literature seems to indicate that adults are concerned about youths' wasting time, the answer "to waste time" was given 48% of the time by respondents over the age of 35. Only 2% of the respondents under 35 answered similarly, but younger respondents often used the terms "to fill time" or "to kill time" as an answer. The overwhelming answer from people under 18 was, "because it's fun."

Discussion

The major impact which age seemed to have on video game playing, was the preference for older players (especially those of age 40+) to concentrate on fewer games. Because older respondents did not generally acknowledge any computer skills, it may be possible to explain that they therefore found video game playing more challenging than relaxing. As Groos (1901) stated, game playing may teach people necessary skills for the future. Given the technological climate in our society, young people are more adaptable to using technology, and therefore, the skills they develop by playing video games will aid in their technological awareness and adaptability.

Though many leisure researchers have suggested that status, prestige, and occupation influence leisure activities (Clarke, 1956; Reissman, 1954; Havinghurst and Feigenbaum, 1959; Gerstl, 1961; Bishop and Iheda, 1970), the only possible "status" indicative of video game playing is computer literacy. A preference for entertainment in the home was not correlated with level of activity for respondents, therefore, there was no impetus to extract occupational status and/or prestige.

With regard to the second question posed, it appears that the popular writings and even the video game industry may be overreacting to the amount of money spent on video games. While younger players did in fact play more often, and a greater number of games, the amount of money was less than the popular press would lead one to believe. When comparing the amount of money spent on video games with the amount of game playing, it appears that, not only are young people acquiring certain skills which allow them to play longer, but that their investment of 25 cents may indeed last longer. Based on the amount of money spent, it is impossible to state that a positive relationship with other "addictive" behaviors (or compulsive gambling) is present, but if the study were replicated, it would be advisable to have a category of the length of time an individual spends playing games. If the popular press is correct, that there may be young "video all-stars," who may play all day on 25 cents, another dimension to the study would have to be included. However, if the amount of time playing games was significant, the finding would confirm the "skills" value of video game playing.

The data suggest that Stephenson's "Play Theory" (1967) has some credibility when discussing video games: however, traditional game playing theories seem to tip the scale in their favor. Though individuals do "rock the boat" to be in the forefront of change by playing games, the socialization element needs to be qualified. It appears that as a player becomes more comfortable with the technology and therefore demonstrates more skill, game playing becomes more "relaxing," and (as demonstrated by female respondents) the technology becomes a mere adjunct to the gaming situation. In this case, socialization into a technologically-comfortable stratum occurs.

It was expected that women would be found to play much less than men, given cultural patterns of male encouragement and expectation of play (Lieberman, 1977, p. 126), but this did not become apparent. However, the need for game playing and the types of games played by different sexes was discerned to show that there may indeed by a sex bias within games (e.g., women preferring to play Ms. Pac Man).

While self-report to the question "Why do you play video games" is in no way statistically correllated to the other data, it is interesting to see that adults (supposedly the group reported by the popular press to have the highest concern for their children's waste of time) say they waste time when playing. Perhaps individuals of different ages have different perceptions about what "wasting time" is, and possibly, age may redefine the perceived use of game playing.

CONCLUSION

Based on the findings of this study, it appears that video game playing does indeed teach necessary skills for survival in a technologically-based society, and that younger people are not as apprehensive as older persons are of the use of technology for traditional purposes. One question remains to be answered, and that is whether or not video game playing substitutes interface with machinery for interpersonal behavior. Given that respondents to this survey generally acknowledged that games were more "challenging" if they did not possess computer skills, it seems likely that greater experience with technology may relegate video games to more "relaxing" pastimes.

Similarly, the term "addiction" may be used too liberally, given the amount of play and the amount of money spent on games by younger respondents. The perceived use of video games may eventually do away with the stress young people feel when coaches, parents, etc., encourage them to compete interpersonally. With video game playing, there is no fear of friends' rejection or failure, and as computer skills become more prevalent, the technology may appear to be an adjunct to traditional interpersonal situations, not a replacement for them.

REFERENCES

"Battle for America's Youth." (1982). *New York Times* (Jan. 5), 2.

Bishop, D. W., and Iheda, M. (1970). "Status and Role Factors in the Leisure Behavior of Different Occupations." *Sociology and Social Research 54*, 190–208.

Clarke, A. C. (1956). "The Use of Leisure and its Relation to Levels of Occupational Prestige." *American Sociological Review 21*, 301–307.

"Electronic Games Help the Handicapped." (1982). *Science Digest* (April), 44.

"Electronic Games: Who Wins or Loses?" (1981). *New York Times* (Aug. 31), 16.

"Games Exercise Mental Abilities." (1982). *Play Meter* (Dec. 1), 44.

Gerstl, J. E. (1961). "Leisure, Taste and Occupational Milieu." *Social Problems 9*, 56–69.

Groos, K. (1901). *The Play of Man*. New York: Appleton.

Havinghurst, R., and Feigenbaum, K. (1959). "Leisure and Life Style." *American Journal of Sociology 64*, 347–353.

Huizinga, J. (1955). *Homo Ludens*. Boston, MA: Beacon.

Levy, J. (1978). *Play Behavior*. New York: John Wiley and Sons.

Lieberman, J. N. (1977). *Playfullness: Its Relationship to Imagination and Creativity*. New York: Academic Press.

Meyersohn, R. (1969). "The Sociology of Leisure in the United States: Introduction and Bibliography, 1945–1965." *Journal of Leisure Research 1*, 53–68.

Neulinger, J. and Breit, M. (1969). "Attitude Dimension of Leisure." *Journal of Leisure Research 1*, 255–26.

Reissman, L. (1954). "Class, Leisure, and Social Participation." *American Sociological Review 19*, 76–84.

Stephenson, W. (1967). *The Play Theory of Mass Communication*. Chicago, IL: University of Chicago Press.

"Town Zaps Video Games." (1981). *Christian Science Monitor*, Dec. 15, 17.

"TV Games Zapping Kids' Minds?" (1982). *New York Daily News* (Nov. 10), 28.

"Using Electronic Games to Challenge Kids." (1981). *Christian Science Monitor* (Dec. 15), 17.

"Video Games—Who's In Charge?" (1982), *Dial* (June), 6.

"Video Games May Aid Brain Injured." (1982). *Science News* (Sept. 12), 168.

"Video Games Train Army." (1982). *Science Digest* (July), 89.

"Wasting Time." (1982). *New York Times* (Jan. 24), 18.

PART III

ARTIFACTS

14

The Kung Fu Movie Genre: A Functionalist Perspective

DAVID J. GRAPER

University of Pennsylvania

Since the early 1970s there has been a seemingly endless string of foreign-produced, low-budget, martial arts movies or "Kung Fu" films appearing primarily in the more run-down theaters of many America cities. (The term "Kung Fu" film generally applies to martial-arts action films, mostly Chinese in origin, which hinge on extremely well-choreographed, elaborate fight scenes in which the actors/combatants employ a variety of oriental fighting skills.)

The Kung Fu film has generated little but derision from both critics of film and the public at large, who tend to see it as one of the more base manifestations of popular culture.

> Kung Fu films are poverty row cinema, generally critically despised and berated for what is seen as their sensationalistic concentration on violent action at the expense of such comfortable attributes as character development, nuance, and even narrative tension (Glaessner, 1974, p. 15)

However, given the apparent popularity of these films, mainly among individuals of the disenfranchised ethnic and economic groups of the cities, it seems that these films present us with a unique opportunity to examine a specific film genre in the context of a specific audience.

This paper discusses the findings of a study (Graper, 1982) investigating the possibility that Kung Fu movies, in the context of the lower-class audiences who watch them, serve to integrate this class into the larger American class structure through their characterizations and narratives. It examined the assumption that, through the structuring of the characters and narratives of the Kung Fu movie, a conceptual order is communicated to the lower-class audiences of these films that justifies both the existing social order and the audience member's position in that order.

A content analysis was conducted using 30 Kung Fu films viewed primarily in Philadelphia and New York City theaters specializing in Kung Fu movie exhibition. Audio-taping the films while viewing them proved to be the most efficient and least obtrusive method of recording the information presented in the movies, so each film was viewed once and taped during this viewing. The narrative material was then transcribed scene by scene, and each of the characters in the film coded.

The analysis was divided into two parts, the first dealing with the characters depicted in the movie narratives. Character sex, nationality, dominant occupation, class, and other data were coded in order to examine the demographic makeup of the symbolic Kung Fu world. The information on character goals, means, and success in obtaining goals was cross-tabulated with character roles (i.e., hero, villain, etc.) to see which goals were sought and which means employed by good and bad characters and how successful they were in achieving their respective goals.

Investigating the casting of characters in these films, it was found that the majority of characters were cast in roles whose class could not be discerned. Well over half of the populace of the symbolic Kung Fu world were either involved in gang-related organizations or were depicted as teachers, students, or practitioners of the martial arts. As might be expected, violence was the most frequent means employed by both heroes and villains in Kung Fu movies, but their goals differed significantly. For heroes, the primary goals were mostly other-oriented and interpersonal in nature (the most frequent goal being vengeance for the death of, or injury to, a loved one, followed by various goals attempting to honor or help other people). The villains' main goals, on the other hand, were usually of an economic or political nature and were *personal* rather than *social* (the villain almost always was shown seeking wealth or power, frequently at the expense of the common working people in the story).

The second part of the analysis, dealing with narratives, examined aggregates of narratives transcribed from the films in order to ascertain dominant themes and plot types. The methodology used was created by Vladimir Propp in his study of Russian folktales (Propp, 1929) and expanded upon by Will Wright in his structural analysis of American Westerns (Wright, 1975). The narrative transcriptions were distilled into lists of sequential constituent narrative elements (or what Propp called "functions"). Constituent elements were one-sentence statements about single actions or attributes of a character or characters which subsumed similar thematic elements appearing in many different narratives. Examples of such constituent elements would be "The hero comes to town," "The hero possesses a unique skill," or "The villain threatens a friend of the hero." The attributes and actions of characters described in such constituent elements outlined the basic recurring interactions of character types in stories, providing overviews of the general plot direction of groups of stories, without the extraneous elements peculiar to each individual narrative.

A list of constituent narrative elements outlining the plot of each film was created, and the lists for all the movies were compared. Similar lists were grouped together, and through repeated comparison, grouping, and collapsing of the lists of elements, two major types of Kung Fu movie narratives emerged: the first was labeled the "Struggle to Achieve" variation, while the second was termed the "Superman" variation.

In the first variation, the "Struggle to Achieve," the hero was depicted as helpless in the face of the villain but, after much time spent in training, as able to defeat him. In this category of Kung Fu movies, the most significant elements in the progression of the narrative dealt with the arduous process of acquiring a Kung Fu teacher, slowly learning the martial arts, and becoming a Kung Fu master. An example can be provided from one of the films studied, entitled *The Seven Grand Masters*. In this story, a young peasant boy spends the majority of the film following the Kung Fu teacher across China, begging to be taught the teacher's Kung Fu skills. Despite repeated rejection, he persists and is finally accepted by the teacher, who consequently subjects him to a long period of almost sadistic physical training. The hero never gives up in his struggle to be a Kung Fu master and, years later, acquires a fighting mastery superior even to that of his teacher. Having mastered the teacher's unique brand of Kung Fu, the hero seeks out his father's killer (a Kung Fu master in his own right) and challenges him to a duel of honor. Amidst repeated flashbacks to the years spent diligently practicing, the hero and the villain pair off in a highly stylized fight scene that ends in the villain's death.

In the second variation, the "Superman" variation, the hero is depicted as superpowerful from the start of the story and spends the entirety of the film working his way through a series of lesser battles with the villain's men to finally fight and defeat the villain himself. This variation concerns stories about an evil group (usually a criminal gang) and their activities and the appearance of a superpowerful hero who arrives on the scene to right their wrongs. The films of Bruce Lee are good instances of films belonging to this variation, an example being *Return of the Dragon*. In this film, the helpless owners and workers at a little Chinese restaurant, unable to deal with the harassments of the local mob by themselves, send for Bruce Lee to help them save their business. Lee individually fends off the bullies sent by the mob in a series of one-against-ten fistfights, and eventually duels with and defeats the mob's purportedly unbeatable hired killer. After smashing the gang, Lee accepts the people's thanks and, like the archetypal Western hero, walks off into the sunset.

The significance of these findings can be most usefully viewed not from the perspective of mass-mediated communications as directly "affecting" audience members, but rather within the context of how mediated messages serve to *avoid* change. As Gerbner maintains,

> the most profound effects of communication can be found not in making sales, getting votes, influencing opinions, and changing attitudes, but in the selective maintenance of relatively stable structures and policies that define the common perspectives of society (Gerbner, 1972, p. 158).

From this larger perspective, the ability to broadly and systematically *maintain* the desirability of certain goals and ways of thinking can be understood as being of great importance to those classes of individuals in a society with the most to gain from keeping things the way they are.

There is obviously a great incentive on the part of those in the upper, more favored classes to perpetuate what to them is a most advantageous system, and, assuming that the less favored, subordinate classes would not remain in their disadvantaged position with respect to the upper classes on their own accord, certain social mechanisms must be called into play to preserve the status quo.

The most blatant mechanisms of law enforcement (and maintenance of the social structure) are embodied in the naked force of the police and military. However, these agencies are only infrequently called upon to repress any large scale uprising of the lower classes, the vast majority of people situated in the lower classes being kept in their place by a much more subtle, yet more pervasive and powerful force. It is widely thought that this force is embodied (at least partly) in the myths propagated by the mass media.

It is here hypothesized that mass-mediated messages function to maintain the status quo in the class system by "integrating" the individuals of each class into society. By socially integrating individuals, it is meant that media messages provide a means by which individuals orient themselves to their place and role in the societal structure they live in. Wright (1975), in his analysis of American Western films, understood the integration of individuals into society through media messages as occurring generally across *all* classes. Given the broad-based appeal of the Western films he studied, this seems a reasonable set of conclusions. But while larger, broad-based message systems like Westerns can be seen as demonstrating and justifying the individual's role in the context of the general American economic and social system to all people, it seems reasonable to expect that smaller, more localized message systems used by narrower subgroups in a society address the problems in justifying the status of that target subgroup in the larger society. Therefore the research reported here was based on the premise that Kung Fu movies, popular with the lower class of American society, can be analyzed in terms of how they function to integrate their specific audience into society.

Given this framework, the analysis of characters in Kung Fu movies showed that problems in the Kung Fu movie world stem not from inequalities in the class system but rather from individuals belonging to criminal gangs, agencies existing outside the obvious class structure. It was hypothesized that through overemphasizing the responsibility of such groups for problems encountered in the world, attention is diverted away from the true class nature of the problems faced by the lower-class audience member. Also, by casting villains as pursuing economic and power goals while heroes seek interpersonal, non-economic and non-power goals, it seems that these films show the lower-class audience member that money and power are not worth desiring. Given that members of the lower class are barred from the wealth and power available to members of the upper classes, it would be socially integrative for them to embrace the belief that they do not want what they cannot have.

The two narrative variations uncovered in Kung Fu movies were seen as functional in maintaining the integration of members of the lower class into the class structure by portraying the individual's control over his environment as either unrealistically alterable or unrealistically unalterable. The first variation, showing the hero's successful herculean efforts to obtain the training he needs for vengeance, subtly argues that one can successfully change one's lot in life if one is only willing to work hard enough for it. Since achievement is open to all who have the will to struggle for it, the credit or blame for a person's life situation is placed on the person himself rather than the economic class he was born into. The blame for any individual's problems, it argues, rests only with the individual himself, and hence the problems of the lower-class audience member cannot be blamed on his inferior position in an unfair class system but rather on his own unwillingness to change his lot in life. This variation portrays the individual as having a control over his environment that the lower-class audience member probably does not have.

The second variation, portraying the hero as a superpowerful character, presents the lower-class audience member with an opposing message: rather than affirming that problems can be solved if one is willing to work hard enough, this variation asserts that such problems *are* insurmountable for the common man and can only be solved by some superpowerful outside agent or agency. As symbolized in the threat of the insuperable gang or invincible hired killer, only the superpowerful hero can hope to deal with power on such a grand scale. Likewise, successfully battling the problems in a society (purportedly caused by evil individuals as opposed to inequalities in the class structure) is no job for common men; the task is too great for anyone besides the super-powerful. Collective action is fruitless, this message contends, so the common man must be resigned to letting more powerful agents or agencies solve his problems for him.

The two variations of the Kung Fu movie, therefore, provide two different orientations for the lower-class audience member to adopt in understanding his position in society. Both orientations function to keep this audience member in his socially-defined position and help to maintain the existing social class structure. The movies tell him to either "put up or shut up": either (1) recognize your powerless state in society and accept it, hoping that someone more powerful will take care of things, or (2) recognize your inferior state in society as your own fault, and either work hard to improve yourself or remain silent. Both explanations circumvent the class nature of the problems of the socially disenfranchised, and may perpetuate the apathy of individuals in this class through their contrasting assessments of the individual's power over his environment.

In sum, the Kung Fu movie world, with its selective characterizations, narrative emphasis on individual effort and achievement, and de-emphasis on the utility of group activities and solutions, can be understood as functioning to maintain the existing class structure by helping to distract the lower-class audience member from perceiving the social nature of his problems, and at the same time imbuing him with beliefs that serve to keep him satisfied (or at least apathetic) about his inferior position in the class structure.

REFERENCES

Gerbner, G. (1972). Communication and the Social Environment. *Scientific American* (Sept.), 153–160.

Glaessner, V. (1974). *Kung Fu: Cinema of Vengeance*. Loudoni Lorrimer.

Graper, D. J. (1982). "An Analysis of the Character Portrayals and Narrative Structures Presented in Kung Fu Movies: A Functionalist Perspective." Master's thesis, University of Pennsylvania.

Propp, V. (1929). *Morphology of the Folktale*, 2d ed. Austin, TX: University of Texas Press.

Wright, W. (1975). *Six-Guns and Society*. Berkeley, CA: University of California Press.

15

The Body and Femininity in Feminine Hygiene Advertising

BERKELEY KAITE
Carleton University, Ottawa

This paper analyzes the emergence and growth of the feminine hygiene market with an emphasis on the relationship between the nature of this market and women's participation in the labor force (see Kaite, 1981). In 1921, following women's involvement in World War I, the first feminine hygiene product, sanitary napkins, was developed. Tampons were introduced prior to women's participation in industries and occupations related to the Second World War. And feminine deodorant sprays, or vaginal deodorants, appeared in 1966 when women were responding to the occupational demands of the growth of the multinational corporation. This correspondence between the emergence of specific products and the participation of women in wage labor suggests a relationship between these two phenomena. The appearance of women in the labor force generates a specific type of consumer, a wage-worker consumer: one who, in an increasingly alienated work place, interacts more often with machines than with people, and, in the face of skills erosion, must confront managerial discipline that is sexist in content and demands the presentation of a "cosmetic self" as a way of ensuring success on the job. Social control of women, seen in this instance with the exercise of discipline and control in the work place, is realized through its internalization by those upon whom it is executed, such that socially ordered compulsions of behavior become automatic on the part of the individual. The consumption of feminine hygiene products represents one example of the sexual control of women, one that denies the female but exalts the socialization of the biological, that which is feminine. Their use also relies on the self-control of women: such "secret" products allow for women to be the final arbiters of their own self-discipline. This is suggested both in marketing techniques and imagery in advertisements for those products.

Advertising is one way of symbolically organizing society. It mediates between production and consumption. We consume the meaning of an ad, the purpose of which, economically speaking, is that we shall consume properly. A semiological analysis of advertisements for feminine hygiene products demonstrates that the "problem that women bleed" has remained constant but has assumed varying forms. The phenomenon has shifted from one wherein it was

perceived as a barrier to total health and hygiene to a problem for the construction and maintenance of an ever-elusive feminity: to be female is to bleed; to be
feminine is to be without blemish, without blood. The task for women is that of
regulating their bodies and related social conceptions. That certain products
are useful is not denied; the decoding of ads, however, lends access to speculation about why women consume redundant products and how, ideologically,
they come to understand and organize their work force experiences. The
mythicizing effects of advertising involve the construction of the subject in
terms of a reconciliation of what she knows and how she acts in a social totality.
The gender relations of dominance require that women appropriate what it
means to be a woman, to be feminine.

This study considers six decades of advertisements for feminine hygiene
products. Nineteen twenty-one was chosen as the year of departure as it was
during that year that the first product, sanitary napkins, was introduced. The
advertising of specific commodities is obviously directed at an identifiable population; therefore, ads for feminine hygiene products were, and are, to be
found in women's magazines or magazines with a female readership. *Good
Housekeeping* and *Ladies Home Journal*, in the 1920s, 1930s and 1940s, were
the most accessible and clearly popular women's magazines. They represented
a good barometer of changes in women's status. As Friedan has written of a
popular women's magazine, "Its contents are a fairly accurate representation of
the image of the American woman presented, and in part created, by the large-
circulation magazines" (1974, p. 29). In the last three decades, however, there
has been a greater selection of women's magazines. Again the selection represents magazines directed at women, or mirror the changing roles women play.
Advertisements from the last decade were chosen from *Chatelaine, Cosmopoli-
tan, Vogue, Self, People, Ms., Homemakers Magazine, Glamour*, and one from
The New York Times (the latter to secure an ad for Rely Tampons before they
were taken off the market). Not all issues of the early magazines were available;
years were chosen based on their proximity to the times when women's involvement in wage work was prominent and the introduction of products (subject to availability), e.g., 1921, 1936, 1939, 1966. For every decade and year of
study every ad in the magazine was analyzed. In the 1920s to 1950s there was
often only one ad per issue, sometimes none. This has changed in the last two
decades. Lately, issues carry as many as 8 ads for feminine hygiene products. In
all, 16 ads from the 1920s, 16 from the 1920s, 19 from the 1940s, 11 from the
1950s, 26 from the 1960s and 42 from the 1970s (a total of 130 advertisements)
were examined.[1]

---

[1]It is interesting to note that, although ads for feminine hygiene products were proliferating by
the 1940s, *Vogue* magazine did not carry any. As this magazine is devoted solely to fashion and
hence women who have some disposable income with which to cultivate a rather expensive sense of
fashion consciousness, the lack of ads supports my claim that feminine hygiene products are designed not for the trendy, but for women who have a definite role in the social work world.

1920s

Advertisements for feminine hygiene products of this decade contain much product information based on the products' physical characteristics and utility. The products, sanitary napkins, and powder napkin deodorants, are part of the "sanitary protection" market. They are designed to aid women with their hygienic and health handicap. The women represented in the ads are other-directed and advised to guard against embarrassment, worry, fear, and self-consciousness. They must, most importantly, not offend their husbands either through bodily odors or during the menstrual cycle. Although the ads reveal factual information about specific products, what they are actually *for* is not mentioned.

Certain euphemisms are used and have relevance for the social construction of the problem "that women bleed." Menstruation in the 1920s was heralded as "women's most distressing hygienic problem" and a "delicate subject." Sanitary napkins were advertised for use for "health's sake and immaculacy," to give women "peace of mind," "freedom from those important fears" and to "end all fear of offending" for "at certain times (women) are seriously offensive to others." The "correct appearance" for women is also used euphemistically and carries a double message. The term implies a notion of "correct" equaling hygienic: a central notion as ads work via the exchange of equivalents. "Incorrect" also refers to the natural order of women's bodily functions before the invention of sanitary napkins. Thus, the identification of the problem of being female and the creation of its attendant needs and anxieties is based on the appearance of a specific product. "Appearance" is related to how one looks, one's social presence. Women "appeared," prior to the introduction of sanitary napkins, in factory and munitions work; "correct appearance" may thus refer to a code of hygiene appropriate to the relievement of that work.

1930s

Products in the 1930s are advertised as offering "protection." Menstruation has moved from the problem of comfort and hygiene to one of protecting oneself from inadvertent signs of blood. But, as the women are often depicted with friends, the message seems to be that they must also guard against others knowing when they are bleeding. Thus, they must protect others from their femaleness.

Tampax (perhaps the "x" was intended to connote scientificity) was introduced in 1936. It is heralded as having been invented by a doctor (female) and is the "civilized" answer to sanitary protection. As Elias points out, civility is equated with restraint of the body and the regulation of individual, social behavior (1978). Thus internal protection, with Tampax, allows the user to exercise restraint over her own self.

One noticeable departure on the ads of this decade involves the portrayal of the subjects. They appear to be young and single, often alone or with friends, but not part of a social network. They are not depicted in social gatherings. They are more stylized and are modeling themselves, not a situation. Images of women are delineated into different aspects of the same self. Different person- alities of the same person are presented. Thus, one Kotex ad depicts three pic- tures of a woman engaged in three different activities: she is carefree (skipping), adventuresome (piloting a plane), and glamorous (modeling a long gown). There is a double message contained within ads of this type. Kotex developed three kinds of sanitary napkins to satisfy the needs of different women and vary- ing days of the menstrual cycle. Hence, the separate images of the individual woman or three assorted women on the same page. But what this ad also dem- onstrates is the emergent individualism in women contained within the dis- crete personalities. The ethos of individualism says that we can choose what- ever personality we want to be: the sport, the worker, the glamour "girl." One Kotex ad claims "There is no average woman . . . every woman is a law unto herself." We are appellated as part of a group but as individuals within that group. Our bodies are the same (as are their functions), but the construction of femininity is ostensibly of our individual design. The "laws" of femininity are, however, socially ordered and involve a denial of all that is essentially female. Women are enlisted in participating in that denial by choosing which "woman" they want to be. The choice is limited however to three different kinds of Kotex (regular, junior, or super) just as there are social limits on what we might choose and still remain feminine.

1940s

In this decade the ads move away from imparting information about the practi- cal utility of menstrual products to imputing their psychological utility. Thus ads rely on images and less information than was formerly the case. Hence the voice of the ads is stronger, more assertive ("This tampon was really your idea"), imploring women to buy appropriately and consume the correct images. The images are ones which equate comfort with lightness, softness, and confidence. The possibility of being burdened with menstruation and carefree at the same time is mentioned for the first time in a Kotex ad in this decade. The acquisition of carefreeness is promised upon purchase of the product.

Women are depicted with men for the first time. They are instructed to be "in the know" about Kotex (and in fact are portrayed as lacking of pertinent knowledge as they are often guilty of not possessing the rules of social behav- ior), and this knowledge is aligned with appropriate rituals of social etiquette. These ads contain suggestions about behavior designed to usher in conceptions of the modern woman. Mothers and daughters are represented together sharing knowledge about "life as women." Goffman (1976) notes that women tend to be pictured more often (than men) akin to their daughters (and them- selves in their younger years), implying that there is a cycle of femininity and that it is learned; information is passed on from mother to daughter and femininity is worked at, modified and perfected. One aspect of incipient femininity involves escaping from the private life of physical blemish (bleeding) so that it doesn't interfere with the social life which contains the secrets of femininity. A Kotex ad reminds us that women have "secrets" but also "secret longings" to deny their femaleness and escape from womanhood. The "safety shield" in Kotex presumably provides a place away from the dangers of being a woman. It is our responsibility to protect others from that impending danger and thus Tampax is useful as "sharp eyes cannot tell" when it is in use.

Along with the scientific-sounding names of Meds and Tampax there are "scientific" illustrations of the internal workings of tampons. These illustrations correspond with the scientific nature of the waged work the women in the ads are involved in: two are technicians or mechanics and one is an ambulance nurse. These depictions reflect the nature of women's work during the war and the need for convenient menstrual products which are easily disposed of and which offer "invisible protection." But although everything is revealed in the illustrations nothing is explained, except with such phrases as "safety center" and "300% of their weight in moisture."

1950s

Although women were active in wage work during the 1950s, oppression was embedded in the "problem that had no name," the loss of an identity for women (Friedan, 1974). If it was women's burden in the 1940s to engage in supporting the war effort, in the following decade their burden was to be beautiful. This burden involved an obsessive concern with the self, an innerdirectedness which, by Friedan's estimation, was unsuccessful. That concern typified the anxiety surrounding what it was to be a woman. The attempt at identifying the sources of women's discontent was undertaken by many and corresponded ideologically to the complacency of the decade. Women could afford to concentrate on their femininity; that was to be their main occupation.

Women's sphere in the 1950s, although not solely domestic, pointed to a delineation of private concerns, related, as reflected in the ads of the decade, to an exaltation of femininity. The *Modess . . . because* ad was first introduced in 1949 and that year won the best national ad of the year award in the United States (Delaney et al., 1976, p. 111). The ad claims that Modess contains a "new design," perhaps signifying a "new design" for femininity. This new design points to the domination of nature, the improvement upon nature, which is bad, and the resultant conception of the natural, which is desired and good. The ad is ingenious as it relies totally on the shared understanding between the producer of the ad and the consumer. No information is released in our reading of the ad, but the knowledge is there: simply, *Modess . . . because*.

The first mention of fashion and its equation with feminine hygiene occurs in the 1950s. Many of the women in the ads of this decade are struck in esthetic, ethereal poses, looking much like figurines in fantasy settings and fantastic clothing. They are inactive and appear ineffectual; sanitary napkins offer "ease" and bring "an entirely new experience in lasting comfort." Similarly, a woman's "monthly time" need not interfere with "theatres, dances, club meetings": with Tampax she may appear "fresh, poised and at ease" at all times. Secrets are mentioned ("what is her secret?") but the taboo is resurrected and women are advised not to discuss the secret, but just try Tampax for themselves. This implies not only the equation of freshness with femininity but also that femininity is something ethereal, changing, not easily imparted with words: its substance is not known but felt. This also corresponds to the tenet of individualism; it is each woman's responsibility to shape her femininity according to her own mood, desires or inclination. However, this is done within a particular standard. For example, another Tampax ad claims:

> You're always the fair lady. it isn't just the way you dress, the way you wear your hair, the way you talk . . . and listen. There's a special *look* about you, a look of confidence, a kind of serenity that people sense . . . and like. It's always yours, wherever you go, whatever you do. Even on those few days each month, it never leaves you—because you rely on Tampax.

With Tampax the essence of femininity receives its fullest expression as something internal, undetected, but sensed.

1960s

The introduction of vaginal deodorant sprays in 1966 gave new meaning to the concept of natural feminine freshness: with their use, women could be fresh all day, every day. The problem of "intimate feminine" odors is now seen as affecting all women, not just married women, and is a new area of domination. This signifies control of the body, not just its emittance, and thus control is extended from a few days of the month to all month. Demure is advertised as a necessity for women "whose days are filled with people and places and things to be done." As women made in-roads into the work force in the 1960s, the challenge of the control of this new "body" of workers became apparent. Control is exercised in the form of discipline which demands that workers focus on the presentation of self. However, most women workers interact not with people but machines. The emergence of the cosmetic self satisfies the demand for socially pleasing female workers, but what we really have is workers engaged in a form of anonymous intimacy; personally grooming themselves (in this case in intimate detail) for a world in which they, as individuals, are highly replaceable or anonymous. These products promote the idea of anonymous intimacy for the social woman in the social office. As well, hygiene in the office is perceived as a problem for the people women work with, thus the need for a new kind of sanitary protection effective everyday. A regimented labor process also requires convenient forms of internalized discipline. Vaginal deodorant sprays are more convenient and quicker to use than vaginal suppositories, perhaps one reason why suppositories are designed and advertised for "marriage problems," while sprays are for women whose days are filled with people, places, and things to be done. FDS saw the need for the total sanitation of women, for "total freshness," and asserted that "feminine hygiene sprays" would "become as essential to you as your toothbrush."

The "Modess . . . because" ads were still appearing in the early part of the decade, as were ads for Fems "feminine napkins" ("So soft you forget them. So safe that you can."). But towards the end of the 1960s ads began to equate menstrual products with feelings of courage and freedom. The notion of courage implies a sense of self-motivation which is really social control displaced onto the subject. Similarly, freedom is an attribute acquired by willing subjects. The subjects in the ads, however, are all wearing white and thus the implication is that they have the freedom to control their bodily functions in the correct way: white equals the absence of blood.

1971–1981

From the 1920s through the 1960s, the euphemistic signifier for menstrual paraphernalia was "sanitary protection." In the 1960s and early 1970s the term shifted to plain "protection"; by the late 1970s the signifier became "feminine protection." The "problem that women bleed" has thus moved from menstruation as a health or hygiene problem to the problem of the nature of femininity itself. Feminine hygiene products were once advertised to protect a woman's sanitary state; they are now advertised to protect the state of femininity. Femininity is socially constructed as are conceptions of the body and its processes.

Femininity in our culture is acquired. It involves (among other things) manipulating the body to achieve a streamlined, deodorized "freshness." "Freshness" is perceived as being natural; it is only one side of nature, the cultural side. Culturalized freshness denies the other side of nature, its potential to destroy, decay, rot. Nature is held up as eternal, unchanging, and good; thus the (culturalized) natural is also. Thus the domination of nature reaches a natural status.

The development of a new line of feminine hygiene products—panti shields or panti liners—represents the natural domination of the body that is total, i.e., it encompasses every day of the month. Perhaps their creation was in response to the demise of vaginal deodorant sprays. The need still existed for constant regulation of the female body, but with the removal of products like FDS from the market, new products were offered to answer the need. Hence, panti shields "for a whole month of little problems." Panti shields are presented as another product of women's fashion essentials and as necessary to "total freshness." Frequently the models are shown standing in front of the backdrop of a calendar, the same woman in three different sets of clothing. The calendar signifies the days of the month one should use panti shields (every day) and the resultant freshness (newness) imparted by the product. This freshness is evident from the model's clothing and the fact that she dresses differently every day. Indeed, Carefree Panty Shields are advertised for the "fresh-dressed woman every day." The phrase "fresh-dressed" is hyphenated, drawing the words and concepts together: freshness-dress-fashion. Some ads assert that "freshness" is the same as "just showered" and panti shields are for that "just showered freshness anytime." Again, what is really natural is replaced by the cultural version: the antiseptic body. For example, one ad shows a fully made-up woman, post-shower, representing the naturalization of the cultural. Ads for deodorant panti shields describe the scent as "fresh," obscuring the fact that anything fabricated is not natural or fresh. But to be fresh is to be feminine: "you enjoy feeling fresh and feminine."

The euphemisms in the 1970s connote images of the female body as a carrier of alien substances and danger. This notion fits under the rubric of the general euphemism "feminine protection." Women, it is clear, must protect their femininity from their femaleness: the domination of nature becomes natural. Tampons and sanitary napkins "pull moisture in," "trap it deep," "hold it," "lock it in," "repel moisture," "direct the flow," "block the flow," "prevent leakage or bypass." These are all things done to enemies, aliens, things dangerous. Prior to the 1960s, women were admonished against offending others and had to protect others from them. Bodily sanitation had to be assured. The advertisements of the last two decades display the notion that femininity must be protected. Thus the progression has been from control by others to self-control. This self-control is an internalization of female oppression which is often subtle but forceful as the text indicates. The very name "shield" connotes violent imagery.

SUMMARY

Menstruation has been socially constructed as a problem. Although "menstruation" and "period" are mentioned in ads of the last decade, the essential signifier, blood, is conspicuously absent. Blood is euphemistically referred to in a number of ways: maxi days, heavy days, fluid, moisture, accident, discharge, and spotting or staining. Thus menstruation is a problem of many names.

The problem that women bleed has remained constant throughout the decades under study but is expressed in varying forms. With the public identification of menstruation as an area of investigation, through the marketing of sanitary napkins, women's menstrual process was endowed with mystery, fear, shame, and embarrassment. This is related, of course, to the morality of the time: these things were not talked about openly. Advertising revealed the problem but what is left out of the ads is just as important as what they contain. Hidden in the ads is the notion that menstruation is a health handicap. The referent in ads of the 1920s, 1930s, and 1940s concerns controlling women's physicalness, ensuring physical comfort, regulating the body itself and denying essential femaleness. The denial of what is female has remained to the present. But beginning with the 1950s, the emphasis in advertising is on the psychological comfort imparted through the products, not just denying femaleness but dominating it and creating the natural order of femininity. Williamson (1978, p. 103) notes that nature is the primary referent of culture, the raw material of our environment. "If a culture is to refer to itself, therefore, it can only do so by the representation of its transformation of nature—it has meaning in terms of what it has changed." Like frozen orange juice, feminine hygiene products improve on nature. The "natural" is justification for whatever society approves of. Thus, the "problem" moved from one of strictly hygiene to one of protecting femininity. Femininity is socially constructed, however, and involves the cultivation of the body so that it is without blemish, without stain. Blood stains, and thus presents a blemish on the face of femininity.

Williamson (1978, p. 124) states that "the importance of 'the natural' increases directly in proportion as society's distance from *nature* is increased, through technological development." Berger constructs a similar argument with respect to the removal of animals from their natural status, with "the disappearance of animals from daily life" and their incarceration in zoos (Berger, 1980, p. 19). Like the isolation of animals and their consequent imprisonment and observation, aspects of femininity are isolated as culture dominates nature. Like animals behind bars, what we have, in a sense, is femininity in captivity. With the lessening of control over women's biological functions and sexuality, men have redefined aspects of women's sexualness. Integral to that sexualness is the capturing and regulation of modes of femininity. In this sense, fashion is used as a form of social control. The recent development of a cosmetic line for men offers products which enhance masculinity; female cosmetics (and feminine hygiene products) are essential to femininity.

What the foregoing tells us about the oppression of women is that it is structural and ideological in its complexity. It can be identified, however, that the control of women by others, and hence the concern with offending others, has been internalized and emerges as self-motivation and self-assurance on the part of the subject. It is also apparent that the social control of women has roots in biology, but, as radical feminists overlook, the socialization of the biological as well. The media reflects and reinforces the gender relations of domination: the notion that women's bodies are fearful and evil is asserted aggressively. It is safe to assume that if the body is considered loathful then the person is too.

REFERENCES

Berger, J. (1980). *About Looking*. New York: Pantheon.
Delaney, J., Lupton, M. J., and Toth, E. (1976). *The Curse*. New York: E. P. Dutton.
Elias, N. (1978). *The Civilizing Process: The History of Manners*. New York: Urizen Books.
Friedan, B. (1974). *The Feminine Mystique*. New York: Dell Books.
Goffman, E. (1976). *Gender Advertisements*. New York: Harper and Row.
Kaite, B. (1981). "The Intimacy of Commodities: Social Control, Subjectivity and Feminine Hygiene." Unpublished M.A. thesis, McMaster University.
Weiner, L. (1974). "The Housewife's Hymnal: A Case Study of the Ladies' Home Journal." Paper presented at the Second Annual Berkshire Conference on the History of Women, Radcliffe College.
Williamson, J. (1978). *Decoding Advertisements: Ideology and Meaning in Advertising*. London: Marion Boyars.

16

"And Next Week—Child Abuse!" Family Issues in Contemporary Made-for-TV Movies

ELLA G. TAYLOR
University of Washington, Seattle

ANDREA S. WALSH
Clark University

While real-life American families in the 1950s experienced infidelity, abuse, and divorce, Lucy agonized over whether Ricky would let her sing in his band, and Bud Anderson lost sleep over not telling Dad he'd lied at school. Despite the popularity of the anguish-ridden daytime soaps, social-problem drama was not considered desirable prime-time fare—by studios and most audiences alike. By the 1970s, however, the tide had turned. Any weeknight could bring 96 wrenching minutes of mental illness, drug abuse, problem pregnancy, anorexia nervosa, family violence, or rape (punctuated by commercials, of course) into America's living rooms. The social problem TV-movie had arrived. And from both audience and studio reactions, it looked like it was here to stay. This paper explores the thematic evolution of the social problem made-for-TV movie, from the 1970s to early 1980s, through the interpretation of several prototypical films.

Our theoretical approach to this study conceptualizes popular culture as a historical dynamic between audiences and producers. The creation and reception of TV movies, for example, constitute an interactive process, embodying the power relations and cultural conflicts of the larger society. Media creations succeed and fail not simply due to the manipulations of industry moguls, but also because of the ways in which they relate to the daily lives, social experience, and fantasy needs of audiences. Cultural analysis taps into the dream life—conscious and unconscious—of viewers. Taken together with other tools of social history (demography, oral history, artifact reconstruction), the analysis of popular culture is invaluable in interpreting a particular era. For the 1970s and 1980s, the evolution of common themes and narrative structures in made-for-TV social problem dramas provides a window on the culture and consciousness of individuals and families in America.

We have analyzed over 40 contemporary TV social-problem dramas, exploring the history of the genre, its defining characteristics, and its development in the light of changes in public perceptions of social issues over the last decade.

Television movies have been gathering momentum on prime-time schedules since the late 1960s, when stocks of old theater films began to dwindle. To the networks, plagued by soaring production costs and fearful of the growing competition from pay- and cable-TV, producing their own movies has proved a profitable alternative to episodic series, since by comparison they could be made quickly and cheaply. Major stars, too, are attracted by the short-term commitment that brings them top exposure without the grueling routines of the weekly series.

The emphasis on topical social problems in early TV movies came partly as a response to the increased receptivity of audiences, soured on consensus politics by Vietnam and Watergate, to a more critical spirit in television programming. These viewers, young, urban, and affluent, increasingly became the target of new ratings strategies (known in the industry as "demographics"), which sought to attract the highest advertising revenues. In this way, network programmers miraculously lost some of their traditional antipathy to social relevance and controversy. Within the 18 to 34 age group, women in particular are singled out as prime consumers, and this, together with growing acceptance of the feminist movement, gives women's issues top priority in TV movies.

The classic social-problem TV movie dramatizes a well-known, often controversial issue, usually in a family setting. More often than not, the protagonist is white, female, middle class (and less than middle-aged). The "issue of the evening" is one raised to public prominence by the feminist movement (e.g., violence against women, reproductive rights, the "empty nest" syndrome). The narrative (somewhat similar to that of classic 1930s and 1940s Hollywood "women's films") centers on a choice the heroine must make or a transition to which she must adapt.

These films, however, differ from the classic women's films of the studio era in that psychological issues are often presented against a sociological backdrop. In *Born Innocent* (1974) Linda Blair is cast as a teen runaway who, having committed no other "crime" than that of fleeing an abusive and alcoholic family, learns to be cynical and street-wise through the brutality of the institution in which she is forced to live. Victim Elizabeth Montgomery in *A Case of Rape* (1974) encounters a criminal justice system that humiliates and victimizes her. In *Kentucky Woman* (1983), Cheryl Ladd breaks the sexual barrier to become a miner, only to experience ridicule and sexual harassment at work and ostracism in her church. These films seek consciously to educate as well as entertain, and sometimes dramatize their issue by choosing an unsettling or tragic ending. *Mary Jane Harper Cried Last Night* (1977) is a prime example of the classic TV social-problem movie.

THE CLASSIC SOCIAL PROBLEM TV MOVIE:
Mary Jane Harper Cried Last Night (1977)

Child abuse moves into prime time in *Mary Jane Harper Cried Last Night,* a powerful evocation of suburban family violence. Pampered young divorcée Rowena Harper (Susan Dey) cannot cope with living and parenting alone. Early scenes capture Rowena's loneliness and frustration (at her ex-husband and at the world) as she lashes out at the most immediate and powerless target, her frightened four-year old daughter, Mary Jane. The camera counterposes the middle-class orderliness of Rowena's living room with the escalating violence within.

This film consciously seeks to correct popular stereotypes of family violence. Rowena is not a demon, merely a confused, frightened, and psychologically damaged young woman. The setting isn't Harlem or Watts; it could well be Great Neck or Short Hills. Like its late 1970s companion pieces, *Battered* and *Violent Strangers* (both 1978), *Mary Jane Harper* depicts family violence as a phenomenon crossing class and racial lines.

A dramatized sociology of child abuse, this film delivers appropriate insights before each commercial. When a terrified and guilty Rowena brings her bruised daughter to a hospital, she is met by Dr. Angie Bucchieri (Tricia O'Neil), a female Quincy of working class-Italian background. Bucchieri is no "bleeding heart," however. She's *been* there—as a former abused child in an urban slum. Risking her job, Angie involves Dave Williams (Bernie Casey) a dedicated young black social worker, with the Harper case. Williams, however, seems more frustrated by the "system" than Bucchieri: "We need more hotlines, more supportive services." And as a well-trained therapist he knows that "children who abuse become abusing parents."

Rowena is defensive and guarded around Williams, however, seeking solace instead in her wealthy, protective, and seductive father (Kevin McCarthy), a respected community businessman who assures her that her problems are minor. After all, "his girl" can do no wrong.

The situation worsens, however, as abuse turns to neglect and the disaster much feared by the audience occurs. Seeking help for herself, Rowena leaves Mary Jane alone in the house while a lighted cigarette catches fire on a blowing curtain. With the neighbors' aid, the child is rescued, and a shocked Rowena returns to face arrest and prosecution.

The crusading advocacy of the Bucchieri-Williams team is no match in court, however, for her father's wealth and influence. With a little help from his lawyer friend, Rowena regains custody, on the condition that she seeks psychological help. Here, too, Daddy provides and the circle closes upon the fragile young mother. Rowena's therapist, too, purchased by her father, is clearly within his circle of influence. In an especially poignant scene, a weeping Rowena tells the therapist of her father's seductive touch, her subsequent shame, and her mother's emotional abandonment of her. However, as Rowena Harper begins to explore the roots of her rage, the therapist, unable to believe her portrayal of her well-respected father, ignores her and terminates the session. "Just another crazy female" reads the look on his face.

As Rowena grows more desperate and enraged, the pace of the film quickens to that of a mystery or crime drama. Terrified by her own potential for violence, the young mother contacts the local Parents Anonymous chapter. However, their "up-front" attitude is more than Rowena can handle. As the level of violence in the Harper home escalates, viewers may wonder if the child, now mute with fear, will survive her mother's next outburst.

In the final scene, Rowena becomes increasingly enraged at Mary Jane's accusing silence and terrified of herself. She throws her daughter impulsively into the car and heads up the highway with no clear destination. In a lucid moment, she phones Parents Anonymous from a motel room but hangs up in hysteria without telling them her location. The film cuts between a traced phone call, a police car chase, and the gathering tension in the highway motel. Will Rowena be able to control her rage? Will the cops arrive in time to save Mary Jane? *Mary Jane Harper Cried Last Night*, unlike most TV movies of its genre, ends tragically. The police arrive to find a delusional Rowena rocking her dead daughter.

This film, despite its sociological formula, is a powerful depiction of family violence and the stigma of incest. And lacking the "truth conquers all" ending of such "relevant" series as *Quincy*, the audience confronts a world in which the caring compassion of self-help groups and the crusading advocacy of proletarian professionals are no match for the ineptitude of the courts, the power of wealth and the trauma of incest.

As the late 1970s became the 1980s, the classic social problem drama declined and a more psychological narrative emerged. *Memories Never Die* and *Another Woman's Child* (both 1983) illustrate this emergent sub-genre: the "family redemption movie."

THE "FAMILY REDEMPTION" MOVIE:
Memories Never Die; Another Woman's Child (1983)

Memories Never Die tells the story of Joanne (Lindsay Wagner), a woman returning to her husband and family after a suicide attempt and a six-year battle with depression in a mental hospital. In her absence, her husband Howdy has installed a governess/housekeeper, Louise, a "Mrs. Danvers" martinet whose Victorian views on child-rearing ("We have no secrets in this house") create a constant source of friction with the more liberal Joanne. Louise also harbors a secret passion for Howdy of which he is unaware. Hospitalized after a coronary attack, Howdy calls on his wife to return and reunite the family. Joanne, ambivalent and apprehensive, but nonetheless determined to try, finds her path strewn with difficulties. Her own past (as the daughter of a mother who "thought that children were like porcelain dolls") and her prolonged seclusion in the mental hospital are further complicated by persistent intimations of an unknown but menacing Event connected with her suicide attempt. The film, while firmly grounded in realism, also nods in the direction of the mystery genre, compounding the fearsome quality of mental disturbance.

The major obstacles, however, come from within the family itself. Joanne becomes the focus of a barrage of hostilities—from her daughter Kathy, whose anger at her abandonment has festered through the years, nourished both by Louise and by Howdy's manipulative (and childless) sister Rita. Howdy has been unfaithful to Joanne in years past, and she is "not sure I will have the courage to trust you again," but he affirms his love and is willing to be patient. Sustained by his faith and the acceptance of her small son Sean, but most of all by the continued support and therapeutic insight of her doctors Joanne gathers strength and, exasperated at the constant attempts to victimize her, angrily confronts Louise and Rita. "*I* don't get myself worked up . . . *you* get me worked up! What I feel is honest-to-God anger, a perfectly normal emotion!" The encounter precipitates a crisis in which Joanne finds herself reliving the mysterious event, her attempt to kill herself and her two children years before. Howdy succumbs to another heart attack on the scene, and Joanne saves his life with some on-the-spot medical attention. "Getting things out in the open" proves cathartic for all concerned, and the family draws closer together, beginning anew with mutual assurances of love and commitment.

In *Another Woman's Child*, Terry (Linda Lavin) struggles to accept her husband's illegitimate 12-year old daughter from a brief affair he had with a woman who has now died. Her loss unresolved, the child has quickly transferred her affections to Michael, Terry's husband, but she steadfastly rejects Tery's tentative overtures. Terry herself is ambivalent and defensive, hampered by her own anger at Michael's infidelity and the arrival of someone else's child when she herself was unable to conceive.

After a turbulent period of silent hostilities punctuated with bursts of open aggression, Terry opens herself to the support and psychological insight of a close friend, who happens, conveniently, to be a therapist. Sending husband and housekeeper away, she closets herself at home with the child. They spend a long night locked in emotional combat. Then the girl abandons her defenses and gives way to grief at the loss of Mother while Terry keeps vigil outside her bedroom door. Michael returns home to find them lying in each other's arms on the bed, exhausted. "What happened?" he asks, amazed at the change. Terry smiles serenely up at him. "We're working it out."

The family has always been a central metaphor in television entertainment. At the same time, the character of family imagery in TV has shown itself sensitive to the sharp and varied changes experienced by many American families since the Second World War. Unlike the wacky bliss of TV families in the 1950s and 1960s, ("Leave It To Beaver," "I Love Lucy," "The Dick Van Dyke Show"), the episodic series of the 1970s began to echo the signs of real family crisis suggested in the sociological and clinical literature of the decade. Shows with domestic settings ("Maude," "One Day at a Time") rarely featured "intact" families according to the stereotype of the nuclear family. Enduring primary relationships of the warm, solidary kind associated with family bonds appeared almost exclusively in the "workplace families" of shows like "The Mary Tyler Moore Show," "Taxi," "Barney Miller" and "Lou Grant," continuing today in series like "Hill Street Blues" and "Cheers."

The "family redemption movies" of the early 1980s rework themes of domestic difficulty. Like many others, *Memories Never Die* and *Another Woman's Child* deal with families that fall apart, come together again, or constitute themselves anew. Like many contemporary families, they are riddled with trouble and conflict. Unlike many contemporary families, their problems rarely stem from welfare cuts, joblessness, or homelessness. Both these films are about affluent, middle class households with interesting, not to say glamorous occupations—Joanne paints, Terry designs jewelry, both husbands are successful professionals. Joanne spends six years in a private mental hospital and maintains a separate apartment, while her husband pays for a live-in housekeeper without complaint. Terry woos the new addition to her home with a barrage of expensive toys.

Trouble for these families means personal relationships gone awry, because of inadequate or misguided parenting, selfishness, or simple incomprehension. Conflict is defined almost exclusively in psychological terms, beginning and ending within the family boundaries. Aside from the benevolent intervention and guidance of therapeutic agents of one kind or another, the domestic unit is almost hermetically sealed from community or wider social institutions. Unlike the classical social problem movie, the public sphere is hardly visible, as if society were composed of families and therapists, and perhaps a couple of friends. What we have here is indeed a "triumph of the therapeutic."

"Family redemption movies" typically chart the difficulties of personal change with varying degrees of complexity, bring matters to a head with a crisis, and resolve the problem, more often than not, with a cathartic experience of the kind undergone by Joanne, in which past trauma is relived and thereby mastered, bringing redemption and new hope for the future. Such films usually end on a positive note, answering to the exigencies of the two-hour narrative form, the viewer's need for affirmative closure, and the peculiar optimism of American psychology. At stake is not only the unity and survival of the family, but the articulation of progressive, liberal-egalitarian values about parenting. (Joanne's permissive but firm authority compares favorably with the rigid autocracy of the sexually-repressed governess.)

Still other TV films of the early 1980s combine elements of the classic social problem drama and "the family redemption movie." While these films do present individual narratives in the light of larger social issues, they do so in a less explicit or didactic fashion. *An Invasion of Privacy* (1983) is a classic example of this type of film, weaving together both psychological and sociological strains.

Social Problems and Personal Redemption: *Invasion of Privacy* (1983)

Invasion of Privacy focuses on the genre's most popular theme: rape. Valerie Harper stars as Kate, a divorced artist with a child spending a winter "away from it all" in a rambling house in rural New England. The heroine seeks an escape from the urban rat-race and a chance to re-involve herself in an art career that had been "on hold" during several years of homemaking.

The small town proves not an escape, however, but a microcosm of problems all its own. The townspeople are hostile and suspicious—what's an attractive educated young divorcée doing there? Harper has a brief affair with a policeman (very unstereotypical in his lack of "macho") and becomes friendly with the town dentist and his family—young hip emigrés to the boondocks. Just as life begins to improve, she is brutally raped in her home by a local man, whom she recognizes and charges with the crime. He, of course, claims she seduced him.

The rest is classic TV rape-drama with a bit of prime-time feminism. Harper encounters disbelief from the townsfolk and betrayal from her pseudo-liberal dentist friend (Didn't she frequent bars? And how could "nice old Luther" do anything like that?) The female paranoia classic of films like *Gaslight* (1944) (and usually confirmed in the movie's ending) surrounds the main character. Kate is isolated and vulnerable; even people close to her don't believe her. Her home, once a haven, is a source of constant terror and painful memory.

Yet a loyal female friend, the dentist's wife (Carol Kane), stands by her, and a jury populated by solid country women convicts "good old Luther." Kate leaves the rural hamlet for the city, however. Yet, in an end-mood characteristic of "woman-in-transition" dramas, she is wiser, stronger, more able to be alone. And the rapist is safely behind bars, at least until the next made-for-TV movie. While the ending is affirmative, it isn't overly upbeat or saccharine and does not gloss over the pain of her life transition. This film combines aspects of the classic social problem drama and a version of the "family redemption movie" in which a newly divorced or widowed woman must deal with living, loving, working, and parenting alone.

By 1984, the classic social problem drama has declined and the "family redemption movie" and its sociological variants are on the rise. As the landscape of larger social and economic issues shrinks, the psychological and familial terrain expands. Today our TV screens are peopled by more single-parent, dual-career, and reconstituted families. Ozzie and Harriet are no longer with us. Feminism—and the social changes it generates—has begun to shape mass media fantasy (although perhaps not always in the ways feminists themselves would prefer). Yet the solutions to personal problems are individual, familial, and therapeutic. Rarely do we see a TV movie which educates us about deep-seated (and more intractable) social problems. These family dramas are redemptive, depicting miraculous personal transformations by the final commercial. Mothers are reconciled with children they abandoned long ago (*Running Away*—1983), divorced couples are civil, even friendly (*Divorce Wars*—1982) and drug abusers magically see the error of their ways (*Cocaine: One Man's Seduction*—1983). The social problems presented often lack controversy, reflecting a single issue, consensual politics. Few of us, after all, are *for* incest, child abuse, or rape. More divisive issues (e.g., abortion) are often presented in an open-ended fashion designed to offend no one. Although more aesthetically pleasing, these films are politically ambiguous.

The significance of this ongoing evolution in TV movies—from sociological to psychological drama—is double-edged for studios and audiences alike. On the one hand, it reflects a more liberal definition of "family," and provides a variety of households (single-parent, gay, and lesbian, reconstituted) with images and narratives to which they can relate. On the other hand, it presents conservative solutions to deeply rooted problems: psychotherapeutic individualism and quintessential American optimism. By evading or neglecting potentially divisive issues in public debate (e.g., unemployment, militarism, abortion), all of which are less demonstrably, but equally implicated in "family misery," these films are conservative by omission. It's all in the family, often the WASP family, and it's all going to improve soon with perseverance and a little "professional help." "We're working it out," "It's a beginning," "We're gonna try again." These are the comforting end-phrases of today's made-for-TV movies.

FILMOGRAPHY 1970–1984—BY THEME

Adolescent Issues
  Born Innocent (1974)
  The People Next Door (1970)
  Go Ask Alice (1973)
  Sarah T.: Portrait of a Teen-Age Alcoholic (1975)
  The Best Little Girl in the World (1981)
  The First Time (1982)

Family Violence
  Battered (1978)
  Violent Strangers (1979)
  Mary Jane Harper Cried Last Night (1977)
  Little Gloria, Happy At Last (1983)
  The Legend of Lizzie Borden (1975)

Abortion/Problem Pregnancy
  My Body, My Child (1982)
  The Choice (1981)
  Brand New Life (1973)

Rape/Sexual Abuse
  Cry Rape (1973)
  Case of Rape, A (1974)
  Invasion of Privacy (1983)
  Something About Amelia (1984)
  When She Says No (1984)

Illness/Disability/Death
  First, You Cry (1978)

Dark Victory (1976)
Brian's Song (1971)
Little Mo (1978)

Mental Illness
Memories Never Die (1983)
Will There Really Be A Morning? (1983)

Aging
A Piano for Mrs. Cimino (1982)
Benny's Place

Divorce
Divorce: His; Divorce: Hers (1973)
The War Between the Tates (1977)
Breaking Up (1978)
Breaking Up Is Hard to Do (1979)

Retardation
Nunzio (1982)

Homosexuality
That Certain Summer (1972)
A Question of Love (1978)

Midlife
My Father's House (1975)
Queen of the Stardust Ballroom (1975)
Cocaine: One Man's Seduction (1983)
The Women's Room (1980)
Mother and Daughter: the Loving War (1980)

Women and Work
Muggable Mary: Street Cop (1982)
Nurse (1980)
Kentucky Woman (1983)
Games Mother Never Taught You (1983)
Question of Sex, A (1984)
Women At West Point (1979)

Infidelity
Torn Between Two Lovers (1979)
The Family Man (1979)

Civil Rights/Race Relations
Autobiography of Miss Jane Pittman, The (1974)
Judge Horton and the Scottsboro Boys (1976)
Farewell to Manzanar (1976)

Holocaust/Anti-Semitism
Skokie (1982)
Remembrance of Love (1983)
Playing for Time (1980)

Prostitution
Money On the Side (1983)
Portrait of an Escort (1982)
Portrait of a Stripper (1979)
My Mother's Secret Life (1984)

Modeling/Beauty
Bare Essence (1983)
Miss All-American Beauty (1982)

Inspirational Biography
A Woman Called Golda (1982)
A Woman Called Moses (1978)
Eleanor and Franklin (1976)
Portrait of A Rebel: Margaret Sanger (1980)

Mystery/Horror
Amazons (1984)
Terror On the Beach (1973)
Look What Happened to Rosemary's Baby (1976)
Illusions (1983)
Don't Go To Sleep (1983)
The Possessed (1977)

17

The Moral Dilemma of Reporting Human Rights: U.S. Television Networks' Coverage of Central America, 1977–1980

JARICE HANSON
University of Massachusetts, Amherst

CHRISTINE M. MILLER
Indiana University, Bloomington

The coverage of human rights presents an agenda item for the global audience. During the presidency of Jimmy Carter (1977 to 1980) the issue of human rights was considered one of primary importance. In a global context, Carter emphasized:

> The search for peace and justice also means respect for human dignity. All the signatories of the U.N. charter have pledged themselves to observe and to respect basic human rights. Thus, no member of the United Nations can claim that mistreatment of its citizens is solely its own business. Equally, no member can avoid its responsibilities to review and to speak when torture or unwarranted deprivation occurs in any part of the world (Public Papers of the Presidents, 1977, Vol. 1, p. 449).

He also stated that he recommended the entire United Nations' Human Rights Division be moved back to New York "where its activities will be in the forefront of our attention and where the attention of the press corps can stimulate us to deal honestly with this sensitive issue" (Public Papers of the Presidents, 1977, Vol 1, p. 450).

During the Carter Administration violations of human rights were reported in Latin America, the Middle East and the Far East; they became salient world issues. This study, based upon a content analysis conducted through the use of *Television News Index Abstracts*, discusses the networks' coverage of Central America during the Carter Presidency. The media began to cover human rights related issues more than they had in the past, because the Carter Administration placed such an emphasis on human rights. Along with such coverage came a number of problems. For example, how might a visual medium, such as television, create images for human rights-related stories. How does one interpret human rights? In what ways did the television coverage influence foreign policy?

While this paper concentrates solely on the television network evening news' coverage of human rights in Central America (Nicaragua, Guatemala, El Salvador, Panama, Honduras, and Costa Rica) it does not indicate that only Central American countries were prime human-rights violators. Violations occurred in every part of the world. This study was limited to Central America because of proximity and the various upheavals during the Carter Administration: El Salvador and Nicaragua. Also, it was in Central America that the press corps lost one of its noted newsmen during a demonstration.

Any analysis of human rights must deal with the problem of definition. Deciding whether a media story relates to human rights issues has usually depended upon the use of the "Big Three" terms: torture, arbitrary arrest or summary execution (Rosenblum, 1981, p. 193).

For the purpose of this study, human rights is defined as outlined by the *Universal Declaration of Human Rights*, a declaration proclaimed by the General Assembly of the United Nations in 1948. Article 3 states that "everyone has the right to life, liberty and security of person." In Article 4, "No one shall be held in slavery or servitude" while Article 5 states that "no one shall be subjected to torture or to cruel, inhuman or degrading treatment or punishment." Of course, the precise rights of people in some communities or countries differ from the precise rights of people in other communities/countries. It is for this reason that the formulation of human rights remains ambiguous and not narrowly defined.

METHOD

This study used the *Television News Index and Abstracts,* which has been tested to reveal a high degree of reliability as a source of data about international news coverage (Larson and Hardy, 1977). Key words in the *Index* related to human rights include words such as *torture, assassination, political assassinations, violence, disappearances, repressed,* or *oppressed.* These words are synonymous with violations of human rights in the context of this study. However, the researchers did read all abstracts to ascertain whether the words used were contextually defined as human rights topics. For example, *terrorist* was sometimes used within the connotation of a human rights event, but sometimes also used for a descriptive process which related to other types of events.

The content analysis was conducted on only weeknight reports, Monday through Friday, of ABC, CBS, and NBC, by a page-by-page analysis. The often shorter and information-abbreviated weekend reports were not included, as often such reports were pre-empted. In addition, weekend coverage often consists of an assemblance of material gathered during the week.

The term "human rights" was not an index word for the *Index*. Therefore, a page-by-page search ensured both contextual and complete reports. The variables considered were:

- amount of time spent on news items
- relationship of the item to a human rights issue
- percentage of human rights-related stories to the total coverage
- number of reports filed from a field location (to estimate possible visual information)

Items such as news placement or correspondents reporting the story, did not figure prominently in the analysis, because of the nature of world events at the time, i.e., Iran and South Korea, and the availability of seasoned reporters. Similarly, blackouts on visual information and news satellites influenced the correspondents' coverage at certain times[1] and therefore, some visual materials were not possible to categorize.

RESULTS

It is possible to see the number of items relating to Central America by referring to Table I. The number of news stories relating to Central America in the first year of the Carter Administration was surprisingly low, given the amount of political unrest in Nicaragua and Panama. All of the events covered in 1977 related to unrest in El Salvador, one of the prime violators of human rights—but only 40% of those stories made any reference to human rights.

In 1978 the number of stories increased considerably, and so did the number of stories related to human rights. While NBC carried the fewest stories about Central America, it did cover the greatest percentage of human right stories, and did so in a much shorter amount of air time. CBS and ABC reported almost the same number of stories (27 and 28 respectively), with the same percentage devoted to human rights (78%). the number of reports issued from the field did not indicate that any network had the potential for covering a greater number of visuals from the field than the others (NBC—16; CBS—15; ABC—18).

The greatest number of stories in 1978 dealt with the political unrest in Nicaragua during the Somoza Regime, the Sandinistas, and political asylum given to fleeing Nicaraguans by Panama. Seventy-nine percent of the stories related to human rights, including such issues as the appeal by Somoza to President Carter for help; the foreign policy of President Carter; reports by Amnesty International regarding human rights violations; OAS arbitration; martial law; and violations of Panama and Costa Rica's borders.

---

[1] Specifically, the satellite used by American newspersons was made unavilable by the Somoza regime in Nicaragua. Control over the satellite was threatened periodically, but seized only once, according to the *Index*. Still the threats were a delaying tactic which influenced the availability of visual information.

Table 1. Network Coverage of Central America, 1977-1980

Year	Network	No. of News Items	No. of Field Rpts.	Time	No. of Human Rights (H.R.) Items	Time	% of H.R. Items	Total for Yr.
1977	NBC	0	—	—	—	—	—	
	CBS	3	2	6:16	1	2:20	33%	
	ABC	2	—	:40	1	:30	50%	5 stories; 2 H.R. (40%)
1978	NBC	19	16	61:08	16	39:60	84%	
	CBS	27	15	55:36	21	61:20	78%	
	ABC	28	18	63:08	22	53:50	78%	74 stories; 59 H.R. (79%)
1979	NBC	22	13	38:05	19	36:05	86%	
	CBS	18	7	21:46	15	21:16	83%	
	ABC	18	9	33:03	15	32:00	83%	58 stories; 49 H.R. (84%)
1980	NBC	23	18	36:00	23	36:00	100%	
	CBS	29	9	27:00	29	27:00	100%	
	ABC	19	5	19:33	18	19:13	94%	71 stories; 70 H.R. (98%)

The longest individual stories in 1978 dealt with the problems of press coverage, such as the censorship of the main opposition newspaper in Nicaragua, *La Prensa*, the Somoza ban on foreign correspondents' access to the news satellite, and on the human interest story about NBC producer Don Critchfield and two cameramen who were caught in political unrest in Managua. The drama of three American newsmen caught in crossfire had no visuals from the scene but did provide an element of "you are there reality."

In 1979 NBC surfaced as the leader in Central American coverage with 22 news stories, 19 of which related to human rights (86%). NBC also had the greatest number of stories filed from a location (13). CBS and ABC each covered the same number of stories (18), and devoted the same percentage to human rights issues (83%). However, CBS had the fewest number of stories filed from the field (7) and devoted the least amount of air time to issues in Central America (21 min. 46 sec.).

Again, the two countries primarily covered were El Salvador and Nicaragua, with the latter receiving the most coverage. And again, the number of human rights-related stories increased percentage-wise (84%).

The number of reports from the field decreased in 1979, probably due to the events in Nicaragua as Americans attempted to leave the country. Reports about the death of ABC reporter Bill Stewart did not command a large portion of air time from CBS or NBC, but ABC devoted portions of almost ten minutes to his murder and the human rights violations related to that event (approximately one-third of its total coverage for the year). The death of Stewart also precipitated a "mass exodus" of reporters beginning in late June.

Also in 1979, Amnesty International, the Red Cross, and OAS were mentioned more frequently than in previous years. As El Salvador became more of a focal point from August to September, the Human Rights Commission was covered in greater detail in nightly newscasts.

By 1980, 100% of NBC *and* CBS nightly newscasts referred to some aspect of human rights when covering Central America. The emphasis changed in this year from Nicaragua to El Salvador and the number of stories increased with NBC covering items 23 times, CBS 29, and ABC 19 times.

Even though the coverage by CBS increased significantly in terms of the number of stories (18 in 1979 to 29 in 1980), the number of field reports remained low (9), and the total amount of air time was not significantly improved over 1979 (1979, 21 minutes 46 seconds; 1980, 27 minutes). The coverage by ABC dropped, not in terms of the number of stories, but in terms of air time devoted to any of the Central American countries. No material to correlate this drop in the amount of air time with the death of Stewart was suggested throughout the news abstracts.

The stories about Nicaragua in 1980 primarily focused on the assassination of Somoza and Carter's policies toward the country, while the stories relating to El Salvador primarily centered around Carter's granting of aid and the discussion about military advisors. In December of that year, the bodies of three Catholic nuns and an American social worker were found murdered, and every story aired that month discussed human rights violations and the suspension of U.S. aid to El Salvador. Ninty-eight percent of the stories filed in 1980 dealt with human rights issues.

DISCUSSION

The results of the analysis show that a concentration of television reports during the years of the Carter Administration, with regard to Central America, focused on events in Nicaragua and El Salvador. Generally speaking, when other Central American countries were mentioned, the news story discussed how that country was coping with the violence in Nicaragua or El Salvador. Throughout the Carter Presidency, the emphasis given to human rights was brought to bear upon network coverage, with human rights issues covered increasingly throughout the Carter Presidency; by 1980, two networks related stories to human rights events exclusively. An interesting note is supplied by the news abstracts provided by CBS on December 19, 1980, in which bloodshed in Central America was linked to the election of Ronald Reagan and the fear in Managua that foreign policy would be severely changed, with human rights suffering.

The relationship of media coverage and foreign policy has been discussed by Cohen in *The Press and Foreign Policy* (1963), which concentrates on print media and more recently by Larson. Both studies state that the press acts as an *observer*, a *participant*, and a *catalyst* with relation to foreign policy (Larson and Hardy, 1977, p. 18).

In terms of television networks' coverage of human rights-related issues in Central America as an *observer*, it may be possible to relate the findings of this study to the way in which the networks decide to report the stories *from* Central America. For example, the length of stories and the frequency of reports increased for each network when Americans were involved, such as the murder of Bill Stewart, Americans fleeing from Nicaragua, or the murders of the nuns and social worker in El Salvador.

Interestingly, each network would occasionally make reference to events on prior days—even though that network did not cover the original story. Networks assume their audiences would get the news from sources other than their own evening news.

In terms of television news acting as a *participant* in foreign policy, it may be possible to look at some of the methods used by the Carter Administration to see that foreign policy be made available for media coverage. As stated earlier, President Carter requested the U.N,'s Human Rights Division be moved back to New York to facilitate media coverage. Likewise Rosenblum says:

> Since the end of the Ford Administration at the insistence of Congress and President Carter, the U.S. State Department has revealed more information about human rights abuses abroad. Embassies were ordered to pay close attention to the

subject and desk officers in Washington made new contacts with experts in the field. New laws required the State Department to issue reports on the condition of human rights in countries which were to receive military aid. Administration officials at times have been brutally forthright in criticising abuses giving reporters legitimate pegs to write at length on the subject (Rosenblum, 1981, pp. 201-202).

While the results of this study could make no reference to the terminology used by the correspondents (due to the material available from the *Abstracts*), Dahlgren and Chakrapani (1982, p. 58) have documented some of the ways in which the audience's perception about news content may be influenced by reporter terminology:

> Somoza's position was further undermined by an embarrassing loss of support from the Carter Administration which had criticized him for human rights abuses and cut off military aid (NBC Nightly News, 7/6/79).

Terms which take the pejorative approach, such as "embarrassing loss," contribute to the audience's understanding of the issue at hand. This becomes critical when discussing the impact of American news upon other cultures.

According to Larson and Hardy (1977, p. 18) "network television news fills a more important role as a catalyst in the foreign policy process than it did prior to 1963." One way in which television news accomplishes this is through its presentation of visual material; it is in this way that human rights suffer greatly. Reporting on the issue of human rights has had less impact than it might because it is done with words, not news film, video, or pictures (Rosenblum, 1981, p. 197). Visual material related to human rights is difficult to attain because the subject material itself is not particularly visual in nature. The result is that human rights violations, *because* of violence or terrorist activities, are made to represent human rights—and the message given to the audience becomes somewhat frayed; the reporting appears to deal with the event of violence rather than the issue at hand.

Finally, the amount of coverage given to foreign policy issues in relation to other news stories about Central America must be addressed. The U.S. has had enormous influence over the development of media in other countries (Tunstall, 1977). Likewise, the availability of electronic news-gathering equipment (ENG) and satellite technology has made it possible for the visual material produced for the U.S. networks to be seen around the world. The Western approach to news coverage, which concentrates on events rather than processes, has become such a controversial subject, that the New World Information Order has cited the problem as one of global importance.

In the analysis by Larson and Hardy (1979, p. 33), they indicate that in network news coverage for the period 1972-1979, the geographical area of Latin America (which they define as all countries and territories in the Western Hemisphere south of the United States) ranked eighth out of nine areas in terms of the amount of attention given to the region by nightly newscasts. It should be noted however, that Larson's account is for the total number of stories, with no qualification given to special interests, such as human rights. For the period covering 1972-1979, Larson and Hardy (1977, p. 24) estimate that Latin America received a total of 14.1% of all coverage of *international events* reported by the U.S. networks. During this same time period, the networks were devoting a total of 9 minutes, 22 seconds (this is an average) of air time to international news. They found that "only about twenty of the nations of the world are mentioned in more than two percent of the international news stories on each network" (Larson and Hardy, 1977, p. 30). The countries covered most frequently were the Soviet Union, Great Britain, France, China, West Germany, and Japan. When developing nations were cited, they were usually engaged in some sort of conflict.

CONCLUSIONS

This study shows the number of human rights-related stories did increase in number during the Carter Presidency, but as the studies by Larson and Dahlgren-Chakrapani indicate, the total amount of time devoted to the Central American issues by the networks remains minimal. While television may indeed act as a catalyst for foreign policy by bringing issues to the audience, certain problems arise as television observes and participates in the newsgathering process.

Making non-visual stories visual is a problem in human rights coverage, because the only visuals available may connote violence and/or terrorist activity which could be viewed as an event rather than a process; thereby, television may offer information to the audience which it may or may not interpret correctly. The bias for the stories relating to Americans may re related to human rights, but the *type of coverage* may not necessarily explore the process involved.

Clearly examination of the visual and audio material from the networks would assist in the interpretation of the approach of the correspondent and provide an assessment of the image-laden visuals. While the bias of the Western news media cannot be ignored, it could be explained with the hopes of improving coverage of non-visual material in the future.

Further research needs to address the limitations of the technological methods of newsgathering and the impact of such technologies on the international news flow. It would be interesting to note what types of visual materials are sent to different cultures and to monitor the description given to them.

As television becomes more and more predominant as a major source of information for the world, further research will be needed in order that we as communicators understand the impact of the technology and the ways in which people make sense of the media.

REFERENCES

Cohen, B. (1963). *The Press and Foreign Policy*. Princeton, NJ: Princeton University Press.

Dahlgren, P., and Chakrapani, S. (1982). "The Third World on TV News: Western Ways of Seeing the 'Other'." *In* W. C. Adams (Editor), *Television Coverage of International Affairs*. Norwood, NJ: Ablex.

Larson, J. F., and Hardy, A. (1977). "International Affairs Coverage on Network Television News: A Study of News Flow." *Gazette 23*, 241-256.

Public Papers of the Presidents of the United States, (1977). *Jimmy Carter*, vol. 1, Washington, DC: U.S. Government Printing Office.

Rosenblum, M. (1981). *Coups and Earthquakes*. New York: Harper Colophon Books.

Tunstall, J. (1977). *The Media Are American*. New York: Columbia University Press.

18

The Coverage of El Salvador in *The Globe and Mail*

VERONICA SCHILD
University of Toronto

This essay examines how the reality of the war in El Salvador is interpreted in the Canadian newspaper, *The Globe and Mail*. It is based on a study of the content of news reports on El Salvador, and covers the period from October, 1979, to September, 1980, as well as a sporadic examination of editions for the period from October, 1980, to March, 1982. By examining the first period of reporting, from October, 1979, to September, 1980, I reconstruct the persistent and compelling mode of interpreting the Salvadorean reality followed by *The Globe and Mail* (referred to below as *The Globe*).

People present in educational meetings about El Salvador sponsored by a local Canadian committee of solidarity with El Salvador expressed an initial resistance, at times quite strong, when faced with an interpretation of what goes on in El Salvador that differed from the one they had acquired through the news media, particularly through *The Globe*. They asked questions like, "which version should I believe, yours or the newspaper's?" Or, "you say one thing but the media say another." Alternatively, they challenged what was being said on the basis of a presumed knowledge of the "facts," with questions like, "how can you say that the United States should stay out of this conflict when the communists are threatening to take over?"

Clearly, those raising such questions already had a version of what was happening in El Salvador which they had acquired through the news media. Also, and more important, they took this version for granted. The alternative version being presented to them in the solidarity meetings openly challenged this knowledge.

Recognizing the difficulty in *knowing* the "facts" of the El Salvadorian war, this paper examines how news is constructed so that people's resistance to conflicting information becomes understandable. Indirectly, this paper supports Gramsci's conception of hegemonic rule. Thus, it will be implicitly argued that hegemonic rule is a process of domination through "passive consensus," and that the news media participate in this process.

THE CONSTRUCTION OF NEWS

The news media reinforce the dominant mode of constructing reality by not challenging taken-for-granted knowledge. Newsworkers participate in the process of domination despite their best intentions by virtue of the ongoing, routine work which they perform as members of their profession. Thus, to engage in the production of news in the context of the rules and practices of professional journalism is tantamount to participating in the process of hegemonic rule.

The production of news constitutes a particular way of "framing" reality.[1] A frame is understood as the "principles of organization which govern events—at least social ones—and our subjective involvement in them" (Goffman, 1974, pp. 10-11). In other words, they organize "strips" or segments of the everyday world. The characteristics of the frame, i.e., its particular principles of organization, and what it makes accessible, determine what we know about a specific reality. Furthermore, they are determined by the rules of professional journalism. These include a commitment to "truth," to "credibility, accuracy, and concern for public interest" (Hohenberg, 1973, p. 5). They also include a definition of what is newsworthy, i.e., what section of a social continuum is made accessible as a news event, and whose actions qualify as the facts of the events.[2]

The practices through which newsworkers accomplish the framing of a particular reality include means of identifying and establishing reliable sources of events, means of verifying the certainty of events, and means of recording them. In other words, once the newsworker establishes a particular frame, she must find sources who can reconstruct the details or facts of "what actually happened."[3]

The discursive practices through which newsworkers accomplish the "fleshing out" of a frame include techniques such as the use of categories which have the effect of transforming a lived reality into something else. These categories do not merely purport to reflect "what actually happened," they also suggest new levels of "signification," new meanings (Barthes, 1972).

---

[1] My understanding of how news is produced (briefly outlined in this essay) is inspired by Dorothy Smith's work on the production of ideological discourses. See, for example, her "The Ideological Practice of Sociology" (1974a), and "The Social Construction of Documentary Reality" (1974b). Also, Gaye Tuchman's important study of the news media, *Making News* (1978) has been very influential for the development of my approach.

[2] Wallace Clement's (1975) and Herbert Gans's (1980) studies suggest that the news media tend to define what is newsworthy, and who is a reliable informant, in relation to the society's "elite."

[3] Because the news media and other institutions share the same principles—based on the legitimizing theory of capitalism, liberal democracy—interpretations of "what actually happens" tend to be of the same type. Only when a breach of trust occurs between the news media and another institution, or branch of government, will the former attempt to redefine a particular frame somewhat more independently. Ultimately, though, the mode of interpreting and its basic assumptions remain unchanged.

THE GLOBE AND MAIL

The Globe is regarded by some sectors of Canadian society as a source of accurate information; its format and style identify it as a "prestige" newspaper. *The Globe's* format is modeled on that of *The New York Times;* it maintains correspondents in prominent places and relies heavily on the Anglo-American news agencies for most of its international coverage. Its style and vocabulary assume a distinct level of literacy, i.e., the type acquired through a middle-class education. *The Globe*, therefore, assumes that its readership knows how to decode the information (images, symbols) it provides. In this sense, *The Globe* and its readership share common assumptions, and a common mode of interpreting reality.

The case of *The Globe's* coverage of the war in El Salvador illustrates the implicit assumptions shared by *The Globe* and its readership. Following is a reconstruction of the framing of El Salvador's reality by *The Globe*. The emphasis is primarily on discursive techniques, i.e., the use of categories, themes, and images to construct the news events in a form that is knowable for the readers. The concern is to reveal the shared assumptions that give the news events that knowable character.

EL SALVADOR IN *THE GLOBE AND MAIL*

After a period of silence broken by brief accounts here and there, El Salvador "entered" *The Globe* one day after a coup d'etat replaced the military government of General Carlos Humberto Romero with a military civilian junta on October 15, 1979. On October 16 *The Globe* carried an account titled, "Military and civilians taking power: El Salvador President ousted."[4] It mentioned that, according to "informed sources at the presidential palace," the ousted government was criticized for its failure to control "the left and right wing violence" that has been sweeping El Salvador in recent months. Also, that General Romero's policy of giving the opposition "enough rope to hang itself" meant that during demonstrations the army stayed in the barracks and the "demonstrations generally turned into vandalism." The account concluded with the suggestion that most anti-government groups want radical reforms but that "their ideologies and methods differ."

What emerges from this account is an image of the ousted General as ineffectual—too lenient—in his handling of the opposition. The assumption made is that government is legitimate, and that disturbances that threaten it must be controlled, something that General Romero has failed to do. A con-

---

[4] The page number of accounts mentioned in the text are not cited. Unless otherwise specified it is to be understood that the accounts appeared in the International section of *The Globe*, i.e., in pages 12, 13, 14, or 15.

trasting view is found in Liisa North's *Bitter Grounds: Roots of Revolt in El Salvador* (1981). She suggests that "the extensive and indiscriminate violence unleashed by General Romero became an embarrassment to the Administration of Jimmy Carter" (North, 1981, p. 80).

This account introduces various themes or features of what became in the following months a persistent interpretation of the war in El Salvador. The dominant one is that El Salvador is a country torn by "left wing" and "right wing" violence. What brings this violence about is not relevant in this context. Rather, violence is to be understood as an objective feature of that part of the world; it is simply there. But it must be contained because it continually threatens social order. Another theme, is, therefore, one that links social order to repressive measures like military interventions and curfews. The assumption is that at least in El Salvador repression has a legitimate purpose. The existence of an opposition that makes radical demands is, like the existence of violence, another objective feature of El Salvador. Thus, El Salvador, like other societies has its dissenters, or malcontents.

On October 17, *The Globe* carried a rather brief follow-up of the situation in El Salvador. Titled, "State of siege follows coup in El Salvador," it stated that the government propsed an "ambitious program of economic and social reforms aimed at defusing the country's political crisis," "the extreme violence gripping the country for the past two years continues," and that at least three "were killed in clashes of extreme left and the army" on the previous day. The passive form used to describe the killings manages to conceal who actually did the killing, who was killed, and also where the killings took place. The passive form is a technique for decontextualizing an actual occurrence and transforming it into an objective fact. It is used consistently in the accounts of El Salvador to describe the deaths of "leftist guerrillas" and "civilians."

The account also mentioned that "troops moved against striking workers in a factory." Here again, a particular occurrence, "striking workers in a factory," is decontextualized and transformed into a feature of the Salvadorean environment. Furthermore, in the context of the account, the strike acts as a reference to the theme that links repression with social order. A contrasting description of what happened stated that:

> A large and heavily armed contingent of combined security forces, accompanied by armored vehicles, broke into the locals of four groups of striking workers in the capital, killing seven, wounding and beating an undetermined number, and detaining 90 (Wipfler, 1980, p. 118).

The Globe's account further indicated that "fearing more leftist violence, a curfew was established." Thus, the theme mentioned above is reinforced once more. Also, the phenomenon "leftist violence" emerges as a theme in its own right, displacing somewhat the theme "left wing and right wing violence."

On October 18, *The Globe* carried an account titled "El Salvador fighting leaves 10 more dead after day of rioting." It stated that "at least 10 more [were] killed in troops-leftist clash." Also, that people in the town of San Marcos "defied" the martial law, and set up roadblocks and burned tires. And, that "San Marcos residents reported seeing hooded men and women firing from hills and atop buildings at soldiers called in to crush the rebellion."

The account seems to suggest that three different types of people were involved in this event: people in the town, residents of San Marcos, and hooded men and women. Who killed whom, and why, is not made clear. In fact, the account is, when examined carefully, almost unintelligible. Nevertheless, the dominant themes are present in it: "leftist violence," and "repression:social order." The use of the categories "riot" and "rebellion" reinforce the theme "repression:social order." Riot is "by definition civil disorder" legitimizing the intervention of security forces.

The dominant themes were present again in an account that appeared on October 24, titled, "Heavy fighting leaves 23 dead in El Salvador," that stated that 23 were "killed in clash of troops and leftists" who tried to "storm" the newspaper office.

Also a brief account on November 2 titled "Opposition Grows to El Salvador Junta," stated that "at least 18 people were killed in clashes," "at least 7 guardsmen" died in an "ambush," and "at least 12 died when armed leftists hurled incendiary bombs at guards" in a market area. It concluded that the military opened fire to "defend itself." A contrasting description stated that

A group giving a comic street play mocking the Government was trapped and fired upon in the central market area by heavily armed Treasury Police, who killed 30 players and onlookers, and wounded dozens (Wipfler, 1980, p. 118).

Keeping an account of "leftist violence," or "leftist activity," seems at first glance to be the predominant feature of the reporting of El Salvador by *The Globe* in the period of October, 1979 to September, 1980. The repetition of the main themes constituting the prevalent frame seems to be carried through at the sake of intelligibility. A brief account that appeared on December 20, titled "Salvador leftists killed," stated that the military had killed 25 "leftists" who opened fire at them in a coffee plantation. Four were wounded and 16 captured, and there were an unspecified number of military casualties. "Leftists" had taken over the plantation and were demanding higher wages for the laborers. When asked by the military to "leave peacefully they opened fire instead."

The account makes a distinction, first of all, between those who work in a plantation (the laborers) and "leftists" who demanded higher wages for the laborers. Why, for example, the military was present in a coffee plantation at the time of what appears to have been a labor unrest is not made clear. Nor is it clear why laborers themselves were not demanding higher wages. What is clear, though, is that the dominant themes "leftist violence" and "repression:social order" are present in the account.

The predominance of these themes, i.e., the particular frame, is such that other important developments like the gradual disaffection and ultimate resignation, in January 1980, of the moderate members of the ruling Junta, are relagated to the status of afterthoughts, in accounts that describe the latest "leftist activities." For example, on January 5, 1980, *The Globe* carried an account titled "El Salvador guard post raided." It stated that approximately 40 "well armed leftist guerrillas" attacked the National Guard headquarters "as El Salvador struggled to cope with a grave political crisis triggered by a mass resignation of top government officials." To conclude, it stated that the "moderate to left-of-center" politicians quit when Mario Andino, accused of being responsible for a "swing to the right which could lead to civil war" refused to leave or be dismissed by the junta.

A "leftist" attack on the National Guard headquarters takes precedence over the government crisis. Also, the resignation of the moderate members is not linked to the performance of the junta. An alternative account describes this occurrence as:

> The internationally-respected civilians in the October junta found that they were being used as a reformist camouflage to keep repression out of sight of the rest of the world. Unable to control the armed forces or to persuade the landlord class to accept the necessary reforms—specifically, a genuine agrarian reform and a sharing of political power with the country's popular organizations—they resigned (North, 1981, p. 82).

According to *The Globe's* report, all of El Salvador, not just the junta, "struggled to cope" with the crisis. This discursive technique, the personification of the country, allows for a distinction between "leftists" and the rest.

Another example of the subordination of the developments in the "crisis" situation to the prevalent "frame" is found in an account of January 12, titled, "Leftists seize Panamanian Embassy in El Salvador." The account is structured in the familiar form, with "leftist activity" dominating the leading paragraph. It stated that earlier that week the Christian Democrats agreed to form an alliance with the military junta, after the latter backed the Christian Democrats' government plan. The plan included the nationalization of agricultural exports and banking, a "push" for land reform, and the restructuring of the armed forces and the police. This plan, the account stated, was similar to the October 15 declaration of the original junta. Still, "the leftists are known to want more radical and immediate changes," the account concluded.

"Leftist activity" takes precedence once more over new developments in the government "crisis." In fact, the account conceals a great contradiction. It states that there is no real difference between the original and the new plan of government. Why, we may ask, must a government that has defined itself as centrist and reformist all along, as the news accounts have implied, agree to be so again?

The framing of the reality of war in El Salvador in terms of the themes "leftist violence" or "leftist activity" is well established at this point. The reshuffling and resignation of more civilians and the transition of some, notably the Minister of Education, from the government to the underground movement and the passing of entire troops, in more than one instance, from the army to the "guerrilla" side, are occurrences that do not conform to the particular framing of the Salvadorean reality, and therefore are not transformed into news events.

The established frame is reproduced, at this time, in investigative accounts as well. Ian Brodie, sent by *The Globe* to El Salvador, produced an account on February 8, titled "El Salvador turmoil increases steadily as junta's rule pleases no one." It stated that as violence increases steadily in El Salvador, the conflict becomes increasingly like that of Nicaragua. In other words, it is more vicious and bloody. Since the new year, "clashes claim an average of 10 lives a day. Triple the figure of a year ago." But, "unlike Nicaragua's point of unity, the overthrow of Somoza, El Salvador has none." Furthermore, a "wishy-washy" five-man junta replaced General Romero, and when three civilians resigned they were replaced with three "equally ineffective people" who try to be "reasonable and moderate." The junta "upsets" the left and "frightens" the right. And the left and right are "at each other's throats more than ever."

Furthermore, El Salvador is so "poverty-stricken," that "the majority may be assumed to support the left," although the middle class supports the right. The right-wing militants include "Orden," a 50,000 strong paramilitary group that controls "subversion" in rural areas; "Union of White Warriors," a group that tortures and executes left leaders; and "Faro," the armed muscle of big land owners. The left-wing militants include "The Popular Liberation Front," the "Popular Revolutionary Block," and an assortment of "guerrilla groups," most of which have coalesced in the "United Front." The "ruthless" operations of the left groups, kidnappings, ransackings, and taking over of embassies, have amassed a "war chest" of $45 million or more.

Also, the account adds, "there are arms everywhere." The middle class and the wealthy "sleep with revolvers and hand grenades," and "students carry Cuban guns in their knapsacks." Coffee rots in the plantations because of an "impasse between pickers and owners." And also, "tourism is down."

The Archbishop, the most liberal critic, "staunch defender of human rights," is tired of right wing excesses and has declared that "the time for legitimate violence may be approaching." The account concluded by stating that the United States supports the junta's program for social and economic reform, something that has been received with "hostility" by the right, and "pettifogging" by the left. And, that left-wing militants "operate with impunity from the University in San Salvador," which is an armed camp which the National Guard has not dared invade so far."

Although there are more details to be found in Brodie's report than in those accounts constructed from wire service material, it manages to reproduce the established "frame." Everything in this report points to the centrality of "leftist activity" for understanding the utter chaos in El Salvador. For example, while it mentions the purpose of each right-wing militant group, and thus somehow legitimates them, it does not do so with left-wing ones. What makes them all alike, according to the report, are their "ruthless" operations. Thus, while right-wing groups engage in reactive violence, they kill "leftist leaders," control "subversion," and protect landlords; left-wing groups engage in "leftist violence."

The framing of the reality of El Salvador by *The Globe* is, at this time, parallel to that of the State Department, and to that of the dominant sector of the Salvadorean society. For almost 12 months of reporting, *The Globe*'s headlines on El Salvador fall into two main types. They either refer to "leftist activity" or "body counts," sometimes to both. In late 1981 this changed, that is, the "frame" was altered somewhat. This change must be understood with reference to the actions of other institutions, primarily of the United States government. The new Reagan Administration proposed a sudden reinterpretation of the war in El Salvador in geopolitical terms, as part of the East-West conflict, and increased considerably the amount of military aid to the Salvadorean junta. Also, General Haig produced a report known as the "white paper," documenting the supply of communist arms to the Salvadorean guerrillas, that was revealed to be unfounded. These actions resulted in the news media's, *The Globe*'s in this case, gradual erosion of trust in the official interpretation of events in El Salvador.[5] *The Globe* assigned a special correspondent, Oakland Ross, to produce investigative accounts of the situation in El Salvador. The purpose was to develop a more independent version of the situation. Specifically, they aimed to discredit suggestions about the origins of the guerrilla's arms. Increasingly, Ross's reporting took on the form of a "crusade," particularly in early 1982 on the eve of the upcoming "democratic" elections. Suddenly the news accounts on El Salvador migrated to the front pages, appearing on the front page more than once. These were sometimes accompanied by photographs of guerrillas wielding American-made M-16s or Belgian arms (the captions pointed this out).

Ross's reporting had a sense of urgency and a definite moral edge to it. He was out to vindicate the misinterpretations of the war in El Salvador. As mentioned before, his reports filled the front pages of *The Globe* on the eve of the presidential elections and for some time after. Then, the attention of *The Globe* shifted to the British-Argentinian "conflict." El Salvador was once again relegated to the back pages of the newspaper.

THE CONSTRUCTION OF EL SALVADOR BY *THE GLOBE*

The Globe's persistent interpretation of the situation in El Salvador was accomplished through practices which managed to transform a concrete social process into an objective phenomenon, a source of facts and events. These practices

---

[5] Also, in early 1981 Canadian Foreign Minister Marc McGuigan had suggested that he was opposed to the shipment of offensive weapons to El Salvador from "anywhere," but added that he would not condemn the United States for doing so. Ultimately, he reasoned, Canada did not have "a serious obligation to Central America" because it was not "an area of traditional Canadian interest."

included, first of all, establishing a network of reliable informants, people whose claims with respect to specific occurrences could be taken to be objective and true. These sources were primarily government officials, police and army officials, diplomatic personnel, and individuals affiliated with international organizations. They were very rarely peasants, workers and other ordinary people. In other words, the informants used by the news media, i.e., by the wire services and by *The Globe* (because it accepts the wire services materials as the "raw data" of its reports) happen to be those charged with producing the "official" version of what happens in El Salvador for the Salvadorean government and the State Department. In this sense, the news media in general and *The Globe* in particular partake of the dominant mode of interpreting reality.

The specific discursive practices that accomplished the decontextualization of particular occurrences in El Salvador and their transformation into news events consistently politically oriented the reader in his/her understanding of the reality of war. Categories like "leftist activity," "leftist violence," "riot," "civilians," and others had the effect of detaching lived situations where people organized, acted, killed or were killed from the eventual account of those situations; "what actually happened" was thus concealed, not disclosed, for *The Globe's* reader. For example, the accounts made constant reference to the deaths of civilians and guerrillas as having occurred in "cross-fires." Other sources reveal that in these seemingly incessant "cross-fires" 3,272 peasants, 392 workers, 724 students, 136 teachers, 5 paramedics, 2 mayors, 42 professionals, 24 slum dwellers, 35 employees, 5 male religious, 5 female religious, 7 transportation workers, 170 businessmen, and another 2,340 unidentified persons were killed between January 1, 1980, and December 31, 1980 (North, 1981, p. 88). Another example is the use of "leftist activity" or "leftist violence;" it stands for a variety of occurrences including the demands of unionized coffee workers and protests by high school students.

The coverage of Archbishop Romero's funeral and the killings that took place afterwards provides a good illustration of discursive practices "at work" in the transformation of a lived reality into something else. The first account referred to the "panic" that resulted when someone shot at a crowd of 50,000 mourners standing outside the archbishop's funeral. The follow-up account transformed the "panic" into a "funeral riot," and stated that leftists and the junta "blame each other" for the shootings. This second account provides an interesting example of the use of visual images to complement verbal ones. A medium-sized photograph of a burning car and armed young men standing next to it accompany it. Regardless of the fact that the responsibility for the shootings is in dispute, and that, as the last paragraph of the account—suitably enclosed in quotation marks, a device used by newsworkers to distance themselves from the material they use (Tuchman, 1978, p. 95)—states:"a statement signed by a number of priests and nuns accused the government of 'grave distortion of facts and false interpretations.' Shots came from the National Palace's 2nd floor, they added." The photograph seems to have identified the group responsible for the shooting. It portrays disorder and violence, and suggests, at least to those readers familiar with the "clues" acquired through previous accounts about "leftist violence" in El Salvador by *The Globe*, that the young men, obviously leftists— they look poor and carry guns—must have caused the "funeral riot." The statement by the priests and nuns is minimized in this way, and the shooting of mourners becomes transformed into something else, namely, another instance of "leftist violence."

The Globe's readership "knows" how to decode the newspaper's accounts; they share common assumptions, a common background of knowledge and consequently a common mode of decoding images and symbols. *The Globe's* commitment to keeping its readers informed must therefore be understood as an invitation to recognize what is known beforehand. Thus, the readers' acquired knowledge, about the reality of war in El Salvador, for example, is constantly reinforced, never challenged.

REFERENCES

Barthes, R. (1972). *Mythologies,* trans. by A. Lavers. London: Jonathan Cape.

Clement, W. (1975). *The Canadian Corporate Elite.* Toronto, Ontario: McClelland and Stewart.

Gans, H. (1980). *Deciding What's News.* New York: Vintage Books.

Goffman, E. (1974). *Frame Analysis.* Philadelphia, PA: University of Pennsylvania Press.

Hohenberg, J. (1973). *The Professional Journalist.* New York: Holt, Rinehart and Winston.

North, L. (1981). *Bitter Grounds: Roots of Revolt in El Salvador.* Toronto, Ontario: Between the Lines.

Smith, D. E. (1974a). "The Ideological Practice of Sociology," *Catalyst* (No. 8), 39-54.

Smith, D. E. (1974b). "The Social Construction of Documentary Reality," *Sociological Inquiry 44,* 257-267.

Tuchman, G. (1978). *Making News.* New York: Free Press.

Wipfler, W. (1980). "El Salvador. Reform as Cover for Repression. "*Christianity and Crisis, 40.*

19

News of Talk, News of Riot

GRAHAM KNIGHT
McMaster University

INTRODUCTION

If, as Foucault tells us, power is everywhere, then it should not be more insistently so than in the ceaseless public discourse of news. Demonstration of this is indeed the direction taken by the sociology of news in its recent concern with ideology. Journalistic commitment to objectivity and balance, narrative realism (descriptive empiricism), and a preoccupation with the disruption and restoration of social order have been shown to structure news accounts in such a way that certain types of fact, opinion, and understanding are routinely produced, at the expense of alternatives that are ignored or devalued as bizarre, dangerous, or incredible (see Knight, 1982b). The routine practices of newswork have been shown to produce a discourse that is generally ahistorical; that mystifies social change and contradiction as novelty and discrete conflicts; that reproduces the authority of dominant institutions by relying primarily on bureaucratic sources, and assuming the pertinence and veracity of their data; and that reduces social structure and process to the personalization of disconnected events. (See for example: Altheide, 1976; Chibnall, 1977; Fishman, 1978, 1980; Gans, 1979; Glasgow Media Group, 1976, 1980; Hall, 1973; Hall et al., 1978; Knight, 1982b; Molotch and Lester, 1975; Tuchman 1978).

This critique of news as ideology embraces form as well as content; it extends to the fundamental epistemology of news discourse which takes as "natural" dominant social forms and forms of domination. This inscription of power carries a double significance. News provides a daily document of the practical formation of the state; its preoccupation with deviance, disorder, and conflict represents, obversely, an underlying commitment to the principle and rule of the legal form as the primary instrument of social order and conflict resolution. At the same time, this reproduction of the state in discourse takes on a class character; news talk draws from an understanding of the world that accords chiefly with the concerns, experiences, and interests of the intellectual, professional, and administrative middle class (Gans, 1979).

The concerns of this paper fall within the perimeters of this critical framework; it seeks to examine the powerfulness of news discourse, and, correlatively, attempts to open up the closure in which ideology normally envelops its material. The analysis tries to show how news talk posits one set of subjects as the objects of another, a process of subordination that represents relations of power in the wider political economy and class system. The analysis argues that news privileges discourse, or rather discursiveness, in an objectified, instrumental way as the authority and sign of authority of the professional-administrative middle class and the apparatuses of the democratic state. Because news consists so much of talk about others' talk, it has become a particular discourse that authorizes discourse in general, and in doing so generates a textual alignment of power among the various agents and strata of this middle class.

Journalists, academics, officials, experts, all talk for a living; discourse itself is the mode of livelihood of the middle class. This production of talk takes place, however, under normative and institutional conditions, such that talk produces the talker, just as the talker produces talk. It is normative in the sense that discourse constitutes an ordered field which is governed by codes that develop and display the subjectivity of the speaker. In the case of the official discourse of the middle class, this code is normally a formalistic one that reproduces and mythifies (in the Barthesian sense) the speaker's authority and officiality. It is institutional in the sense that discourse must posit its subjects in ways that are concretized non-discursively, in the context of structured social relations (cf., Coward and Ellis, 1977). In both respects, discourse can be said to reproduce power-in-ideology.

The powerfulness of ideology consists in the way discourse separates and excludes, combines and possesses, permits and prevents, and thereby subordinates some as the practical objects of others—subjectivity's double face. This objectification takes place as the knowing and speaking subject comes to be known and spoken about as a problem, inscribed in which there is a desire for control. For power, as Foucault (1971) shows, is a relation, the continuous production of limits and desire. The productivity and measure of this power is the way in which, through its activity of differentiation and appropriation, discourse embodies what really can and cannot, must and must not, be said about whom. The determination of meaning takes place in that field of relations between the spoken, unspoken, and unspeakable (cf., Machrey, 1978).

HUNGER STRIKERS, RIOTERS, AND TALKERS

On March 1, 1981, Bobby Sands began a fast, or "hunger strike," as it became known in the news media, in the Maze prison near Belfast, Northern Ireland. The purpose of this fast was to press the claim that he and other Irish nationalist inmates, convicted and imprisoned under the sub-state's special "anti-terrorist" laws, be granted the status of political prisoners by being allowed to wear their own clothing, refuse prison work assignments, associate freely within the prison, receive more visits and mail from outside, and receive sentence reductions for "good behavior." Sixty-three days later Sands died from his fast, the first of ten prisoners to die before the fast ended. These hunger strikes and the responses they evoked became the principal focus for news of the Northern Ireland conflict that year. Although violence there had long since become routine news, it was clear that the hunger strikes were taken by the news media as no ordinary instance of collective death.

The analysis below centers on news coverage of the first four deaths, that of Bobby Sands in particular, in the *New York Times*, during a period of roughly two months from the beginning of April to the end of May 1981. The *Times* has been chosen for its influential reputation, stemming from a general respect, nationally and internationally, for the quality and credibility of its reporting as these are measured by prevailing standards of balance and thoroughness.[1] The limited time period under consideration was dictated by the analytical focus on the detailed aspects of the news accounts, a concern with the semiotic rather than the quantitative organization of the text. The first four deaths—those of Sands, Francis Hughes, Raymond McCreesh, and Patrick O'Hara—occurred sufficiently closely together to produce an almost continuous daily narrative. After the death of O'Hara there was a period of several weeks before the fifth striker died, and the news narrative was temporarily broken.

The news story was organized around the developing relationships between four main groups of participants. The first, most obviously, consisted of the hunger strikers themselves. All four were identified together through the reiteration of a number of common themes: by their membership in Irish nationalist organizations committed to the use of open force to achieve the reunification of Ireland independent politically from Britain (specifically the Irish Republican Army (I.R.A.) and the Irish National Liberation Army); by their ages (all under 30); by the grounds for and length of their prison sentences; and by the reason for the fast, viz., the "demand" that they be given "political status", which was said "to turn on such matters of symbolism as the requirement that they wear prison uniforms."[2] At the same time, Sands was separated from the others, and, as the first to fast and die, given more prominent attention. He was introduced as a "leader" of the nationalist inmates, and his candidacy in a par-

---

[1] The analysis is based on the microfilmed final Late City Edition of the *New York Times*.

[2] No explanation was given of the connection between fasting, political prisoner status, and "such matters of symbolism" as clothing requirements, until May 25, after the first four strikers had died.

This report also began to represent the symbolism of these demands in a more practical, rational light by noting (a) that special category status had been granted to terrorist offense inmates before; (b) that several other inmates in the same prison continued to enjoy this privileged status, though the conferral of it had since been stopped so far as new, incoming prisoners were concerned; and (c) that Sands and the other fasters had been convicted under the substate's special anti-terrorist laws that provided for conviction without juries and with weaker evidence than normally obtains in the remainder of the U.K. Thus, the actions of the hunger strikers were re-cast, retrospectively, in a more practical light.

liamentary by-election was the original peg on which the story was hung. Sands' identity was established in two respects. Initially he was identified through the anomaly of his candidacy and subsequent victory in the by-election while being an I.R.A. leader serving a 14-year jail term for a firearms offense, and a hunger striker demanding political prisoner status for himself and others. After this initial frame began to exhaust itself, and as Sands began to approach death, the news discourse began to focus with increasing detail on the condition of his physical deterioration: his failing senses, his corpse-like appearance, his lapse into a coma, his eventual death.

The second group of news subjects consisted of those who responded (in the main supportively) to the hunger strike in the form of public demonstrations that resulted in street violence, defined usually as "disturbances," "riots," "rioting," or "clashes" involving the "security forces" (police and British Army soldiers) on the one side, and what were reported to be groups of (mainly) adolescent males on the other. News of the street violence took the form of reports of actual and anticipated hostilities, and became, at times, the principal focus of the narrative as a whole. From April 20 until the end of May, public violence was discussed in 26 separate reports, and headlined in 14. Additionally, the written text was accompanied by a number of photographs that established visual dimensions of the violence: four shots of "rioters" and "rioting;" one of British soldiers crouching in building rubble to avoid becoming "sniper targets;" six of public rallies and demonstrations (five in support of the hunger strikers, one opposed); and five shots of funerals (of which three were of coffins).

The third group consisted of those who responded to the hunger strike and the street violence in a discursive manner, by calling on the British government in particular to enter into discussion and negotiation with the hunger strikers to bring about a resolution to the conflict and avert further violence. These discursive interventions came from outside the immediate radius of the conflict, and fell into major and minor news items (judging by narrative placement, extent of coverage, headlining, and reiteration in more than one report). There were three major interventions, all before Sands' death: a group of three Irish parliamentarians, two envoys from the European Commission on Human Rights, and a special envoy from the Pope. All three attempted intervention at the site of the conflict. The minor interventions, coming mainly after Sands' death, took the form of appeals to the British government and/or the hunger strikers to negotiate and be willing to compromise in order to resolve the impasse. These came either from American politicians (e.g., Ramsey Clark or Edward Kennedy), or from Catholic churchmen.

The final participant was the British government whose presence in the text took the form of statements by government officials, government ministers, politicians supporting the government, and, most commonly, the British prime minister, Margaret Thatcher. References to Thatcher usually took the form of cited remarks about the voluntary (though nonetheless regrettable) character of the hunger strike, and about the impossibility of granting special political status to those convicted of and imprisoned for "common" criminal offenses. These remarks, reiterated frequently over the period, were generally presented as the reason for the government's refusal to negotiate and compromise with the hunger strikers.

NEWS TALK: POWER AND OBJECTIVITY

Beginning as a news story about the conflictual relationship between the hunger strikers and the British government, the story developed into a discourse about the evolving relationships between all four groups noted above. Beginning as a linear narrative about the intensification of confrontation, hostility, and the breakdown of law-and-order, the story developed, after the death of Sands, into a cyclical discourse of recurrent events appropriated textually in standardized format: a "grim cycle of violence," as one report itself concluded.[3] The analysis concerns this discursive formation with regard to the inscription of power within its oganization and functioning. In large part, it must be recognized that this power consists in the ability and necessity of discourse to transcend the here-and-now of its utterances, and evoke in the reader what is already known about what is already there. This transcendence is particularly important in the highly conventionalized form of the modern news text, where reiteration and redundancy create, intertextually, a doubly powerful effect.

As previous research on the Northern Ireland conflict, and on dissent, opposition, and social disorder generally, has shown, the crux of this discursive activity is the way in which news accounts reproduce uncritically the state's own separation—embedded in its functions institutionally and discursively—of politics and law-and-order (Clarke and Taylor, 1980; Knight, 1982a; Knight and Dean, 1982; Schlesinger, 1978; Tumber, 1982; Wren-Lewis, 1981). Politics embraces a circumscribed sphere of difference and legitimate opposition which is normally confined to the parameters of official democratic procedures. Law-and-order, on the other hand, is defined as a sphere of consensus and universality that incorporates the practices of official social control—the policing of disorder, crime, and deviance in general—whose necessity and legitimacy, as means and especially ends, is rarely brought into question.

---

[3] Although the analysis here is not directly concerned with narrative structure, it should be noted that the death and burial of Sands served as something of a turning point in the narrative's direction, signaling a move away from an emphasis upon the growing likelihood of a serious escalation of civil disorder (e.g., talk of "all-out sectarian struggle"), to an almost resigned emphasis upon the cyclical routine character of the violence (e.g., talk of its being "normal or less than normal by the standards of Northern Ireland," to its being a "ritual" show of protest). Cast as a big news event in itself, the impending death of Sands was framed initially as the probable beginning of something even bigger. When these "all-out" sectarian "assaults" failed to materialize, the narrative fell back to a more cautious revelation of new events and occasional discussion of background, without so much concern to predict future outcomes.

This separation affects intimately the ways in which, and the extent to which, "contra-discourse" can emerge, receive public recognition as credible, and thus begin to challenge the assumptions and claims of dominant official discourse. This is because the separation is profoundly asymmetrical and contradictory. On the one hand, the universality and consensuality embedded in the discourse of law-and-order invest that form of talk with the power of immediacy: The appeal to common sense of the obvious need to act now when law-and-order are threatened. This power is particularly strong when the disruption of social order is most obvious in its presence and effects (and therefore newsworthiness), such as in rioting and violence against people and/or property (cf., Wren-Lewis 1981). Here the separation of political and law-and-order discourse, and the immediate, practical subordination of the former to the latter, are clearest since they appeal to an already known that emanates from the most fundamental already there; the former reproduced intertextually through daily news accounts of crime and punishment, crisis and resolution, disorder and order restoration, etc.; the latter preconstituted in the institutional procedures and separations of the state. On the other hand, the practical subordination of political to law-and-order discourse represents, obversely, the formal privilege of the former over the latter once the context of immediacy is transcended. This power is expressed both in the way the political identifies itself with and elevates discursiveness itself, and in its (the political's) ability to go beyond the here- and-now and enter the discursive space of past and future, of underlying causes and long-term solutions, etc.

The immediate power of law-and-order discourse is mythical in that it signifies a socially naturalized range of practices that are constituted as necessary and inevitable (cf., Barthes, 1973; Hartley, 1982; Knight and Dean, 1982). As a result, its separation from the political does not normally require the character of an explicit labor. Thus we find that the separation of the principal consequences of the hunger strike—the discursive interventions and the rioting—as, respectively, matters of politics and law-and-order, was not registered openly in the news text so much as activated implicitly through the "natural" signifying procedures of the discourse. There was one exception to this, however, the report of May 14. After discussing the latest instances of street violence and the attempt by the I.R.A. to keep it at "a level that could be portrayed as the struggle of an oppressed people, rather than an aggressive show of power," the report continued that "to the despair of many, there was no sign of movement on the political front from any side at all," followed by the remarks of a "moderate Catholic politician" lamenting this state of affairs. The conflict, then, had two "fronts"—the violent and the political—counterposed through the identities of their members: politicians (particularly "moderate" ones no doubt) embrace the political, but are unable to act politically because of the immediacy of the violence from the I.R.A. and its "backers," who thereby exclude themselves from consideration as political subjects, and become a problem of law-and-order. The separation of spheres is, simultaneously, the separation of subjects and their differential inscription into this discourse of power.

Who talks? Who riots? And how do we know them as such? The persistent problem of news is to resolve and re-solve the identity of its subjects and their activity. That it does so in determinate ways is the mark of power in discourse. Those who talked, who attempted intervention discursively in the relationship between the hunger strikers and the state, were generally considered notable enough to be identified by proper name, office (past or present); and cited speech. They were posited, even in those cases where they were not accorded particular prominence, as individual subjects, representatives of authoritative institutions, with fully rational (i.e., humanely rational) motives: to "discuss" the situation, to reach a "compromise definition" of the hunger strikers' penal status, to avoid further loss of life, to prevent "[Sands'] death and the turmoil . . . expected to follow," to act in the "hope (of) eas(ing) the rapidly mounting tensions," to "halt (the) hunger strikes," to issue "an impassioned plea for a 'change of heart.' "

The newsworthiness of these entreaties signifies the work of a class-coded discourse: negotiation, compromise, and an end to violence are institutional instruments idealized in modern society as the bases for restoring and maintaining social order. They express the logic of its dominant institutions: the adversarial system of justice; the parliamentary system of opposition and conflict resolution; and the capitalistic marketplace where those with divergent, opposing interests meet in order to reach agreement through their mutual willingness to talk and compromise. What we encounter in the newsworthiness of these interventions is a fundamental economism of news discourse: like these other institutions, news is promised upon the model of the universal marketplace, the continuous circulation and exchange of commodites realized through the equally continuous circulation and exchange of talk. Talk is the immediate expression and instrument of these institutions' reproduction; talk is the meta-code of the discursive middle class that inhabits and works them.

In the critique of news as ideology, it is commonly argued that both the form and substance of news talk reproduce and legitimate these primary institutions in their powerfulness (Knight, 1982b; Tuchman, 1978). However, while news talk may legitimate institutional structures and formal powers, it may still separate them from their specific inhabitants, the particular personnel that enact those structures and exercise those powers at any moment. At least until the death and burial of Sands, Thatcher's response to this talk of talk and compromise was viewed critically. This was most evident in the editorial commentary of April 29, where the need to maintain an apparently impartial stance was set aside.[4] Thatcher was portrayed as inflexible, and her unwillingness to compromise was seen to strengthen the resolve of the hunger strikers, to provide them with favorable publicity and martyrdom, and thereby increase sectarian hostili-

---

[4] Even in early news event reports there was a hint of mild criticism: Thatcher's remarks were characterized as "terse," and her position as "unyielding." With the re-direction of the narrative after Sands' death (footnote 3); she became "resolute," "steadfast," and "firm."

ties. The commentary referred to Thatcher's "stubbornness," to her "appearing unfeeling and unresponsive," and to her "starchy tone" and "hauteur." Underlying this critical concern was the unspoken, taken-for-granted assumption that her refusal to talk abandoned the very class code that she should embody, both as private citizen—the intertextually established myth of the quintessential English middle-class woman in speech, habits, and outlook—and as the official, public representative of the democratic state. This act of inaction, response of unresponsiveness on her part devalued the position and appearance of the state, reducing it ideologically to the same plane as the hunger strikers. Abstracted by the news from its real historical context, a dichotomy was formed in which the immobility of each side was seen to nourish the other.

This controlled rebuke of Thatcher centered on her having effectively made herself an equal (non-)partner in what ought to be an unequal relationship; by failing to talk of compromise, she undermined the powerfulness of the discursive form and, therewith, the authority of the democratic state and its discursive middle class.[5] (In the marketplace, after all is said, the abstract equivalence of buyer and seller is normally transformed into concrete inequality once agreement is reached, an inequality which, as Marx recognized, is already there, concealed from open view by an ideology of individualism and voluntary exchange.) Thatcher's negative stance—"stressing only what Britain won't do," as the April 29 editorial phrased it—undermined the moral authority that normally adheres to the democratic state (the ideological form of its democraticness); and that normally constitutes the "already there" of its acceptable power—the authority to initiate resolution. The legitimacy of this power derives not only from eschewing action without prior talk, but also, at the same time, from its not appearing exclusively rationalistic and powerful. The economism of the discourse is one-sided and incomplete by itself; it functions properly only in relation to its obverse—humanism. When the news discourse distanced itself from Thatcher's refusal to talk, it did so not only because this action of hers contravened the rule of economism—the need to compromise to

---

[5] As the actions of the hunger strikers were framed initially in idealistic terms, i.e., as symbolic rather than practical, then so too was the critique of Thatcher's (in)actions. This centered on the concrete aspects of the hunger strikers' demands which were seen by the discourse as a matter of penal reform separate from the question of special political prisoner status. Having noted that Thatcher was "right in refusing to yield political status Bobby Sands," the April 29 editorial continued that there were other issues on which the British government could "honorably yield." The editorial then raised "the petty question of prison clothing" asking why those engaged in the protest should not be allowed to wear ordinary clothing rather than prison-issued uniforms.

In the absence of any historical account of the relationship between the hunger strike, the concrete demands, and political status, this question seemed plausible enough. The report of May 25, however, began to re-cast the government's position as well as the strikers in a more practical light (though it failed to mention that the earlier conferral of political status had been brought about by a hunger strike also), by noting that free association within the prison led to the reinforcement of political cliques and factions, and that the freedom to wear civilian clothing allowed the prisoners to dress in paramilitary uniforms.

realize self-interest—but also because it stood as the sign of the absence of humanism as well. This was evident in the editorial's opinion that Thatcher's position made her seem "unfeeling" and "unresponsive," and that to end the conflict would take "courage but also compassion."

These criticisms of Thatcher, by the discursive interveners and the news editorialist, should be taken as complementary. They signified an attempt to restore the balance of economism and humanism, to reaffirm the sensitive substance of the state's rational form, and thereby restore the appearance of universality and full rationality. At the same time, these actions also disclosed a desire to restore the interveners' own form of authority, discourse itself, and realign the fragments of the discursive class as a whole within the sphere of political power that is realized. This restoration and realignment consisted simultaneously in the exclusion of those who rioted (and fasted) from the authority of discursiveness, and their reappropriation as the objects of discursive policy.

In contrast to those who talked, those who rioted remained nameless, without office, and speechless in the conventional sense. In part, the discourse enlisted the participants themselves to justify this absence of comparable identity. Their namelessness was seen to express an anonymity that was actively desired: the rioters "wear ski masks to preserve their anonymity" when "engaging" soldiers and police. Nonetheless, this appears as an admission of criminality. Moreover, proper names do not represent subjects so much as simply designate an abstract form (this individual rather than some other) that requires concrete substantiation; thus the presence of the names of the discursive interveners required also the presence of their offices and speech to create a sense of real subjectivity. The non-identity of the rioters, in regard to the ways in which the talkers were established: the absence of their proper names, offices and speech, spoke not so much to their own complicity in the structuration of the story, as to the way in which the discourse established them as a contradistinction.

The positive identity of the rioters was framed in two ways. First, they were given a collective identity that connoted criminality and dangerousness: "gangs," "mobs," "bands," and "groups" described as "roving," "rampag(ing)," "rioting," "stone-throwing," and "maurading" (sic). Second, they were identified by age: "youth," "youthful," and "young." On both counts, they stood in textual opposition to those who talked, an opposition that represented a real class division. To name subjects is to confer individuality, however abstractly; to ignore age is to imply universality and representativeness. Not only did these two distinguish talkers and rioters, and as political versus law-and-order subjects, they also established the primary link between the latter and the hunger strikers themselves; but as an association of context, sentiment, and symbolism rather than of rational action. Apart from the rioters, the hunger strikers were the only other news subjects to be identifield consistently in terms of collectivity—members of nationalist organizations engaged in concerted symbolic action—and age.

The identity of the rioters is decoded primarily through a myth of youthfulness that similarly evokes a double reading, a dialectic of meaning that reflects the economism/humanism couplet of the discursive interventions. Youthfulness is simultaneously unserious and, in the context of collective violence, tragic. On the one hand, the youthfulness of these rioters was unserious in that it was not insistently political; it reflected the disposition to challenge and rebel as a group in a way that is marginal, evanescent, and non-rational: the "agefulness" of the rioters meant that they were temporary. In this respect, the substance of discursive economism appeared as its very absence. There was, for example, rarely any explicit mention of a rational connection between the actions of these youths and the hunger strikers. Their relatedness was implied by the textual association of the two, by the sharing of contiguous discursive spaces, rather than established in a consistently open manner. News of the violence began on a daily basis on April 20, but it was not until April 26 that the first explicit connection was made between the rioting and the fasts with reference to the former being "fueled by Mr. Sands' hunger strike." This metaphor implied, moreover, that the rioting had some other, unspecified source to which the fasts were adding effect. It was not until April 28 that the rioters were explicitly identified as "sympathizers of a jailed I.R.A. member . . . on a hunger strike."

The inability to ascribe rational motivation is, obversely, the resort to an uncritical naturalism on the part of the news narrative. The rioting was depicted as action for its own sake—symbolic in effect, ritual in organization—emanating from essentially natural forces which, while potentially uncontrollable and sudden, were nonetheless constrained by their ritual symbolism.[6] This naturalism is evident in the metaphors used by the discourse to account for the violence and to speak of its occurrence: "erupt," "break out," "outbreak," "spasm," "flare," "tumult," and "torn by" violence. These metaphors of pathological and geological forcefulness complement, and are constrained by, the metaphors of a naturalized sociality: the symbolic, ritual, and cyclical character of these demonstrations of protest.

On the other hand, the myth of youthfulness is tragic in this context of conflict and violence; it connotes waste and irrationality. On this side of myth we see how humanism derives from its relation to economism: the assessment of human action according to the formula of opportunity cost; what better—more peaceful, more constructive, more enjoyable—way in which these youths could be "spending" their time. Humanism takes on the form of a moral economism of waste, as was most clearly evident in the background report of

---

[6] Unlike the hunger strikers and the government, the symbolism of the rioters' behavior was not given the opportunity to be recast in more rational, practical terms. That the street barricades erected by the demonstrators may have been designed for the practical purpose of keeping the security forces out of nationalist areas to prevent harassment and retaliation was not a possibility raised in the discourse.

May 7. Noting first that Sands, "jailed for terrorist crimes," had joined the I.R.A. at the age of 18, and that other adolescents from the same neighborhood, "seething with . . . hatred," provided further potential recruits for that "illegal organization," the narrative proceeded to evoke the sense of futility and waste by comparing these youths to their American counterparts: "The younger boys, at an age when their American counterparts are learning to throw a baseball, are already throwing stones and bottles at the army trucks." Brought together by the common activity of throwing—physical, natural, youthful—the two were immediately dispersed to opposite poles: the American to the wholesome and normal (throwing as recreation and fun), the Irish to the tragic and abnormal (throwing as violence and hate).

The very grounds on which this comparison was made disclose the powerfulness of discourse at work. That the account did not establish the comparison by referring instead to the unlawful or otherwise deviant pursuits of American adolescents (which surveys and statistics suggest are quite widespread), was not merely a sign of journalistic chauvinism (American journalists give plenty of attention to domestic crime and deviance in other news contexts). Rather, it represented avoidance of the potentially radical, political implications just such a comparison would have begun to make. To compare Irish youths throwing stones and bottles at the official representatives of law-and-order, with American youths engaged in mugging or the use of illicit narcotics, would have begun to demonstrate, not the fundamental, apparently natural, similarity of youthfulness, but rather the radical social difference. It would have established the political character of the former in a way that the baseball comparison, by evoking proximity as well as distance, could not. It would have begun to recognize a contra-discourse challenging the safety of the separation of politics and law-and-order.

This comparison shows, nonetheless, that the rioters were indeed given a discourse, though not in the conventional sense of speech. The speechlessness of the rioters existed only in the conventional sense of an absence of talk: speech as the verbal expression of ideas, as the agency of intent, as the instrument of intellectual labor. The absence of speech in this idealist sense points obversely to the "speechfulness" of the rioters in a radically different, materialist sense: the speech of the body, the coherence of muscle, flesh, limbs, the instrument of physical labor. The real relations of stratification were reproduced in the differential modes of communication allowed to the subjects of the discourse.

Here too the rioters were joined to the hunger strikers by a common sign: the misuse and abuse of the body. Just as the latter talked to us through the passivity of their bodies—self-inflicted deterioration as the ultimate sign of non-rationality: the denial of self-reproduction—so the former talked to us through the activity of their bodies. The rioters came to throw their meaning, their identification, to us, and, insofar as we are inscribed into the discourse as rational subjects who read according to the same elaborated and privileged code, also at us. Within the perimeters of this code, however, this speech of the body is confrontational and problematic; it is the sign of disruption and disorder, opposed to conventional speech, the discursive mode of that privileged political sphere, that attempts to resolve and re-order. This speech of the body is the sign of a subordinate class, though a class not identified as such, but rather in terms of its youthfulness, its Catholic-ness, the shabbiness and low-income-ness of its neighborhoods. It is the speech of regression, of those incapable of speaking otherwise.

By using so visibly the speech of the body—and in a way that transgressed those broad prescriptions for bodily self-discipline—the rioters (and hunger strikers) enabled a double movement of discourse. They allowed for their own exclusion from its privileged sphere as equivalent subjects, and so prepared the way for their reappropriation as the objects of official policy. In the different ways in which the news text posited its subjects—ways that seemed quite natural (would it have been possible to speak without irony of "gangs" of officials, of "outbreaks" of talk?)—it showed a certain complicity in this objectification and the operation of power that accompanied it. However much the story of these riotous youths may have evoked sentiments of anguished concern, it nonetheless looked at them with powerful objectivity, with an object-like regard: whether we attributed their behavior to a deteriorating social environment (bad housing and schooling, unemployment, discrimination, etc.), or to the pathologies of crowd psychology (agitators, copycats, etc.), these youths were constituted as a problem, to be administered and resolved within the authoritative practices of officials and experts, of subjects such as those who warranted identification in the news in terms of names, offices, and cited speech. The humanism of the discursive class, a humanism invoked and reproduced within the official-like regard of the modern journalist, consists in a desire of power.

FINAL REMARKS

Throughout, the hunger strike and its consequences were understood, intertextually, as part of an "ancient sectarian struggle," a frame of interpretation reinforced by references to rioting in "Catholic neighborhoods," and to "heightened tensions" between Catholics and Protestants. At the same time, the hunger strikers were defined usually as nationalists and as members of nationalist and republican organizations, not according to their religious affiliations; and although sectarian violence did occur, prominence was given to news coverage of the hostilities between the supporters of the hunger strikers and the security forces. This dislocation between the general news frame and the particular reporting of news events represents the separation of politics and law-and-order. The persistence of the sectarian frame—when indeed the conflict as a whole had taken on quite new proportions as a struggle between the state and a particular, dissenting community within its boundaries—pointed to the formal privilege and authority of the political as a sphere of discursiveness that transcends the immediacy of the here-and-now. Talk of ancient sectarian struggles displayed the discursive authority of the news text, its ability to speak of that level of underlying causes. The substance of this frame was significant of both the non-rationality (indeed irrationality) of the conflict (it is fundamentally religious), and, therefore, of the need for the state to balance economism and humanism. Confronted by a force that was seen as at once collective, emotional, symbolic, and, above all, natural—those who were "seething with . . . hatred" were those who "break out" in rioting, who erected street barricades as "symbols of sovereignty"—discursive rationality objectified its subjects.

Yet however powerful this objectivity, it came to disclose contradiction. On the one hand, we were reassured by the implicit submission of the rioters (and the fasters) to talk of rational policy (talk of feeling and compassion, talk of penal reform); on the other, we were confronted by an objectivity that was non-rational and natural, with all this implied of autonomy, irresistibility. As rational subjects we ask: why not negotiate and compromise?—to be faced with the self-decay of imprisoned bodies and the violent eruptions of youthful gangs. For those who read by the rules of official-like discourse, the resolution of this division is persistently problematic. For the discursive interveners it involved the resort to a half-measure, the call for greater humanism on the part of the state to remove this object of disquiet. For these subjects the moral authority of the democratic state came to consist in its capacity to act in ways it does not have to. For the state and its political representatives, it involved the outspoken reification of the separation of politics and law-and-order, of the realm of acceptable discursiveness from the immediacy of maintaining public order and the rule of legality. The reiteration in the news of Thatcher's remarks that the strikers were acting from free choice and that crime is crime, not politics, represented more than simply the self-defense of a politician on the run. It spoke to and from that division that the fasts and the riots were threatening: the individuality of choice and the universality of law, a division that emanates from the most fundamental already there, the alienation of labor from labor-power.

In recognizing that news uncritically reproduces dominant social forms, we must recognize that it also reproduces the plays of power and contradiction inherent in those forms (Knight, 1982b). News discourse does not deny this dialectic so much as impose a textual closure that suppresses it. Its modelized realism, its sheer factfulness, its eternal revelation of recurrent events, all these contribute to the ideological power of news. All create a separation of subject and object, of form and substance, without mediation. The closure of news talks works so long as news keeps on talking this way. So long as it promotes the mode of discourse itself, replacing one story with its formal equivalent, authorizing the idealism of the discursive class as a whole, it does not subvert (cf., Baudrillard, 1981). In this way the power of this ceaseless discourse comes to consist in its being quickly forgettable. For if we are to ask how all this talk of hunger strike and riot perpetuates ideology at large, we have simply to ask: who, after all, can now recall the death of Bobby Sands?

REFERENCES

Altheide, D. (1976). *Creating Reality: How Television News Distorts Events*. Beverly Hills, CA: Sage.

Barthes, R. (1973). *Mythologies*. London: Palladin.

Baudrillard, J. (1981). *For a Critique of the Political Economy of the Sign*. St. Louis, MO: Telos Press.

Chibnall, S. (1972). *Law and Order News*. London: Tavistock.

Clarke, A., and Taylor, I. (1980). "Vandals, Pickets, and Muggers: Television Coverage of Law and Order in the 1979 Election." *Screen Education*. (No. 36), 99-111.

Coward R., and Ellis, J. (1977). *Language and Materialism*. London: Routledge and Kegan Paul.

Fishman, M. (1978). "Crime Waves as Ideology" *Social Problems 25*, 531-543.

Fishman, M. (1980). *Manufacturing the News*. Austin TX: University of Texas Press.

Foucault, M. (1971). "Orders of Discourse", trans. by R. Swyer. *Social Science Information, 10* (No. 2), 7-30.

Gans, H. (1979). *Deciding What's News*. New York: Pantheon.

Glasgow Media Group. (1976). *Bad News*. London: Routledge and Kegan Paul.

Glasgow Media Group. (1980). *More Bad News*. London: Routledge and Kegan Paul.

Hall, S. (1973). "A World At One With Itself." In S. Cohen and J. Young (Eds.), *The Manufacture of News*. London: Constable.

Hall, S., Critcher, C., Jefferson, T., Clarke, J., and Roberts, B. (1978). *Policing the Crisis: Mugging, the State, and Law and Order*. London: Macmillan.

Hartley, J. (1982). *Understanding News*. London: Methuen.

Knight, G. (1982a). "Strike Talk: A Case Study of News" *Canadian Journal of Communication 8* (No. 3), 61-79.

Knight, G. (1982b). "News and Ideology." *Canadian Journal of Communication 8* (No. 4), 15-41.

Knight, G., and Dean, T. (1982). "Myth and the Structure of News" *Journal of Communication 32* (No. 2), 144-161.

Machrey, P. (1978). *A Theory of Literary Production*. London: Routledge and Kegan Paul.

Molotch, H., and Lester, M. (1975). "Accidental News: The Great Oil Spill as Local Occurrence and National Event." *American Journal of Sociology*. 81, 235-260.

Schlesinger, P. (1978). *Putting "Reality" Together: B.B.C. News*. London: Constable.

Tuchman, G. (1978). *Making News*. New York: Free Press.

Tumber, H. (1982). *Television and the Riots*. London: British Film Institute.

Wren-Lewis, J. (1981). "The Story of a Riot: The Television Coverage of Civil Unrest in 1981." *Screen Education*. (No. 40), 15-33.

20

An Analysis of Anti-Handgun Propaganda

JERRY M. GOLDBERG
Pace University

A handgun is a firearm designed to be fired with one hand (Shields, 1981, p. 1), and the American public often finds itself inundated by media campaigns and news stories centering on its control. The issue of its regulation rises from the ashes every time an assassin's handgun bullet is directed at a major public figure such as Malcolm X, Robert F. Kennedy, George Wallace, Larry Flynt, Gerald R. Ford, Allard Lowenstein, Michael Halberstam, or Ronald Reagan.

The anti-handgun position is linked in the public mind with liberalism—the Northeast, academia, and urban centers. Pro-handgun forces, exemplified by the 2 million member National Rifle Association (NRA), represent a powerful and well-funded interest group which has succeeded in thwarting most attempts at control. Its support comes most strongly from the South, West, and Midwest, among conservatives and in rural areas.

The difficulties encountered by advocates of handgun control have not been those of numbers alone, because a significant majority of Americans favor additional handgun regulation. Rather, difficulties have stemmed from a paucity of dedication and funds. The more successful pro-handgun advocates can be divided into two main groups, gun owners and gun and paraphernalia sellers. Owners provide the intensity and dedication. Gun sellers provide the bulk of the funding and massive indirect support. The NRA is aided by Colt Industries, Smith and Wesson, Sturm, Ruger and Company, and other manufacturers of handguns and accessories who purchase ads in hunting and gun sports magazines, in the NRA's *American Rifleman,* and on television shows which feature firearms use. They commission or support studies. They provide speakers and print and distribute brochures showing the camaraderie and other joys of "responsible gun ownership." However, there is no industrial support *not* to sell handguns. Recently, though, a new coalition has given a new voice to the anti-handgun forces.

The death of John Lennon in December, 1980, brought new life to anti-handgun forces. *The New York Times* discussed this rebirth last October as it detailed the effects on Handgun Control, Inc., the leading anti-handgun group,

> after John Lennon was killed with a pistol last December in New York City . . . Handgun Control's crowded office . . . had more contributions and telephone calls than it could handle (Herber, 1981, p. 14).

The influx of funds provided the means to purchase full page newspaper ads in major newspapers following the March, 1981, attempt on the life of President Reagan. The Reagan ads, in turn, brought in additional funds and members, and the organization now numbers its membership at a half million (Herber, 1981). The new membership and unaccustomed revenue had provided the anti-handgun lobby with the means of more fully utilizing the mass media to advance their cause.

In the past, analyses of anti-handgun propaganda have been concentrated in pro-handgun publications. Consequently they have been biased against the anti-handgun position, resembling refutations more than analyses. In this study (whose goal is neither affirmation nor refutation), Rank's Intensify/Downplay model (Rank, 1976, pp. 7-19) and Maslow's Hierarchy of Needs model (Maslow, 1976, pp. 35-58) have been utilized. Rank deals with the message—what is *stated* and what is *intensified*—what is *omitted* and what is *downplayed*. His model deals with what the propagandist does. Maslow's model, which is designed as a psychological model and is popularly used in advertising and marketing, affords a means of determining why the distorted picture of reality is to the propagandist's advantage.

Because the handgun control lobby is composed of many organizations, *ad hoc* (such as the National Coalition to Ban Handguns and Handgun Control, Inc.) and broader interest groups (such as the United States Conference of Mayors), this analysis is conducted on an issue basis rather than by the source of the propaganda.

Public opinion polls have important implications in propaganda studies. They make possible the use of Rank's Intensify side under the heading of *association*. We live in a nation where "democracy" and "majority rule" are "God" terms. The extension of this concept is obvious—if most people want it, it must be good. The appeal is also to the bandwagon effect—hop on now before you get left behind. Maslow would say that the need to belong is being satisfied.

Wright conducted an analysis of two polls: the Decision Making Information, Inc. (DMI) study, commissioned by the NRA, and the Cambridge Reports, Inc. (Caddell) study, paid for by the Center for the Study and Prevention of Violence. Both polls were conducted in 1978. Wright (1981, p. 39) noted:

> So far as public opinion on such a complex an issue can be summarized at all, the thrust of majority thinking on gun control seems to be that the government should be just as careful about who is allowed to own and use a firearm as it is about who is allowed to own and use automobiles or other potentially hazardous commodities.

Larry Lowenstein (brother of the slain ex-Congressman, Allard) (1982, p. 4) writing a mass mail letter on Handgun Control stationery utilizes such statistics as, "over 200 million Americans support tougher handgun control laws." In naming no specific study nor the specific controls supported he *omits* that material—he *downplays* to maximize the bandwagon effect.

Another, more blatant, omission is committed by Lowenstein as Wright (1981, p. 39) noted:

> most people anticipate that stricter weapons controls would have little or no effect on crime . . . [These conclusions] are, I believe, fully consistent with all evidence reported in both the Caddell and D.M.I. surveys; they are also consistent with the evidence from NORC, Gallup, Roper, and indeed, all other polls and surveys of which I am aware.

Lowenstein, nevertheless, implies that a reduction of handguns will reduce handgun crime. In omitting the public's lack of faith in the efficacy of handgun control as a cure for crime in his letter he "downplays" contradictory evidence. The exact wording of a question, its relationship to other questions in a series, and similar factors can influence the answers. *Playboy* Senior Editor William J. Helmer gives an example of the type of question rarely but properly asked, "Do you think the government should have the power to prohibit you from keeping a gun in your home or place of business?" (Helmer, 1982, p. 132). The respondent is asked to determine not whether *other* people should have guns, but whether *he* or *she* should have a gun. *Other* people are careless, violent, irresponsible. *He* or *she* is careful, controlled, responsible. The Caddell study was specific in offering different types of control for the respondents to consider. When easy-to-agree-with items such as "a crackdown on illegal sales" are considered, an agreement rate of 88% results. A similar percentage approved of a "waiting period . . . to allow for a criminal records check" (Wright, 1981, p. 32). These are the statistics the anti-handgun lobby loves to cite. It is not surprising that such questions were asked by a control-commissioned pollster.

It is also no surprise that the Caddell study made no attempt to duplicate previous surveys which asked the questions on a personal basis. In 1968, an Opinion Research Center survey found that 52% of the sample expressed a lack of faith in law enforcement agency protection when asked, "Do you think that people like yourself have to be prepared to defend their homes against violence, or can the police take care of that?" When responding to the Harris Poll question, "Do you tend to agree or disagree that the way things are today, people should own guns for their own protection?" In 1971, 49% agreed, 43% disagreed, and 8% had no opinion (Wright, 1981, p. 31).

The issue is complex and the public is ambivalent and confused, and it is in this environment of confusion that the propagandist thrives. Lowenstein and other handgun control advocates *downplay* what is in contradiction by *omission* and take advantage of the *confusion* by offering a simple solution to the problem. In 1981, former DuPont executive Pete Shields, the chairman of Handgun Control, Inc., wrote a book *Guns Don't Die, People Do*. The title is a play on the more familiar NRA unofficial slogan, "Guns don't kill!—People do!" The message is "pro-gun people love guns—anti-gun people love people."

In an attempt to "personalize" the deaths from handguns, Handgun Control has taken a largely emotional approach. Shields (1981, pp. 11-24) describes the origin of his own involvement in the anti-handgun movement which began with his son Nick's death as a random victim of San Francisco's "Zebra Killers." Other members of the Handgun Control board send letters-to-the-editor, have their names on mass-mailed letters, or appear on radio and television shows (Shields, 1981, pp. 133-144). They relate stories, not of the deaths of thousands, but of one single individual. We cannot help but be impressed by the magnitude of the 10,728 who were murdered by handguns in 1979. We cannot *associate*, however, with death on that scale but we can empathize with individual tragedy. Shields quotes others whose children, siblings, parents, and spouses were handgun victims in similar anecdotal fashion. He calls this the "victim's strategy" which is part of every aspect of the work at Handgun Control, Inc. (Shields, 1981, p. 134). Further examples of this technique are to be found in a letter-to-the-editor of *The New York Times* by board member Odile Stern (1981) in which she writes:

> On my desk there is a photograph taken in 1978, the portrait of a young woman smiling, my daughter. Her features have not aged, her youthful face will never change, frozen into death by a bullet, three years ago.

Similarly, Lowenstein produces a letter on Handgun Control stationery noting that:

> Right now *one in five Americans* will be victimized by handgun violence during their lifetime and that includes you or your loved ones—your husband, wife, daughter or son, mother or father, brother or sister . . . Last year over one thousand New Yorkers died because of senseless handgun violence. One of those slain was my own brother, former Congressman Allard Lowenstein (Lowenstein, 1982).

Both writers *intensify* using *association*. Handguns equal murder. Safety exists in the absence of handguns. Banning or minimizing handgun ownership equates with love of family. On the Maslow scale the appeals are to safety and belonging.

Statistics, too, are selectively utilized. Handgun opponents readily discuss the numbers of Americans who are murdered with handguns (10,728 in 1979, or 5 per 100,000 population). But, they fail to draw any comparisons which might minimize the impact of their statistics on any segment of the population. Helmer (1982, p. 182) notes that the rate of murder is identical with the death rate for women on oral contraceptives. Yet a demand for a ban of contraceptives has not resulted in a coalition of a half million active members. He also notes that advocates of handgun control do little to provide the demographic statistics which would convince the white middle class that *their* chances of being victimized by handgun violence is far less than the one in five to which Lowenstein referred should their concerns tend to be personal rather than societal.

> most of [the] killings are of the bedroom-and-barroom variety and involve a rather select group of white hillbillies and black or brown slum dwellers given to offing

one another at truly impressive rates . . . [most] are drunk or on drugs . . . in cities the majority have police records and a substantial percentage initiate the fight themselves. Your average sober citizen in a nice white suburb is about as likely to get hit by a bullet as by a lightning bolt, unless he shoots himself with the pistol he bought for self protection (Helmer, 1982, p. 182).

Another example of *omission* is evident throughout anti-handgun propaganda. The number of handguns has increased each year. Shields, himself, provides the statistics for 1969 to 1979, as well as the number of handgun murders from 1972 to 1979 (Shields, 1981, p. 174). If the number of handgun deaths increases as a result of an increase in the number of handguns, the number of deaths should have increased each year as handguns have increased in number. Shields (1981, pp. 40-41) writes,

> Here are the blunt facts in handguns in circulation in America:
> - 40 to 60 million now.
> - 2.5 million more produced and sold each year.
> - At current rates, approximately 100 million in circulation by the year 2000.
> - A new handgun sold every thirteen seconds.
> - One in five Americans with access to a handgun. *Given these facts, is it any wonder that one of us is murdered with a handgun in the United States every fifty minutes.*

Here Shields *omits* and *diverts* as he makes the reader complete the syllogism—limit handguns and handgun murders will decline. Shields chooses to omit the statistics that, of the years listed, handgun murders were the highest in 1974 and lowest in 1977 despite the fact that the number of guns had increased each year.

A final area of statistical maneuvering is found in the use of the studies of weapons substitution by Zimring. Quoting Zimring, the United States Conference of Mayors' Handgun Control Project publication notes:

> Serious assault with a gun is five times as likely to cause death as a similar attack with a knife, the next most dangerous weapon, and gun robberies are four times as likely to result in the death of a victim as are other kinds of robbery (Adviani and Drake, 1975, p. 5).

However, Hardy and Kates examined Zimring's findings and concluded:

> Though Zimring purports to be comparing the lethality of gun versus knife wounds, he includes in the latter not only deep stab wounds inflicted with stilettoes, ice picks, butcher knives, etc. but also slash wounds and those made with small pen or pocket knives or even beer-can openers (Hardy and Kates, 1979, p. 124).

Hardy and Kates (1979, pp. 124-125) continue their analysis of Zimring's findings and reject the suggestion that *homicidally intended* attacks would be less lethal in the absence of handguns. A robber who would have a handgun would hardly choose a penknife or beer-can opener if handguns were not available. It is logical, they maintain, that such an individual would choose a long-bladed stabbing weapon and such a weapon is, according to medical studies, equally lethal in the case of penetrating abdominal wounds. While fault might be found with the use of statistics only on *abdominal* wounds for comparison, Zimring's study still has methodological flaws omitted by the Conference of Mayors study. These omissions of the methodological indictments of Zimring's work *downplays* that which is in opposition to the thesis being posited. To include the indictments is to risk minimizing the appeal to safety.

Pro-handgun advocates are wont to cite the Second Amendment of the Constitution which states, "the right of the people to keep and bear Arms, shall not be infringed." Shields (1981) attacks the concept that the right to keep and bear arms is an *individual* right. He argues, first, the pro-gun forces are selective in *their* use of the Constitution as the initial 13 words are deleted in most of their argumentation. Those words are, "A well regulated Militia, being necessary to the security of a free State."

He argues that the Supreme Court has rejected that argument and cites five specific cases: U.S. v. Cruickshank (1875); Presser v. Illinois (1886); Miller v. Texas (1894); U.S. v. Miller (1939); and U.S. v. Tot (1942). He cites a 1975 statement of the American Bar Association in support—after making certain to point out that the ABA is not a doctrinaire liberal group (Shields, 1981, p. 137).

Shields is using *repetition* to drive home his point. Further intensity is gained by *association* as his position is made identical with those of two of the most prestigious legal institutions in the country—the U.S. Supreme Court and the American Bar Association.

Shields (1981, p. 56) considers the NRA position on the Second Amendment and takes their claim to a right to bear arms to the point of absurdity as he argues:

> In fact, if we follow the N.R.A.'s current constitutional argument to its logical conclusion, then we could say that any American has a constitutional right to own *any* type of weapon—a bazooka, a tank, even a warplane!

No NRA publication or spokesman has ever advocated the right of the citizenry to own heavy weapons, yet Shields has shifted the focus of the argument from .22 Barettas and .44 Ruger Magnums to weapons of mass destruction. Even those who would like the sense of protection a handgun in the night table might afford would probably be repelled by the idea of a Panzer in their neighbor's family room.

The NRA has long been successful in gaining mass support for its stands against gun control. It has always been able to convince its members to respond with letters, telegrams, phone calls, and petitions to voice opposition to anti-gun legislation. Senators Tydings and McGovern lost long-held seats in the United States Senate following massive NRA activities to unseat them. To many gun owners, gun control isn't *an* issue, it's *the* issue and elected officials are loath to forget that fact.

Handgun Control Inc. is currently conducting a campaign which is seemingly directed against pro-handgun congressmen. In his book, Shields (1981, p. 169) discusses the "victim strategy" using TV ads showing a woman discussing the death of her grandson, whose picture was displayed next to her. The message was:

> If I'd done this before, maybe my grandson would be alive today. Brian didn't die in Vietnam. He was just seven and a half when he was killed with a pistol by a man who assaulted him and then took his own life. Since 1970, 192,000 Americans like Brian have been killed with handguns. Not in Vietnam—here at home. Now the National Rifle Association wants to repeal the few laws we have to control pistols. And Congressman Findley agrees with them. I'm sure he's a nice man, but how else can we ever get Washington to care if we don't defeat the congressmen who don't seem to care? So I won't be voting for the National Rifle Association's congressmen this year. I'll be voting for the Brian's in our lives. It can't help my grandson. He's dead, but it's not too late for yours.

Congressman Findley survived the ad, but his 70% victory in 1978 was reduced to 56% in 1980, a year when a Republican president carried many candidates on his coattails (Shields, 1981, p. 169). The message is clear: Paul Findley killed Brian because he supports the NRA position. This is the use of *association*. The ultimate message was delivered on November 3, 1982, when Paul Findley lost his seat in the election (*New York Times*, Nov. 4, 1982, p. A24).

In New York, Senator Alphonse D'Amato is the target of a current campaign. That is the focus of the Lowenstein (1982) letter. It states that D'Amato is sponsoring a bill (the Federal Fireams Reform Act, also known as the McClure-Volkmer Act) which would reduce federal control over firearms. That is true. It also states that the NRA gave him $16,259 in political contributions in 1980. That is also true. But the letter condemns D'Amato for taking such an action which Lowenstein (who signed the letter) says *"endangers the lives of the very people he represents."* The letter continues:

> Why did he do it?
> Perhaps its because he received $16,159 from the National Rifle Association's Political Victory Fund in the last election. Perhaps that's also why he hired a former N.R.A. lobbyist as his chief legislative assistant.

Lowenstein has resorted to an *ad hominem* attack as a *diversion* in which he implies that D'Amato's actions were determined by greed, not conviction. It is just as likely that the NRA has given its support to D'Amato because his position on matters of gun control coincides with theirs. D'Amato has responded to the letter campaign saying that his position on gun control was well known before the campaign. Senator D'Amato won the 1980 election by a plurality, not a majority, in a race against two liberal candidates (Jacob Javits and Elizabeth Holtzman). It is unlikely that D'Amato will benefit from a divided opposition when he runs for reelection in 1986. He will also lose any vote-getting ability a popular president running on the same ticket might bring. D'Amato's ardor may cool enough so that he does not fight as hard, if at all, for the pro-handgun side of the issue. And, if D'Amato·is right—if the letter campaign is but "an effective fund raising gimmick" (Clines and Weintraub, 1981)—he and other pro-gun candidates may find themselves opposed by powerful, well-funded pressure groups with "big bucks" to back *their* candidates. The campaign may raise sufficient funds to put anti-handgun candidates "over-the-top" through the use of the media on *other* issues. They may use campaign funds from anti-handgun groups to stress other issues important in their states and districts. But, regardless of the issues which led to the successful campaign, when they get into Congress each will be one additional anti-handgun vote while their opponent's defeat subtracts one vote from the pro-gun majority. The future political victims may be the Tydings and McGoverns of the pro-gun side of the controversy.

The future has always been impossible to determine with total accuracy. But, some insight is possible from an examination of the signs. The seeds of a powerful new lobby were planted long ago; they are just beginning to take root. The issues are there and handgun opponents are just beginning to exploit them. They are becoming increasingly effective as they have brought the issue down to a personal level. Within a few years they may equal the NRA in membership, funding, and influence. Then the propaganda war will become even more intense. Just as England, Japan, and France have not become dictatorships because they restrict handgun ownership, the extension of handgun control laws will not make criminals law-abiding, lunatics sane, nor the fearful less concerned with threats to their well-being. Complex problems require complex solutions. The question is whether or not the public will demand such solutions or succumb to the propagandist and deal in terms of absolutes where truth and reason are the ultimate victims.

REFERENCES

Adviani, J., and Drake, W. R. (1975). *Handgun Control . . . Issues and Alternatives*. Handgun Project of the United States Conference of Mayors. Washington, D.C.

Clines, F. X., and Weintraub, B. (1981). *New York Times* (Nov. 6).

Hardy, D. T., and Kates, D. B., Jr. (1979). "Handgun Prohibition and Crime." In D. B. Kates, Jr. (Ed.), *Resricting Handguns—The Liberal Skeptics Speak Out*. Croton on Hudson, NY: North River Press.

Helmer, W. J. (1982). "Guns and Rhetoric," *Playboy* (Mar.).

Herber, J. (1981). *New York Times* (Oct. 22).

Lowenstein, L. (1982). (Letter on Handgun Control Stationery).

Maslow, A. H. (1976). *Motivation and Personality*, 2nd ed. New York: Harper and Row.

Rank, H. (1976). In D. Dieterich (Ed.), *Teaching About Doublespeak*. Urbana, IL: National Council of Teachers of English.

Shields, P., with Greenya, J. (1981). *Guns Don't Die—People Do*. New York: Arbor House.

Stern, O. (1981). (Letter-to-the-Editor). *New York Times* (Oct. 22).

Wright, J. D. (1981). "Public Opinion and Gun Control: A Comparison of Results from Two Recent Surveys." *Annals of the American Academy of Political and Social Sciences, 455*, 24-39.

PART IV

INSTITUTIONS

21

The Role of Values in Supreme Court Opinions as Legal and Cultural Force

CANDISS BAKSA VIBBERT
Purdue University

Supreme Court opinions justify judicial decisions (Jones, 1976, p. 121). As Charles A. Miller (1969, pp. 11–12) states: "Judicial opinions are the most permanent and public manifestation of the work of the courts. . . . The function of opinions is to convince the judge, the parties, and the public that cases are rightly decided." In the Supreme Court, this conviction—that cases are "rightly decided"—has been associated most often with the reasoning processes employed by Supreme Court Justices in their opinions (see Gottlieb, 1968). Reasoning is commonly agreed to be a crucial, if not the "essential element of the judicial process" (Miller, 1969, p. 11). Since Supreme Court Justices are highly cognizant of this expectation for reasoned opinions, their opinions utilize the forms of legal reasoning and the norms of the legal tradition. The Supreme Court is a legal institution—thus, it strives to fulfill those legal expectations: but the Court is not *merely* a legal institution. The Supreme Court is also a symbol of American culture (Miller, 1978, pp. 11–49), and an institution for the preservation of the "social-political bonds of the nation" (Miller, 1969, p. 189). Supreme Court opinions justify judicial decisions not only as the right legal decision in a case, but as a case which is "rightly decided" in the legal environment for a cultural community of Americans.

The concomitant functioning of the Supreme Court as legal authority and cultural guardian is accomplished through the justificatory role of values in Supreme Court opinions. The values of Americans are rhetorical resources for the Court; values are a resource of legal justification with cultural force. This paper illustrates the strategic use of value appeals in four Supreme Court cases from the 1982 summer term: *Board of Education v Pico; Nixon v Fitzgerald; Enmund v Florida; and New York v Ferber*.[1] These cases deal respectively with

---

[1] Since all of these cases are from the same term, they are all recorded in the same volume of Supreme Court opinions. The citations are as follows: *Board of Education v Pico*, 73 L Ed 2d 435–481; *Nixon v Fitzgerald*, 73 L Ed 2d 349–395; *Enmund v Florida*, 73 L Ed 2d 1140–1173; and *New York v Ferber*, 73 L Ed 2d 1113–1139. In the paper, references to these cases are contained under headings which identify the case and the majority or dissenting opinions. Consequently hereafter, citations from these opinions include only the page numbers for reference.

school library censorship, presidential immunity, the death penalty, and child pornography. These highly controversial cases—selected, indeed, because they represent cultural as well as legal conflict—reveal the centrality of value claims to justify decisions as both legally "right" and as culturally appropriate.

In three of these cases, the Court was sharply split. Though the issues change, the fundamental clash is constant. Through an analysis of the language of the majority and dissenting opinions,[2] the polarization of value appeals in this conflict is apparent. The foci in each analysis are upon: (1) the selection of language to appeal to American values; (2) the use of those values as reasons supporting the legal authority and cultural appropriateness of a decision; and (3) the rhetorical strategies which the appeals to particular values reveal.

SUPREME COURT SCHISM: PRINCIPLE v PROCESS

Dissension in our highest Court is not a novelty (Grossman and Wells, 1980, p.231) nor given the composition of our current Court is it particularly surprising. Grossman and Wells (1972, p.50) characterize the Supreme Court as "a hybrid institution, combining in an often uneasy alliance the cultures of law and politics." The uneasiness which may accompany the coordination of ideals and pragmatism became a major obstacle in three of the cases investigated here: *Board of Education v Pico; Nixon v Fitzgerald;* and *Enmund v Florida*. The vote in each case was a squeaky five to four.

The dissension in these cases involves more than a split about what the Court's decision ought to be. The language selected to justify the opposing positions reveals a fundamental tension about what values should guide the Court in its decision-making, decision-justifying process. Regardless of the varied issues, the opposing opinions opt either for the priority of democratic process or democratic priniciple as the guiding tenet for judicial decision. While, in a legal sense, both the structure of democracy and the ideals of democracy are "principles" for judicial justification, the term, "principle" is used recurrently by one camp to refer to high, democratic ideals. Thus here, the schism between principle and process depicts the hierarchical differences revealed in opinions between the priority of American ideals—principle—and governmental structure—process.

These opinions, then, bifurcate principle from process in order to prioritize them. Both the sanctity of principle and the sanctity of process are esteemed political values. However, the hierarchical importance accorded them in the opposing opinions poses different rhetorical problems for their use as a justificatory framework. The adherence to principle as the highest priority in democracy appeals to abstract values as the basis for conviction. The problem

---

[2] There is, of course, only one majority opinion. However, in *Board of Education, Nixon*, and *Enmund* there are multiple dissenting opinions. This paper investigates only the first dissent which is signed by all of the dissenting justices.

facing those Justices who give priority to principle inheres in the remoteness of abstract values from daily life. To be persuasive, principles must seem attainable and must have some connection with daily life. Principle needs to be visualized in some fashion. Conversely, the adherence to process is replete inherently with concrete referents: the electoral process, the branches of government, the roles and responsibilities of those governmental branches. In addition, particular persons are associated frequently with various processes of government. To be persuasive, process must appear to embody values which subsume particular individuals and particular acts. Although identified through tangible, specific referents, political process—as a justificatory value—needs to be depicted holistically as a means to democratic ends. The process must appear to embody abstract American values (see Perelman and Olbrechts-Tyteca 1969, pp. 77–79).

These opinions reveal a variety of rhetorical strategies with which to accomplish these goals. An opinion which gives priority to principle embodies principle in a physical structure—a library—in *Board of Education;* in *Nixon,* the opinion visualizes principle through a mythic drama; and in *Enmund,* principle is equated with the social wisdom of Americans. An opinion which gives priority to process equates process with parental control over education in *Board of Education;* in *Nixon,* the opinion mystifies the presidency through depersonalization of that office; and in *Enmund,* process is simplified as the antithesis of and protection from murder.

BOARD OF EDUCATION v PICO

The removal of nine books from a school library upon the direction of the local school board sparked these proceedings. The majority holds that this action is unconstitutional because it violates the constitutional rights of students. The dissenters contend that such removal is consonant with the educational control of a school board.

Majority Opinion

Principle is idealized in this opinion. The First Amendment is accorded ultimate priority. Brennan, who authors this opinion, expresses the importance of that principle in social terms.[3] He states:

> Just as access to ideas makes it possible for citizens generally to exercise their rights of free speech and press in a meaningful manner, such access prepares students for active and effective participation in the pluralistic, often contentious society in which they will soon become adult members (447).

To maintain democracy, Brennan implies, society must place a high value on access to ideas.

---

[3] The majority opinion is authored by Brennan, and joined by Marshall, Stevens, and Blackmun. White concurred in the judgment.

This ideal assumes priority, says the opinion, over the responsibilities of school boards. The opinion states: "The discretion of the States and local school boards in matters of education must be exercised in a manner that comports with the transcendent imperatives of the First Amendment" (445). The opinion, thus, expresses principle as both a legal and cultural reason for this decision. The First Amendment is a legally imperative principle and the maintenance of democracy hinges upon the protection of that principle.

Though the maintenance of democracy is a strong appeal, it is, still, abstract. Brennan concretizes principle through a value-laden depiction of school libraries. School libraries become the tangible embodiment of American ideals. School libraries, says Brennan, have a "unique role." They are "voluntary," "a matter of free choice," "an opportunity for self-education and individual enrichment," and are the "the principle locus of such freedom" (448). Law and society, suggests the opinion, ought to protect school libraries. School libraries are portrayed as a visible representation of high principle.

The provision of a tangible form for principle through appeals to cultural values—"free choice," "self-education," and "individual enrichment"—depicts principle as the daily fare of American life. Libraries are familiar structures and Americans can envision the consequences of removing books from their shelves. In a quotation from Madison, the opinion vivifies the desired perceptions:

> A popular Government, without popular information, or the means of acquiring it, is but a Prologue to a Farce or a Tragedy; or, perhaps both. Knowledge will forever govern ignorance: And a people who mean to be their own Governors, must arm themselves with the power which knowledge gives (447).

The implication is clear: to reject this decision—to leave the source of popular information unprotected—is to invite political doom.

Dissenting Opinion

The cultural and legal importance of democratic process is stressed in this opinion. Of the majority's decision, Burger says:[4] "It is a startling erosion of the very idea of democratic government to have this Court arrogate to itself the power the plurality asserts today" (461). The dissent further charges that the decision mandates that school boards acquiesce to "the demands of teenagers" (463). According to the dissent, the decision of the majority is legally unprecedented and politically irresponsible.

As evidence for this political irresponsibility, the dissent states that "the plurality fails to recognize the fact that local control of education involves democracy in a microcosm" (462). As depicted in this dissent, this microcosm represents democratic process. The opinion describes that process in detail:

---

[4] The dissenting opinion is authored by Burger and joined by Powell, Rehnquist, and O'Connor.

People elect school boards, who in turn select administrators, who select the teachers. . . through participation in the election of school board members, the parents influence, if not control, the direction of their children's education (462).

This description serves two functions. It portrays the interrelationship between the components of the microcosm—it is a process. And, it attaches cultural importance to that process—parental say over the education of their children. This dissent equates democratic process with the capability of parents to raise their children.

The appeal to this cultural value is expressed, also, in a more legalistic fashion. Says the dissent: "A school board is not a giant bureacracy far removed from accountability for its actions; it is truly "of the people and by the people' " (462–463). The justification for the priority of democratic process in this opinion is based upon two appeals: the political and legal sanctitiy of school districts as processionally democratic, and the opportunity for parents to influence those controls. Together, these appeals provide a legal and cultural basis upon which to accept the position endorsed.

NIXON v FITZGERALD

In 1968, A. Ernest Fitzgerald was dismissed from his job as "management analyst with the Department of the Air Force" (353). The Civil Service Commission investigated Fitzgerald's dismmisal and concluded that it "had offended applicable civil service regulations" (356). Evidence cited in the majority's description of this case indicates that then-President Nixon, endorsed—perhaps ordered—the dismissal, not because Fitzgerald was incompetent, but because he was disloyal (355–356). Fitzgerald named Nixon in a civil suit for liability damages. The majority opinion holds that presidents are absolutely immune from such civil suits. The dissenting opinion contends that the personal culpability of presidents can be debated and decided in court.

Majority Opinion
Political process—viewed here as a macro rather than a micro-process—is portrayed in this opinion in lofty terms.[5] The presidency is described as "unique" (363–364) and "special" (367) and is said to make "sensitive and far-reaching decisions" (364) of "singular importance" (365). The presidency functions, states the opinion, "to advance compelling public ends" (369). Through the use of value-laden terms to describe the responsibilities of a president, the opinion attempts to deflect attention away from the man and onto the sanctity of the office.

The terms selected to describe presidential duties, then, function to depersonalize the issue. It is not Nixon, but all presidents, whom this opinion dis-

---

[5] The majority opinion is authored by Powell and joined by Burger, Rehnquist, Stevens, and O'Connor.

cusses. Just as importantly, social roles and responsibilities and not personal actions are featured. Through this depersonalization, a mystical quality can be attached to the presidency. As Powell states: "[the Constitution] establishes the President as the chief constitutional officer of the Executive Branch, entrusted with supervisory and policy responsibilities of utmost discretion" (363). Presidents are described in abstract and glowing terms. The presidency, implies the opinion, is to be revered.

In contrast with the presidency, the safeguards built into the democratic process against presidential misconduct are specified in detail. Those safeguards include: "impeachment," "the constant scrutiny by the press," "vigilant oversight by the Congress," "a desire to earn re-election," "the need to maintain prestige," and "a President's traditional concern for his historical stature" (368). This contrast between the specific checks in the democratic process on the president and the lofty responsibilities of the office further strengthens an appeal to the cultural mystique of the presidency. Though hounded by the press, the Congress, and the public, presidents still must perform their awesome duties. As the opinion states, "the sheer prominence" of the presidency entails "unique risks" (365).

The depersonalized, mystical portrayal of the presidency imparts a legal and cultural importance to the protection of that office. In the language of this opinion, the case involves "policies . . . implicit in the nature of the President's office in a system structured to achieve effective government" (362–363). The opinion is justified through the combination of an appeal to the need for legal protection of the presidency and a need for cultural reverence for the office.

Dissenting Opinion

This dissent, as might be expected, grants priority to principle.[6] The dissent expresses the guiding tenet in this case as: "The principle that government shall be of laws and not of men" (375). While that statement is highly valued, it is especially abstract—the Court cannot point to a constitutional amendment representing that ideal. To provide this principle with an understandable form, the opinion depicts the case through the elements of a cultural myth. The dissent, through its language choice, portrays a villain, a victim, and a hero. Of course, in the tradition of American myths, the dissent argues that the villain should be punished, the victim should be given restitution, and the hero should be honored (see Klapp, 1962; Frye, 1957). Through the depiction of the case in mythic terms, the opinion both appeals to cultural values and provides a visualizaion of the abstract principle embraced.

The decision of the majority is described as "frivolous," (387) "bizarre," (392) and "perverse" (392). Perversity becomes a predominant theme of the opinion for the majority is said to have "abandon[ed] basic principles" (376). The major-

---

[6] The dissenting opinion is authored by White and joined by Brennan, Marshall, and Blackmun.

ity opinion is perverse, implies the dissent, because it sanctions the villain. The villainous deed is described as "a trumped-up reduction" which is "contrary to the civil service laws" (373). The perverse Court and the president become associated. The opinion states that the majority's decision "concludes that whatever the President does and however contrary to law he knows his conduct to be, he may, without fear of liability injure federal employees or any other person within or without the government" (374). By casting the president as someone who may flaunt the law and harm innocent persons, the opinion develops a villainous persona for the president. This negative role is intensified when the dissent states that the majority's decision: "places the President above the law. It is a reversion to the old notion that the King can do no wrong" (374). Americans hold that Kings certainly can do wrong, and our myths reinforce the idea that when Kings, villains, or presidents do wrong, they ought to be punished.

The hero in this narrative is principle—the supremacy of law over all individuals. Law safeguards society. The dissent argues, "This principle of individual accountability is fundamental if the structure of an organized society is not to be eroded to anarchy and impotence" (376). Moreover, law rescues the victims of villainous deeds. The specific victim in this dissent is Fitzgerald, but the opinion extends the possibility of victimage to every citizen. In closing, White states, "I find it ironic, as well as tragic, that the Court would so casually discard its own role of assuring 'the right of every individual to claim the protection of the laws' " (394). As potential victims of a despotic president, Americans well know how this story should end. The myth is tragic, the implication is, because the cultural values it embodies have been violated. The decision is tragic, says the Court, because the sanctity of law has been eroded.

ENMUND v FLORIDA

Earl Enmund was the driver for a group of robbers who not only robbed but killed two persons at their home. Both opinions state that the evidence indicates that Enmund remained in the car throughout the crime. Enmund was convicted of first-degree murder and sentenced to die. The majority holds because Enmund was an accomplice who did not intend to kill, the death penalty is an excessive punishment. The dissenters contend that if Enmund is convicted of murder, he can be put to death.

Majority Opinion
The Eighth Amendment is the principle which the majority employs as the legal justification for this decision: the constitutional directive against cruel and unusual punishments.[7] In contrast to the abstract nature of principle, the crime in this case is abhorrent, heinous, and—through the publicity of the media—all

---

[7] The majority opinion is authored by White and joined by Brennan, Marshall, Blackmun, and Stevens.

too real. In all probability, murder has more vivid appeal for Americans than does the Eighth Amendment.

Whatever the reasons, the majority opinion attempts to provide a more understandable form to the principle it espouses by expressing this principle as the social wisdom of Americans. This equation of principle with social wisdom is accomplished in several ways. As one strategy, the opinion pinpoints juries as a tangible reflector of American values. White says, " 'The jury is a significant and reliable objective index of contemporary values' " (1149). Hence, the opinion employs the decisions made by juries as evidence that Americans believe that the death sentence for accomplice felony murder is excessive. The Court states: "Society's rejection of the death penalty for accomplice liability in felony murders is . . . indicated by the sentencing decisions that juries have made" (1149). Juries become the tangible expression of principle, and juries (as Americans) reflect the wisdom of adherence to principle.

The opinion also points to the social role and social values of prosecutors. White states, "Prosecutors, who represent society's interests in punishing crime, consider the death penalty excessive for accomplice felony murder" (1151). Once again, as portrayed here, society has the wisdom to adhere to principle in the meting out of punishments.

Finally, and perhaps most compelling, is the translation of principle into a cultural maxim. By expressing legal principle as a maxim of American life, the opinion captures cultural truths in the fashion they are most often expressed: "Putting Enmund to death to avenge two killings that he did not commit and had no intention of committing or causing does not measurably contribute to . . . ensuring that the criminal gets his just desserts" (1154). That criminals ought to get their just desserts is, indeed, a cultural truism. This expression encapsulates values with which Americans can identify. Hence, it may impart a sense of justice to the Court's decision. Together, the association of principle with the values reflected in legal bodies—juries and prosecutors—and the expression of principle as a maxim justify this decision as legally and culturally wise.

Dissenting Opinion

The importance attached to democratic process in this opinion is illustrated in an interesting way through the judgment made about the case.[8] In general the dissent rejects the Supreme Court's decision; the specific judgment about the case is that it should be remanded for reconsideration by the lower court. The trial judge, says the dissent, held the "erroneous belief that the petitioner had

---

[8] The dissenting opinion is authored by O'Connor and joined by Burger, Powell, and Rehnquist.

shot both victims while they lay in a prone position" (1173). Thus, the judge discredited the evidence that Enmund remained in the car "when the fatal shots were fired" (1173). For the correction of judicial error, the dissenters employ the machinery of the judicial process. Process is highly valued.

The dissent counterpoises the sanctity of democratic process—here, the state judicial and legislative process—with the crime which process seeks to control—murder. O'Connor typifies Enmund as a person who is "responsible . . . for the murders of the Kerseys" (1168). The majority's decision, states the opinion, "prohibits a State from executing a convicted felony murder" (1154). There are no mitigating circumstances. The opinion simplifies the grounds for decision: Enmund is a convicted murderer. This simplification has both a legal and cultural appeal. If Enmund is convicted of murder, he can legally (at least in Florida) be sentenced to die. If Enmund is a murderer, then, culturally, the death penalty may be his "just desserts."

This simplification of Enmund as a murderer functions as a shorthand or enthymematic representation of the importance of democratic process. Murderers are caught and tried through institutional procedures. The unstated appeal that murderers ought to be punished reinforces the also unstated conclusion that processes are important. The strength of American values associated with murder and murderers encourages audience completion of the argument and acceptance of the dissenter's position.

The sanctity of the state's procedural powers is reinforced explicitly through the dissent's rejection of the Court's decision. The majority's decision is said to "interfere" with the "determination of the degree of blameworthiness [which] is best left to the sentencer" (1169). Democratic process, implies the dissent, has been violated through interference by the Supreme Court. The Supreme Court's role is to review the conviction and restart the procedural machinery if there is error.

In each of these opinions then, value appeals perform a crucial role in the justificatory process. The appeals to values function on several levels. The hierarchical importance attached to either principle or process provides a value-laden framework for a case as a whole. Within that framework, values are employed—through language choice—to provide cultural and legal reasons for the acceptance of a particular position. Additionally, through appeals to particular values, these opinions craft rhetorical links among the elements of a case, the decision, those specific values and general politically-valued goals. The acceptance of the values appealed to in these opinions is an essential component in the acceptance of the reasoning process and the decision.

In the final case considered here, value appeals function as a sanctuary wherein the process-principle schism has no authority. Unfortunately perhaps, the atypical issue in this case offers, at best, a momentary respite from the Court's internal conflict. However fleeting, *New York v Ferber* represents a unanimous Supreme Court.

NEW YORK v FERBER

Ferber was the proprietor of a bookstore selling sexual materials. An under-cover police officer purchased two films from Ferber. These films primarily "depict[ed] young boys masturbating" (1119). Ferber was indicted for distributing child pornography. The Supreme Court considered the constitutionality of the New York statute under which Ferber was indicted.

Majority Opinion

This opinion is heavily against child pornography and for the protection of children. By directing attention to "children," the opinion develops a vivid and value-laden contrast: protecting children is good; harming children is bad. This antithesis defines the political, cultural, and legal values to which all members of the Court can submit.

After a succinct statement of the constitutional issue, the opinion begins: "In recent years, the exploitative use of children in the production of pornography has become a serious national problem" (1117). The use of the term, "exploitation," recurs in the discussion of child pornography. Furthermore, child pornography, says the Court, is an "abuse of children," (1123) the "sexual abuse of children," (1124) and is "harmful to the physiological, emotional, and mental health of the child" (1123). Above all, emphasizes the opinion, child pornography is "evil" (1127). Indeed, the evil character of child pornography "overwhelmingly outweighs" (1127) all other considerations. Through the identification of a common enemy, the Court finds the grounds for cooperation (see Burke, 1970).

The Supreme Court, thus, cooperates with those states which seek "to combat the problem" (1118). The stakes, says the Court, are high. The opinion says, "A state's interest in 'safeguarding the physical and psychological well being of a minor' is 'compelling' " (1122). Society, too, has a compelling interest. White continues, "A democratic society rests, for its continuance, upon the healthy well-rounded growth of young people into full maturity as citizens" (1122). Just as the negative values of child pornography are epitomized by the term, "evil," the Court adds that "the protection of children" is "a sacred trust" (1123). The crusade against child pornography is given the sanction of the Supreme Court.

The depiction of this case as a crusade against evil provides a cultural justification for the legal arguments in the opinion. The Court argues that the constitutional standards for obscenity do not apply in matters of child pornography. Those standards, states the Court, "bear(s) no connection to the issue of whether a child has been physically or psychologically harmed" (1125). In addition, though the New York statute does not provide exclusions for academic or educational materials that might depict children in sexual activities, the Court argues that the "legitimate reach" of the statute "dwarfs its arguably impermissible applications" (1133). While this approach is not unknown in the Court, it does reinforce the portrayal of child pornography as an enormous evil.

Hence, value appeals function as a diversionary tactic in *New York*. The opinion dissociates child pornography from the principles of the First Amendment for two reasons: (1) the Court argues that obscenity standards construed under the First Amendment do not apply; and (2) the concurrences reveal that conflict remains in the Court about just what kinds of expression the First Amendment protects and what it does not (see Brennan: 1135). There appears to be no other legal principle applicable; instead, the Court crafts a principle from American values about children. While the Court upholds the state's authority to indict distributors of child pornography, the emphasis is upon the eradication of evil by any and every means. The political process through which this eradication is accomplished is portrayed as secondary.

THE ROLE OF VALUES IN SUPREME COURT OPINIONS

Based upon this non-random sampling of Supreme Court opinions, the importance of value appeals as a rhetorical resource for the Court is suggested. Though the Supreme Court has the authority to interpret the Constitution, it has no power to enforce those interpretations as "the law." Supreme Court opinions bridge the gap between judicial decisions and "law" by portraying values as the force which legitimizes a decision. Through the use of language to appeal to our values, Supreme Court opinions attempt to transform judicial decisions into American "law."

In Wallace's terms (1963), values provide "good reasons" to accept Supreme Court statements as "law." As has been noted, values as reasons function at several levels. Values are expressed as political goals which law ought to serve. Values are expressed as the personal motivations which bond individual Americans to the cultural community. Value appeals are employed to express a compelling rhetorical synthesis of the specific elements of a case. Appeals to American values provide "good reasons" for the Supreme Court because they enhance the legal and cultural personae of the Court as an American symbol of justice.

Values, obviously, are appealed to as often in dissents as in majority opinions. And, there is scant evidence to suggest that majority opinions are more prescient in their selection and reflection of American values than are dissenting opinions. Indeed, after reading these analyses it would be unremarkable if some persons did not judge some of these dissents to be more "persuasive" than their majority counterparts. To a large degree, Supreme Court opinions generally may function to reinforce the values that particular segments of society already hold. But, in reinforcing those values, majority and dissenting opinions alike remind Americans that our cultural values are an essential ingredient of our laws; and they remind Americans that the cases accepted by the Supreme Court are contemporary value conflicts.

The role of values in Supreme Court opinions is to convince Americans that cases are "rightly decided" (or perhaps, decided for the "right" reasons) despite the popularity of a particular position. Appeals to American values provide reasons for Americans to regard Supreme Court decisions as a force for the protection of our law and our values. Despite the varied positions reflected in these opinions, value appeals are employed to provide the legal authority and cultural appropriateness necessary for "law" to be a force which binds society.

REFERENCES

Board of Education v Pico, (1982). 73 L Ed 2d: 435–481.

Burke, K. (1970). *The Rhetoric of Religion: Studies in Logology*. Berkeley, CA: University of California Press.

Enmund v Florida. (1982). 73 L Ed 2d: 1140–1173.

Frye, N. (1957). *Anatomy of Criticism: Four Essays*. Princeton, NJ: Princeton University Press.

Gottlieb, G. (1968). *The Logic of Choice: An Investigation of the Concepts of Rule and Rationality*. New York: Macmillan.

Grossman, J.B., and Wells, R.S. (1980). *Constitutional Law and Judicial Policy Making*, 2nd ed. New York: John Wiley & Sons.

Jones, S. (1976). "Justification in Judicial Opinions: A Case Study." *Journal of the American Forensic Association* 12, 121–129.

Klapp, O. (1962). *Heroes, Villains, and Fools*. Englewood Cliffs, NJ: Prentice Hall.

Miller, A.S. (1978). *The Supreme Court: Myth and Reality*. Westport, CN: Greenwood.

Miller, C.A. (1969). *The Supreme Court and the Uses of History*. Cambridge, MA: Belknap Press of Harvard University Press.

New York v Ferber. (1982). 73 L Ed 2d: 1113–1139.

Nixon v Fitzgerald. (1982). 73 L Ed 2d: 349–395.

Perelman, C., and Olbrechts-Tyteca, L. (1969). *The New Rhetoric: A Treatise on Argumentation*. Notre Dame, IN: University of Notre Dame.

Wallace, K. (1963). "The Substance of Rhetoric: Good Reasons." *Quarterly Journal of Speech* **49**, 239–249.

22

From Ford to Carnegie: The Private Foundation and the Rise of Public Television

RALPH ENGELMAN

Long Island University, New York

The Ford and Carnegie foundations wrote the book, chapter and verse, on public television. A noncommercial U.S. television system would not have assumed its present form or even come into being, without the patronage of these two powerful private philanthrophic institutions. Public television (née educational television) emerged initially as the carefully nurtured offspring of the Ford Foundation, later as the adolescent stepchild of the Carnegie Corporation of New York. Ford launched the so-called fourth network in the 1950s and 1960s. The landmark report of the first Carnegie Commission on Educational Television provided the blueprint for the Public Broadcasting Act of 1967, which marks the transition from the "foundation years" to the "federal years" of public television (Network Project, 1971, pp.15–16).

Although Ford and Carnegie support of public television is well known, the "foundation years" warrant closer scrutiny. The two foundations virtually controlled—indeed orchestrated—the rise of public television at each stage in its development until 1967. Their role contradicts several legends about the emergence of public television. The first is that a group of independent educators laid the original foundation for public television. The second is the myth of a Carnegie Commission on Educational Television made up of a disinterested cross-section of prominent citizens operating outside the political arena. Finally, the notion that public television is politically neutral must be discarded.

THE FORD FOUNDATION LAUNCHES EDUCATIONAL TELEVISION

At the outset the Ford Foundation was not the sole advocate of noncommercial television. Support came from old educational radio hands and from FCC Commissioner Frieda Hennock, among others. But it was the Ford Foundation that commanded educational television's forces from the early 1950s until 1967.

Ford created two agencies in 1951: The Fund for the Advancement of Education, its research arm, supported studies establishing a rationale for educational television; and The Fund for Adult Education (FAE), its tactical arm, laid the political and institutional foundation for a noncommercial television system. When the Ford Foundation entered the picture, not a single noncommercial television station was on the air. Furthermore, educational broadcasters, who had failed to establish a significant presence on AM radio, had little clout. Television, to use contemporary communications parlance, was a new technology. The public was generally unaware or indifferent to its educational potential. Against this background the Ford Foundation waged a campaign on a series of fronts.

The Fund for the Advancement of Education sponsored a series of seminal studies. Some explored in-school use of television on the primary, secondary, and college levels. In addition, the Chelsea Closed-Circuit Television Project pioneered the first experimental use of educational television for the urban poor in a Spanish-speaking neighborhood in New York City. The Fund's own evaluation of the project concluded that educational television could meet the special needs of ghettos with "hard core educational or cultural problems" and that, moreover, it could serve "as a form of psychotherapy" and "as an instrument for the development of community leaders" (Network Project, 1971, pp. 9–10). This study anticipated *Sesame Street* and the Children's Television Workshop. More broadly, it suggested the potential of noncommercial television as a powerful social instrument beyond the classroom. Thus an ambitious agenda for educational television, more "public" than "instructional" in the traditional sense, was already at play in the 1950s.

In 1951 the Ford Foundation created the second entity, the Fund for Adult Education (FAE). Its task was nothing less than to put together from scratch a rudimentary educational broadcasting system in the United States. The most pressing task was to get the Federal Communications Commission to reserve television channels for noncommercial use. The failure of the Communications Act of 1934 to set aside educational channels for radio had permitted commercial interests all but to eliminate educators from the AM spectrum. The Ford Foundation was determined that this chapter of broadcasting history not repeat itself.

A look at early educational television organizations reveals the deftness with which the FAE laid the political groundwork for a favorable FCC decision. At its very first 1951 meeting, the FAE awarded key grants to what were then two rickety organizations: the National Association of Educational Broadcasters (NAEB) and the Joint Council on Educational Television (JCET). Ford money enabled the nearly defunct NAEB to become educational television's principal trade association and Washington lobbyist, which it remained until its demise more than a quarter of a century later. The reconstituted JCET supplemented the NAEB's lobbying efforts by parading an elite group of educators, labor leaders, and politicians before the FCC and congressional committees to testify on behalf of educational television. In addition, the FAE drew up plans for a National Citizens' Committee for Educational Television (NCCET) to spread the gospel of educational television to the American public as a whole.

The flurry of Ford-inspired and Ford-financed activity paid off. In 1952, the FCC set aside 242 television channels—80 in the VHF band and 162 in the UHF band—for noncommercial use. This measure marks the birth of educational television in the United States, and the assurance that it would have a foothold on the television dial. The FAE's follow-up was swift. Before the year was out it set up the Educational Television and Radio Center (ETRC). ETRC, initially a program exchange center housed in Ann Arbor, Michigan, would eventually grow to become the National Educational Television system (NET) headquartered in New York City in the 1960s. Today's Public Broadcasting Service (PBS) can be considered a descendant once-removed of the Ann Arbor operation.

Interestingly, FAE's institution-building antedated the existence of a single noncommercial television station. (The first, KUHT in Houston, began broadcasting in May 1953.) Thus, a networking arm for a noncommercial system was set up when nary a station could join it. Only after the FCC's 1952 ruling, and the founding of the Educational Television and Radio Center, did the FAE focus on station organization and activation. Over a three-year period it provided financial support and technical assistance for the construction of 35 stations across the nation. A study by the Network Project (1971, p.8) at Columbia University notes the irony that "a supposedly educational or public system of television was wholly the progeny of a private economic institution."

However, in this period the extent of Ford Foundation machinations on behalf of educational television was camouflaged by an organizational maze—perhaps in part because of the conservative political climate of the 1950s. The Fund for the Advancement of Education and the FAE were Ford Foundation fronts, although each had its own board of directors and staff. Nominally independent organizations like the NAEB and the JCET were refashioned to serve the Foundation's purposes.

> Any organization seeking support from the Foundation needed to discern the foundation's current line on a particular problem area and gradually tailor its grant requests to fit this orientation. This often involved a rather extensive period of instruction by the Foundation regarding the appropriate ways to conceptualize a problem followed by a period of negotiation in which the grantee demonstrated that it had learned its lessons well and understood completely the Foundation's requirements in order to obtain support. The end result . . . entailed an almost unilateral shift of the perspective of the organization to one which matched the foundation's interests in an area (Seybold, 1978, pp.378–379).

The key operatives in the early days of Ford's educational television program—C. Scott Fletcher, Robert Hudson, and James Armsey—often initiated grant proposals, and maintained liaison between the Foundation and its satellite organizations (Hudson 1982; Armsey 1981).

The educational television movement went into high gear after 1958 when John F. White, a protégé of Ford Foundation president Henry Heald, became head of the Educational Television and Radio Center. White was much less the staid educator than his predecessor, Harry K. Newburn, and better equipped to initiate the transition from "educational" to "public" television. White together with James Armsey of the Ford Foundation aggressively promoted the concept of a "fourth network" as a multi-faceted alternative to the three bastions of commercial television.

In 1959, soon after becoming president of ETRC, White moved its main offices from Ann Arbor to New York City, and added "National" to its name. That year White also applied for, and received, a $5 million grant from the Ford Foundation. NETRC continued to promote the incorporation of new stations, which totaled 76 by 1962, a decade after the FCC decision to set aside channels for educational television. NETRC now circulated a 10-hour weekly package of programs which embraced the arts, public affairs, and children's shows. Most programs were produced by the affiliate stations since NETRC had no production staff or facilities of its own. NETRC also contracted programs from independent producers and acquired material from overseas sources. The improvement of programming, so that educational television would be transformed into a major national network of information and the arts, was one of White's two major objectives.

The second was diversification of funding sources. White believed that educational television needed to build a more varied base of support to insure its independence. Opposed to government funding of broadcast operations, he thought that significant support could be provided by public school systems and universities, labor unions and corporations, local community groups and foundations. In order to promote such support, he set up a development department at NETRC. However, White was unable to lessen substantially NETRC's dependence on the Ford Foundation, which he now considers a major failure of his administration (White, 1982). Knowledge that the educational television network was the Ford Foundation's baby hampered supplementary fundraising. In addition, the Foundation imposed a reorganization plan on NETRC that entailed the elimination of its development department.

The restructuring of NETRC in the mid-1960s was a humiliating reminder for White that the Ford Foundation was in charge. The process began in 1962 when the Foundation decided to do its own study of the state of the educational television movement under the direction of James Armsey. In the course of his review, Armsey organized a meeting of NETRC's affiliates in Scottsdale, Arizona. White and his staff were neither informed of the meeting nor invited to attend. Moreover, White was never permitted to read the final report, although it resulted in a far-reaching reorientation of the office he headed. The message to White was unmistakable; the Ford Foundation would make policy, his job was to carry it out.

In 1964, the president of the Ford Foundation, Henry Heald, redefined NETRC's function on the basis of the Armsey report. For the time being, he said, the Foundation would remain educational television's principal financial supporter. Now that a network infrastructure was in place, Ford would apply its resources to the development of quality programming. Heald announced the first of a series of $6 million annual grants to transform NETRC into a program production center. The Foundation required that White abandon many of his traditional activities. James Armsey felt that a development department was no longer necessary in light of Ford's renewed commitment of support. NETRC would cease receiving Ford grants for instructional television; NAEB would take over station origination and support services; and radio development would end—after which the programming center would be known simply as National Educational Television (NET).

There was much to be said for the Ford Foundation's new emphasis. Most educational television programming had been parochial and poor in quality. The origination of improved programming was clearly the next task for establishing the legitimacy and permanency of a noncommercial television system. And the central office of educational television needed to streamline its operations and focus its energies to carry it out. White continued with the new assignment; however, he was troubled. For one thing, the Ford Foundation had blown the whistle on his attempts to diversify funding sources. For another, the Foundation, through Armsey, was acting as an arbiter and censor of programming content. Armsey required that half of NET's shows be devoted to public affairs, and, in general, he watched NET like a hawk. However farsighted the Ford Foundation leadership may have been, it exercised its near-absolute control over the growth of "public" television in a highly manipulative and authoritarian fashion.

Paradoxically, the Ford Foundation intervened so aggressively in NET's affairs in the mid-1960s because it was eager to relinquish its role as prime sponsor of educational television—but only after its survival was assured. The Foundation, however, was not quite ready to loosen its control over a movement it had carefully built since the early 1950s. A programming model and a plan for permanent financing had yet to be established. With these things accomplished, the fourth network would be able to stand on its own.

THE BUNDY-FRIENDLY ERA AND THE CARNEGIE COMMISSION

In 1966, McGeorge Bundy became president of the Ford Foundation, after six years in the White House as national security advisor to Kennedy and Johnson. At the same time Fred Friendly ended his 16-year career at CBS. Bundy asked Friendly to become the Ford Foundation's television consultant, and to conduct a far-reaching review of NET. David Davis replaced James Armsey as the Foundation's educational television officer. The Foundation's line on educational television became sharply focused: "make it fly so we can get out" (Davis, 1981, p.42).

The new Foundation leadership came up with two bold scenarios for the future of public television: one to resolve noncommercial television's funding problems, the other to establish a dynamic model for future programming. The first initiative, McGeorge Bundy's maiden project as Foundation president, was the satellite plan of 1966. In brief, Bundy and Friendly proposed that a nonprofit corporation be created to develop a domestic communications satellite system. Such a system, instead of using AT&T's telephone lines, could transmit the programs of the three commercial networks at sharply reduced rates. A portion of the networks' substantial savings would be earmarked for noncommercial television. Hence the proposed satellite system would bankroll public broadcasting by providing a permanent and independent source of revenue. Moreover, by providing a means of simultaneous interconnection which noncommercial stations could afford, NET would be transformed into an authentic network. The August 15, 1966, issue of *Newsweek* cited Bundy's characterization of the proposed satellite system as "a people's dividend, earned by the American nation from its enormous investment in space."

The 80-page Ford Foundation proposal ran up against a barrage of criticism during hearings of the Senate Communications Subcommittee in 1966. Leading the pack of critics was AT&T, whose spokesman exchanged harsh words with Bundy. Officials of Comsat, the corporation chartered by Congress in 1962, claimed it had a monopoly on domestic satellite service. The networks opposed the plan on the grounds that they would be forced to subsidize a competing television network in the name of public service. The proposal threatened too many vested interests to gain speedy acceptance in Congress or at the FCC. However, the satellite plan succeeded in giving communications satellites greater prominence as matters of national policy. But Bundy and Friendly failed to obtain the financial fix for NET that would get the Foundation off the hook.

The second Bundy-Friendly initiative—the *Public Broadcasting Laboratory* (*PBL*)—was even more controversial. Its purpose was to establish an original model for public affairs programming, so that public television would be recognized as an indispensable part of the American broadcasting system. Friendly had quit CBS over its refusal to preempt an "I Love Lucy" rerun in order to carry Senate hearings on the war in Vietnam; public television, he thought, could fill the vacuum created by commercial television's failure to carry out its social responsibilities.

Late in 1966 the Ford Foundation earmarked $10 million for "PBL," the name of a public affairs magazine to be broadcast live Sunday nights on the NET network. The show was to give expression to the political and cultural crisis of the 1960s.

Av Westin, hired by Friendly as executive director of "PBL," indicated his intention "to stir things up, to challenge the status quo of both commercial and educational television" (*Saturday Review*, November 11, 1967). From its debut in 1967 until its demise in 1969, "PBL" highlighted controversy and confrontation. The theme of the first broadcast, for example, was racial conflict; it featured a play in which whites were caricatured by blacks in "whiteface." Another

"PBL" broadcast aired Felix Greene's *Inside North Vietnam,* a sympathetic portrayal of the "enemy," which brought protests from Congress. As Barnouw (1968, pp.292–294) recalls, the thrust of "PBL" was "anti-war, anti-racist, anti-establishment." Perhaps public broadcasting could become an electronic gadfly, exposing injustice and strengthening the body politic.

The highly publicized launching of "PBL" added momentum to attempts in 1967 to find a permanent niche for noncommercial television in the nation's communication apparatus. In 1967, President Johnson, in his State of the Union message, called for the transformation of educational broadcasting into a vital public resource. The speech was broadcast live on 70 educational radio stations through a special NET hookup financed by a special Ford Foundation grant. February, 1967, saw the publication of *Public Television: A Program for Action,* the report of the Carnegie Commission on Educational Television (1967), which had been established in 1965 by the Carnegie Corporation of New York. The report gave currency to a broad concept of *public* television, which had been implicit in the Ford Foundation's support of educational television. The Carnegie Commission laid out an ambitious plan to make public television a national institution supported by the taxpayer. The centerpiece of the proposal was a federally chartered, nonprofit, nongovernmental agency which would administer public television's funds and assure its orderly growth. From this idea sprang the Corporation for Public Broadcasting (CPB). Although Congress did modify certain features of the master-plan, it can nonetheless be considered a not-so-rough draft of the Public Broadcasting Act of 1967. The thrust of the study, and a remarkable number of its recommendations, were enacted into law. The institutional framework for public television as we know it today is in large measure attributable to the Carnegie Commission report.

Thus the Carnegie Corporation of New York, another eminent private foundation, entered the picture at a critical juncture in the history of noncommercial television. As the Ford Foundation before it, the Carnegie Corporation showed itself adept at setting an agenda and then implementing it in the political arena. A second foundation presided over the final—and most difficult—task of facilitating the transition from the foundation years to the federal years of public television.

THE THIRD FORCE AND THE EASTERN ESTABLISHMENT

Silk and Silk (1980) argue that nonprofit institutions, especially private foundations, play a key role in the Eastern Establishment's approach to public policy. The rise of public television seems to fit their hypothesis.

The roots of the Establishment of the American Northeast go back to a network of families and institutions in Colonial America. The great industrial empire builders of the nineteenth century—Andrew Carnegie, John D. Rockefeller, and Henry Ford, among others—entered and further influenced the character of this elite group. They added the privately endowed foundation

to the roster of Establishment institutions like the Episcoplian Church and
Harvard University. The foundations that bear their names have played an important role in shaping social policy, including public broadcasting, in the
twentieth century.

Andrew Carnegie articulated the ethos behind nineteenth-century philan-
thropy in his celebrated essay on "The Gospel of Wealth." A third force was
needed to mediate between the disruptive forces of popular democracy and industrial capitalism. Those that profit most from our great social system should
temper its inequities so that, in Carnegie's words, "the ties of brotherhood may
still bind together the rich and the poor in harmonious relationship" (Silk and
Silk, 1980, p.106). Carnegie updated the Protestant Ethic for the age of industrial capitalism. He identified nonprofit organizations as agencies of the "third
sector": libraries and museums, churches and colleges, endowments and foundations. Such bodies could help maintain the nation's social fabric independent
of the twin evils of unruly popular movements from below or state control from
above.

Carnegie's heirs continue to preach "the gospel of wealth," albeit in a more
sophisticated fashion. Characteristic of our own day is the language of social
science. After the Second World War, the Ford Foundation had promoted
"behavioral science" as a means of strengthening the social fabric during a period of rapid social change. The prospect of social disorder—of urban decay,
racial conflict, and economic instability—was the context in which the Ford
Foundation issued its famous 1949 report upon which its postwar programs
were based. The "hidden political agenda" of the Foundation was a new legiti-
mation crisis for the social system and its elite—as the United States increasingly became a mass society characterized by a lack of participation and a
declining faith in the system (Seybold, 1978, pp.385–398). The response to the
crisis was technocratic. Now the enlightened application of behavioral science
and modern technology was seen as the means to bridge the gap between the
haves and the have-nots.

According to Seybold (1978, p.392), the essence of the Ford Foundation response to postwar problems resided in "containing social problems and chan-
neling discontent." It created mechanisms through which grievances could be
aired, brought into the mainstream, and eventually rectified—within the
framework of the existing social structure. Such mechanisms—and public television is one of them—were meant to rekindle faith in the democratic nature of
American society. The Silks have stressed that inclusivity is the hallmark of the
modern Establishment, that by demonstrating its openness and responsiveness
it aspired to remain "the only game in town" (Silk and Silk, 1980, pp.10–11).
Social engineering could not be left to the vagaries of the political process; a
socially responsible elite needed to exert leadership to assure stability and
progress.

The rationale and very language of the Carnegie Commission (1967) report
suggest how much public television owes to the ethos of the Eastern Establish-

ment. It stressed the potential of television as a broad vehicle for public enlightenment and social amelioration. The Carnegie Commission (1967, pp. 13–15, 92–98) pleaded for the use of "a great technology for great purposes." Public television's greatest task was to strengthen a society "proud to be open and pluralistic."

The Carnegie Commission's objective of fostering a sense of community among all strata was rooted in Andrew Carnegie's "gospel of wealth." The desire to exploit the "great technology" of television reflected the technocratic perspective grafted onto the old faith, as did the 1966 satellite proposal. The Carnegie Commission also echoed the example of the "PBL" series sponsored by the Boston Brahmin, McGeorge Bundy, at the Ford Foundation: had not the Establishment, facing mounting criticism, reaffirmed its legitimacy by giving the counter-culture and anti-war movement a piece of the action? Characteristically, despite harsh strictures against commercial television, the Carnegie Commission sought to supplement the existing system, not dismantle it. Public broadcasting was situated between unchecked commercialism on the one hand, and popular discontent over unmet needs on the other. The Corporation for Public Broadcasting (CPB), established by Congress in 1967 as a nonprofit and nongovernmental agency, was designed to serve as a third force in American broadcasting.

POSTSCRIPT: THE FAILURE OF THE FORD FOUNDATION GAME-PLAN

The attack of the Nixon Administration on public television signaled its failure to become a secure national institution insulated from partisan politics. However, as examination of the Ford Foundation suggests, one should guard against the facile view that Nixon was the serpent who introduced the forbidden fruit of politics to public television.

Any study of public television's fate after 1967 must examine the charge that the Public Broadcasting Act of 1967 violated the Ford-Carnegie approach, that federalization tied public television too closely to the state. A more fundamental question is whether any "third force"—including public television—can contain and transcend political conflict. Or is the very notion of a third force distinct from the private and public sectors ultimately a chimera?

Public television did not simply spring, Medusa-like, from the head of the liberal Establishment through its nominally neutral agencies, the Ford and Carnegie foundations. Its expansion came about as a result of the political ascendancy of that Establishment during the Kennedy and Johnson administrations. True, public television came of age in 1967 replete with inner tensions, with complex left-liberal-conservative crosscurrents. The balance of power between different visions and interests—a basic institutional equilibrium—was based upon the flexible support of the Eastern Establishment and of two successive liberal administrations. Few within public broadcasting anticipated that with the 1968 elections a period of liberal political ascendancy would be coming to an end. The election of Nixon reflected a significant power shift in which the hegemony of the "Yankees" of the Eastern Establishment was challenged by the "Cowboys" of the Sunbelt. The liberal Establishment would not remain "the only game in town." The high hopes engendered by the Public Broadcasting Act of 1967 faded in the months to come. Instead of moving into its final phase, the carefully orchestrated Ford/Carnegie game-plan for public television was off-track.

REFERENCES

Armsey, J. (1981). "An Interview with James Armsey." James Robertson Oral History Project. Archives of the Corporation for Public Broadcasting, Washington, D.C.

Barnouw, E. (1968). *The Image Empire. A History of Broadcasting in the United States,* Vol. III— from 1953. New York: Oxford University Press.

Carnegie Commission on Educational Television. (1967). *Public Television: A Program for Action.* New York: Bantam Books.

Davis, D. (1981). "An Interview with David Davis." James Robertson Oral History Project. Archives of the Corporation for Public Broadcasting, Washington, D.C.

Hudson, R. (1982). "An Interview with Robert Hudson." James Robertson Oral History Project. Archives of the Corporation for Public Broadcasting, Washington, D.C.

Network Project. (1971). *The Fourth Network.* New York: Network Project.

Seybold, P. (1978). "The Development of American Political Sociology—A Case Study of the Ford Foundation's Role in the Production of Knowledge." Ph.D. dissertation, State University of New York at Stony Brook. Ann Arbor, MI: University Microfilms.

Silk, L. and Silk, M. (1980). *The American Establishment.* New York: Basic Books.

White, J.F. (1982). (Interview with the author.)

23

Broadcasting as a Reflection of the Politicizing of German Culture

ALEXANDER F. TOOGOOD
Temple University

The March, 1983 West German federal elections saw 90% of the registered voters casting ballots. Such a turnout, where voting is not compulsory, places West Germany amongst the most participatory and "political" of the world's democracies. In such a climate, one must question the relationship between broadcasting and politics. Despite constant bickering about budget, programing, and rival technologies, the most distinctive characteristic of West German broadcasting is the delicate balance between the espoused goal of independence and the reality of a real political presence.

After World War II, the allies were wary of a strong centralized government such as that which had proved such a fertile breeding ground for the Nazi party. A solution was attempted in giving the conquered nation a diffusion of power based on an earlier model of local and provincial authority with the inherent pride that German's still feel for their regional roots. So that, while the overall political structure is federal, matters such as internal security, education, and broadcasting were firmly entrusted to separate state authorities. The most dramatic of such constitutional provisions occurred in terms of an important broadcasting decision. Twenty years ago, the usually politically adept Konrad Adenauer attempted to establish a federal television network. His efforts were rebuffed by the highest federal court.

With each of the Federal Republic's states taking charge of broadcasting matters, individual public corporations were established. Most of these serve a single state, although in one instance, three states offer a joint venture through inter-state agreement. As each state reflects an accident of history—ranging from vast rural expanses to concentrated industrial might to two city states—the subsequent broadcasting bodies vary widely in size and audience coverage. This also effects income; half the financing is from a steep monthly receiver licensing fee distributed to each corporation in relation to its potential audience, with the other half from advertising revenue.

The resultant regionalism belies some realities of broadcasting; in particular, the need for a nationwide television network service. In resolving such a dilemma, the country has devised a unique broadcasting pattern. The first network, ARD, is a cooperative venture from these nine separate entities, who provide programming in proportion to their size. Each station maintains its autonomy by being permitted to opt out of the network feed; an important consideration in political matters, especially when conservative sensibilities might be offended. Most opting out, infrequent as it is, has occurred in the conservative south.

To establish a second television network, which is legally obliged to compliment, not compete with the first, the separate states showed a rare form of unity whereby all 11 of them signed an inter-state treaty to establish a separate broadcasting entity. Although national in its scope, it is important to remember that its actual being occurs only through the good will of each separate state, thereby maintaining the legal nicety that broadcasting remains a local concern.

To complete the broadcasting pattern, each state corporation runs its own local television service as the third program, and offers at least two radio channels as well as following the European tradition of public broadcasting in providing a feast of peripheral entrepreneurial activities in "cultural" and popular entertainment.

It is within the structure of the broadcasting organizations that we see the political influence. The current pattern centered on the public corporation was established after the war. It is, indeed, a cultural graft. The British, in their northern sector of Germany, were the first to appreciate the value of broadcasting in the devastated nation. It was to be expected that they would turn to the model of the BBC. With the British sector established, both the French and the Americans opted to provide national uniformity in broadcasting rather than promote their own individualistic broadcasting systems.

It is important to note that this corporate model, unfamiliar to both America and France, was also alien to the German tradition. Subsequent problems can often be attributed to the cutting of this foreign cloth to fit the domestic form. In particular, the British tradition of the independence of such public bodies with minimum political interference has had great difficulty in being transplanted. Germans have always meshed politics with their every day existence. It is often startling to the outsider to find that such matters as school curricula or professorial appointments are judged more for their political allegiances than from objective academic criteria. Such a national characteristic soon infected broadcasting.

One of the main avenues for political intrusion is in the corporate system of governance. Most have two councils; one at the top of the organizational pyramid to give policy, and a smaller one to handle general administrative matters including budget. The original concept was that these councils would reflect the social composition of each region. Although differing in size, they typically include representation from religious sects, academe, cultural institutions, the press, trade unions, youth organizations, women's groups, and political parties. The last was to be a distinct minority representation. Yet, of all of these groups, it is the political parties which provide the most effective organization, research, and lobbying efforts. The political parties provide a unifying rallying point for a council's activities. This political focus was given a stronger importance in the two largest state corporations in 1954 when the council structure was changed to mirror parliamentary representation. All members of these two councils are appointed by the political parties in direct proportion to seats held in the legislative body.

These elements were not initially troublesome. The allies insured that the first councils had minimum political input, and that the chief executive, the *Intendant*, was chosen for his professional expertise in broadcasting or journalism. Political representation in either the social group council or in the initial phase of the direct parliamentary representation model was made up of old political loyalists gracefully put out to pasture. Indeed, instead of bringing difficulties to the system, such old professionals made valuable contributions through their well-tooled skills of discussion and compromise.

Toward the end of the 1960s, the problems emerged, and can be traced to the change of national government in Bonn. Until this time, broadcasting had been neutral in its political comment because of a stalemate between the conservative government and the comparatively liberal broadcasters. Then, suddenly, the Christian Democrats were out of office for the first time in 20 years. As a conservative opposition they became obsessed with the favorable treatment being given to the new government by the broadcasters. Exacerbating the situation was the unrest of the times; conservative elements felt that social disturbances that could incite the masses should be kept off the air waves. A further grievance that was to emerge some years later was that conservatives always feel that the majority of broadcasting employees have socialist sympathies. This was usually accepted as a *fait accompli*. However, the 1980 federal election saw the issue reach crisis proportions. The conservaties offered a candidate who proved particularly vulnerable to ridicule. The resultant coverage was patently biased. It also encouraged research into other areas of television manipulation such as camera angle or image size, and it was found that the socialist candidate, the then-chancellor, was receiving far more favorable coverage. A ready solution to all such problems was seen in political control of broadcasting.

The broadcasting councils are very influential in German broadcasting. They are not those cozy, quiet, comfortable bodies found in other parts of the world with a similar public corporation structure. The role of the council has, unquestionably, increased in the past 20 years as the outcome of the interest of both major political parties in getting their own people into positions of influence. The councils have always had a vital role to play in German broadcasting. But while the period immediately following the war saw each council concerned with working with broadcasters to better the broadcasting system, the current intent is to control broadcasting. Parliamentary representation has changed from grand old men and the pensioned-off reliable worker to the brash, young, inquiring politician trying to make a mark for himself or herself.

The councils have two important functions: the making of policy, and the selection of the corporation's *Intendant* or Director-General and usually other senior executives. Policy has been construed to include programming; a position that has been supported by the federal courts. While denied the prior restraint of direct censorship, councils' right to review programs that have been aired has been found to have a cooling effect on controversy. A further avenue for the "raised eyebrow" control of programming is inherent in the reliance on the license fee which is set by each of the individual states. Deliberation over such fees provides politicians with a ready invitation to comment upon the programming practices of their stations.

In the choosing, and subsequent evaluation for reappointment, of the *Intendant*, the councils exert their major impact. Most recent appointments to this top broadcasting position were politicians who were well versed in political games, or individuals who it was hoped would prove malleable. This gave a new breed of *Intendant*. Until recently, not one had come up through the ranks of broadcasting. Indeed, none had prior broadcasting experience. All were from national or local parliaments or from the closely allied legal profession.

It was thought that the 1977 selection of a new *Intendant* for the influential second network might provide an opportunity to break out of this mold. The inside favorite was Dieter Stolte, a man with decades of top broadcasting experience, who was a deputy to the then *Intendant* as head of entertainment programming. He was unacceptable to the socialists. A compromise candidate, who placated all political factions was found in the recently retired German ambassador to London. Not only was he seen as a stop-gap candidate, but also as representing political realities. It might be helpful to have an individual who knew his way around the corridors of Bonn. Furthermore, the network hoped that the appointment of an international figurehead might give the organization prominence in national and international circles.

The past two years have seen changes. The ambassador proved no great success. Dieter Stolte is the new head of the second network. State corporations have turned to practicing broadcasters for their leadership. Yet, it is overoptimistic to see such developments as a contrite change of heart. Often they are part of the political manipulation. The 1982 appointment of the new *Intendant* in Berlin saw a bloodletting in the council that proved a precursor of the national political scene. The socialists thought they clearly had the reappointment, only to be outvoted by a coalition of conservative elements. (This on-going controversy occupied front-page newspaper coverage for a full week, stressing the importance that Germans place on such a politically sensitive subject as the choosing of the chief executive of the local broadcasting station.)

A year earlier, a political independent with a strong broadcasting background was appointed as *Intendant* in Frankfurt. However, the event was reported in *Variety* (Dec. 3, 1981) as "simply throwing a bone to an angry dog. Next year, the station's job of program director will be open, and since the program director has more control over what kind of programming emanates from the station, choosing a socialist for this job would of course influence the shows." This statement takes on greater significance when placed alongside a unique structural characteristic of the broadcasting system.

There is an unwritten, but strongly binding, rule that there will always be political balance throughout the corporate structure. The result is a chain of command where the head of a department will be of one party, the deputy of another; and within the corporate hierarchy, each step is supposed to alternate between the two major parties, with troublesome areas covered by an independent or a member of a minority party. Such a system is devastating to employee morale, and it tends to dissuade many talented individuals from a career in broadcasting. In a speech to a German-American Chamber of Commerce meeting in York in 1981, the Chairman of the Board of the German conglomerate Bertelsmann AG presented chilling examples of individuals of high principles frustrated in their efforts for professional careers or advancement in broadcasting. He summarized the system: "When it is a matter of considering the promotion of a studio manager or a news editor, for these openings, lists of sympathizers are maintained and updated at party headquarters."

There are other avenues for political influence. Some of these obtain in the unique structure of the first network. There is such a delicate balance of the many conflicting elements that extreme pressure from any one of them would destroy the system. The provision for opting out, or the threat to do so, provides an element of real persuasion which frequently results in pre-production pressure to modify program content. Each corporation wants national distribution, but compromise tends toward blandness in programming and the extolling of the safe, the acceptable, and the dull.

The inter-state cooperation that forms the essence of national broadcasting presents a basic dichotomy: the broadcasting system relies on agreement; political process demands opposition. Each state broadcasting system represents the interests of its dominant political party. Meetings to conduct the business of the first network spend more time debating political differences than in formulating broadcasting policy. One advantage is that major issues are often left to a small team of apolitical experts.

Within the political rivalries lies the German equivalency of a "fairness doctrine." As the network programming originates from different regional centers the public affairs programming reflects the politics of the area. This supposedly exposes the nation to the wide variety of public opinion. However, it hardly provides for all sides of an issue, and the capability of opting out of the network feed while assuming sole responsibility for programming a third station means that each state system functions more through the tyranny of the majority than through the plurality of democracy.

All this is not to argue that the situation is at a crisis stage. Indeed, recent pointers suggest a maturing of the system. Professionals have been appointed as *Intendanten;* there were no loud outcries of biased reporting in this recent 1983 election; and the threatened destruction of the first network structure through the political rivalries in the most northern corporations was resolved with the prodding of a federal court. Nonetheless, the political aspects of broadcasting remain a dominant thrust, and there is an awareness of an increase in the politicizing of the process. This must remain a major concern for German broadcasters, for German politicians, and for those interested in the very fabric of German society.

24

Communications Multinationals in Subsaharan Africa: The Recording Industry in Kenya and Nigeria

ARNOLD S. WOLFE
Triton College

The recent development of the recording industry in subsaharan Africa has gone relatively unnoticed in the scholarly community. Ndeti (1975, p.56) writes that recording is now an important industry in Kenya. A number of Kenyan records have, in fact, found a world market. Kenyan recording artists, such as Kelly Brown, are reported to have recorded hundreds of songs on records distributed throughout the world ("Kenya's Envoy of Soul," 1979). "Singles" (45 rpm records) recorded by another Kenyan, James Wahome, have sold 60,000 units in his homeland (Armstrong, 1979, p. 24). In 1979 an estimated 300,000 recordings manufactured in Nairobi were exported to such countries as Malawi and Nigeria (Armstrong, 1979; Andrews, 1980, p. 290). In Nigeria a "top Afro-rock" group, Osibisa, recently agreed to have the country's "leading indigenous recording company" release the group's records in its home country ("Osibisa 'Comes Home,' " 1981). And in 1982 Collins, (1982, p.65) estimated that the Nigerian recording industry would press 20 million long-playing records, a full 80% more than it produced as recently as three years before.

This paper examines the academically neglected issue of the recording industries of Kenya and Nigeria. As will be shown, the market for recordings in these two countries is not equally shared among the firms in each nation. A significant feature of these markets appears to be that a small group of firms dominates each. What is more, the majority of firms in each dominant group are foreign-owned, or multinational, enterprises.

THE RECORDING INDUSTRY OF NIGERIA

In their study of U.S. communication industry trends, Sterling and Haight (1978, p.38), note that: "Constant statistics are few and far between in the recording business." The paucity of information on Nigerian recording is, if anything, even greater. Nevertheless, a composite picture of the industry may still be drawn. This can be seen in Table 1.

Table 1. Key Artist[a] Ownership, Vertical Integration[b] and Horizontal Integration[c] in the Nigerian Recording Industry

Firm	Artist	Vertical Integration	Horizontal Integration
EMI (Nigeria)	Olumide Adeyinka Fela Anikulapo Kuti Harry Mosco Santana Fuju Sound[d] Sonny Okusuns	Plating, Processing and Pressing Plant Design and Artwork Printing and Lithography Tape Duplication Jackets and Sleeve Labels Tape, Blank Loaded and Raw	licensed: WEA (US); Ice, RAK, Creole, Rolling Stones, Ballistic (UK) Dynamic (Jamaica)
Decca (West Africa)[f]	Chief Commander Ebenezer Obey Vicky Edimo Fred Fisher Oriental Brothers Dr. Orlando Owoh	Plating, Processing and Pressing Plant	—
Phonodisk	Gbebume Amas Osibisa	Recording Studio	—
Odofin Irohin Ayo	Last Days Gospel Group[e]	—	—
Adetona	—	—	—

PolyGram	Recording Studio	*licensed*: Hansa (W. Germany), Polar (Sweden), WEA, Motown, Tamla, RCA, Solar (all US)
		Manufacturers, head cleaners and demagnetizers, needles
		Browser boxes, display racks, record divider cards
		Tape, Blank Loaded and Raw
Record Market	—	—
Senn-Sound	—	—

Bibliographic Sources; "African Carnival Comes to Stay," (1981); Akano, (1977); " 'Country Boy' Harry Mosco," (1982); "Drumbeat Reviews," (1977); "Drumbeat Reviews," (1978); Ebony, (1981); Ezenekwe, (1976); "Last Days Gospel Group Celebrates," (1981); Lawson, (1977); Billboard Publications, (1983, p. 243); Billboard Publications, (1980, p. 307); "Obey's Joy of Salvation," (1981); "Osibisa 'Comes Home,' " (1981); "Reviews," (1979); "Santana Sound Releases Soon," (1981); "Vicky Edimo Thanks You Mothers," (1981); "Yet Another Star—From Phonodisk," (1981).

Discographic Sources: Fela Anikulapo Kuti, *Confusion* (EMI 008N); Idem, *Shakara* (EMI 0004); Sonny Okusuns, *The Gospel of Sonny Okusuns: Ozziddi* (NEMI(LP) 0530); Idem, *Third World* (NEMI(LP) 0500); Oriental Brothers, *International Band Obi Nwanne*. Afrodisia Records (a subsidiary of Decca(West Africa)) Ltd. (DWAPS, 2090).

[a]Defined as an African musician whose musical activities have been the subject of press reports or reviews in any available source during the period approximately January 1977 to the present.

[b]Refers to the ownership on of the part of the recording manufacturer of goods or services it offers for sale to other firms in the industry.

[c]Defined as contractual agreements reached with other recordings firms outside Nigeria to distribute their recordings as their exclusive licensed agent within Nigeria.

[d]Formerly contracted to Odofin Irohin Ayo Records.

[e]Formerly contacted to Adetona Records.

[f]Taken over by PolyGram.

This picture of the industry shows that the factors of production in Nigerian recording are not equally divided among the industry's competing firms. EMI (Nigeria) and Decca (West Africa) emerge as dominant. Ten of thirteen key Nigerian recording artists record for one of the two.[1] Both own the industry's only means of phonograph record manufacture—the plating, processing and pressing plants listed in column 3 of Table 1. EMI possesses the industry's sole means of manufacturing prerecorded tapes—the tape duplication listing in column 3. Included among the foreign "labels" EMI distributes in Nigeria are those owned by or associated with Warner Communications, the giant U.S. communications conglomerate, which in 1981 sold more recordings in America than any other firm ("The Year-End Charts," 1980, YE8,9).

A PROFILE OF MULTINATIONAL CORPORATIONS IN NIGERIAN RECORDING

Multinational corporations (MNCs) clearly dominate indigenous enterprises in the Nigerian recording industry. Such subsidiary enterprises represent a form of direct foreign investment on the part of their multinational parent firms. (See Table 2.) As Table 2 shows, the corporate parent of EMI (Nigeria) is significant in size. In 1979 in a ranking based on annual sales, EMI ranked 194th among the top 5000 European industrials. With annual sales approaching $2 billion the British MNC is, according to Stopford et al. (1980, p. 367) "the world's largest record manufacturer," owning "recording and pressing facilities in every major market," and in 1981 taking in approximately 20% of all revenues accruing to recording firms worldwide. In the 1960s its market share was even greater, due to the popularity of such artists as the Beatles and the Beach Boys, whose recording rights it owned. (See Stopford et al, 1980, p. 368 and Peterson and Berger, 1975, pp. 167–168.) From then to the present, its wholly-owned subsidiary, Capitol Records, helped solidify its share of the all-important U.S. market (Peterson and Berger, 1975, pp.167–168; Billboard Publications, 1980, pp. 8, 12). Recently ("The Year-End Charts," 1981) *Billboard* ranked Capitol fourth in U.S. sales.

Precisely what components of EMI's operations are included in each of the product groups listed in Table 2 is not certain.[2] According to Europe's 5000

---

[1] Decca's musical operations were taken over by PolyGram in 1980. The fate of key artists contracted to Decca could not be ascertained.

[2] *Europe's 5000 Largest Companies* (1981) does not specify output for listed firms beyond the broad product categories reproduced in footnote a of Table 2. From the more extensive company profiles in Stopford et al. (1980), however, a clearer picture of the most significant activities of a given firm may come into view. Neither source is ideal. The former contains data on a greater number of firms than the latter but is more schematic in its presentation. The drawback of the latter source may be illustrated by the absence of any data on Decca. A search of corporate annual reports, U.S. Securities and Exchange Commission 10-K Reports and 8-K Reports yielded no data on Decca and incomplete data on EMI (principally because only its U.S. subsidiary is required to file 10-Ks). Even so by combining data from these sources, it is possible in some cases to "flesh out" the bare bones descriptions contained in *Europe's 5000 largest Companies*.

Table 2.   Multinational Corporations in the Nigerian Recording Industry

Firm	Product Groups[a]	Rank Among European Manufacturers 1979	1978	1979 Annual Sales[b]
EMI	1-2-3-4	194	174	$1,932,000,000
Decca[c]	1-2-3	889	812	405,556,000
Philips[d]	1-5	7	5	17,402,094,000
Siemens[d]	1-3	9	6	16,177,688,000
PolyGram (Neth.)	1-2	277	225	1,310,209,000
PolyGram (W.Germ.)	2-6	787	n.a.	455,050,000

Source: *Europe's 5000 Largest Companies* (1981); Jones (1980).
[a]Product Group Code: 1-Electrical Machinery, Apparatus and Supplies; 2-Printing, Publishing and Allied Industries; 3-Professional and Scientific Instruments; 4-Communications; 5-Industrial Chemicals; 6-Plastic Products.
[b]Worldwide.
[c]Taken over by PolyGram, 1980.
[d]50% participant in PolyGram.

largest companies (1981), EMI manufactures "electrical machinery, apparatus and supplies." The firm is one of the U.K.'s leading electronics companies. (Stopford et al., 1980, pp. 367–369). In "communications" EMI is the "largest [film] distributor in Europe," owns the third largest film production company in the U.K. and a 50% interest in one of that country's largest television production companies. Its "Defense Electronics Division" makes "professional and scientific instruments," a product category which would subsume the output of a U.S. subsidiary in medical and industrial electronics. An "Entertainment and Leisure Division" oversees the operations of EMI-owned cinemas, hotels, restaurants, and live theaters. And among its "principal associated companies" are two of primary interest here: Record Manufacturers of Nigeria and EMI (Nigeria).

As of 1980, EMI owned 25% of the former and 40% of the latter. To what extent does EMI control these firms? The bond between associated companies and their parents is likely to be tightly interwoven when the mode of management within the divisions of the parent firm is highly centralized. This appears to be the case with EMI. Stopford et al. (1980, p.267) note that all its recording interests outside North America are managed from the firm's London home office.

Decca, considerably less powerful worldwide than EMI, reported 1979 sales of more than $405 million and ranked among the top 18% of European industrials. Active in the manufacturing of electrical machinery, apparatus, and supplies; printing, publishing and allied industries; and professional and scientific instruments, Decca wholly owned its West African subsidiary, headquartered in Lagos (*Europe's 5000 Largest Companies*, 1981, p.30).

Like EMI, PolyGram is "well-connected." Its parents are two of the largest firms in Europe—Siemens, a West German electrical and electronics giant, and Philips, a Netherlands-based electronics, industrial chemicals, and scientific instruments conglomerate. Siemens and Philips each own equal shares of PolyGram GmbH (*Gesellschaft mit beschränkter Haftung*, or, "Limited Liability Co."").

Largely because of this arrangement it is difficult to ascertain PolyGram's annual sales or the contribution they make to the revenues of its parent firm. PolyGram GmbH is, according to Stopford et al. (1980, p.939), "the largest producer of records in Germany . . . The company also produces TV films, publishes music and has a limited number of retail outlets." PolyGram BV (*Beslotene Vennootschap*, or "Privately Owned Corporation") is based in the Netherlands and not only produces recordings but films and other audiovisual programs. It also exploits music copyrights (Stopford et al., 1980, p.783). The revenues for PolyGram GmbH and PolyGram BV are divided equally between Siemens and Philips. But *Europe's 5000 Largest Companies* (1981, p.30) does not indicate whether the revenues listed for Siemens and Philips include those derived from PolyGram operations.

Philips' annual reports are not much more helpful. Philips Gloeilampenfabrieken (1980, p.4) noted that in 1979 the firm began to treat PolyGram as a "non-consolidated associated company" for accounting purposes. Revenues from PolyGram's operations are reported but are not broken down by geographical area.

Note, too, that while Table 2 lists PolyGram (Netherlands) and PolyGram (West Germany) as participants in "printing, publishing and allied industries" (a category that may encompass music recording, music publishing, or both), the latter firm manufactures "plastic products," while the former is listed as a producer of "electrical machinery, apparatus and supplies." This does not jibe with the corporate profiles of the two subsidiaries in Stopford et al. (1980, pp.783,939), but rather compounds the difficulties in asserting anything definitive about PolyGram.

Investigation into the question of linkages between PolyGram and either—or both—of its parents' African subsidiaries would be helpful. Worth noting in this connection is the 60% participation of Philips in Philips (Nigeria) and Philips' full ownership of Philips (Kenya) and Philips Electrical Lamps (East Africa), Philips (Uganda), and one other fully-owned Tanzanian subsidiary, Philips Electronics (East Africa) (Stopford et al., 1980, p.786–787). Whatever linkages may exist between PolyGram and these East and West African subsidiaries merits fuller inquiry. Siemens has no such subsidiaries operating either in Kenya or Nigeria.

THE RECORDING INDUSTRY OF KENYA

Statistics on Kenyan recording are even more scant than on its Nigerian counterpart. Andrews (1980) has made the most significant contribution to date, and it is primarily on his work that the following discussion is based. To facilitate discussion data are presented in Tables 3 and 4.

In market structure, the recording industry of Kenya resembles its Nigerian counterpart: Both industries are oligopolistic. According to Andrews (1980, p.290), the combined market share of A.I.T., CBS (Kenya) and Phonogram (East Africa) is 60%, "with the fragmented remainder being held by hundreds of smaller independents."[3] The market structure of phonograph record pressing is monopolistic, as is the market structure for the manufacture of prerecorded tapes. Both means of production are owned by Phonogram. Phonogram also acts as a licensee for several U.S., U.K., and West German recording firms.

In this last respect A.I.T. is closely competitive. This apparently indigenous firm is a licensee for three of the five major U.S. recording companies—MCA,

Table 3.   Major Firms, Vertical Integration[a] and Horizontal Integration[b] in the Kenyan Recording Industry

Firm	Vertical Integration	Horizontal Integration
A.I.T. Records (Kenya) Ltd	Music Publisher Importer, stereo and tape system accessories (e.g., cleaners, 45 rpm adapters); head cleaners and demagnetizers	licensed: MCA, RCA, Stax, Fantasy, United Artists, Capital (all US); EMI (UK), Teal (S. Africa)
CBS Records (Kenya) Ltd		licensed: CBS, Epic, Island, WEA (all US)
Phonogram (East Africa) Ltd[c]	Plating, Processing and Pressing Plant Tape Duplication	licensed: De-Lite, Motown, RSO (all US); Hansa (W. Germany); African, Isa (not determined)

Sources: Andrews (1980, pp. 288, 290); Billboard Publications (1983, p. 233); Billboard Publications, 1980, p. 24).

[a]Refers to the ownership on the part of the recordings manufacturer of goods or services it offers for sale to other firms in the industry.

[b]Defined as contractual agreements reached with other recordings firms outside Kenya to distribute their recordings as their exclusive licensed agent within Kenya.

[c]Renamed PolyGram Records Ltd.

---

[3] Phonogram (East Africa) has since changed its name to PolyGram. Phonogram had been a wholly-owned subsidiary of PolyGram in any case.

RCA, and Capitol.[4] Its relationship with the South African-based Teal label appears to be more substantial than what generally obtains between a label licensee and licensor: Armstrong (1978), in an informal survey of Eastern African recording industries, noted that A.I.T. stands for Andrews International and Teal.

Andrews (whose work is utilized in this discussion) is, in fact, sales director of A.I.T. (Andrews, 1980, p.290). As is evident from Table 3, A.I.T. is an importer of ancillary goods, such as record cleaners and 45 rpm adapters, which are sold to retail consumers as well as to recording firms. As a record manufacturer A.I.T. is reportedly export-oriented and, according to Armstrong (1978), maintains active trade relations with the recording markets in Zambia, Malawi, and Nigeria. Seychellois recordings are also produced by A.I.T.

Table 3 is more limited in scope than Table 1, because of the dearth of data on indigenous Kenyan artists and their contractual relations with the companies for whom they record. This necessitates the exclusion from Table 3 of a key artist column and the more truncated listing of firms. Noteworthy in this respect is the absence in the table of two firms which as recently as 1978 were major participants in the Kenya recording industry. EMI (Kenya), which, in one form or another, had been prominent in East African recording since the 1920s, "was completely knocked out of the business in 1978" (Collins, 1982, pp.64–65). Reportedly the industry's "biggest" MNC, EMI (Kenya) also relied on export trade. Accounts are widely divergent, but the firm is said to have shipped between 100,000 to nearly 500,000 albums yearly to Nigeria alone. Its dependence on Nigeria was apparently so great that when the latter banned the importation of records in 1978, the firm found itself unable to overcome the loss of sales volume and left the industry (See Collins, 1982 and Armstrong, 1978). It may be speculated that by then EMI (Nigeria) had grown to a point where it could serve the export markets in Sierra Leone, Liberia, and Cameroon that its Kenyan counterpart had formerly served.

The other major firm now absent from the Kenyan scene is J. K. Industries, which, under license from Philips, formerly manufactured at least two brands of cassette tape (Armstrong, 1978). J. K. may have left the industry after failing to renew its licensing agreement with Philips, a speculation fueled by the actions of another Kenyan firm, East Africa Records. East Africa Records, the record-pressing division of PolyGram, began producing cassettes in 1979 after acquiring "much of the . . . equipment of a liquidated cassette factory" (Andrews, 1980, p.290). Although the source does not specify, the factory may have been owned by J. K. PolyGram is half-owned by Philips, J.K.'s former licensor.

---

[4] The two other U.S. majors are CBS and WEA. (See Gronau and Horrigan, 1980, pp.20–24; and "The Year and Charts, 1981) Together, the six major U.S. firms, with respect to recordings they either released or distributed, accounted for 93.3% of all "charted" singles and 96% of all charted albums in 1981. The charts rank-ordered the 100 most popular records in each category.

Table 4.   Recordings Sales in Kenya, 1978-1979[a]

Type of Recording	Units Sold (in 000s)	Percent Change[b]	Retail Value (in US $)	Percent Change
Disc Albums, 1979	180	− 16.3%	$1,727,027	− 30.1%
Disc Albums, 1978	215	—	2,469,594	—
Disc Singles, 1979	2,500	+ 4.1	3,716,216	− 26.6
Disc Singles, 1978	2,400	—	4,864,865	—
Prerecorded Tapes, 1979	65	+62.5	747,500[c]	+62.5
Prerecorded Tapes, 1978	40	—	460,000[c]	—
Total, 1979	2,745	+ 5.4	6,190,743	− 20.6
Total, 1978	2,655	—	7,794,459	—

Source: Andrews (1980).
[a]Includes imports.
[b]To nearest 0.1%.
[c]Calculated on the basis of a retail price of $11.50 per unit. See Andrews, 1980, p. 290. All other amounts are from Andrews.

While J. K. may no longer serve the record market, it appears to continue in business; Kenya Records and Tapes, however, is no longer listed in current publications.

Turbulence on the supply side of recordings was not limited to Kenya in 1978 and 1979. In 1979, and for the first time in a quarter of a century, sales in the U.S. market fell ("The Blues in Vinyl," 1979, p.67). Profits of CBS (Kenya)'s parent were off more than 45% (CBS Inc., 1980, p.4). PolyGram profits declined by nearly the same amount (Philips Gloeilampenfabrieken, 1980, p.4). And for the year ending in March 1980, Decca lost $22 million (Jones, 1980, p.9). That year also label after label changed hands.[5] In addition to the loss of Kenya Records, EMI (Kenya) and J. K., the Kenyan industry suffered a similar recession in sales (see Table 4).

As shown above, album sales dropped at a rate approaching the major's losses. Sales for the industry as a whole may have been worse had not the Kenyan government rescinded a 20% retail sales tax it had imposed in 1978 (Andrews, 1980, p.290). (It is largely for this reason that the retail value of prerecorded tapes sold has been calculated on the basis of the same average price per unit for both years.) The dramatic rise in prerecorded tape sales in 1979 represented 12% of that year's recording revenues. For the industry this "breakout" of tape has both positive and negative aspects. On the plus side, such firms as CBS must be encouraged at the demand for this new product dif-

---

[5] One label merger of interest to the Kenyan industry was the 1979 takeover of United Artists Records by Capitol Industries EMI. That same year Thorn Ltd, a U.K. electronics firm, took over EMI. For an account of the former, see Seyell (1979). Thorn's merger with EMI is summarized in Stopford et al. (1980, p.368).

ferentiation, especially since the cassette market in Kenya is still, according to Andrews (1980), in an "embryonic stage." As Andrews notes, however, for every prerecorded tape sold in Kenya 100 blank tapes are sold. The pirating of recordings by cassette, Armstrong writes (1978), is practically industrial in scale. In the same report Armstrong notes the passage in the Kenyan Parliament of legislation outlawing such practices. The measure may well be the first legislation of its kind in Africa. The losses from piracy can be significant: Collins (1982, p.65) estimates that it absorbs half of Nigeria's prerecorded music market sales. The future profit potential for the industry in both African countries is imperiled as a result.

MULTINATIONAL CORPORATIONS IN THE KENYAN RECORDING INDUSTRY

CBS (Kenya) is a relative newcomer, having entered the industry in 1979 (CBS Inc., 1980, p.17). Its parent is the U.S.-based CBS Inc., a diversified communications conglomerate that consists of four principal divisions—the Records Group, the Broadcast Group, a division that includes the largest American recordings-by-mail service, and a divison active in magazine and book publishing. The Broadcast Group embraces the CBS Television and Radio networks; the third division also manufactures musical instruments, amplifiers, and toys and operates a nationwide chain of high-fidelity audio equipment retail stores (CBS Inc., 1980).

CBS (Kenya) is the CBS/Record Group's "first majority-owned record company in Africa" (CBS Inc., 1980, p. 17). The enterprise represents, according to CBS (1980) "part of a long-range development plan to broaden the (Group's) sales base and talent pool." CBS management is sanguine about the prospects for Africa as a whole. "Expanded penetration on that continent . . . is planned for the future." The Group's International Division, of which CBS (Kenya) is part, had by 1979 already established its market power on another continent. It recorded its "best sales year ever" to become "the number one record company" in Europe (CBS Inc., 1980, p.16). Such success enabled the Group to generate more than $1 billion in sales during 1979. Revenues for CBS Inc. as a whole that year were $3,729,701,000 (CBS Inc., 1980, p. 2,4). Were the firm based in Europe its sales would make it the 95th largest industrial there (*Europe's 5000 Largest Companies*, 1981).

The data presented in the foregoing pages suggest certain unanswered questions. In a study of foreign investment in Kenya, Eglin (1978, p.98) writes:

> Traditional international trade theory would suggest that in a static world of perfect competition and free movement of capital and labour there would be no incentive to undertake direct foreign investment, since it is assumed that a comparative advantage in production is not transportable across national boundaries.

Clearly some of the largest recording companies in the world have chosen not to establish branch operations in either African state we have addressed. What then, have been the determinants for those companies that have—especially considering the theoretical absence of benefits in exchange for the cost incurred by the firms examined? Eglin continues:

> The existence of direct foreign investment has therefore been explained . . . by the identification . . . of monopoly advantages, which are available to enterprises and can be embodied in production or marketing activities outside their home economies.

Recorded music, however, is not merely an economic entity. It is a cultural artifact. To properly evaluate the performance of industries that supply such artifacts, special criteria apart from those applied generally to other industries may be required. In his text on the structure, conduct, and performance of American industry, Caves (1977) refers to performance as the "normative appraisal of the social quality of the allocation of resources that results from a market's conduct." Industrial market structures that exhibit allocative inefficiency, he suggests, *perform* poorly. Similar criticism may be levelled at market structures that are unnecessarily un-"progressive,"—that fail to raise the quality and variety of the goods they produce; or inequitable—that fail to allocate goods and services with reasonable equity to the markets they serve. Market structures that "waste factors of production by leaving people idle"—labor, of course, being the chief production factor in question, may also be said to perform poorly. (Caves, 1977, p.14). To evaluate the recording industry of any country according to these criteria is entirely appropriate. To efficiency, progressiveness, equity, and full-employment, proposed is a fifth criterion, viz., that a recording industry—in any particular country—should preserve and extend the indigenous musical culture of that country.

In this connection and with particular reference to Kenya and Nigeria, the following questions become pertinent. How have the recording industries in Kenya and Nigeria *performed?* Have they allocated their factors of production with reasonable efficiency? Have they been progressive in terms of such standards as raising the quality and variety of the goods they produce? What have been the effects on employment of the market structure of the industries in these two nation-states? And have they protected and extended the indigenous musical cultures of their respective nations?

To ask this last question is to inquire into the marketing and input policy of each industry as a whole, as well as to inquire into such policies of particular firms that comprise it. Marketing policy for a recording firm is in large measure a function of how the firm allocates its resources to the promotion and advertising of particular recordings or particular artists. Thus, which recordings by which artists from which companies have received what measure of marketing support? Is the policy of EMI (Nigeria), for example, to allocate a greater measure of its marketing resources to recordings by local recording artists or to those produced by foreign artists who have recorded for its overseas parent?

Input policy refers chiefly to company policy relative to the acquisition and development of recording artists. We need to know which, of the local available pool of musicians are signed by what companies. What are the policies of CBS (Kenya), for example, with respect to signing and developing local musical talent? Has the firm established a pattern of signing and developing artists who are more "traditional" or more westernized in their musical orientation? What has been the cumulative effect of the firm's—and the industry's—activities on the indigenous musical culture of Kenya?

Such questions call for the expertise of musicologists, sociologists, and cultural anthropologists. It is hoped that the preceding discussion will provide interested scholars with the beginnings of the database required to address them.

The structures of both the Kenyan and Nigerian recording industries have been shown to be oligopolistic, with MNCs dominating both markets. Such enterprises have been considered direct foreign investments and the foreign-based MNCs that made them have been profiled. It has been noted that the means of reproduction of recordings—the plating, processing, and pressing plants for records and the duplication facilities for tapes—are controlled by MNCs in both countries. Whether ownership of such means is the single most important determinant of the market power that has accrued to those enterprises is another question deserving research. Yet another is ascertaining why the Kenyan recording market seems to be able to sustain only one plating, processing, and pressing plant, while its Nigerian counterpart maintains two. The likelihood of scale economies would doubtlessly account for the high degree of concentration in each case. But the actions of the PolyGram subsidiary that resulted in its capture of a monopoly position in tape duplication, taken away from an apparently indigenous firm, would suggest that corporate strategy more than technical factors had a stronger hand in shaping the Kenyan recording reproduction market into its present monopolistic position. In this, Phonogram's monopolistic position in Kenyan plating, processing and pressing and oligopolistic position in the Kenyan output market loom large. Further study of Phonogram may even shed further light on the determinants of EMI's decision to shut down its Kenyan Branch.

Finally, the question of whether a phenomenon not unlike "brand loyalty" may play a part in accounting for the dominance of multinational corporations in Kenyan and Nigerian recording should be raised. In addition to recordings, PolyGram, EMI, and CBS each produce films and television programs and each of these firms is associated with the manufacture or retailing of audio equipment on which these same recordings may be played. The penetration into both cultural and non-cultural sectors of subsaharan African economies of goods and services produced by European and U.S. based MNCs may engender in locals a brand loyalty—a consumer-goods colonialism—that might favor any product, including a recording, made by or associated with highly-visible European or American MNCs. Such an intangible asset, should it be found, would tend to enhance the competitive position of multinational recording enterprises over their indigenous counterparts.

REFERENCES

"African Carnival Comes to Stay." (1981). *Lagos Weekend* (July 17), 86.

Akano, R. (1977). "Sonny's Silvery Smile." *Spear* (April), 32–33.

Andrews, R. (1980). "Kenya." In Billboard Publications, *International Buyer's Guide, 1980-1981*. New York: Billboard Publications.

Armstrong, J.C. (1978). "The Record Industry in Eastern Africa: An Introduction." Overseas Operations Division, Processing Services, U.S. Library of Congress.

Armstrong, J.C. (1979). "Sound Recordings—East Africa." *LC Acquisition Trends* (Feb.), 23–27.

Billboard Publications. (1983). *International Buyer's Guide, 1983-1984*. New York: Billboard Publications.

"The Blues in Vinyl." (1979). *Newsweek* (Aug. 13), 67.

Caves, R.C. (1977). *American Industry: Structure, Conduct, Performance*, 4th ed. Englewood Cliffs, NJ: Prentice-Hall.

CBS, Inc. (1980). *1980 Annual Report*. New York: CBS.

Collins, J. (1982). "Seventy-Five Years of African Recording." *Africa Now* (May), 64–65.

" 'Country Boy' Harry Mosco." (1982). *Drum* (Nigeria) (Feb.), 19.

"Drumbeat Reviews." (1977). *Drum* (Nigeria) (March), 46.

"Drumbeat Reviews." (1978). *Drum* (Nigeria) (June), 29.

Ebony, B. (1981). "Decca, Shanu-Olu on 'War Path' over Orlando Owoh." *Lagos Weekend* (July 10), 14.

Eglin, R. (1978). "The Oligopolistic Structure and Competitive Characteristics of Direct Foreign Investment in Kenya's Manufacturing Sector." In *Readings on the Multinational Corporation of Kenya*. Nairobi: Oxford University Press.

Europe's 5000 Largest Companies. (1981). Oslo and New York: A.A. Ókonomisk Literatur and Dun & Bradstreet International.

Ezenekwe, A. (1976). "The Other Side of Fela Anikulapo Kuti." *Spear* (June), 4–7, 9.

Gronau, K., and Horrigan, T. (1980). "Record Companies: Who Really Owns Them." *Songwriter* (July), 20–24.

Jones, P. (1980). "U.K. Decca Losses May Reach $22 Mil." *Billboard* (March 15), 9.

"Kenya's Envoy of Soul." (1979). *Drum* (East Africa) (March), 30.

"Last Days Gospel Group Celebrates." (1981). *Lagos Weekend* (July 24), 8.

Lawson, S. (1977). "Obey Reigns Still as King of Juju." *Drum* (Nigeria) (Aug.), 20.

Ndeti, K. (1975). *Cultural Policy in Kenya*. Paris: Unesco Press.

"Obey's Joy of Salvation." (1981). *Lagos Weekend* (July 24), 8.

"Osibisa "Comes Home.' " (1981). *Lagos Weekend* (July 24), 9.

Peterson, R.A., and Berger, D.C. (1975). "Cycles in Symbol Production: The Case of Popular Music." *American Sociological Review* **40**, 158–173.

Philips Gloeilampenfabrieken. (1980). *Philips Annual Report, 1979*. Eindhoven, Netherlands: NV Philips Gloeilampenfabrieken.

"Reviews." (1979). *Drum* (East Africa) (April), 34.

"Santana Sound Releases Soon." (1981). *Lagos Weekend* (July 31), 12–13.

Seyell, M. (1979). "Capitol/EMI Purchases United Artists Records." *Rolling Stone* (March 22), 11.

Sterling, C.H., and Haight, T.R. (1978). *The Mass Media: Aspen Institute Guide to Communication Industry Trends*. New York: Praeger.

Stopford, J.M., Dunning, J.H. and Haberich, K.O. (1980). *The World Directory of Multinational Enterprises*. New York: Facts on File.

"Vicky Edimo Thanks You Mothers." (1981). *Lagos Weekend* (July 31), 12–13.

"The Year-End Charts." (1981). *Billboard* (Dec. 26), YE-8-9.

"Yet Another Star—From Phonodisk." (1981). *Spear* (June), 28–29.

25

Contemporary Canadian Communication Issues: An Alternative Plan

THOMAS L. MCPHAIL
University of Calgary

INTRODUCTION

As Canada moves into the 1980s, telecommunications technology is racing ahead of policy-makers and many in the Canadian business sector. Major shifts and changes in business procedures and home information services will evolve with the implementation of videotex/teletext services, direct broadcast satellites (DBS), fiber optics, cellular radio, and laser technology, to name a few. With or without effective regulation policies, the wave of telecommunications innovations will continue to impact upon Canadian society at an increasing rate.

A major question is, for whose benefit will all these changes take place? Where does Canada stand in the Information Age? How can legislative bodies, such as Canadian federal and provincial governments, the major regulatory agency—the Canadian Radio-Television Telecommunications Commission (CRTC)—as well as the national broadcasting system—the Canadian Broadcasting Corporation (CBC)—face these issues and plan strategically for Canada's future in the Information Era?

While information is becoming a packaged and marketed consumer commodity, there is generally little thought or planning given to information beyond its raw economic power; yet most concede that the Information Age will have a powerful effect on the individual, political, social, and cultural facets of Canadian life.

A major underlying theme in the range of Canadian communications issues has always been that of Canadian identity. Both communications structures and content play an organic role in defining Canadian society. Few Western countries have struggled to the extent Canada has to define, study, protect, and encourage its own national identity. The questions, "What is Canadian culture?" and "How do we preserve it and promote it?" are at the core of Canada's past, present, and future approach to communication issues.

Beyond the issue of national identity, Canadian industry and government policy-makers should shape Canada's role in response to the satellite industry, transborder data flows, technological changes and impact on industry and labor, and finally, aspects of international communication markets.[1]

HISTORICAL BACKGROUND

Canada has been investigating communication issues of national concern for decades. Yet the numerous reports and studies of public policy for communications have incited a minimum amount of action within government and industry.

One such report, *Instant World: A Report on Telecommunications in Canada* (1971) was compiled by a study group called "Telecommunications." With the cooperation of government officials, industry spokespersons, and university faculty, Eric Kierans, the first Canadian Federal Minister of Communications (in 1969), organized the broad ranging Telecommission to examine the present and future issues in telecommunications, and to address accompanying social changes. A major observation from the study was that some Canadian information was being stored exclusively in U.S. databanks. At that time, the Canadian insurance industry relied on computerized information from Hartford, Conn.; Canadian hardware-makers used a Columbus, Ohio, databank for prices and stock quotes; and real estate information for four major Canadian cities was held in a Detroit databank.

In addition to this first deleterious aspect of transborder data flow, the 1969 report noted that a continental system existed covering services between the U.S. and Canada. For example, telephone rates were established by the TCTS (TransCanada Telephone System), the six member companies which shared the U.S. border, and AT&T (American Telephone and Telegraph). However, because regulatory bodies such as the CTC (Canadian Transport Commission), the Department of Communication, and the COTC (Canadian Overseas Telecommunications Corporation), were not coordinated in agreements, ad hoc policies developed.

Instant World (1971, p.96) also addressed the issue of cultural privacy:

This holds that cultures which may be intrinsically rich and satisfying but which are relatively weak in contemporary terms, can neither assimilate inexpensive foreign-produced media content, nor afford to produce material of equally commanding audience impact on their own.

---

[1] Canada has been reluctant to pursue with either sophistication or aggressiveness the international markets. Although international markets provide a window for future sales, the Federal Government has been negligent in developing any policy or strategy in this area. A good example is the recent Federal Government extension of funding for Telidon for a two-year period involving $23 million. Within the $23 million, only $1.2 million will be spent on international marketing. This is clearly about 10% of what is required, particularly in head-to-head competition with Prestel, Antiope, and various teletext/videotex systems from IBM, Apple, Commodore, Radio Shack, etc.

The study recommended that Canada undertake extended Research and Development (R&D) efforts to meet Canada's specific media needs. Other recommendations included: the development of multi-disciplinary executives in the industry for effective futuristic planning, as well as multi-lateral discussions involving governments, industry, and universities.

At the management level, the Telecommission advised the expansion of facilities to accommodate Canada's regional diversity, the integration of networks, and, particularly, the development of coast-to-coast digital transmission systems with linked databank and information processing organizations.

The main thrust of *Instant World* (1971, p.169) is:

> To redress the balance, authorities—federal, provincial and municipal alike—may find it worthwhile to collaborate in addressing themselves to these problems so that the greatest possible benefits can be derived from the individual regional, provincial and national opportunities that Canadian computer/communications systems may be expected to provide with a significant impact on social cultural, political and economic activity.

Eight years after the Telecommission study, the Consultative Committee on the Implications of Telecommunications for Canadian Sovereignty, under the direction of Chairman J.V. Clyne, submitted another report. The Clyne (1979) report asserted that Canada should work at being a leader in the field of telecommunications and that its position in the field should be a major focus of public policy. With the concern that Canadian sovereignty was being jeopardized in two fields, the Clyne report (1979, p.5) stated,

> First, Canadians are already being swamped with foreign broadcast programming and a new approach to the problem is urgently required; at the same time, there is a danger that foreign interests may achieve a predominant share of the market for dataprocessing services, and far too much of the information stored in databanks will be of foreign origin. Second, Canada is heavily dependent on imports in telecommunications technology. In certain sectors, such as satellites and information exchange, Canada is in the forefront of competitive technological developments. The exploitation of these developments requires public support that does not entail a vast expenditure of public funds.

The recurring theme in the Clyne Report was the urgent task of the Canadian government to preserve Canadian sovereignty and to capitalize on opportunities in the communications industry.

In *The Information Revolution and Its Implications for Canada* (Sarafini and Andrieu, 1980), the complexity of communication issues was documented. Because of the fragmented nature of the Canadian economy with its foreign subsidiaries and domestically controlled firms, Canada is vulnerable to conflicting interests. Jurisdictional disputes exist among the various levels of government, the public lacks awareness of the developing issues, and the small Canadian market cannot provide a strong industrial base for Canada's high technology and electronics industries.

Recently the Science Council of Canada (1982) reiterated the issues and many of the same recommendations of these previous studies in *Planning Now For An Information Society: Tomorrow is Too Late*.

While the Science Council's report recommended government support of R&D for such things as robotics and specialized computers, it stressed:

> The creation of a national telecommunications system to provide the infrastructure for the future cultural and economic development of Canada means that telecommunications policy development will require serious attention by the relevant provincial and federal government agencies. (Science Council of Canada, 1982, p.53)

Finally, in the first major federal document on culture since the Massey-Levesque Commission (1951), the Applebaum-Hébert Report (1982) outlined Canada's position with respect to the development of a federal cultural policy.[2] It provides a detailed analysis of policies in seven areas: heritage, contemporary visual arts, applied arts, publishing, sound recording, film, and broadcasting; and it probes general issues of funding, government and culture, and international cultural relations.

The report's two major and controversial recommendations were: that the CBC hand over almost all TV production to independent producers, eliminate commercials, and drop its affiliated stations; and that a federal system of arm's-length funding be developed for all major cultural agencies such as CBC, the National Film Board (NFB), the Canadian Film Development Corporation (CFDC), and the National Arts Center (NAC).

In light of these two recommendations, one can see, as Ganley (1979, p.4) suggests, a basic attitudinal difference between not only the U.S. and Canada, but the U.S. and the rest of the world:

> The Canadian governments and the governments of Western European nations and Japan, as well as many developing countries view the swift changes taking place in the communications and information field as primarily political events. The U.S. on the other hand, has tended to see them largely as technical and commercial problems, which it has had plenty of technicians, engineers, businessmen, and capital to solve. And when the U.S. has seen them as political problems, it has viewed them in isolation rather than as part of a whole.

---

[2] Canada does not have a cultural policy; rather it has developed a series of cultural industries and agencies in an *ad hoc* manner that are expected to have a positive influence on the overall Canadian cultural scene. Beginning with the establishment of the Canadian Broadcasting Corporation (Radio) in 1936, down to the creation of such government agencies as the National Film Board (films), Canadian Film Development Corporation (feature films), Telesat (satellites), and Canadian Content Rules, all reflect a mix of culture by regulation and culture by arms-length funding. Both the Massey-Levesque Commission and the Applebaum-Hébert Committee document the failure of the *ad hoc* approach.

CANADA'S POSITION IN THE HIGH-TECH RACE

While plagued with unresolved communications issues, *ad hoc* policies, and current economic woes, Canada has demonstrated its capacity to produce world-class high technology products. Canada's significant players in the high-tech race are Mitel, Northern Telecom, Gandalf, Spar Aeorospace, as well as the Telidon and NABU technologies. While the economic recession is affecting the 300 firms engaged in manufacturing, software development, and consulting in Canada's Silicon Valley North, sales continue to increase for Canadian products and services. Gandalf Technologies (data communications) and Mitel (telecommunications) are experiencing increases in research and development and plan major new products for the world market.

The success of Mitel and Northern Telecom in the international market is due to management skills and the development of innovative microcomputer-type products. In the next five years, Northern Telecom plans to spend $1.2 billion in research and development to integrate data processing, voice and data communication for office electronics.

NABU (Natural Access to Bidirectional Utilities) is a manufacturing company which has produced a home computer that is cable-compatible with Telidon. Whereas NABU uses cable, Telidon runs via telephone lines. Using cable, NABU has great access to Canada's high percentage of cabled homes, and the broadband cable system allows high resolution graphics (useful for teleshopping) and faster delivery than Telidon.

SATELLITE DEVELOPMENTS

Since the 1957 launchings of Russia's Sputnik I satellite and America's Explorer I, satellite hardware and software have evolved quickly through various stages. NASA, which has clearly held the monopoly on launching satellites, now uses its space shuttle, a reusable vehicle which reduces launching costs. Canada uses NASA services.

As satellites with expanding capabilities increase in number, the need for earth-based satellite hardware will grow. In Beakley's Report, (1982, p.70), the Yankee Group states,

> The proliferation of earth stations for domestic satellites is due to a number of factors: common carriers continuing to integrate the satellite facility into nationwide long distance networks, with specialized common carriers concentrating on inter-city routes; the proliferation of private networks; and the TV market, of which CATV is the major user of satellite services, with dramatic increases expected due to the proliferation of high capacity (54 channels and more) cable systems in major metropolitan markets.

Satellite hardware and software (particularly DBS) promises to grow into a multi-billion dollar industry within the next decade (Beakley, 1982, p.70). The future demand for satellite services will necessitate the international cooperation of communications policy-makers. Isolationist and protectionist regulations will hinder the flow of information services and jeopardize international relations as well as the internal development of nations adhering to such policies.

Canada has been a leader in satellite technology since the launching of its first broadcast satellite in 1972. According to the Science Council of Canada Report *Planning Now for an Information Society: Tomorrow is Too Late*, (1982, p.14–15):

> With the majority of our population thinly distributed along the U.S. border, Canada has long recognized the importance of exclusively Canadian transportation and communication systems from a transcontinental railway in 1883 to a trans-Canada radio network in 1927, a trans-Canada telephone network in 1932, a domestic geostationary communications satellite in 1972, and the first nationwide digital data system in 1973.

Our ability to meet the communications needs of such an expansive and diverse nation is becoming more difficult, particularly as satellite technology brings with it a plethora of communications services, issues, and opportunities.

Canadian leadership in the satellite industry began with Telesat, Canada's three domestic communications satellites, the Anik A series, launched in 1972, 1973, and 1975. The first Anik C was launched in August 1982, the second in April 1983, and the third in 1984. Anik C satellites use higher power than Anik A's and can be received by smaller earth station antennas; the Anik C service is the first commercial DBS service in the world.

However, Anik C is being tilted away from Canada's north to serve U.S. customers, and to profit Canada's TCTS. Yet this action conflicts with the federal government's financial support designated to provide satellite services to remote areas of Canada.

The powerful DBS satellite, Anik C, with its 16/14 gigahertz band has spread fear among Canadian communications policy-makers and broadcasters. The Canadian broadcasting industry is worried because DBS offers a potential range of communications services that will undermine their fragile advertising base and will by-pass local stations. Policy-makers are concerned chiefly with the impact of the high volume of foreign software, which will further impose foreign norms, values, and perspectives on Canadian society.

In 1972, Canada-U.S. letters of Agreement prohibited reciprocal use of satellites except in some exceptional circumstance. However, in June 1982, Communications Minister Francis Fox gave approval to Telesat Canada to provide Argo Communications Corp., a U.S. satellite carrier, with six channels on the Anik C satellite. Fox's agreement with the Secretary of State for External Affairs enables authorized satellite communications companies in the U.S. and Canada to negotiate with each other for the carriage of telecommunications traffic between the two countries by domestic satellites operating in the fixed satellite service.

These negotiations indicate a move towards liberalizing communications between the U.S. and Canada, and may be headed towards the first stage of a "continental communication pact."

Telesat's claim that the tilting of the satellite will not inconvenience Canadians, overlooks what the Canadian Industrial Communication Assembly believe is a great demand for Canadian business services. Canada may become even more dependent on the U.S. for satellite applications, while at the same time, Whitehorse and Halifax will receive weaker satellite signals from the tilted Anik C. As Canada's north and remote areas continue to be underserved, illegal earth stations (estimated to number 4,000) will proliferate to pirate programming from U.S. satellites in order to fill the vacuum in available Canadian alternatives.

In spite of the profits gained by Telesat-TCTS, Anik C may exacerbate the erosion of Canadian communication objectives to preserve Canada's national sovereignty. The legitimate objectives of Telesat-TCTS may conflict with the cultural and social objectives of the Canadian government and the taxpayers who have subsidized the Canadian satellite program.

While Canada's Anik C satellites have secured a leading position for Canada, the global scale expansion of the satellite industry now under way will more than quadruple the world's capacity for long distance communications in this decade. Canada cannot afford to lose its leading position through inadequate and *ad hoc* telecommunications policies, or through a protracted dependency on foreign countries to supply Canada with hardware and software.

Because satellites expand the capabilities of other technologies, they have helped produce media hybrids such as cable networks, superstations and DBS systems. Within the last ten years, domestic satellite systems have become a significant link in the chain of communications sevices. Beakley, (1982, p.69), Corporate Director of Research and Development for Scientific Atlanta, observes,

> There will be a trend toward integrating satellite, cable fiber optics and microwave into coherent networks with distributed control. Satellites will cover rural areas, oceans and cities, and rates for satellite communications will drop compared to the prices of paper, gasoline and transportation.

Beyond integrating these media, Beakley predicts satellites will revolutionize telephone communications via business networks and rapidly expand the data processing industry. In addition to the threat to the traditional newspaper and publishing industries, satellites have thwarted the dominating influence of broadcasting networks and are challenging telephone companies' monopolies as well.

TRANSBORDER DATA FLOWS (TBDF)

Canadian telecommunications links with countries around the world will multiply in the next several years. As satellites are launched to provide network services to American and Canadian markets, the earth stations to receive foreign programming will become more accessible and available in Canada. From this scenario, two major policy issues are apparent: transborder data flows, and the issue of access by Canadian to foreign (U.S.) television through cable or DBS.

While unrestricted TBDF may promise benefits for some Canadian businesses, a number of potentially dangerous problems arise, such as privacy. Because of U.S. influence in Canadian life, unlimited data flows would exacerbate efforts to develop and maintain national and cultural sovereignty, including Canada's efforts to create its own data bases.

According to Barry Lesser (1982, p.206)

> The issue of transborder data flows is, in fact, a whole series of issues involving such questions as loss of jobs, (to the United States) because of centralization of computing facilities by U.S. multi-nationals operating in Canada; the implications for a domestic satellite industry in Canada if U.S. satellites are used to provide Canadian services; privacy; foreign control of vital parts of the telecommunications and computer infrastructure; balance of payment problems; and access to information by Canadians and by government in Canada.

Unrestricted use of satellites for transborder communications is deterred by Canada's need to protect the revenues of the Canadian communications industry and its broadcasting networks. Although the U.S. seeks to pursue an open-skies policy, the principle of shared revenues between the U.S. and Canada is vital for Canada, and it necessitates a complex allocation of customers and the accompanying accounting procedures. Lester (1981, p.15) states that the benefits are not limited to revenues received by the telecommunications carriers for their services but include such other factors as direct Canadian labor payments, annual capital expenditures in Canada for equipment, payment of taxes and support for Canadian R&D.

However, in spite of such benefits, dangers to Canadian sovereignty are undiminished, not the least of which is the concern for the loss of job opportunities for Canadians. Canada is among the few countries to have attempted to calculate the cost in terms of balance of payments deficits, loss of jobs, and loss of managerial opportunities, of having data processed in another country. Ganley (1979, p.21) notes that Canadians have estimated that imported costs (TABLE 1) to Canada will have risen to about $1.5 billion annually by 1985, up from about $155 million in 1975; and 23,000 directly related jobs will have been lost to the Canadian economy in the process, simultaneously decreasing the need for Canadian middle and upper managerial positions.

In addition to the loss of jobs for Canadians, unregulated transborder data flows also mean loss of control by Canadians over Canadian data. W.E. Cundiff observes,

> Many American branch offices of Japan, European and other foreign companies have well-established computer communications to their head offices half-way around the world. Rather than establish communications lines between Canada and these far remote points, Canadian subsidiaries merely tie-in across the border to the existing network for their corporate data transactions. This sort of activity is

Table 1.   Canadian Projections of Losses Due to Imported Computer Services

	1975	1978	1980	1985
Cost of Imported Services	$155M		$560M	$1.5B
Proportion of Outside Services Required	30%		41%	52%
Estimated Job Loss	4,400	7,500	11,000	23,000
Percentage of Canadian Data Processing Jobs Repre- sented in Losses-Approximations		6%	8%	14%

Adaptation from: Canada, Computer/Communications Secretariat, *The Growth of Computer/ Communications in Canada* (Revised draft), Ottawa, March 1978. These figures include purchased computing service (15%), in-house personnel (45%), in-house c/c equipment (21.5%), other costs (14.5%), and data transmission (4%). The percentages are for 1975.

frustrating to a Canadian organization like Teleglobe in its attempt to build an international gateway, and market international telecommunications directly between Canada and foreign centers. (Cundiff and Reid, 1979, p.16).

Technical and logistical problems also arise, leading to such regulatory questions as deciding where communications becomes computing in networks. While regulations would affect the marketing, planning and financial aspects of multi-national concerns in Canada, Canada needs input into decisions affecting its own expertise in data services, software and hardware networking, and the development of databases.

In October 1981, two major American satellite data services companies, American Satellite Corporation (ASC), and Satellite Business Systems (SBS), requested transborder network connections with major Canadian cities. The ASC application proposed the alternative use of the U.S. Westar satellite and one of Canada's Anik systems, allowing a division of revenues so that each carrier could cover its costs. The SBS application proposed the use of the SBS system and SBS earth station facilities. While Canadian facilities could be controlled and owned by Canadians, all network functions were to be managed by SBS.

The FCC approved these two applications, but negotiations with the Canadian government stalled the implementation of the services. At that time, former Canadian Senior Assistant Deputy Minister of Communications, Jean Fournier, recognized that transborder traffic could be profitable in terms of revenue sharing for Canadian carriers. Ahern and Sternad (1982, p.80) note that beyond technological and economic benefits, Fournier stated, "The Canada-U.S. market is a vitally important source of revenue for Canadian carriers; there is a real danger that without an appropriate framework, U.S. satellite services would dominate Canada-U.S. traffic".

When a data-pact was finally reached between the U.S. and Canada, it outlined several conditions. Domestic satellites could be used for transborder services, provided Intelsat facilities could not provide the service, or it would be uneconomical or impractical for American or Canadian companies to use the international system. Earth stations used in Canada were to be owned and operated by Canadian entities, and the satellite services in Canada and the U.S. would be required to negotiate the division of revenues.

Beyond the issue of data services, the U.S. placed applications for transborder videoprogramming, of which two proposed the receipt of Canadian television programming in the United States. As in the case of data flows, the Canadian government was initially unwilling to consent to the distribution of U.S. satellite programming in Canada. While negotiations have extended now to Canada's reception of U.S. pay TV series, there are several reasons for Canada's continuing review of the issues of TBDF. There has been no formal policy to date covering a comprehensive approach to the control and access to Canadian databases, and to Canadian content in satellite and cable information exchanges.

These concerns are not unique to Canada. An Independent Broadcasting Authority (IBA) Research Report (Wober, 1981, p.3) revealed similar reservations in the United Kingdom regarding international satellite programming. Two major sources of opposition were: (1) the concern that increased programming choice will reduce the quality of satellite broadcasting to the lowest common denominator; and (2) the competition with existing interests (i.e, copyright infringement via use of VCR's, etc.). A third concern outlined in the United Kingdom report pointed to the "survival of the fittest" and largest, organizations within an open-skies situation. According to the report, broadcasts of these large organizations

> would influence cultures and political systems so that if this would debase European culture and destroy the European press, the wisest policy decision of all might simply be to suppress it (i.e., DBS) now. Since spectrum scarcity was no longer a usable excuse for regulation, societies should find a "new set of legal principles based upon other generally recognized societal values" with which to regulate events. That this applies already to the practice of terrestrial television is made clear by contributors to a volume edited by Gerbner. But the problems would be much more acute with unfettered satellites. For example, Cuba could put up a station and rain down Russian propaganda (packed with Moscow circuses and gymnastics) upon the helpless U.S.A.

CANADIAN CULTURE AND SOVEREIGNTY

Of primary concern to communications policy-makers is the protection of Canadian cultural identity in the face of potential U.S. cultural influence.

Within both the industrial and business sectors, U.S. cultural imperialism takes the form of lost employment if Canada relies too heavily on U.S. databases, information sources, hardware, and software. Importation of U.S. programming may also inhibit the development and growth of domestic Canadian satellite video services and video programming.

The status of the nation's hardware and software sectors also relates to the issue of Canada's sovereignty. Less than 10% of Canada's hardware sector is Canadian-owned, making that industry a branch plant operation which imports or manufactures hardware in Canada via subsidiaries of multinationals. The software sector, (computer services, etc.), is 80% Canadian-owned by companies such as Datacrown, Systemhouse and Canada Systems Group. However, the relationship of telecommunications to these industries is changing rapidly.

In developing new research and development programs, industry and government must recognize that software costs, in both human and financial terms, exceed those of hardware to a significant degree. As hardware costs dwindle, the gap between software and hardware costs will increase.

Beyond the need for Canadian hardware and software is the issue of the quality and quantity of Canadian content in programming. Canadian broadcasting policy to date has been characterized by two key concepts: "a single broadcast system," in which privately owned broadcasting is to cooperate with the state-owned network; and "balanced programming," to strive for a balance between inexpensive U.S. (and other foreign) programming, and Canadian productions of equal quality and audience appeal. Section 3 of the Broadcasting Act (Canada Broadcasting Act, 1968, p. 203) states government objectives to be a "single system", to be "effectively owned and controlled by Canadians" so as to "safeguard, enrich and strengthen the cultural, political, social, and economic fabric of Canada".

In the wake of increased U.S. program reception via videocassette players, recorders, videodisc players, satellite dishes, and videotex/teletext services on home computers, it will be impossible to regulate Canadian content in the future. But if Canada is to retain a programming presence in its own broadcasting and telecommunications system, it should channel technological and creative resources into the production of competitive and marketable Canadian programming.

Canadian cultural sovereignty and Canadian content issues ultimately depend on economic factors. Canadian broadcasters compete for American programs which are expected to draw large audiences and thus larger advertising revenues. In its licensing and content regulation procedures, the CRTC has often gone against the best interest of Canadian producers. For example, one CRTC ruling permits a Canadian station to substitute its own advertising for that of a U.S. station whenever the two stations are broadcasting the same show at the same time. This encourages Canadian producers to purchase U.S. produced shows for prime time slots.

Unfortunately, communications policy continues to deal with these issues with either national defensiveness or economic expediency, and both on an *ad hoc* basis. The Science Council (1982, p.53) elaborates on this problem, stating Canada's need to develop a network capable of serving national and international needs using the nation's economic resources efficiently:

This may be more difficult than it looks initially, for Canada has considerable re-dundancy in its network today because of its technical expertise in the transmission field, the rush to provide hardware solutions for what are essentially issues of sovereignty and, of course, the existing industrial structure. The transformation of the existing technological and institutional structures into an integrated structure may be more difficult for Canada to achieve than for most other nations. With the exception of the U.S. and Canada, the telecommunications structure in most countries is government owned and operated. Canada has a mixed public and private telecommunications structure under divided jurisdiction and regulation.

NATIONAL STRATEGY AND THE SATELLITE QUESTION

Melody (1979, p.3) laments the wasted potential of Canadian satellites when he states that it is:

restrained by the need to accommodate the vested economic interests of the carriers that own and control the land-line microwave and cable technologies. The history of satellites is one of wasted technical potential and outrageous economic inefficiency in order to preserve the near monopoly market dominance of the established telecommunications carriers.

As each generation of new satellites is launched, the gulf between the promise of technology and the threat to cultural identity is being exacerbated.

The confusion over how to approach issues of Canadian content, hardware and software, or research and development, has precipitated further reluctance on the part of government and other regulatory bodies to solidify a national telecommunications strategy. For example, although Canada was a pioneer in the use of satellites with its Anik series and with Telidon, it has hesitated to build and expand its early leads.

Unprecedented opportunities may be explored within the framework of a comprehensive broadcasting and telecommunications policy. Such a policy will have to accommodate the new competitors, rapidly changing technology, and international opportunities.

For example, Canada's present relationship with the United States consists of sporadic agreements regarding isolated sales; Canada's Telidon is being loosely marketed across Canada; and marketing opportunities there have been a series of unrelated contracts demonstrating Canada's lack of a coherent communications marketing strategy.

One such contract was between Infomart, an international leader in the development and operation of videotex/teletext information system and the Buick division of General Motors. Using the Infomart Telidon System Software, (ITSS), Buick will provide instant product information such as pictures of new cars, accessories, pricing details, and maintenance information for its dealers and customers across the U.S. The Buick deal is the first application of Telidon to the automotives industry, and will involve the linking of Telidon terminals to Buick's computers in Flint, Michigan, to serve 2,000 Buick dealers across the U.S.

Meanwhile, ITSS is in operation in 12 locations on four continents. Other U.S. users include Time Inc., Digital Equipment Corp., and the Los Angeles Times. Infomart also has a 50% interest in Videotex America. As a result, Canada's Telidon technology has a foot in the door of the U.S. market, and it is gaining recognition on the international scene as well. However, as a government funded project, Telidon's status is tentative.

Canada also has gained a foothold in the U.S. cable market. Canada's largest cable company, Rogers Cablesystems Ltd. has U.S. cable franchises in New York, California, Oregon, and Minnesota. Maclean-Hunter Cable TV Ltd. operates systems in New Jersey. Moffat Communications has systems in Texas. Capital Cable TV Ltd. of Edmonton has franchises in Colorado, and Toronto's Cablecasting Ltd. has operations in Georgia and California.

Another company, Telescan Electronics and Communications Inc. of Toronto was established recently to exploit opportunities in satellite broadcasting in the U.S. and Canada. The company is offering tiered cable services to U.S. apartment dwellers using programming taken from U.S. satellites.

Ironically, the U.S. responses to Canadian-owned U.S. cable franchises have been ones of protest, because the U.S. companies feel they are discriminated against by the Canadian government since they cannot own cable systems in Canada.

While the Canadian Broadcasting Corporation (CBC) markets its productions around the world, efforts to penetrate the American market have had limited success. According to the CBC Annual Report (1982, p.15), the burgeoning of U.S. cable channels has awakened interest in arts programming, and a growing international market awaits CBC-produced ballets and serious music specials.

Marketing opportunities are also available to the National Film Board (NFB) of Canada which has distribution offices in several major cities around the world. However, to this point, NFB films have not had substantial success breaking into major American television or cable networks. Applebaum and Hébert (1982) stress that the NFB and CBC should plan for the present and long-range potential of new satellite systems. In particular, their report noted the need to establish closer coordination with Telesat in order to stimulate the development of new technological systems to.serve Canadian programming objectives.

How can Canada best approach a comprehensive communications policy which would encompass the challenges of production, the dangers to sovereignty, the opportunities of the international market, and other major issues facing the telecommunications industry?

A CONTINENTAL COMMUNICATION PACT (CCP)

Numerous reports, studies, and commissions have attempted to address the issues affecting Canadian communications. However, the recommendations from these efforts have yet to be compiled and translated into effective communications strategy. Instead, there exists a series of *ad hoc* and disjointed short-run and frequently conflicting policies. Government involvement in the satellite industry has been characterized by a lack of concern for Canadian software, and even less for evaluation of the social impact of various satellite programs.

Meanwhile, DBS, cable, videotex, and TBDF are growing on a continental scale precipitating a continental information communication grid. This now necessitates a public policy requiring a "Continental Communication Pact (CCP)" with the United States. Such a pact would broaden the market for Canadian products, both hardware and software, so as not to be swamped by foreign, mostly American, products. To have the CBC and CTV carried on all U.S. cable systems, or new pay services, First Choice and Super Channel, carried on U.S. satellites, would financially aid the Canadian services and redress the current imbalance. In addition, it would provide guidelines for Canadian cable companies such as Rogers, Maclean-Hunter, and Cablecasting, with franchises in the U.S. The U.S. networks are carried on Canadian cable systems and U.S. pay services are being received by a growing number of Canadian-based television receive-only earth stations (TVRO's); now the major question is why not have a reciprocal agreement to benefit Canadian manufacturers and software merchants?

There is a greater hope for the marketing of Canadian programming in the U.S., albeit the demand is not yet proven. From the CBC Annual Report (1982), it is apparent that a market does exist for Canadian productions, particularly those relating to the arts. An information pact would outline the strategy for the promotion of CBC, NFB, and CFDC productions on American networks and theater screens.

With regard to satellite technology, Canada is being forced into a pact with the U.S. over the issue of future DBS services. Both Canada and the U.S. are seeking to reserve prime satellite orbital slots for future use. While the FCC is planning to establish a DBS system with up to 13 services, Canada is requesting 6 slots with full frequency bandwidth of 500 mhz reserved for each service. Canada's request raises the problem of maximum spacing, 15 or 16 degrees between each satellite, which will be necessary to accommodate the proposed Canadian services, yet it will also mean that the U.S. will be left with only 4, mainly unfavorable, slots. Negotiations will require adjustments to the requests of both countries, although the U.S. favors a system where applications are granted on expression of demand and first-come, first-served.

Yet once again, Canada is demonstrating concern for the preservation of its sovereignty by seeking an orbital slot for each of its five time zones and an additional slot for French programming for Quebec. While Canada does not have the economic resources to develop these services immediately, it is seeking to prevent the U.S. from absorbing all the available slots now. (It is to be remembered that other smaller countries, particularly in South America, are hoping to use DBS services in the future, and are looking at the same spaces that Canada and the U.S. are hoping to capture.)

The issues of both content and hardware/software sovereignty could be addressed by the negotiation of a joint satellite serving both the American and Canadian public. Canadian strategy on this point would involve a bilateral agreement with the United States regarding the division of revenues from the joint satellite network; the equity of content/carrier status; and the equal division of American and Canadian programming services provided by the satellite, plus shared R&D.

In light of the complicated nature of forming a CCP, Canada and the U.S. will do well to examine, as a model, the Canada-U.S. Auto Pact of 1965. That agreement was signed to provide duty-free trade by manufacturers in automobiles and parts between the U.S. and Canada. At the time of the pact, Canada's position in the automobile industry was weak; it was incapable of competing in the international market because of the expense to duplicate U.S. cars in Canadian subsidiaries. The auto pact promised to redress the deficit in the sectoral balance of trade and expand production in Canada.

While on the surface, it appeared to be a sectoral free trade pact, it was inevitably viewed differently by each country. According to Beigie (1970, p.5) the agreement integrated the industry in the two countries increasing imports from the U.S. to more than 40% of the Canadian market in 1968 from 3% in 1964; and 60% of all vehicles produced in Canada during 1968 were exported, compared with less than 7% in 1964. The price of Canadian cars came closer to U.S. cars, and Canadian production increased dramatically.

The major problem with the Auto Pact was that from the onset, the objects of the two countries were different, and thus by 1969, both governments decided to evaluate their mutual discontent and reassess the pact. Essentially, the pact was *an ad* hoc measure to allay specific pressures, and questions of long-term complications were tacitly avoided. In addition, the pact was negotiated between Congress and Parliament, with little input from the public.

In approaching a CCP, Canada and the U.S. should avoid the errors and problems inherent in the Auto Pact. An agreement satisfactory to both countries would depend on consideration of each country's objectives, as well as such variables as market forces, wage parity, government power, trade imbalances, and cultural and economic resources. Ultimately all stakeholders in the communications industry should be considered and consulted prior to the formation of a CCP.

The CCP will strengthen the position of the diverse Canadian cultural industries; the CCP is consistent with the emerging narrow-casing, rather than broadcasting, or tiering approach of the evolving cable/satellite, hybrid communication systems blanketing North America. The *status* quo is really a closet communication policy giving Canada the worst of both the hardware and software dimensions of the communication world. Unless a bold initiative, such as the CCP, is taken to recognize and protect the Canadian presence within the North American continental framework, then, over time, many of the current deleterious aspects of Canada's cultural and broadcasting areas will simply increase.

REFERENCES

Ahern, V. and Sternad, S. (1982), "Governments Need Regional Coordination, Communication." *Telephony* (May), 80.

Applebaum, L., and Hébert, J. (1982). *Report of the Federal Cultural Policy Review Committee.* Minister of Supply and Services, Ottawa.

Beakley, G. (1982). "Special Report on Satellites." *Communications News* 3, 73.

Beigie, C.E. (1970). "The Canada—U.S. Automotive Agreement: An Evaluation." Canadian American Committee, Canada.

Canada Broadcasting Act. (1968). Statutes of Canada: Part I Public General Acts, 16–17 Elizabeth II Chapter 25, pp.203–237. Roger Duhamel, Queen's Printer, Ottawa, Ontario.

Canadian Broadcasting Corporation (CBC). (1982). Annual Report 1981-1982. (Published in accordance with the provisions of the Broadcasting Act, Part III, Section 47.)

Clyne, J.V. (1979). *Telecommunications and Canada.* Consultative Committee on the Implications of Telecommunications for Canadian Sovereignty. Ottawa, Ontario: Minister of Supply and Services.

Cundiff, W.E., and Reid, M. (1979). *Issues in Canadian/U.S. Transborder Computer Data Flows,* Institute for Research on Public Policy. Toronto, Ontario, Butterworth & Co.

Ganley, O.G. (1979). "The United States-Canadian Communications and Information Resources Relationship and Its Possible Significance for Worldwide Diplomacy." Working Paper, Program on Information Resources Policy, Harvard University, Cambridge, MA.

Instant World: A Report on Telecommunications in Canada. (1971). Ottawa, Ontario: Information Canada.

Lesser, B. (1982). "The Implications of the Federal and Provincial Proposals for Regulating Telecommunications: An Economist's Perspective." *In* R. Buchan and C. Johnston (Eds.), *Telecommunications Regulation and the Constitution.* Montreal, Quebec: Institute for Research on Public Policy.

Lester, R.M. (1981). "Communications and Transborder Information Flows." Conference Board of Canada, Business Outlook Conference, unpublished paper.

Massey, V. and Levesque, G.-H. (1951). *Royal Commission on National Development in the Arts, Letters and Sciences.* Ottawa, Ontario: E. Cloutier, Printer to the King.

Melody, W. (1979). "Are Satellites the Pyramids of the 20th Century?" *Search* 6 (No.2), 2–9.

Science Council of Canada. (1982). *Planning Now for an Information Society: Tomorrow is Too Late.* Minister of Supply and Services, Ottawa. (Report No.33).

Serafini, S. and Andrieu, M. (1980). *The Information Revolution and Its Implications for Canada.* Communications Economics Branch, Department of Communications, Minister of Supply and Services, Ottawa.

Wober, M. (1981). "Pyramids or Chariots—The Satellite Question." Independent Broadcasting Authority, Audience Research Department, Special Report.

26

The Language of Education and Revolutionary Policies in Formerly French West Africa

J. R. RAYFIELD
York University

This paper discusses language and education policies in West African countries (former French colonies) and proposes the hypotheses that: (1) the continued use of the French language as the only official language of the country and the only medium of instruction in the schools has perpetuated and even increased the inequalities in the political, economic, and social systems that were inherent in the colonial system; and (2) those countries committed to socialism, democracy, and/or economic and cultural independence have been the most active in reforming the educational system by (a) restructuring the school systems, (b) initiating comprehensive adult literacy programs, and (c) introducing African languages as the medium of instruction.

Biarnes (1980, pp.5–6) sums up the situation in all former French colonies:

> Everywhere, bureaucratic bourgeoisies and soon *compradores,* trained in the schools of the former colonial power and claiming to be either socialists, or, more logically, liberals, installed themselves in power, headed by leaders in three-piece suits, gradually replaced by other leaders in military uniforms. Very rapidly, and by increasingly authoritarian methods, they seized for themselves, at the expense of the rural masses and with the indifference or complicity of nearly all the rest of the world, the largest part of the national income, which, in most cases, they were admittedly incapable of increasing in proportion to the growth of the population.

The French colonizers entered Africa in the last quarter of the nineteenth century to control a new source of raw materials and military manpower and to check the advance of the British who had started the same process a little earlier. As few Frenchmen were willing to live and work in West Africa, the colonial civil and military administrators established schools in which Africans could be trained as interpreters, clerks, soldiers, and transport workers. Instruction was only in French; apparently the use of an African language, even one such as Malinke or Wolof, which were widely used as *lingua francas,* was not even considered. The French language was presented, by the attitude of the teachers and the material in primers and readers, as the vehicle of the greatest civilization in the world; by mastering it, intelligent and ambitious Africans could participate, if only marginally, in this civilization. Of course they would willingly abandon their own rudimentary languages in which their primitive cultures were expressed. Older Africans still remember the humiliating punishments they received for speaking their own languages in school.

The only schools which taught literacy in African languages were a few set up by Catholic missionaries. The colonial administration disapproved of this practice; first they forbade the schools to teach anything but religion, and later they closed them down as soon as they could establish their own schools (Harding, 1971).

However, the administrations did not interfere with the Koranic schools, probably because they failed to see them as a threat to their aim of implanting French values on the Africans. These schools, however, were of great importance in the maitenance of Africans' values and pride in their own culture. (Santerre, 1980 and 1971) Their main function was to teach students to memorize and later to discuss the Koran, and to study other Muslim literature. Although many children learned only to "read" Arabic phonetically, some did acquire a deeper knowledge of the language, which for several centuries had been a *lingua franca* in the Sahel area, used for trade between the medieval African kingdoms and the Arab world, and even for communication between the rulers of the various kingdoms. Many students learned to apply the Arabic script to their own languages. Even today, many West Africans throughout the area use Arabic script for everyday purposes. There exists a rich literature in African languages using the Arabic script.

The importance of the Koranic schools, then, lies in the fact that the French colonial administrators thought that they were giving illiterate primitives the opportunity to enter the fringes of a great civilization, to which the key was literacy in the French languages, whereas in actuality the Africans, through the Muslim religion and its literature, were already participants, however marginally, in another great civilization, and many of them were literate.

A further consequence of the trade and cultural network extending throughout West Africa and connecting with the Arab world was that success in the French educational system was not the only way to fame and fortune. Many herdsmen, traders and local rulers of West Africa became wealthy and powerful without speaking a word of French. This situation continued after independence and is important to the present day.

The schools set up by the colonial administrations were exactly like those in France in both structure and curriculum. No provision was made for teaching oral French to the great majority of children who came to school without knowing so much as a French word. Most children dropped out after a few months. Those who managed to get through the elementary cycle usually had to repeat two or three years, and thus were too old to take the examination for entry into the very few available secondary schools; they had learned nothing of use to them; they were unqualified for most available jobs and too proud to return to peasant life.

The small minority of Africans who went all the way through the school system were the children of those who had succeeded in acquiring an education in
the early period of colonization. French was spoken in their homes, and many
began their education in the few schools in the capital cities set up for the children of French colonial officials. In this way the colonial elite was perpetuated
into the period of independence that began with the liberation of Guinea in
1958. (The other countries became independent in 1960.) It was the graduates
of the few colonial secondary schools, especially William Ponty in Dakar, who
led the movement for independence and remained in power as leaders of the
new republics. Houphouet-Boigny of Ivory Coast, Sekou Touré of Guinea,
Léopold Senghor of Sénégal, and Ahidjo of Cameroon were still in power 20
years later. (Senghor and Ahidjo recently retired and handed over power to
their chosen successors.) The others were overthrown by coups, but their successors had the same background, except that they had risen from the ranks of
the army rather than the civil service.

By the mid-1960s, even the elite were dissatisfied with the educational system. (The mass of the people had never had any illusions about it.) It was exor-
bitantly expensive in proportion to the national income, and ineffectual even
with its limited aims of providing manpower for the lower ranks of the civil service. Even if the aim of training the sons of the elite to be administrators were
admitted to be the sole aim, it was still ineffective; engineers, architects, physi-
cians, administrators, and even secondary school teachers still had to be
imported from France. As for the masses, what was the point of educating them
at all? There were no employment opportunities for those who completed some
or even all of the elementary cycle. There had been little industrial development during the colonial period, and with mechanization and the completion of
the building of roads, railways, docks, and airports, even fewer workers were
needed than in the earlier period of colonial government. The few rural children who attended school were withdrawn from the labor force, where they
were urgently needed, and from traditional forms of education and apprentice-
ship, so that they were worse off than if they had not attended school at all.
They were still taught the values of French civilization from which they were
excluded; they learned to be discontented with their own culture, and were in
no way prepared to develop a new one.

The most obvious way in which schools promoted French culture and deni-
grated African culture was through the curriculum, and it was this factor which
the new governments tackled first. African history and geography were substi-
tuted for French. Children read about Sundiata instead of Charlemagne; elementary readers featured Mamadou and Bineta helping their parents in the
fields and the kitchen instead of the French equivalent of Dick and Jane going
to the supermarket; the arithmetic book characters counted yams instead of ap-
ples. But the basic system was unchanged.

The basic problem was never squarely faced. There was no lack of development plans; every ministry drew up a series of five-year or seven-year develop-

ment plans. But these plans did not face the fact that the means to carry them out were unobtainable, even by pawning the country to outside powers or by begging from UNESCO. Hence the often paradoxical plans for education. Erny (1977, pp.48–49) sets out the paradox:

> As, generally speaking, it is not possible, for financial reasons, to reconcile long and thorough schooling with schooling that aims to reach the mass of the people, one must choose between the two. But as, on the other hand for socio-political reasons it is not generally desired to abandon conventional training of a self-styled elite of leaders and managers, the balance will tip on the side of very selective schooling, while many specialists conceive of a "porous" school to minimize repeats and dropouts. The fact is that many states have explicitly ended the quantitative expansion of the primary school and are secretly glad of its contraction.[1]

In all the voluminous and multitudinous writings and speeches of African educators and planners, no really radical changes are suggested.

A typical manifesto is that of a conference of ministers of francophone African countries held in Kinshasa in 1969: the principles on which an elementary education system should be based are: (1) children should not be isolated from their environment and should be able to contribute to its development; (2) the duration of schooling should be adapted to the requirements of each country; (3) class size should be limited; (4) new programs and pedagogical methods should be introduced, so that the children can acquire a level of knowledge equal to that reached in the present system; and (5) elementary education should prepare a child to go directly, or after further training, into the work force or to enter secondary education (Erny, 1977, pp.26–27).

Such a policy does not strike one immediately as impracticable. But we must consider the enormous expense needed to implement it. Funds for universal elementary education of this kind would have to be diverted from other programs. The elite would not sacrifice any of the privileges of the urban rich. Muslim populations, while wanting some of their children to be prepared to participate in the modern sector of the economy, often see government schools as a threat to their religion and moral values (Santerre, 1971). Resources are needed to train teachers. The present generation of teachers wants to recreate the system in which they themselves succeeded. There is a shortage of teachers; many university or normal school graduates refuse to teach, since schoolteachers are paid much less than other graduates with the same amount of training.

However varied their development plans, all the West African countries have one problem in common, the "*exode rurale,*" the mass migration of rural populations to the cities, especially the capital cities of their own and other countries, in search of nonexistent job opportunities and very limited educational opportunities. This migration is often made in stages, from village to

---

[1] All translations are my own.

small town, then on to a large city; young men from even poorer parts of West Africa are often brought in to replace the absent rural workers; then they, in turn, start the process of migration to the cities. True, many of the migrants return to their villages, but, overall, the mass movement is one-way. This results in all the evils of an overlarge and underemployed city population: shanty towns, petty crime, and a mass of potential supporters for any revolutionary demagogue.

All countries have this problem in mind when planning changes in their educational system.

The following is an examination of the relevant individual countries: Ivory Coast, Cameroon,[2] Senegal, Guinea, Mali, Benin, Upper Volta, Niger, and Togo.

IVORY COAST

The Government's external policy is oriented to the West; it maintains particularly close ties with France. Its economic policy supports the free enterprise system. One of its major objectives is gradually to Africanize the private and mixed sectors as qualified personnel become available. (Bolibaugh 1972:96)

As one might expect, the school structure and curriculum have been little changed since colonial times. Because of the "need for skilled manpower," resources have been directed towards higher and technical education. The policy is to improve the extent of the system, making elementary education available to all children, and to improve its quality, so that more children can qualify for advanced training. Ruralization, as everywhere, is also important. Thus a large number of rural elementary schools have been opened in the last ten years. Because of the difficulty in getting trained teachers to man these schools, a system of educational television has been developed, and otherwise poorly prepared teachers have been taught to use it. Programs are taped in Abidjan, and the cassettes are circulated to rural schools.

The language problem has not been tackled. Some educators recognize the difficulty of teaching young children in a language they do not understand, but see no alternative; they cite the fact that over 60 different languages are spoken in the Ivory Coast, none of them predominant, (though Baule is the language of about a quarter of the population, and Dyula is widely used as a *lingua franca* by over half the population). Some neighboring countries, such as Mali and Upper Volta use African languages, but the education authorities are not interested in African language instruction, since their policy favors elitist-type education. All adult literacy programs are in French only, except for a few run by missionaries.

---

[2] Cameroon is not usually included in the culture area termed "West Africa." However, I have included it because it is contiguous with West Africa and it represents a specially interesting case.

A few Ivorian scholars have more recently advocated teaching in one or more Ivorian languages (Kokora, 1977; M'Lanhoro, 1979). M'Lanhoro even advocates the adoption of an Ivorian language as an official language of the country, alongside French. They base their arguments on both practicality and cultural nationalism. But there seems to be no chance of any real attempt to try out their proposals.

CAMEROON

Cameroon has an extra educational problem in that it has two official languages, English and French. The expressed aim of the educators is to make all children literate in both these languages. English is spoken only in one small area in the southwest of the country, and most schools operate in only one European language. Like the Ivory Coast, Cameroon has many African languages, none predominant, except possibly Ewondo, the language of the area of the capital city, Yaoundé.

There is some activity among intellectuals in promoting the national languages. The department of linguistics at the University of Yaounde has developed alphabets for several Cameroon languages; actually the same alphabet can be adapted for half a dozen of the major languages. Plans have even been drawn up for teaching in vernaculars in schools, such as that set out in Maurice Tadadjeu's "Language Planning in Cameroon: Toward a Trilingual Education System" (1975). In Douala, the largest city in Cameroon, Libermann College has always used at least two Cameroon languages as both medium and subject of instruction. Several Protestant churches hold services in one or more Cameroon languages and have printed hymnbooks in them. Books in Cameroon languages are published and although they are mostly grammars and readers for the study of the languages, it can be said that there exists a small but genuine literature in several Cameroon languages.

In spite of these and similar attempts, there is very little real preparation for the introduction of African languages into the Cameroon school system. Little is done in adult education. One reason for this lack of activity is that the school system is more extensive than in other "francophone" countries, and development policies have concentrated on a small area in the south of the country. Thus the people of the south are relatively well served by the school system. In the north, Koranic schools are numerous and of high quality; many of them cater to adult students (Santerre, 1980). Thus the view from the capital is of a fairly satisfactory educational system.

SENEGAL

Like the Ivory Coast, Senegal has maintained its connection with France. Léopold Senghor, its president from the time of independence until his retirement in 1981, has a somewhat paradoxical attitude to French and Senegalese culture. On the one hand, he values his French education, writes poetry and prose in the French language, and has played a leading role in an organization for promoting the French language throughout the world. On the other hand, much of his poetry is about *"négritude,"* the mystic quality of the African, his "participation mystique" with nature. While stressing the irreconcilable differences between African and European cultures, he writes about the one in the language of the other.

Educational reforms were part of a series of general development plans. But even the third plan, for 1972–1973, altered the French structure only slightly. General development plans entailed provision for more and better technical education. But the basic problem of language in the elementary schools was not tackled until the late 1970s, and this was not so much a major objective as it was a spin-off from adult literacy programs in the national languages,[3] which were, again, only part of a nationwide program for rural development and decentralization of authority. The aim was to develop a network of autonomous rural cooperatives, which were to be organized initially by regional development authorities, but were to be continued by the farmers themselves. Thus it was necessary for at least some of the farmers to be literate, so that they could do their own bookkeeping and use scales, surveying instruments, etc. In preparation for this, the linguists of CLAD (Centre Linguistique de l'Université de Dakar) were set to work to devise alphabets for the seven main languages of Senegal, Wolof, Serer, Pular (Fulani), Malinke, Soninke, and Jola (Diagne, 1978). Actually, extensive work was concentrated only on Wolof, the language of the largest ethnic group, about 36% of the population, but spoken by 80% to 90% of the population as a first or second language (O'Brien, 1978, pp. 183–184).

Only a very few Senegalais such as Ousmane Sembène, Pathé Diagne, and Cheik Anta Diop have suggested making Wolof an official language of Senegal.

The adult literacy programs in Wolof, and a few in other languages, seem to be making considerable progress, as reported frequently in the only daily newspaper *Le Soleil*, e.g., Nov. 23, Dec. 12, 1979; Jan. 31, Feb. 1, 1980.

As for elementary school teaching, the minister of education published a long report entitled "We have given teachers a dignified position," in *Le Soleil* of December 16, 1979. He defends the 1971 guidelines for education, claiming that:

> teaching has been adapted to our realities and our needs, systematically Senegalized and Africanized. The national languages have been introduced into our education system. In the next decade they will take on primary importance. New programmes have appeared, and now manuals appear regularly.

---

[3] The term "national languages" is used by the Africans to denote their own languages, in preference to the term "vernacular," which has derogatory connotations. French is called the "official language."

Actually, it was only in 1979 that the first experiments in teaching children to write Wolof were made in half a dozen elementary classrooms, mostly in the Dakar area. Books and television programs were used to teach the writing of Wolof to six- and seven-year olds. Another series of television programs, delivered to the classroom on video cassette, introduced the children to elementary oral French. This method was amazingly effective.

In spite of this, the experiment has been abandoned. Some of the teachers and parents were against it, regarding it as attempt to fob them off with an inferior education and delay or prevent acquisition of proficiency in French. Nobody, except those directly involved in the experiment, mentions the vast quantity of material in pedagogical and psychological journals showing that children who are first taught to read and write their own language, quickly adapt their skills to a second language.

One has the impression that elementary education does not have the first priority with the government of Senegal. There seems to be more emphasis on improving the quality of secondary and technical education.

MALI

The Malian experiments in educational reform are the best documented (Ly, 1969; UNESCO, 1978).

In 1962, two years after independence, an educational reform law was passed with the fundamental objectives "to offer mass and quality education adapted to the needs and realities of Mali, and offer an education which decolonizes the minds and rehabilitates Africa and its own values" (Bolibaugh, 1972, p.41). The structure of the system was changed, providing for fewer years in school and increasing the number of classroom hours per week. In the interests of shortening the period of schooling, the first year (added to the French system, in which the child was introduced to the French language) was eliminated (Bolibaugh, 1972, p.49), but there was nothing to compensate for this. Instruction in African languages was not introduced until the late 1970s and then only in a few schools.

Mali has devoted the main part of its educational resources to adult education, in connection with large programs of rural development. A special department was set up to develop materials for adult literacy programs. It recently produced a film, *Nankorola*, showing a village in a cotton-growing area discussing a literacy program, deciding to adopt it, and attending classes. The last reel shows the villages measuring their fields, weighing their crop, sharing out the profits, and driving the crop to market in their own truck. It appears as if literacy magically causes trucks to appear, roads to be paved, and harvests to increase. Actual results are much more modest. Problems result from insufficient and inadequately trained manpower, lack of communication between the government and the villagers, and the suspicion that national-language education is a poor substitute offered to rural people for the French-language programs offered in Bamako. Nevertheless, the villagers are eager to learn and want to be part of the modern world.

GUINEA

Guinea was the first French colony to achieve independence, the most committed to the greatest degree of economic and cultural separation from France, the first country to carry out a total reform of its educational system and, according to Calvet (1974, p.135) the only country with a policy of "linguistic militantism."

In 1958, the year of independence, the whole structure of the educational system was changed. All schools became "Centres d'Education Revolutionnaires," "the school takes its place in the life of the local community, and fits into its regular curriculum its own contribution to the development of the locality" (Guilavogui, 1975, p.436).

"A necessary step to true cultural decolonization is the revival of national languages" (Guilavogui, 1975, p.440). Thus the first four primary grades of school are taught in one of the half dozen local languages; fortunately most of them are also spoken in neighboring countries and some are lingua francas, so that Guinea did not have to start from scratch in producing pedagogical material in them. Blakemore and Cooksey (1981, p.157) claim that it is still impossible to produce material in African languages. However, their information may be out of date. According to Rivière (1977, p.228), teaching in the local language began in the academic year 1969) (see also Bolibaugh, 1972, p.25).

Adult literacy programs in national languages were also instituted in 1968 (Guilavogui, 1975, p.440). (See also, Kidd, 1976, pp.42–47.)

> The Service National d'Alphabetisation trains the technicians for the National and Regional Literacy Centres; the Academic des Langues is concerned with working out a system of transcription and orthography and with compiling manuals for the study of languages; the Institut Pedagogique National periodically organizes workshops and seminars for the training and further training of teachers who teach national languages in the CERs (Guilavoqui, 1975, p.442).

UPPER VOLTA

The situation at independence in Upper Volta was one of the worst in West Africa.

> with 23% of the national budget, it succeeded in sending to school only 6% of the children with the conventional 6 year primary school (Erny, 1977, p.45).

Instead of immediately tackling the school system, the government concentrated on compensating for its deficiencies by establishing a network of *Centres d'Education Rurale* in 1959, in which young people over the age of 12 would, it was hoped, complete an accelerated primary school program and learn to be better farmers in three years. The scheme ran into problems from the start. The prospective students were too old to be spared from the labor force, but too young to be able to become leaders in agricultural reform. Only boys participated in the scheme. The centers were regarded as an inferior alternative to the colonial type schools and confirmed the suspicions of the rural populations that they were being fobbed off with a cheap substitute for the education available, they thought, to city dwellers (Erny, 1977, p.44–47). Ahmed and Coombs (1975, pp.335–364) attribute the failure of the scheme to the fact that the language of instruction was French, which none of the potential students spoke, and which most of them failed to acquire.

Later reforms concentrated on adult literacy programs. In 1974 the *Office National Permanent de l'Alphabetisation Fonctionnelle et Sélective* was set up to promote literacy in the national languages. As in Mali and Senegal, centers were set up in which literacy programs were operated in selected rural areas as part of local agricultural development schemes. Under the auspices of UNESCO, a committee was set up to advise on alphabets for 13 Voltaic languages.

NIGER

In Niger, as in the other Sahel countries, the school system was grossly ineffective. Between 1957 and 1970, the percentage of school-age children in school rose from 2.2% to 10%, but still most of the children dropped out before completing the primary cycle (Issa, 1978, p.235) and 90% of the population was illiterate in 1963 (Gattinara, n.d.). Both Issa and Hamani (1978) deplore the fact that French is the only language used in the schools, and that competence in that language is the only way to succeed in the modern sector of Nigerian society. Both stress the necessity of teaching in the national languages, not only for pedagogical reasons.

> Just to use these languages in schools and literacy programs would stimulate only a passing enthusiasm. Their use must be accompanied by a redefinition of the relationships between languages and cultures, so as to make the national languages true factors in social progress (Issa, 1978, p.244).

The government of Niger concentrated on adult literacy programs, rather than reform of the schools. In 1964, a National Committee planned transcriptions of the five main languages of Niger: Hausa, Sonhay-Zerma, Kanuri, Tamashek, and Fulani. But literacy programs had already been started in connection with a general plan of agricultural development in the Maredi region of central Niger (Darkoye, 1974). Darkoye stressed the problems: The peasants did not feel the need for literacy while the elite did not want to promote the national languages. (Actually there was a good body of literature as well as pedagogical material in Hausa, mostly published in Nigeria, but in Niger, as in the other "francophone" countries, little use was made of the work that had been carried on in British West Africa since early colonial times.) Belloncle (1978), however, reports that between 1968 and 1973, 3271 peasants were taught in Hausa, which they all spoke. There was a drop-out rate of one third, but 15% emerged fully literate, and many contributed to the Hausa journal *Kasaa may albarkaa* (The land, source of all wealth), which had a circulation of 1000 copies. Salissou Madougou (UNESCO-Cesti, 1973, p.1) lists a dozen journals with circulations between 500 and 2000.

Further progress was made in adult literacy programs from 1968 on. Programs were planned for nomad populations, and by 1969 there were 21 literacy centers in villages and with nomadic groups in Tamashek and Kanuri as well as Hausa and Songhay-Zerma (Gattinara, n.d.).

BENIN

In 1973, when 93% of the population was illiterate in French, and most were also illiterate in their own languages (Mercer, 1976, p.59), one of the first acts of the Revolutionary Military Government was to change the school system completely, with teachings in the national languages.

Benin has the disadvantage of having at least 12 major languages, none except the Fon-Aja group (800,000 speakers) with more than 200,000 native speakers. However, all are of the same language family (Niger-Congo) and some, such as Yoruba, Fulani, and Hausa, are widely spoken in neighboring countries and already possess a considerable literature, both literary and pedagogical (Aguenou, 1973). A Yoruba journal had been circulating in Porto-Novo since the 1930s and Bariba had been transcribed and used by the Sudan Interior Mission.

Adult literacy programs were also started about the same time as part of the revolutionary program of rural development. An anonymous document (13,040-F in the University of Reading (England) Agricultural Extension and Rural Development Centre) sets out the tasks of "all workers who seek to satisfy the cultural and educational needs of rural populations":

to help them to appreciate the value of their languages, training themselves, communicating, expressing themselves and confirming their individual culture;

enabling them to control their own productive activities, through greater mastery over nature and knowledge and appropriate techniques adapted to their environment;

to arouse and encourage attitudes that will speed their liberation from the obscurantist and feudal forces of imperialist exploitation.

In the northern part of the country the Bariba journal *Kparo* has achieved considerable success (Auroi, 1977-1978).

TOGO

The French education system in Togo was modified only slightly by the reforms of 1959 and 1967. 60% of school age children were in school, a higher percentage than in many African countries, but still far from optimal (UNESCO, 1978, pp. 38–39) .

In 1970 an executive Council for National Education was set up, which planned radical reforms. Children were to start nursery school at the age of two. Following this,

At the second level of education, the pupil in the south, in addition to Eve, will learn Kabye as a second language while the pupil in the north will, in addition to Kabye, learn Eve as a second language.

The national languages will be studied up to university level UNESCO, 1975, p.43).

This plan was implemented in 1975 (Takassi, 1977, p.55).

Adult literacy programs were one of the priorities in the second five-year plan, for 1971 to 1975 (Akouete 1973). By that time several programs, run variously by missionaries, volunteers, and the *Service des Affaires Sociales,* had produced a considerable number of adult literates in African languages, and the concern was to build on these new skills in the interests of rural development. In 1972, a monthly journal in Ewe was started, by the collaboration of such government agencies as Agricultural Training, Health Education, and Literacy Program, assisted by international organizations. There was also help from Ghana, which had for several decades produced pedagogical, religious, and general literature in Ewe.

CONCLUSION

There is the recognition in West African countries that French is the language of colonialism—that as long as French is the only official language of a country, that country will remain a colony of France.

The most important difference between the French system of education and traditional African systems is that in the former only a minority of students can succeed. However many students pass the examination for entry into secondary school, the number of places is limited, and only the "fortunate few" can continue their education. In the traditional initiation schools, although the children had to learn many difficult skills and go through harsh ordeals to test their strength and courage, and although these schools were the only path to adult status, nobody failed. So the French education system taught African children, not only that their culture was inferior, but that most of them were incapable of achieving the "superior" culture that was offered in its place.

Some African writers accept that it will always be necessary for Africans to use French as the language of higher education and of international relations. They think that this need not imply the inferiority of their own languages and cultures; after all, citizens of the smaller European countries recognize the necessity of competence in one of the major European languages for such purposes, and do not worry about the status of their own languages. But the more radical writers, aware of the examples of Kenya and Tanzania, which have adopted Swahili as their official language, consider that as long as a colonial language is the only official language of a country, that country retains its colonial status. Most of them suggest only that an African language should be used alongside French as an official language throughout the country. But some go further, advocating the use of one or two African languages—Swahili and Hausa are the favorites—throughout Africa, making these the instrument and symbol of African unity.

All those who have worked with African-language literacy programs are impressed with the psychological effect of literacy in African languages. The new generation of intellectuals, especially those who are working on oral literature at the universities of Dakar and Yaoundé, appreciate anew the value of their traditional cultures, and see new possibilities of economic and technical development without denigrating or abandoning traditional values. The effect is even greater on the rural population. They are excited at the ease with which the children learn to read their own languages, after their experience of failure in the French system. Their new ability to express their thoughts in writing, to weigh their crops, to check their tax demands, to keep their own accounts, to correspond with relatives working far from home—all this gives them a great feeling of confidence and control over their own destiny.

It is clear that revolutionary changes in language and education policies go together and that these are a key factor in African movements for real independence and autonomous development.

REFERENCES

Aguenou, J. (1973). "Benin," In UNESCO-Cesti. "Colloque regional" ["Regional colloquium"]. Paris: UNESCO.
Ahmed, M., Coombs, P.H. (1975). Education for Rural Development. New York: Praeger.
Akouete, B. (1973). "Togo". In UNESCO-Cesti. "Colloque regional" ["Regional Colloquium"]. Paris: UNESCO.

Auroi, C. (1977–1978). "L'alphabétisation rurale au nord Benin: la fin de l'exploitation des paysans" ["Rural literacy programs in north Benin: Ending the exploitation of peasants"]. *Geneve-Afrique*. **16**, 89–108.

Belloncle, G. (1978). "Cooperatives et alphabétisation—Niger" ["Cooperatives and literacy programs"] *Literacy Work*. **7**, (No. 2).

Biarnes, P. (1980). *L'Afrique aux Africains [Africa for the Africans]* Paris: Armand Colin.

Blakemore, K. and Cooksey, B. (1981). *A Sociology of Education for Africa*. London: Allen & Unwin.

Bolibaugh, J. (1972). *Educational Development in Guinea, Mali, Senegal and Ivory Coast*. Washington, DC: U. S. Department of Health, Education, and Welfare.

Calvet, L. (1974). *Linguistique et Colonialisme [Linguistics and Colonialism]*. Paris: Payot

Darkoye. (1974). "Niger." *In* UNESCO, Meeting of Experts on the use of mother tongue in literacy programs in Africa, Bamako. *Final Report* ED/CONF 628. Paris: UNESCO.

Diage, P. (1978). "Transcription and Harmonization of African Languages in Senegal." Contribution to meeting of experts on the transcription and harmonization of African languages, Niamey.

Erny, P. (1977). *L'enseignement dans les pays pauvres [Education in poor countries]* Paris: L'Harmattan.

Gattinara, G. (n.d.). "Alphabetisation et education des adultes" ["Literacy programs and education of adults"]. University of Reading, Literacy Documentation Centre.

Guilavogui, G. (1975). "The Basis of Educational Reform in the Republic of Guinea." *Prospects*. **5**, 435–444.

Hamani, A. (1978). "De la langue vernaculaire á la langue officielle" [From the vernacular language to the official language"]. *Annales de l'Université de Niamey*. **1**, 93–96.

Harding, L. (1971). "Les écoles des Pères Blancs au Soudan Francais" ["The White Borthers' schools in the French Sudan"] *Cahiers d'Etudes Africaines* **XI** (41), 101–128.

Issa, S. (1978). "Le probleme linguistique dans l'enseignement au Niger" ["The language problem in education in Niger"]. *Annales de l'Université de Niamey* **1**, 235–245.

Kidd, J. R. (1976). *The Experimental World Literacy Programme*. Paris: UNESCO Press.

Kokora, P. (1977). "Enseignement en langues maternelles en Coacte d'Ivoire" ["Education in the mother tongues in the Ivory Coast"]. *Annales de l'Université d'Abidjan* Serie D, **10**, 234–246.

Ly, F. (1965). "Mali: Educational Options in a Poor Country." *In* A. Manzoor and P.H. Coombs (Eds.), *Education for Rural Development*. New York: Praeger.

Mercer, M.M. (1976). "Language, Literacy and Rural Development." M.A. Thesis, University of London, Institute of Education.

M'Lanhoro, J. (1979). "Langues nationales et libération culturelle" ["National languages and cultural liberation Colloquim on Black African literature and aesthetics"]. *Colloque sur litterature et esthetique négro-Africaines*. Nouvelles Editions Africaines.

O'Brien, D.C. (1978). "Senegal". *In* J. Dunn (Ed.), *West African States*. London: Cambridge University Press.

Riviére, C. (1977). *Guinea: The Mobilization of a People*. Ithaca, NY: Cornell University Press.

Santerre, R. (1980). "Maitres Coraniques de Maroua Cameroun" [Koranic teachers of Maroua, Cameroon]. Paper presented to Canadian Association of African Studies.

1973 *Pédagogie musulmane d'Afrique noire [Muslim pedagogy in Black Africa]*. Les Presses de l'Université de Montreal.

Santerre, R. (1971). "Aspects Conflictuels de deux systemes d'enseignement au Nord-Cameroun" ["Conflicting aspects of two educational systems in North Cameroon"]. *Canadian Journal of African Studies* **5**, 157–170.

Takassi, I. (1977). "Les Langues du Togo" ["The languages of Togo"]. *Annales de l'Universite de Benin* **4**, 47–56.

Tadadjeu, M. (1975). "Language Planning in Cameroon". *In* R.K. Herbert (Ed.), *Patterns in Language Culture in Sub-Saharan Africa*.

UNESCO. (1978). *Educational Reforms and Innovations in Africa*. (Experiments and Innovations in Education #24.) Paris: UNESCO.

UNESCO-CESTI. (1973). "Colloque regional sur le developpement des journaux ruraux en Afrique francophone" ["Regional colloquium on the development of rural newspapers in francophone Africa"]. Paris: UNESCO.

27

Local Telecommunications, Political Economy, and Enterprise Zones

Russell L. Stockard
Security Pacific Data Transmission Corporation, Glendale, CA

Competition and deregulation are now typical of the telecommunications industry in the United States (McGowan, 1982; Wines, 1981, 1982, 1983), and the resulting abundance of communications channels may indicate that the so-called information economy and the post-industrial society have arrived (Porat, 1978). While the emphasis on service occupations and knowledge-handling tasks and professions may indeed characterize the national economy (two-thirds of the national workforce is classified as service workers), the heralded post-industrial society is a companion phenomenon to the protracted economic crisis of the nation's cities (State and Local Government in Trouble, 1981). Moreover, the economic distress of metropolitan areas is a manifestation of the fiscal crisis of the state, a condition that has generated much of the urge to deregulate practiced by the supply-siders dominant in the Reagan Administration.

Communications policy since World War II has tended to stimulate the growth of telecommunications through government subsidies, purchases, and other industries growing out of electronics have gained in importance as weapons in the increasingly competitive international economic wars being waged among the advanced industrial nations (Chisman, 1982; Mosco and Herman, 1981; Reich, 1982). In order to conduct these trade wars more effectively, a number of economic and communications "strategists" have urged rationalization of conflicting policy elements under the aegis of "information policy" (Dunn, 1982) and "industrial policy" (Reich, 1982). The former considers the impact of the current rush toward deregulation in weighing the possibility of public investment versus private investment in various new technologies; the latter views communications as one of a number of viable U.S. industries for strategic development while recognizing the need to balance the labor and regional economic impacts of a communications policy emphasis. While economic development consequences of international competition are considered by advocates of industrial policy, this approach may face obstacles in implementation, insofar as domestic warfare has broken out among states (and cities) over jobs and business, particularly involving high technology (Schellhardt, 1983a). Companies relying on microelectronic, computer, and communications

293

technologies enjoy a halo in this respect, and are portrayed as the solution to the ills of economically distressed cities and regions. On the most local level, cable television franchise "fever" has only recently shown any signs of waning as city and county governments displayed high expectations about the medium's revenue potential in an era of tax limitation and retrenchment in Federal aid to metropolitan areas (Stoller, 1982).

The deregulation of communications is not taking place in a vacuum, but is merely one manifestation of the Reagan Administration's wholesale removal of federal government intervention in, and funding of, programs in energy, transportation, health and safety, and, most importantly in this context, urban affairs (Sing, 1983a,b). While the dismantling of the communications regulatory apparatus is taking place at the federal and state levels, cities continue to cling to their right to regulate cable television, which is perhaps the most local of the currently operational communication technologies (Stoller, 1982, p.35). This determination may spring in part from the apparent fulfillment of the long-delayed technological promise of urban cable television (Lucas and Yin, 1973), but also from the linking of telematics with economic growth, however misplaced (Chisman, 1982). The irony lies in the setting of the technological and growth aspects of communications: the virtual abandonment of metropolitan areas by the current administration in Washington.

While deindustrialization is not new in the context of metropolitan areas (Bluestone and Harrison, 1982; State and Local Government, 1981; Kasarda and Lineberry, 1980), the resort to high-tech solutions to this particular dimension of the chronic crisis of the cities is. Furthermore, the implicit target of the urban enterprise zone proposals submitted by the Reaganites in lieu of urban policy is high-tech industrial development in depressed urban and rural areas (Shapiro, 1982). This position is consistent with the observation that information industries comprise one of the "largest and most dynamic sectors of the U.S. economy . . . (accounting) directly for about 10 percent of our GNP as well as capital investment and compromise our third largest export sector (after agriculture and aviation)" (Chisman, 1982, p.72). On the other hand, Rubin and Sapp (1981) have observed that the information sector conducts relatively little international trade compared to its domestic activity. They note that about 12% of U.S. exports are attributed to the information sector; more than 97% of the sector's output goes to U.S. sales. Rubin and Sapp also report that the growth in information workers during the century from 1870 to 1970 (8% to 41% of the U.S. work force) could not be attributed greatly to technological innovations; rather, the growth of the public and private bureaucracies, which now constitute more than one-quarter of our total work force, largely explains the growth of the sector. Similarly, Porat (1978) locates workers with knowledge skills in public and private bureaucracies rather than in many competing firms.

Thus, since the communications industry consists of a few very large firms, it appears that cities should not expect to enjoy the benefits of communications industry growth in the form of additional employment in areas where, for instance, new urban cable systems are being constructed (technological innovation). Whatever likely employment growth would probably be confined to corporate headquarters. Furthermore, since bureaucracies require highly skilled personnel to staff their largely professional, technical, and managerial positions, it is probable that such employees would choose to reside outside the inner city, compelling their firms to locate accordingly. Central cities would remain untouched by the wonders of telematics, except as markets for programming transmitted over cable or fiber optics, and would be the preserve of the secondary labor market (Harrison and Hill, 1979).

In light of these probable trends, it appears that a theory of dependency could describe the political economy of metropolitan areas at a historical juncture where high-tech "fixes" for economic distress are hailed by an administration bent on liberating the cities from the yoke of government intervention and assistance, the ostensible goal of the enterprise zone proposals. The application of dependency theory to the metropolis has been by casual analogy or in "tantalizing snippets" (Kasarda and Lineberry, 1980, p.167). While Katznelson (1976) has described urban politics succintly as politics of dependency, Lincoln (1977) has briefly equated the interdependent organizational relations of cities with external dependency suffered by the less developed nations. Finally, Barnet and Mueller's (1974) analysis of multinational corporations explicitly advises U.S. cities to compare their situation to that of the less developed nations, both of which, they claim, are increasingly at the mercy of decisions made by "worldwide behemoths." When Kasarda and Lineberry wrote, they linked a "deepening dependence" of the cities in an era of resource constraints to the federal government, noting that direct federal aid as a percentage of own-source revenue increased sharply, even from 1976 to 1978 (Kasarda and Lineberry, 1980, p.169). Under Reagan, Business Week observed that after a fourfold growth in the 1970s, federal grants-in-aid would be drastically reduced, falling from $88 billion in 1980 to $78.6 billion in 1983 ("State and Local Government in Trouble," 1981, p.136).

Hence, for dependency theory to apply under the New Federalism and urban enterprise zones, the role of high-tech, information industry firms must be viewed as substituting, however imperfectly, for that of the shrinking federal government. The restructuring of what federal aid that still exists has apparently failed, generating criticism of such mechanisms of the administration as block grants (May, 1983), and cities have been forced to turn to state governments that are now themselves deficit-ridden (How Cities Fit into 1983's Legislative Picture, 1983). The question arises, then, of whether enterprise zones could stimulate the growth of urban-based information industry, including such local telecommunications technologies as cable television and low-power television, such that the resulting economic growth would accrue to the benefit of metropolitan areas.

A brief summary of enterprise zones (Weintraub and Fitzsimmons, 1980), as defined by the Urban Jobs and Enterprise Zones Act of 1980, reveals the goal of creation of private enterprise jobs in areas of high unemployment or with a high percentage of families below the poverty level. Although employers would be subject to a number of constraints such as the hiring of at least 50% of their work force from areas designated as zones, they would be entitled to a number of substantial tax deductions (depending on the particular bill) such as elimination of capital gains taxes, a 50% reduction of corporate income taxes, a 5% refundable income tax credit for wages paid to CETA eligible employees, and rapid depreciation allowances (Betts, 1982).

The reliance on incentives that reduce taxes does not meet the needs of high-tech industries currently being lured by states and cities. These industries do not require assistance that might work for the steel and auto industries or traditional small businesses, but rather are concerned with raising capital, finding and keeping skilled workers, and promoting free trade (Hagstrom, 1982; Hormats, 1983). The enterprise zones would not consider regulatory issues influencing municipal cable television regulation such as the current compromise between the National League of Cities and National Cable Television Association on basic cable rate deregulation and simplified franchise renewal requirements (Schley, 1983). At the same time, the NLC-NCTA pact would prevent cities from regulating cable television as common carriers (Huffman, 1983). Finally, despite the possibilities for local community and minority ownership of low-power television (LPTV), almost no licenses have been granted—a condition which the passage of enterprise zone legislation would do nothing to alleviate. Furthermore, the dominance of the application process by large corporations such as Sears militates against the role of LPTV as a generator of local economic development. Thus, the net effect of enterprise zones with respect to high-tech would seem to be the shift of the cities' dependence to the private sector, most likely toward the large conglomerates that dominate information industries in the U.S.

Since the deregulatory thrust of the supply-side Reaganites does not hold promise of decreased urban dependence, what of the polar policy, industrial policy? Briefly, industrial policy at least attempts to rationalize the process of choosing "winners"—industries that can compete internationally while helping to develop the industrial infrastructure. In an information economy, the information infrastructure consists of telecommunications networks such as coaxial cable, fiber optics, telephone company local loops and long lines and other facilities that require relatively high capital investment. The initial building and rebuilding of this communications infrastructure is currently taking place under the management of private sector firms such as Warner-Amex (cable), MCI (long haul voice and data), and Sears (LPTV network): and monopolies such as the recently divested Bell's operating companies. Since vast regions of the nation are covered by the communications infrastructure, the emphasis in industrial policy on balanced regional growth and assistance to workers in retraining and/or relocating for skilled employment would be reduced. On the other hand, careful attention would be required to establish that "jobless growth" (Menzies, 1981) and other post-industrial employment ills did not increase. Where possible, new ownership and/or operating arrangements could be pursued under a comprehensive industrial policy, such as electric utility load management and rural telephone cable television companies. International competitiveness could be maintained through the manufacture and export of telecommunications equipment and other hardware.

While the notion of an overarching industrial policy linking information/communications policy and urban policy is attractive, a number of obstacles exist, particularly the rush toward deregulation prevalent at the FCC and misconceptions concerning the benefits and costs of high-tech industries. Nontheless, such a coordinating strategy could provide cities with control over local telecommunications and thereby decrease their dependence on companies whose decision-makers operate without accountability. This belief is as yet embryonic, but the groundswell can be measured in the attitudes of mayors toward Reagan and Reagonomics in local elections. The President's policies have generated an unusual degree of concern with national issues in mayoral contests (Schellhardt, 1983b).

REFERENCES

Barnet, R.J., and Mueller, R.E. (1974). *Global Reach*. New York: Simon and Schuster.

Betts, R. (1982). "Eight Enterprise Zone Bils Introduced in U.S. Congress." *Minority Business Today* 1 (No.3), 2.

Bluestone, B. and Harrison, B. (1982).*The Deindustrialization of America: Plant Closings, Community Abandonment, and the Dismantling of Basic Industries*. New York: Basic Books.

Chisman, F.P. (1982). "Beyond Deregulation: Communications Policy and Economic Growth." *Journal of Communication* 32 (No.4), 64–83.

Dunn, D. (1982), "Developing Information Policy." *Telecommunications Policy* 6, 21–38.

Hagstrom, J. (1982). "High-Tech Leaders Have Their Own Ideas of What Government Can Do for Them." *National Journal* 14, 861–864.

Harrison, B., and Hill, E. (1979). "The Changing Structure of Jobs in Older and Younger Cities." *In* B. Chinitz, (Ed), *Central City Economic Development*, 15–44. Cambridge, MA: ABT Books.

Hormats, R.D. (1983). "High Technology Industries and the Challenge of International Competition." *National Journal* 15, 94–96. "How Cities Fit into 1983's Legislative Picture." *Western City* 59 (No.2), 12.

Huffman, L. (1983). "NCTA, NLC Announce Pact on Municipal Cable Regulation." *Multi-channel News* 4:1–57.

Kasarda, J.D., and Lineberry, R.L. (1980). "People, Production, and Power: Converging Issues in Urban Studies." *American Behavioral Scientist* 24, 157–176.

Katznelson, I. (1976). "The Crisis of the Capitalist City: Urban Politics and Social Control." *In* W.D. Hawley (Ed.), *Theoretical Perspectives on Urban Politics*, Ch. 9. Englewood Cliffs, NJ: Prentice-Hall.

Lincoln, J.R. (1977). "Organizational Dominance and Community Structure." *In* R.J. Liebert and A.W. Imersheim (Eds.), *Power, Paradigms and Community Research*, pp. 19–36. Beverly Hills, CA: Sage.

May, L. (1983). "9 U.S. Block Grants Misadministered, Social Groups Say." *Los Angeles Times* (Jan. 15) (Pt. 1), 14.

Menzies, H. (1981). "Women and the Chip: Case Studies on the Effects of Informatics on Employment in Canada." Institute for Research on Public Policy, Montreal.

Lucas, W.A., and Yin, R.K. (1973). *Serving Local Needs with Telecommunications.* Washington, D.C.: Rand.

McGowan, W. G. (1982). "The New Competition in US Telecommunications." *Intermedia* 10 (No. 4), 45–47.

Porat, M. (1978). "Communication Policy in an Information Society." *In* G. Robinson (Ed.), *Communications for Tommorow: Policy Perspectives for the 1980s.* New York: Praeger.

Mosco, V., and Herman, A. (1981). "Radical Social Theory and the Communication Revolution." *In* EG. McAnany (Ed.), *Communication and Social Structure,* pp. 58–84. New York: Praeger.

Reich, R.B. (1982). "Why the US Needs an Industrial Policy." *Harvard Business Review* 60, 74–81.

Rubin, M.R., and Sapp, M.E. (1981). "Selected Roles of Information Goods and Services in the U.S. National Economy." *Information Processing and Management"* 17, 195–213.

Schellhardt, T.D. (1983a) "War Among States for Jobs and Business Becomes Ever Fiercer." *Wall Street Journal* (Feb. 14), 1.

Schellhardt, T.D. (1983b). "Mayors Expect Reagan to Be Issue in Races." *Wall Street Journal* (Feb. 10), 33.

Schiller, D. (1982). *Telematics and Government.* Norwood, NJ: Ablex.

Schley, S. (1983). "NLC-NCTA Pact Draws City Opposition." *Multichannel News* 4, 1–38.

Shapiro, H. (1982). "Now, Hong Kong on the Hudson: Saving the Slums with Enterprise Zones." *Newsweek* (April 26), 35.

Sing, B. (1983a). "Decontrol Doubts Grow Amid Gains." *Los Angeles Times* (Feb. 13) (Pt.1), 1.

Sing, B. (1983b). "Decontrol Backers Criticize Quick Promises, Slow Pace." *Los Angeles Times* (Feb. 14) (Pt.1), 1.

"State and Local Government in Trouble." (1981). *Business Week* (Oct. 26), 135–181.

Stoller, D. (1982). "The War Between Cable and the Cities." *Channels of Communication* 2. (No. 1), 34.

Weintraub, L., and Fitzsimmons, E. (1980). "CBC Policy Statement on the Kemp-Garcia Bill." *Citizen Budget Commission, Inc.* 47, 1–6.

Wines, M. (1981). "The Cable Revolution—Tough Choices for Industry and the Government." *National Journal* 13, 1888–1895.

Wines, M. (1982). "The FCC and Its Critics Are at Odds on How to Control the Video Explosion." *National Journal* 14, 1408–1413.

Wines, M. (1983). "Transition to a New Era of Telephone Service Could Be a Painful Passage." *National Journal* 15, 101–148.

Author Index

Subject Index

A

Adenauer, Konrad, 243
advertising, 133, 134, 136, 137
   by anti-handgun lobby, 212, 217
   feminine hygiene in, 161–67
   sexual control of women and, 159–60
African nations
   African languages and, 282, 284–87, 290
   Benin among, 288–89
   Cameroon among, 283
   educational policies within, 280–82
   French language and culture in, 278–80,
      283, 285
   Guinea among, 286
   Ivory Coast among, 282–83
   Kenya among, 259–60, 290
   Koranic schools of, 279, 283
   literacy programs within, 284–87
   Mali among, 285–86
   Niger among, 287–88
   Nigeria among, 249, 252–54, 259, 260
   Senegal among, 283–85
   Togo among, 289
   Upper Volta among, 286–87
agenda setting. *See* opinion formulation
aggression, 136, 137
alcoholism, 115
American Civil Liberties Union (ACLU),
   123, 125
Amnesty International, 180, 182
Another Woman's Child (film), 172, 173

appropriateness, 97–98
Armsey, James, 236, 237
automobiles, 133–37

B

bourgeoisie, 8–9
bleeding, 159–61, 165–67
Bundy, McGeorge, 237–38, 241

C

Carnegie Commission on Educational
   Television, 233, 239, 240–41
Carter, Jimmy, 178–80, 182, 183, 185, 190
Catholics, 127, 128, 183, 195–96
   in Napoleonic era, 4
   in Northern Ireland, 202, 208
certainty, 108, 109
children, 14, 15, 18, 65–66, 114
   child pornography and, 230–31
   cognition of, 65–68, 73
   communication and, 67, 68, 73, 74
   illegitimate, 172
   interaction and, 70–71, 74
   language and, 65–69
   and movies on child abuse, 170–71
   non-verbal responses of, 68, 76
   question processes and, 69–70, 72, 73
   in television study, 66, 70–75
   video games and, 140–41
chi-square analysis, 135, 136